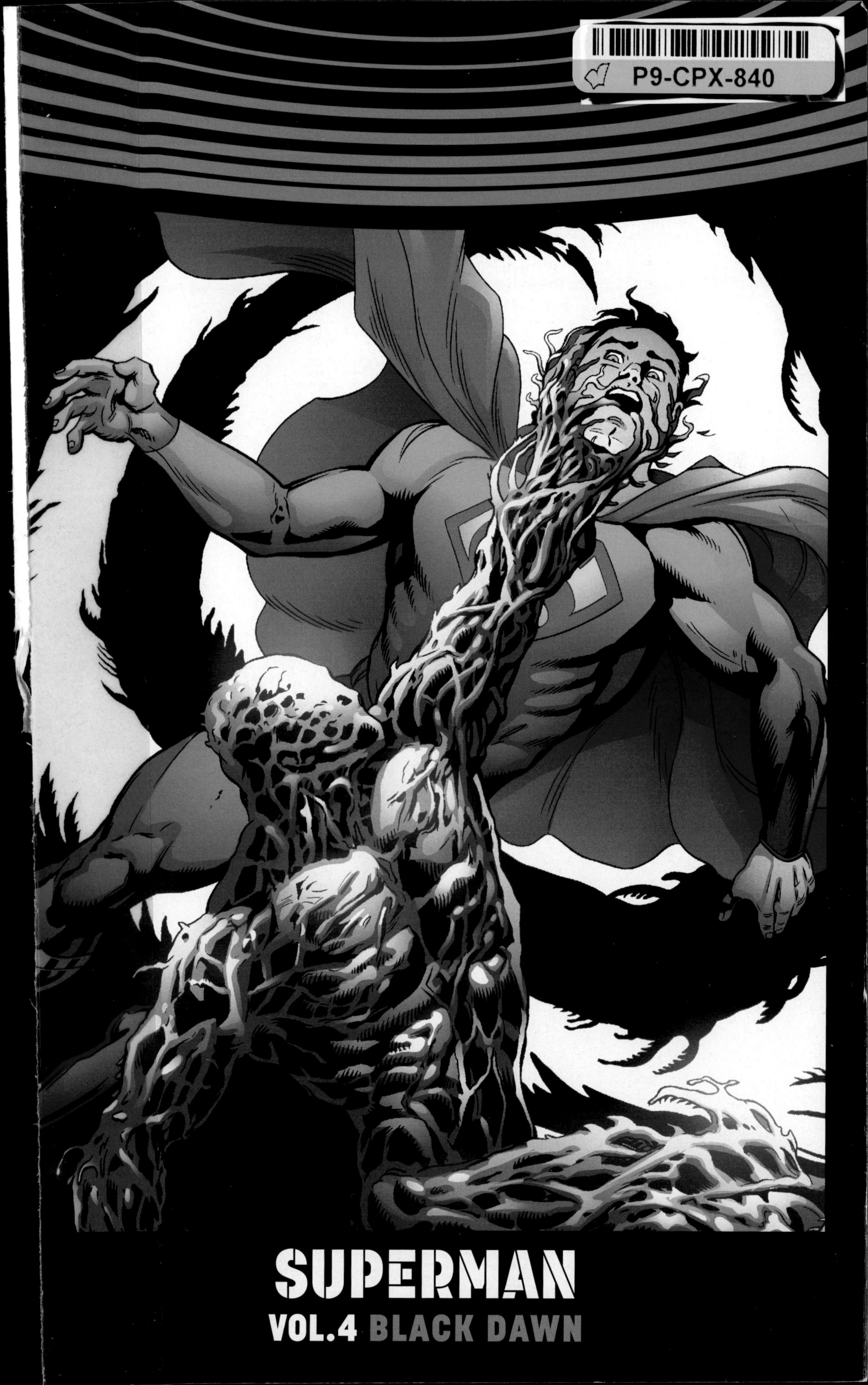

SUPERMAN

VOL.4 BLACK DAWN

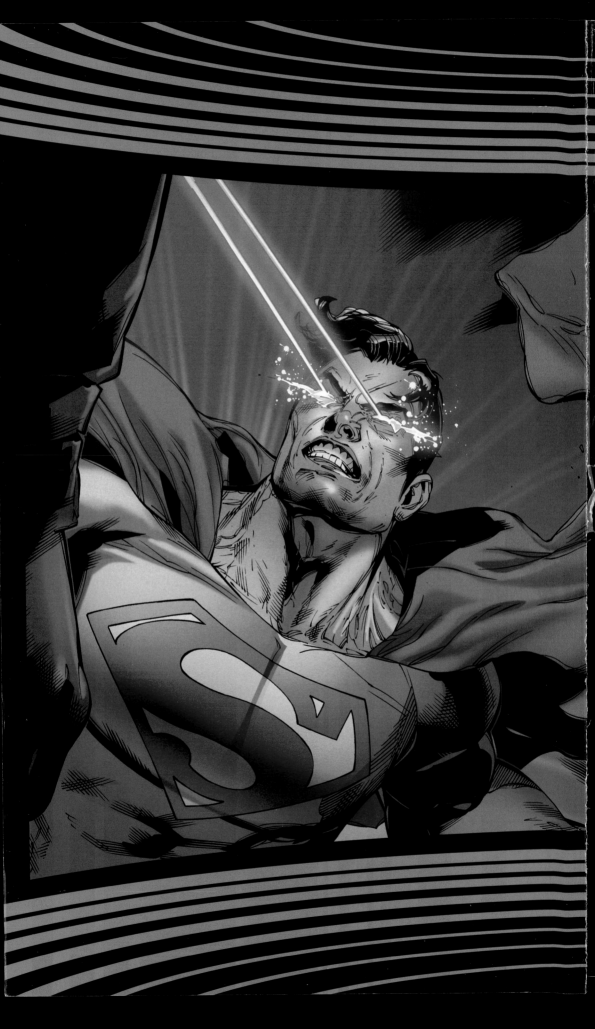

SUPERMAN

VOL.4 BLACK DAWN

PETER J. TOMASI * PATRICK GLEASON * MICHAEL MORECI
writers

PATRICK GLEASON * DOUG MAHNKE * MICK GRAY
SCOTT GODLEWSKI * JAIME MENDOZA * RAY McCARTHY
JOE PRADO * KEITH CHAMPAGNE * SCOTT HANNA
MATT SANTORELLI
artists

JOHN KALISZ * WIL QUINTANA * HI-FI
colorists

ROB LEIGH * DAVE SHARPE
letterers

RYAN SOOK
collection cover art

RYAN SOOK
PATRICK GLEASON and JOHN KALISZ
PATRICK GLEASON, MICK GRAY and JOHN KALISZ
LEE WEEKS and BRAD ANDERSON
original series covers

SUPERMAN created by **JERRY SIEGEL** and **JOE SHUSTER**.
SUPERBOY created by **JERRY SIEGEL**.
By special arrangement with the Jerry Siegel family.

EDDIE BERGANZA Editor - Original Series ✳ **ANDREW MARINO** Assistant Editor - Original Series
JEB WOODARD Group Editor - Collected Editions ✳ **SCOTT NYBAKKEN** Editor - Collected Edition
STEVE COOK Design Director - Books ✳ **MONIQUE NARBONETA** Publication Design

BOB HARRAS Senior VP - Editor-in-Chief, DC Comics
PAT McCALLUM Executive Editor, DC Comics

DIANE NELSON President ✳ **DAN DiDIO** Publisher ✳ **JIM LEE** Publisher ✳ **GEOFF JOHNS** President & Chief Creative Officer
AMIT DESAI Executive VP - Business & Marketing Strategy, Direct to Consumer & Global Franchise Management
SAM ADES Senior VP & General Manager, Digital Services ✳ **BOBBIE CHASE** VP & Executive Editor, Young Reader & Talent Development
MARK CHIARELLO Senior VP - Art, Design & Collected Editions ✳ **JOHN CUNNINGHAM** Senior VP - Sales & Trade Marketing
ANNE DePIES Senior VP - Business Strategy, Finance & Administration ✳ **DON FALLETTI** VP - Manufacturing Operations
LAWRENCE GANEM VP - Editorial Administration & Talent Relations ✳ **ALISON GILL** Senior VP - Manufacturing & Operations
HANK KANALZ Senior VP - Editorial Strategy & Administration ✳ **JAY KOGAN** VP - Legal Affairs ✳ **JACK MAHAN** VP - Business Affairs
NICK J. NAPOLITANO VP - Manufacturing Administration ✳ **EDDIE SCANNELL** VP - Consumer Marketing
COURTNEY SIMMONS Senior VP - Publicity & Communications ✳ **JIM (SKI) SOKOLOWSKI** VP - Comic Book Specialty Sales & Trade Marketing
NANCY SPEARS VP - Mass, Book, Digital Sales & Trade Marketing ✳ **MICHELE R. WELLS** VP - Content Strategy

SUPERMAN VOL. 4: BLACK DAWN

Published by DC Comics. Compilation and all new material Copyright © 2017 DC Comics. All Rights Reserved.
Originally published in single magazine form in SUPERMAN 20-26. Copyright © 2016, 2017 DC Comics. All Rights Reserved.
All characters, their distinctive likenesses and related elements featured in this publication are trademarks of DC Comics.
The stories, characters and incidents featured in this publication are entirely fictional.
DC Comics does not read or accept unsolicited ideas, stories or artwork.

DC Comics, 2900 West Alameda Ave., Burbank, CA 91505.
Printed by LSC Communications, Kendallville, IN, USA. 10/27/17.
First Printing. ISBN: 978-1-4012-7468-9

Library of Congress Cataloging-in-Publication Data is available.

PEFC Certified

Printed on paper from
sustainably managed
forests, controlled
sources

PEFC/29-31-337   www.pefc.org

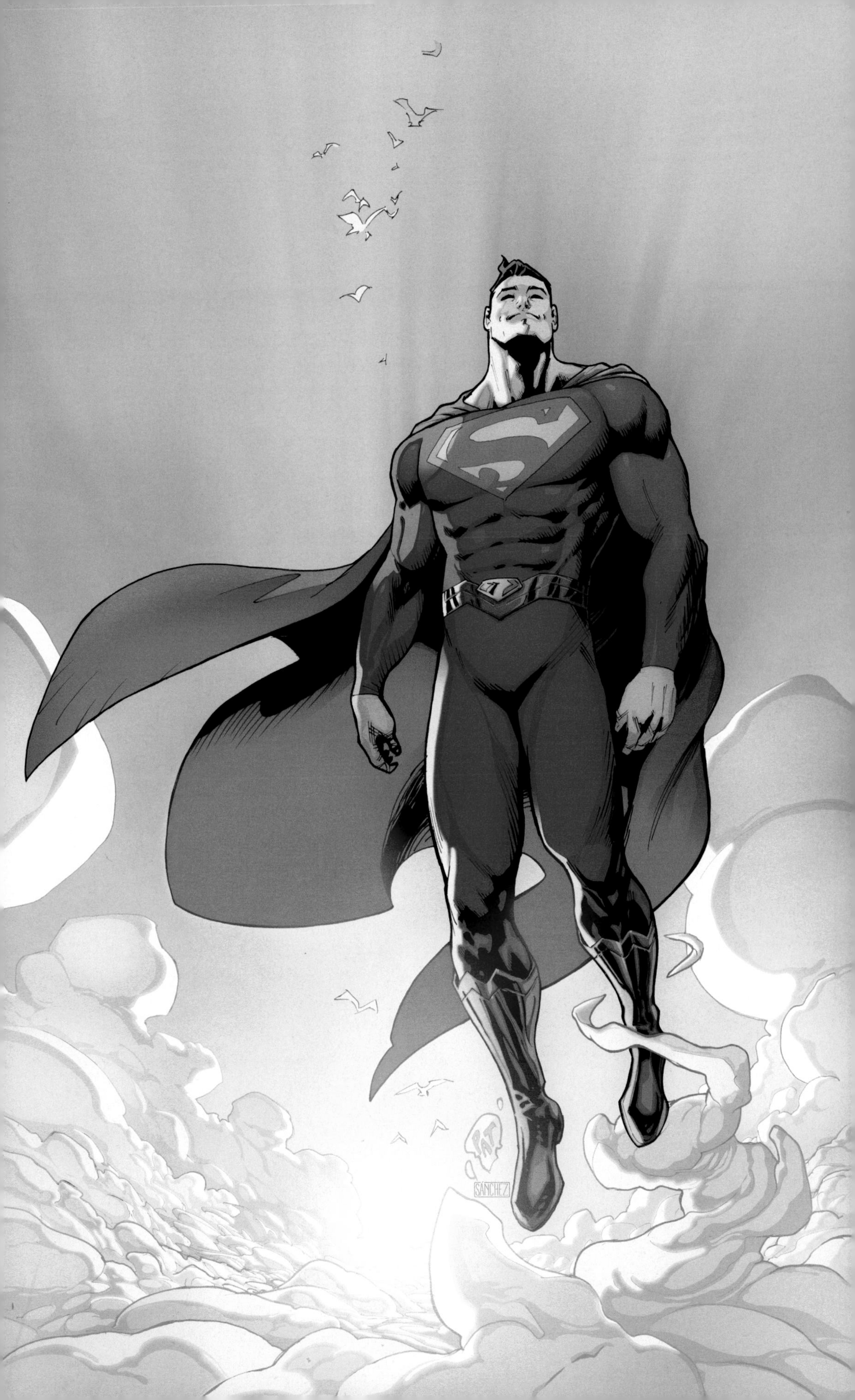
PAT
SANCHEZ

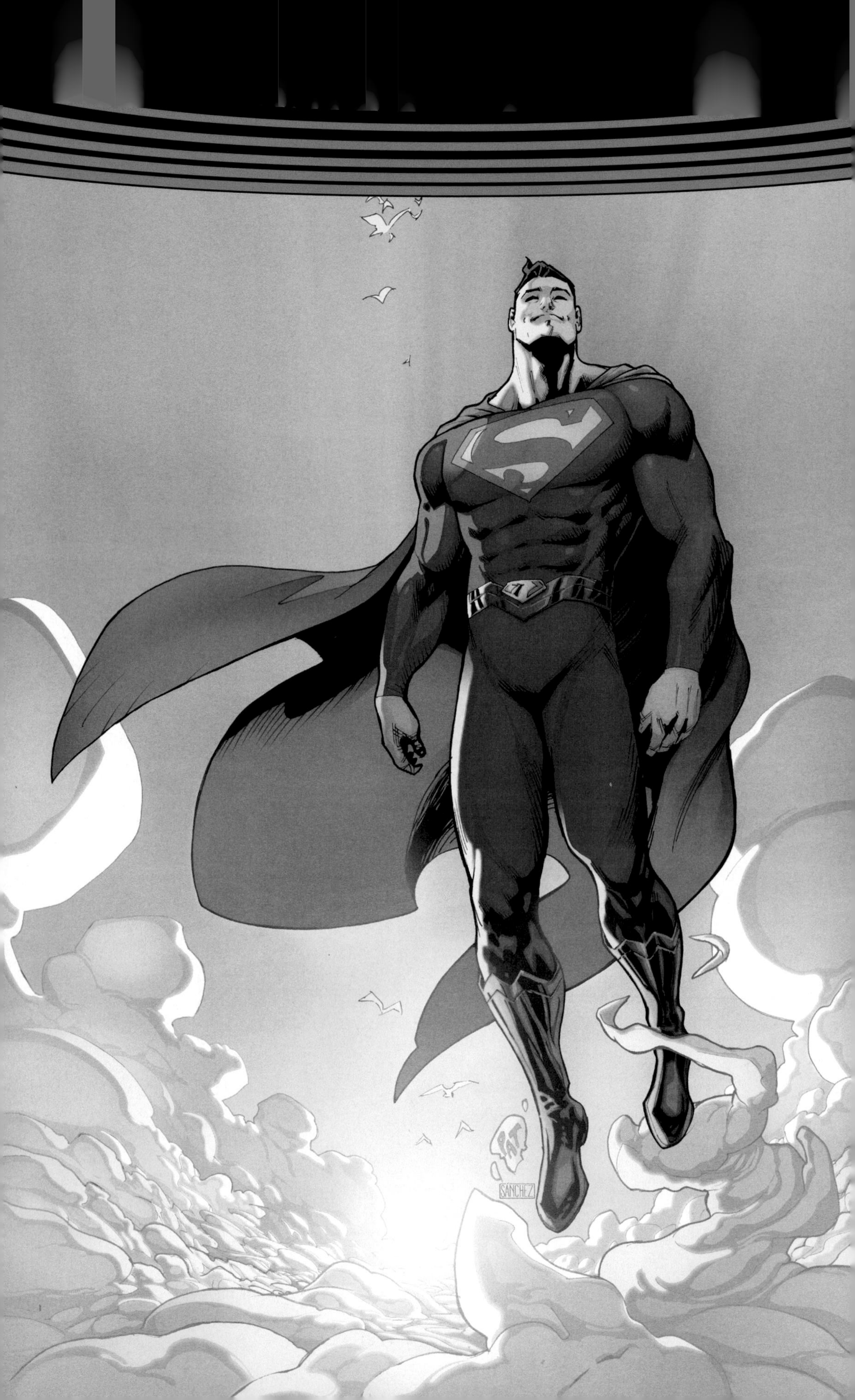
PAT
SÁNCHEZ

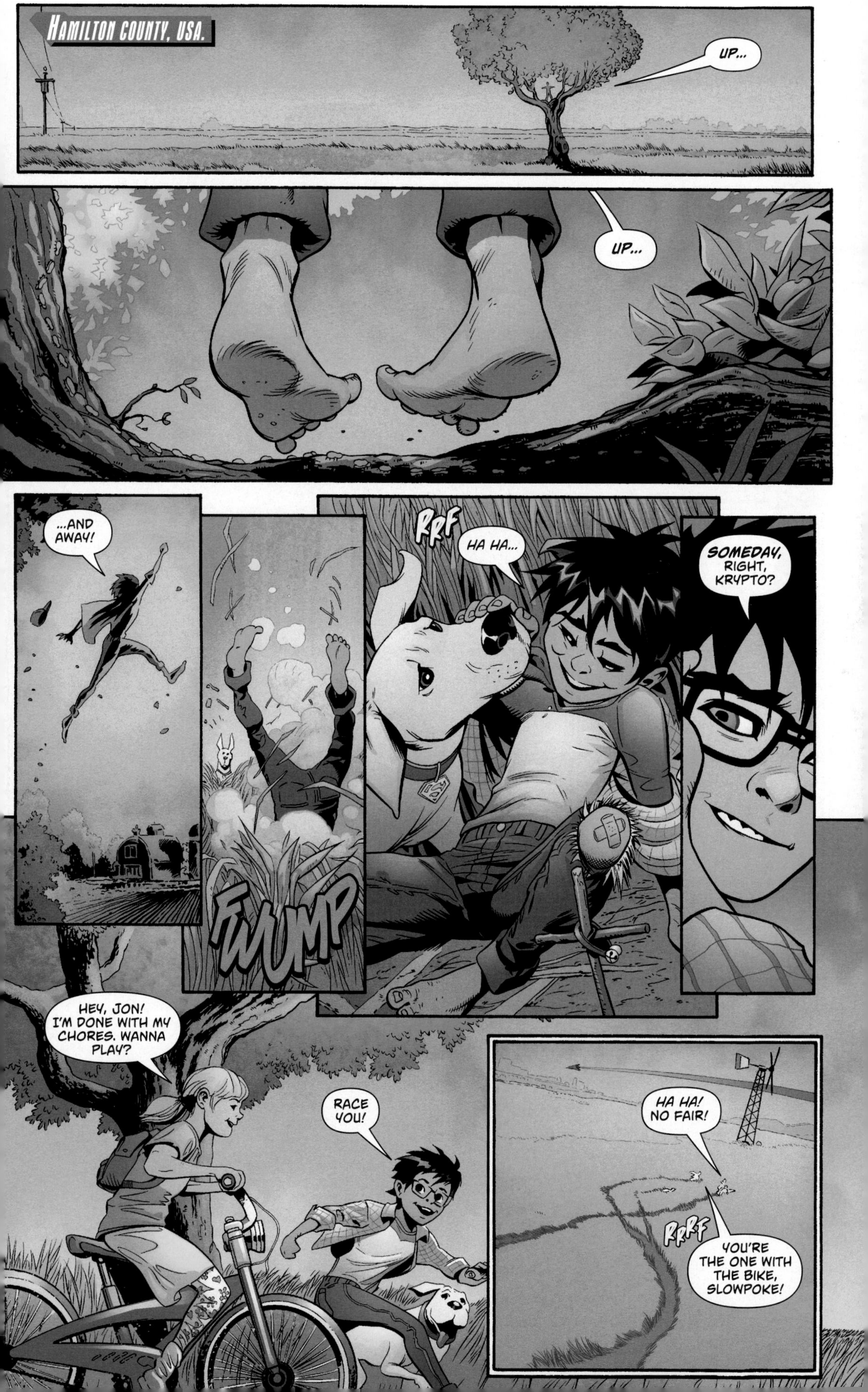
HAMILTON COUNTY, USA.
UP...
UP...
...AND AWAY!
FWUMP
RRF
HA HA...
SOMEDAY, RIGHT, KRYPTO?
HEY, JON! I'M DONE WITH MY CHORES. WANNA PLAY?
RACE YOU!
HA HA! NO FAIR!
RRRF
YOU'RE THE ONE WITH THE BIKE, SLOWPOKE!

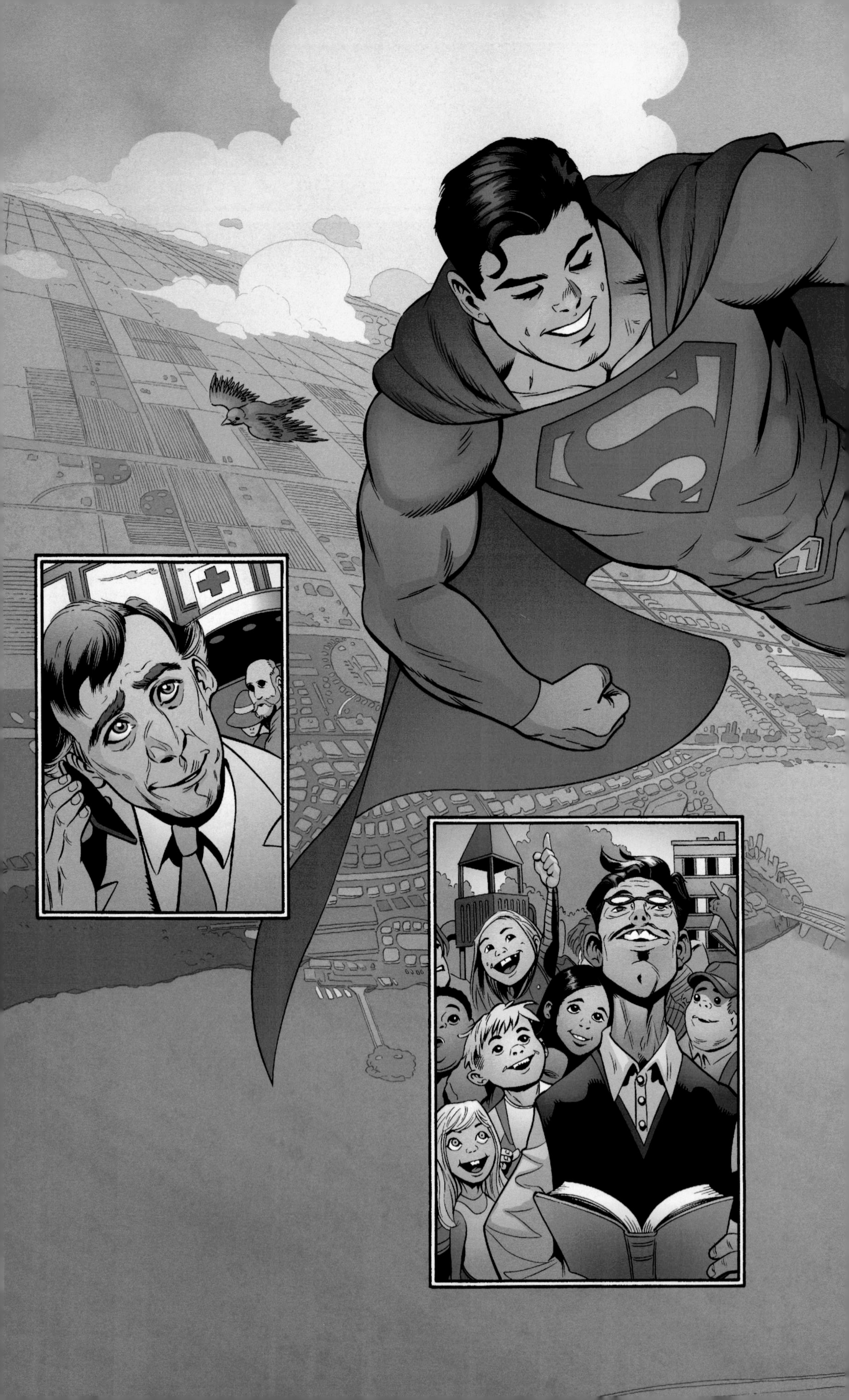

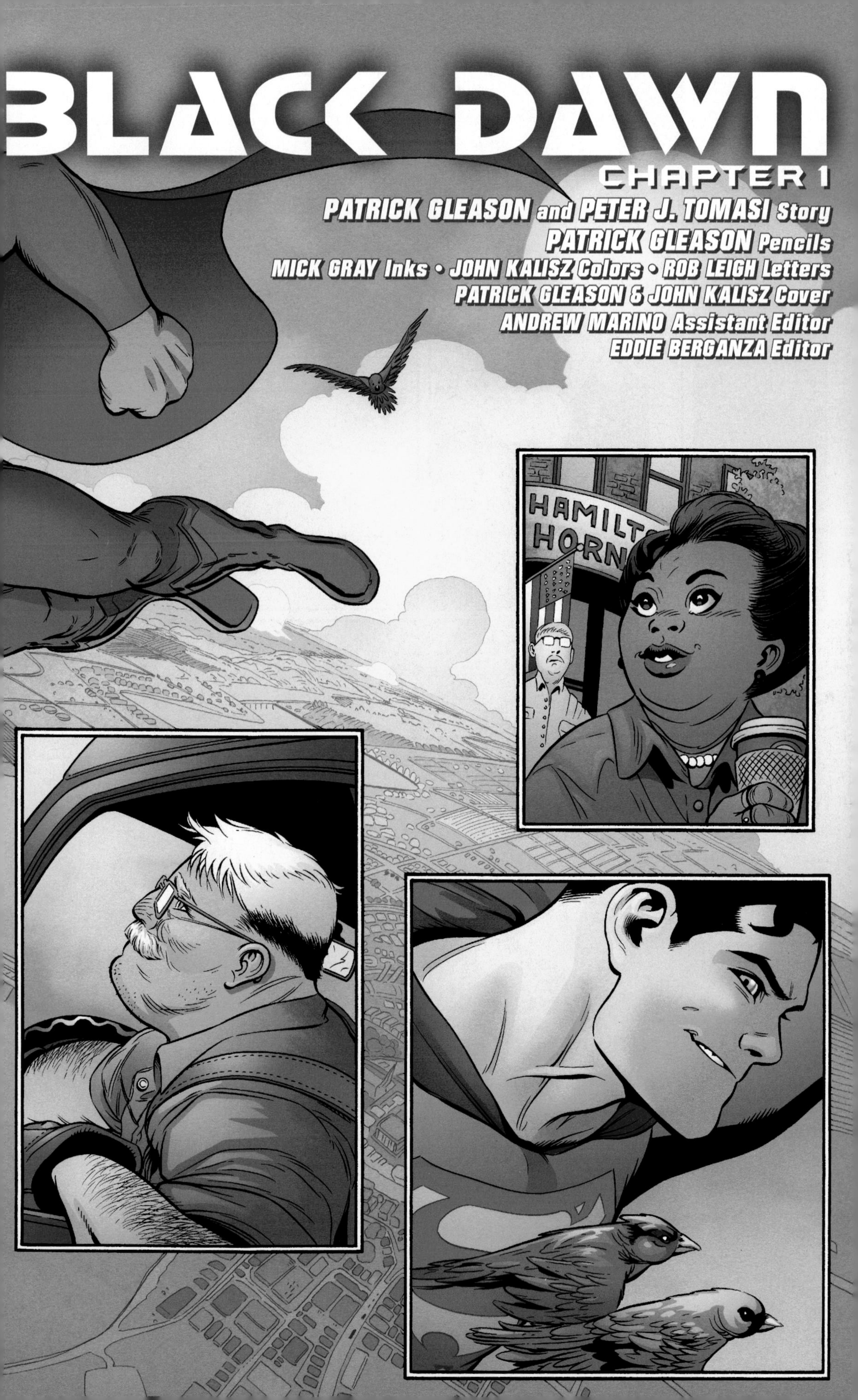
BLACK DAWN
CHAPTER 1
PATRICK GLEASON and PETER J. TOMASI Story
PATRICK GLEASON Pencils
MICK GRAY Inks • JOHN KALISZ Colors • ROB LEIGH Letters
PATRICK GLEASON & JOHN KALISZ Cover
ANDREW MARINO Assistant Editor
EDDIE BERGANZA Editor

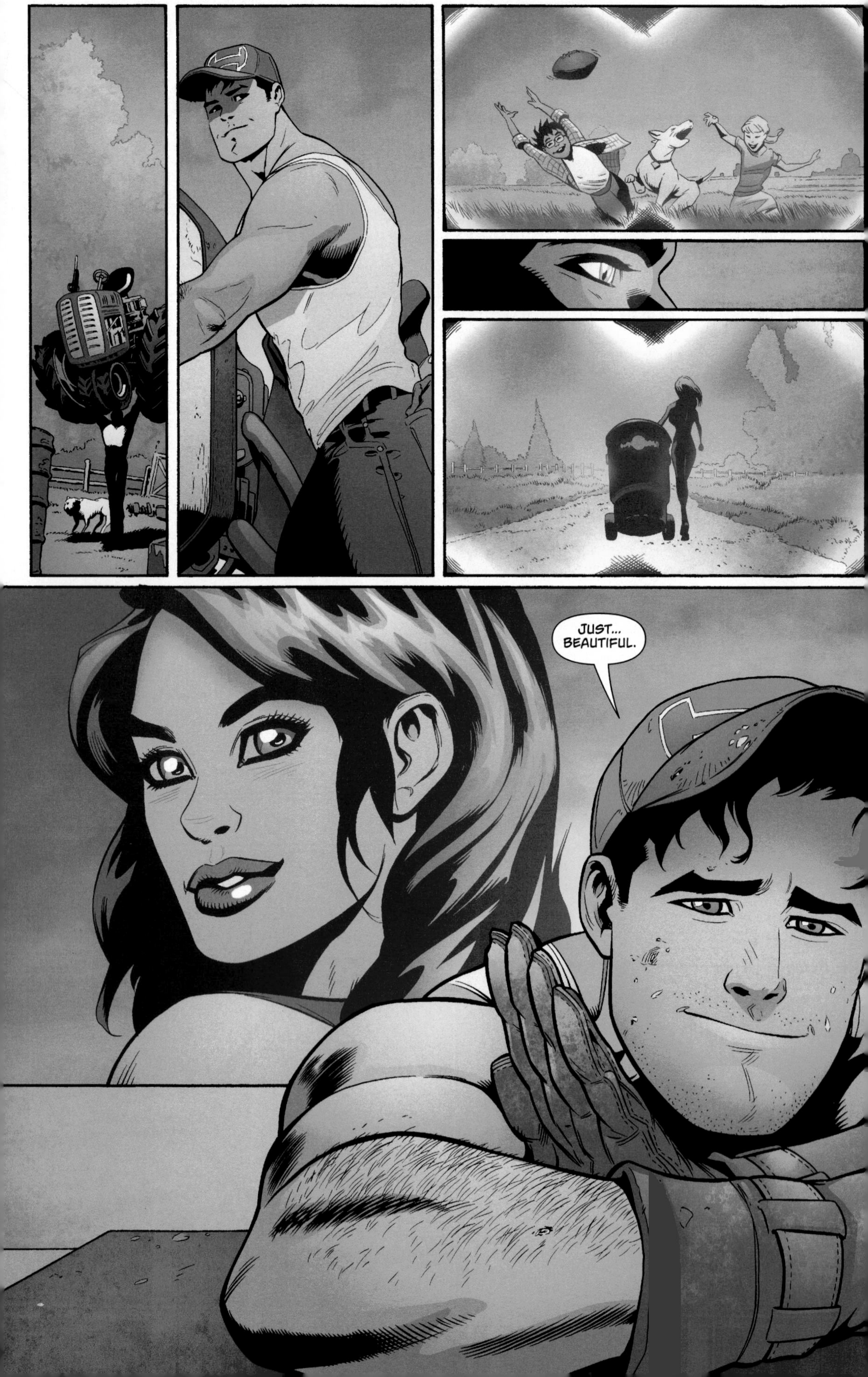
JUST... BEAUTIFUL.

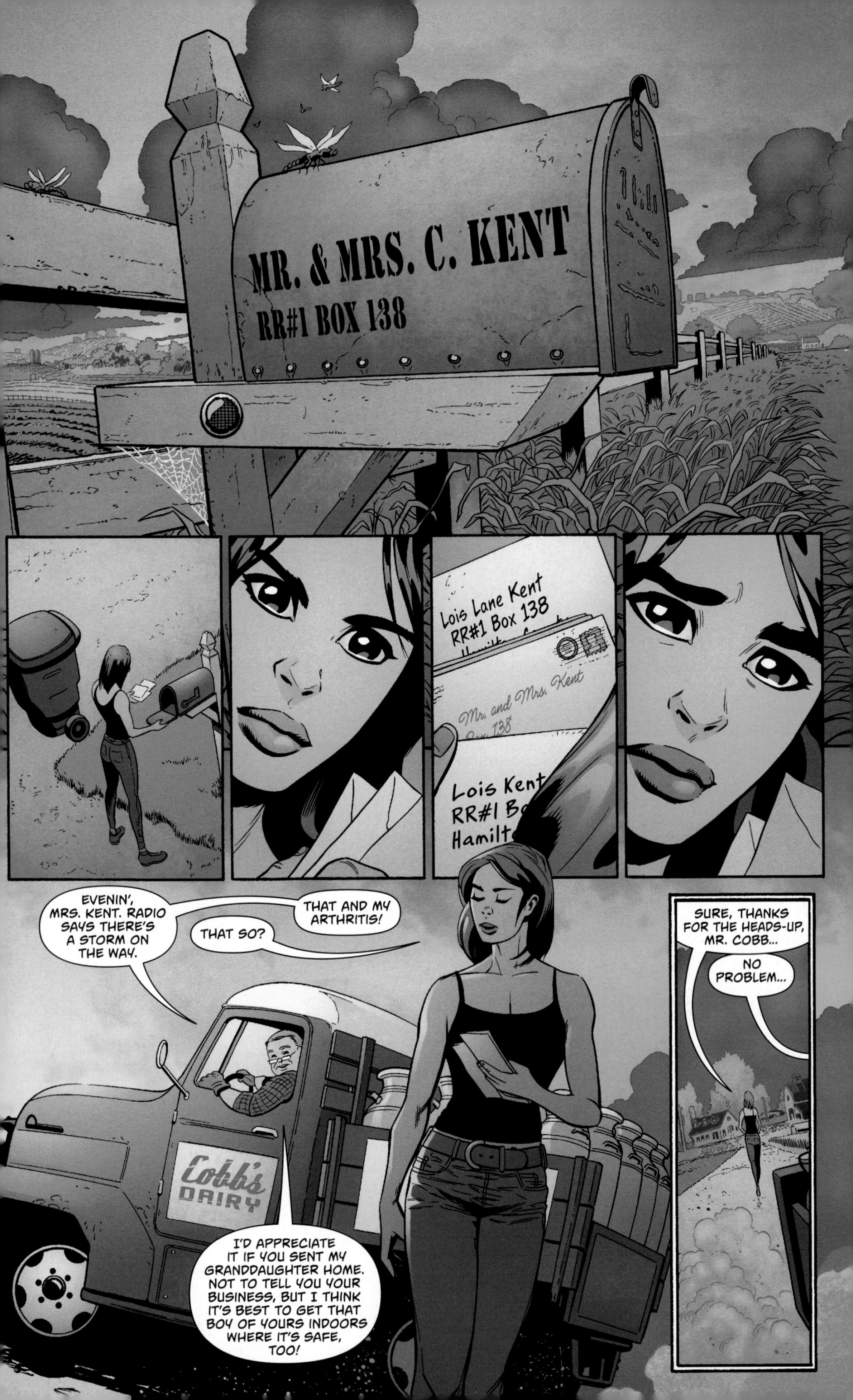
MR. & MRS. C. KENT
RR#1 BOX 138
Lois Lane Kent
RR#1 Box 138
Mr. and Mrs. Kent
Lois Kent
Cobb's Dairy
EVENIN', MRS. KENT. RADIO SAYS THERE'S A STORM ON THE WAY.
THAT SO?
THAT AND MY ARTHRITIS!
I'D APPRECIATE IT IF YOU SENT MY GRANDDAUGHTER HOME. NOT TO TELL YOU YOUR BUSINESS, BUT I THINK IT'S BEST TO GET THAT BOY OF YOURS INDOORS WHERE IT'S SAFE, TOO!
SURE, THANKS FOR THE HEADS-UP, MR. COBB...
NO PROBLEM...

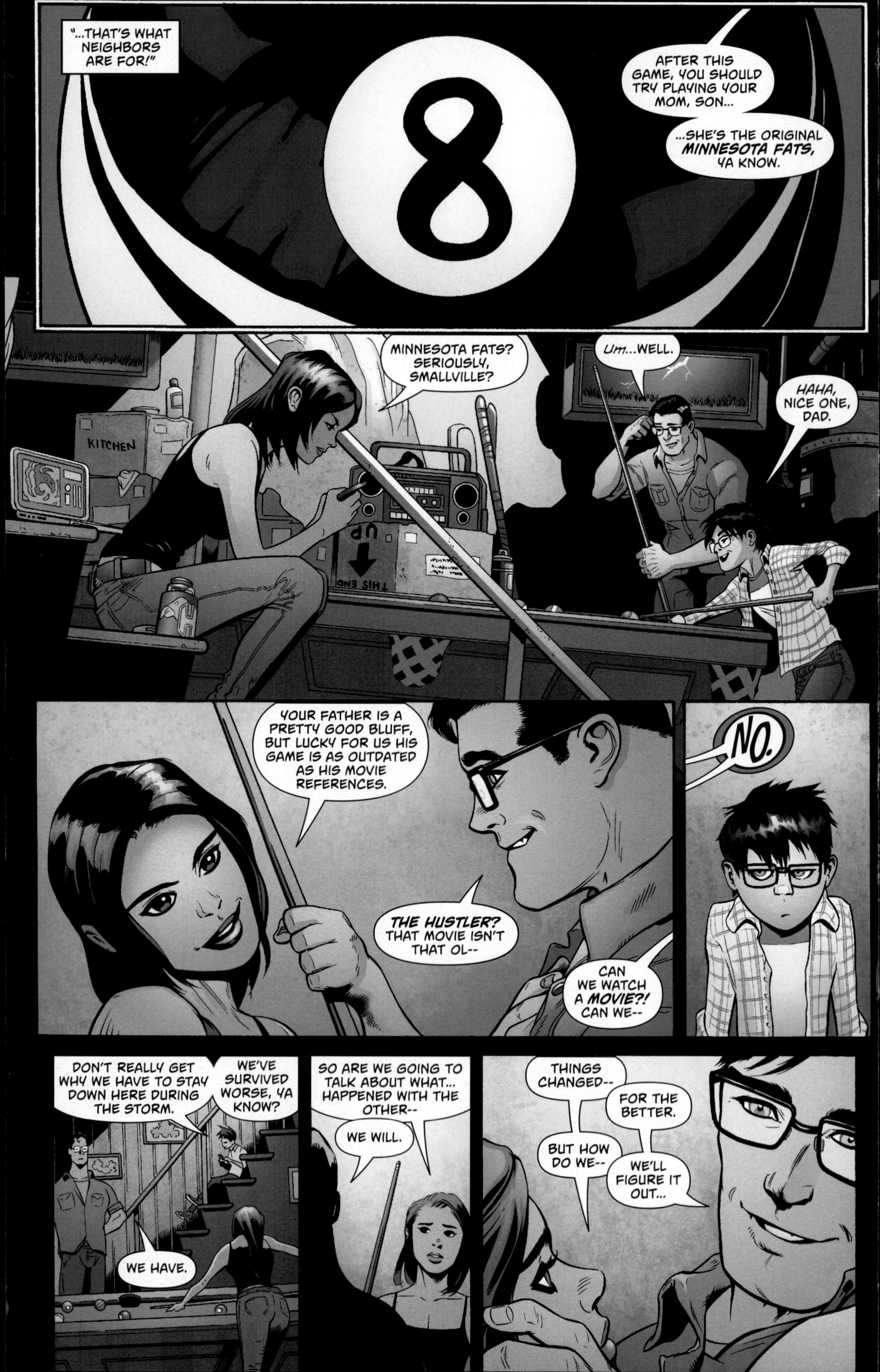
"...THAT'S WHAT NEIGHBORS ARE FOR!"
AFTER THIS GAME, YOU SHOULD TRY PLAYING YOUR MOM, SON...
...SHE'S THE ORIGINAL MINNESOTA FATS, YA KNOW.
MINNESOTA FATS? SERIOUSLY, SMALLVILLE?
UM...WELL.
HAHA, NICE ONE, DAD.
KITCHEN
UP
THIS END
YOUR FATHER IS A PRETTY GOOD BLUFF, BUT LUCKY FOR US HIS GAME IS AS OUTDATED AS HIS MOVIE REFERENCES.
THE HUSTLER? THAT MOVIE ISN'T THAT OL--
CAN WE WATCH A MOVIE?! CAN WE--
NO.
DON'T REALLY GET WHY WE HAVE TO STAY DOWN HERE DURING THE STORM.
WE'VE SURVIVED WORSE, YA KNOW?
WE HAVE.
SO ARE WE GOING TO TALK ABOUT WHAT... HAPPENED WITH THE OTHER--
WE WILL.
THINGS CHANGED--
FOR THE BETTER.
BUT HOW DO WE--
WE'LL FIGURE IT OUT...

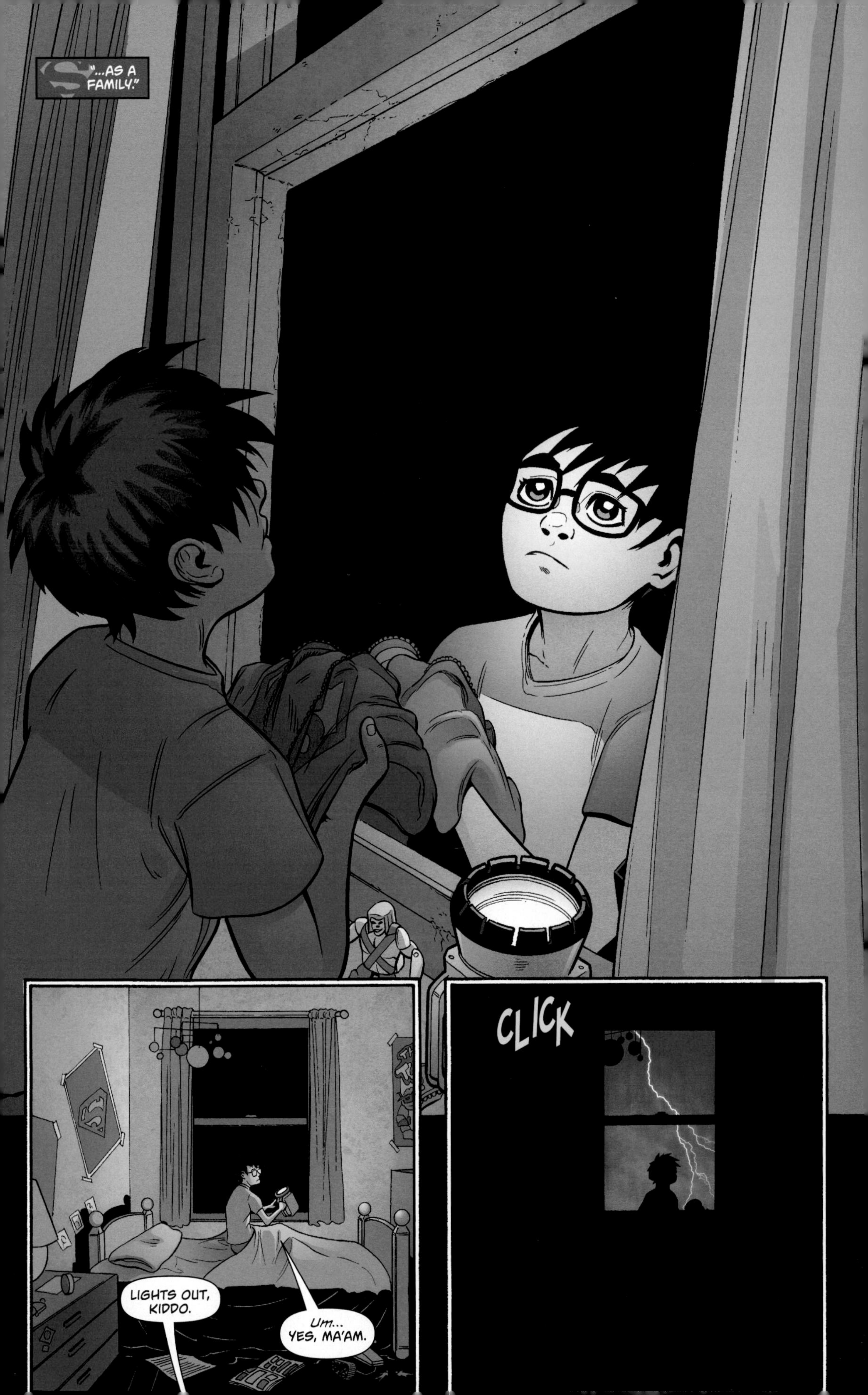
"...AS A FAMILY."
LIGHTS OUT, KIDDO.
UM... YES, MA'AM.
CLICK

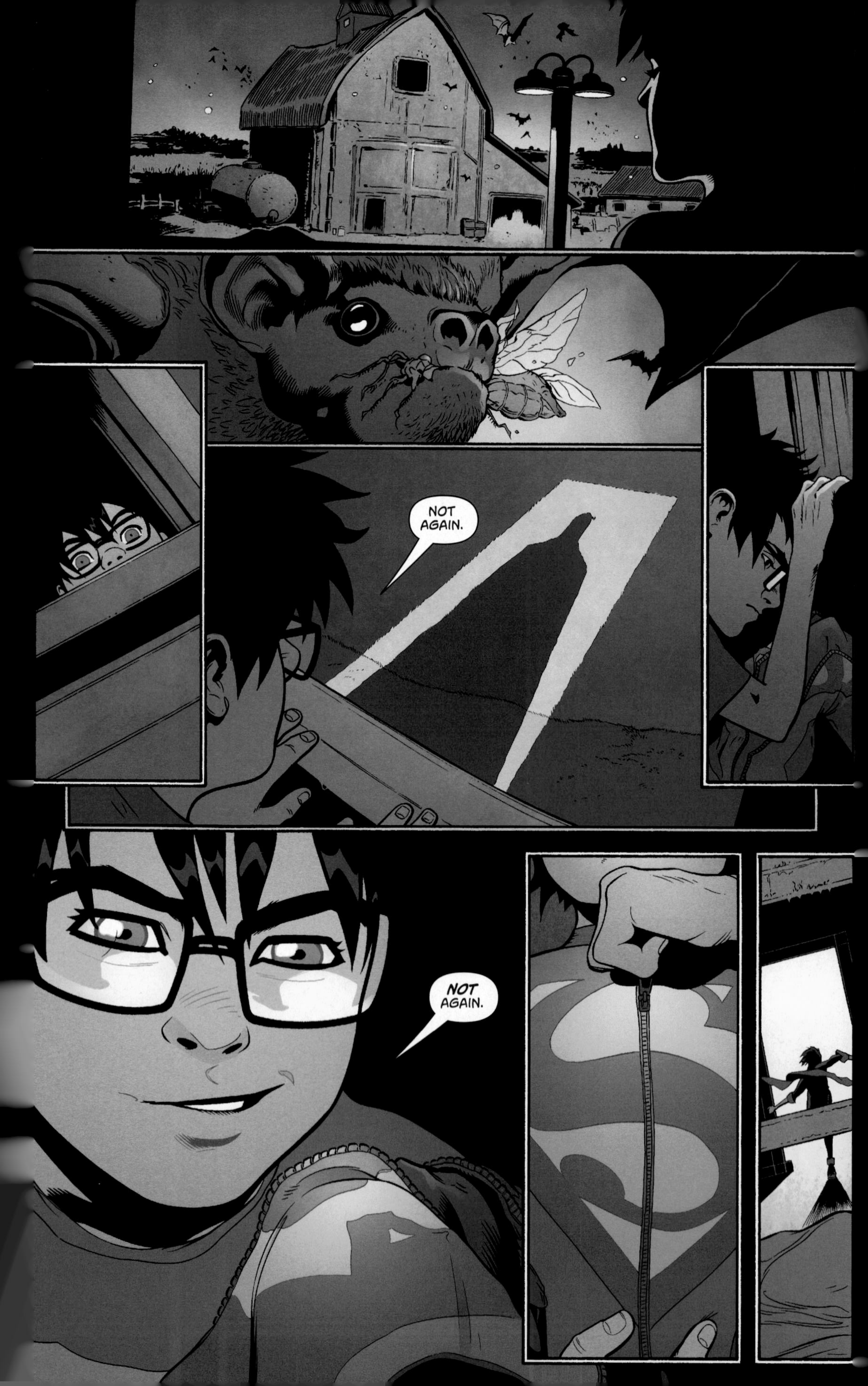
NOT AGAIN.
NOT AGAIN.

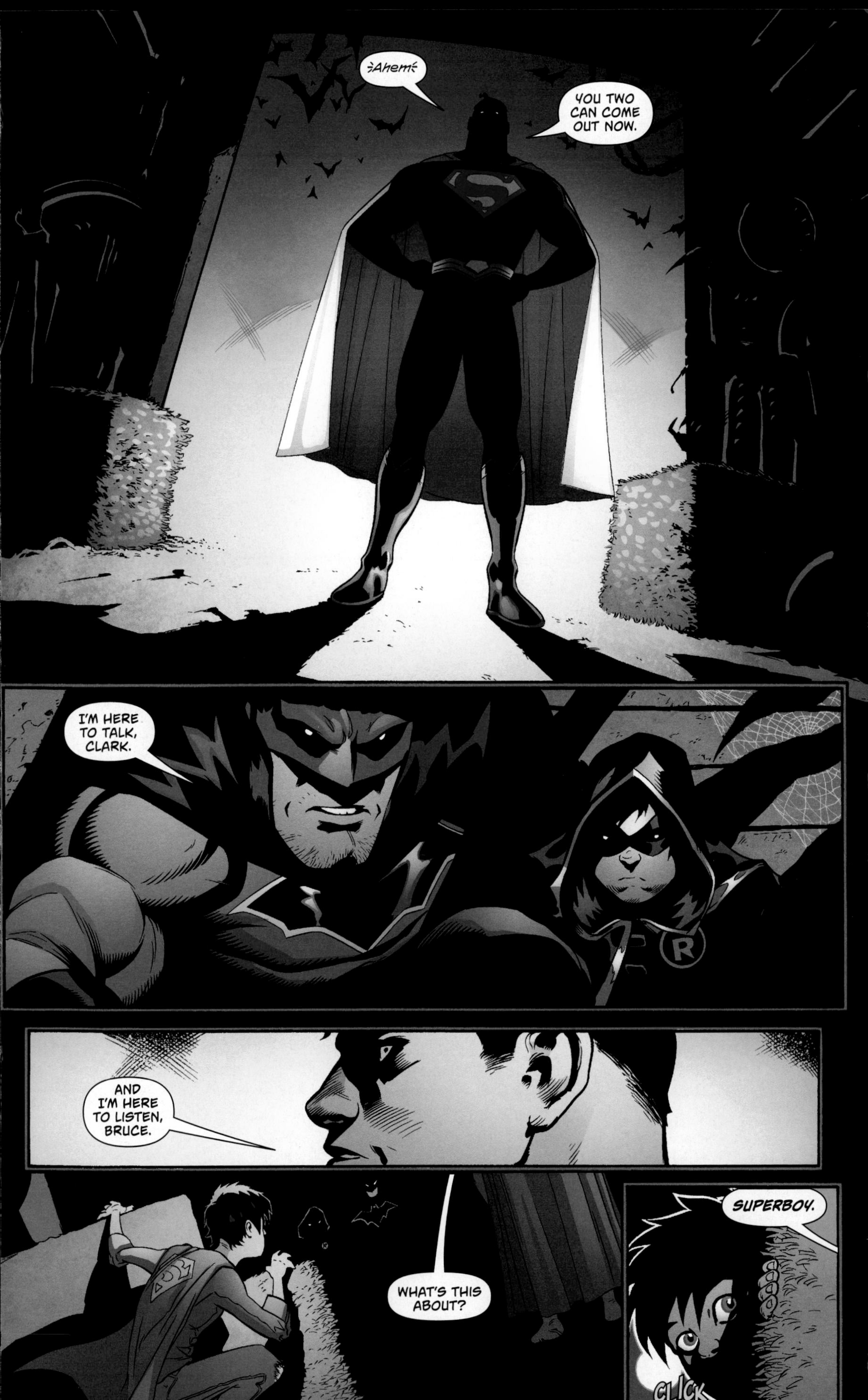

AHEM
YOU TWO CAN COME OUT NOW.
I'M HERE TO TALK, CLARK.
AND I'M HERE TO LISTEN, BRUCE.
WHAT'S THIS ABOUT?
SUPERBOY.
CLICK

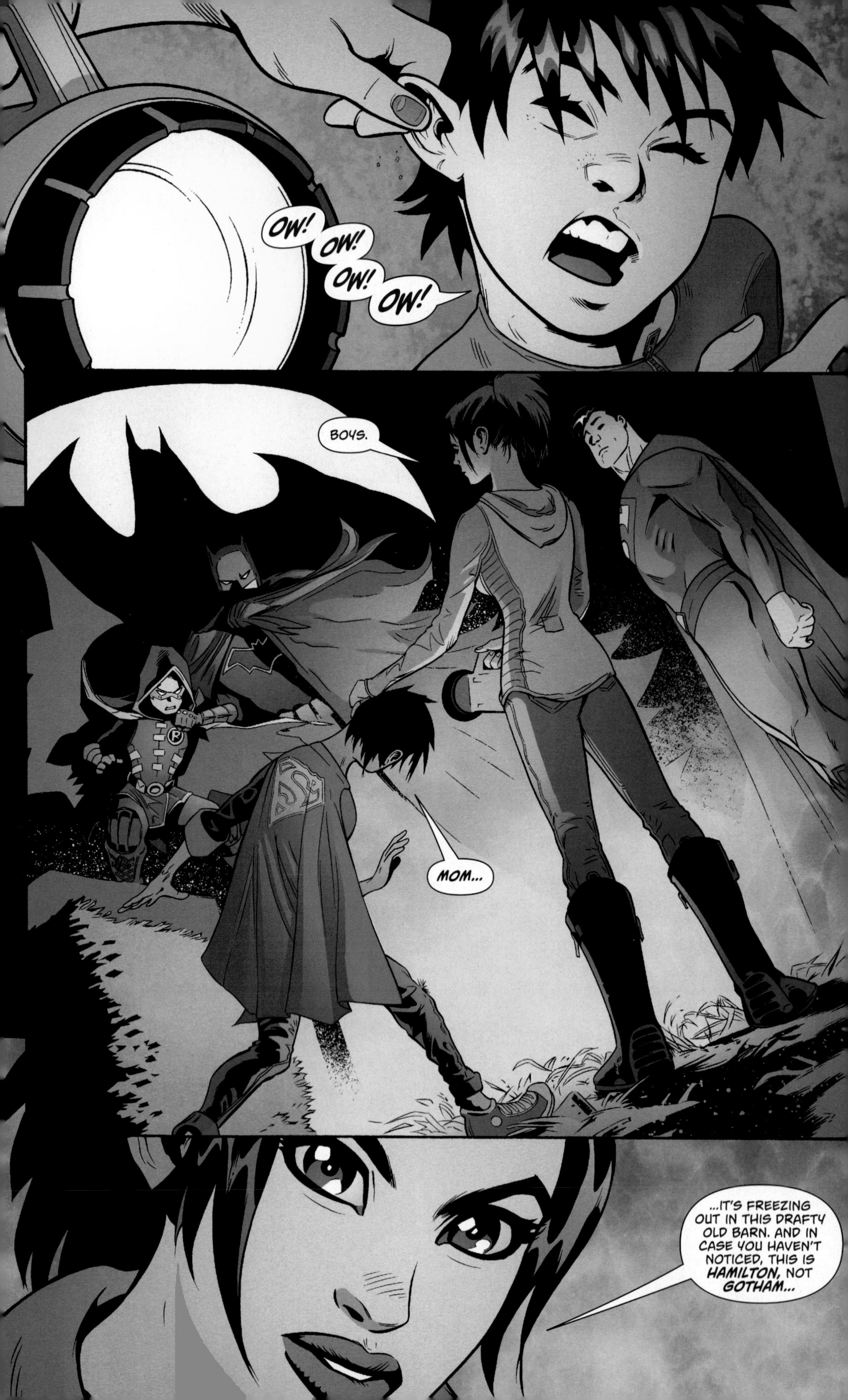
OW! OW! OW! OW!
BOYS.
MOM...
...IT'S FREEZING OUT IN THIS DRAFTY OLD BARN. AND IN CASE YOU HAVEN'T NOTICED, THIS IS HAMILTON, NOT GOTHAM...

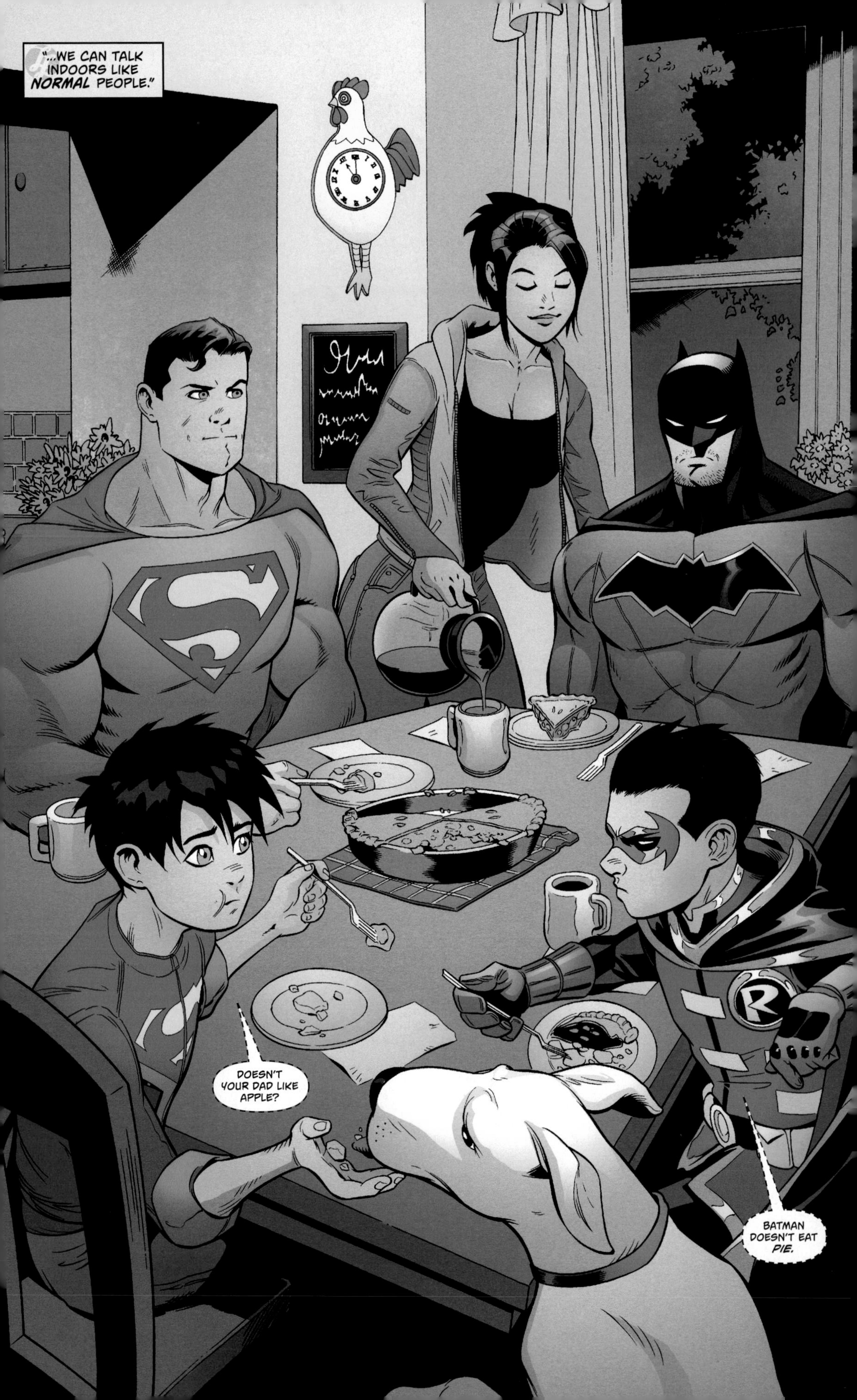
"...WE CAN TALK INDOORS LIKE *NORMAL* PEOPLE."
DOESN'T YOUR DAD LIKE APPLE?
BATMAN DOESN'T EAT *PIE*.

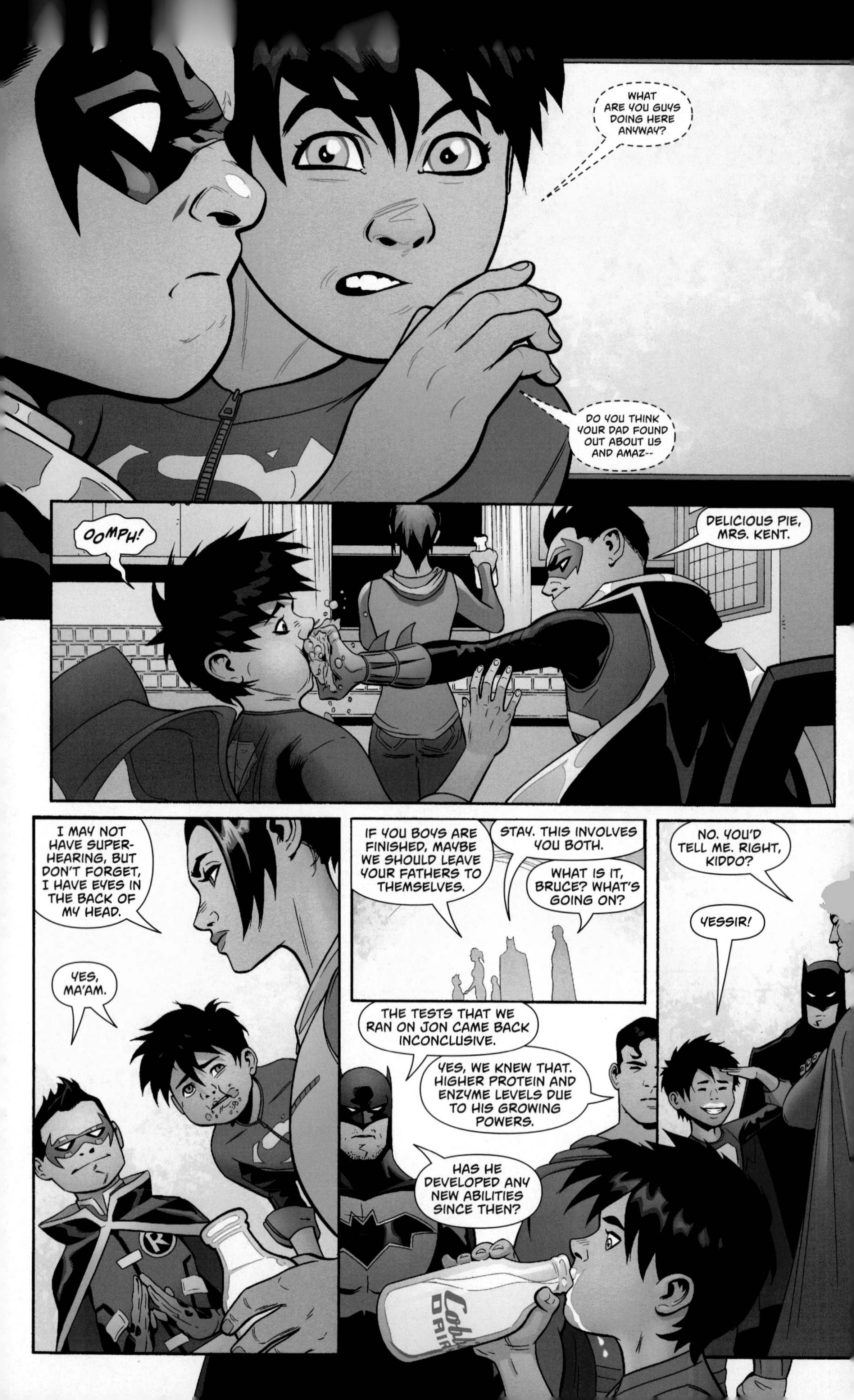
WHAT ARE YOU GUYS DOING HERE ANYWAY?
DO YOU THINK YOUR DAD FOUND OUT ABOUT US AND AMAZ--
OOMPH!
DELICIOUS PIE, MRS. KENT.
I MAY NOT HAVE SUPER-HEARING, BUT DON'T FORGET, I HAVE EYES IN THE BACK OF MY HEAD.
YES, MA'AM.
IF YOU BOYS ARE FINISHED, MAYBE WE SHOULD LEAVE YOUR FATHERS TO THEMSELVES.
STAY. THIS INVOLVES YOU BOTH.
WHAT IS IT, BRUCE? WHAT'S GOING ON?
THE TESTS THAT WE RAN ON JON CAME BACK INCONCLUSIVE.
YES, WE KNEW THAT. HIGHER PROTEIN AND ENZYME LEVELS DUE TO HIS GROWING POWERS.
HAS HE DEVELOPED ANY NEW ABILITIES SINCE THEN?
NO. YOU'D TELL ME. RIGHT, KIDDO?
YESSIR!

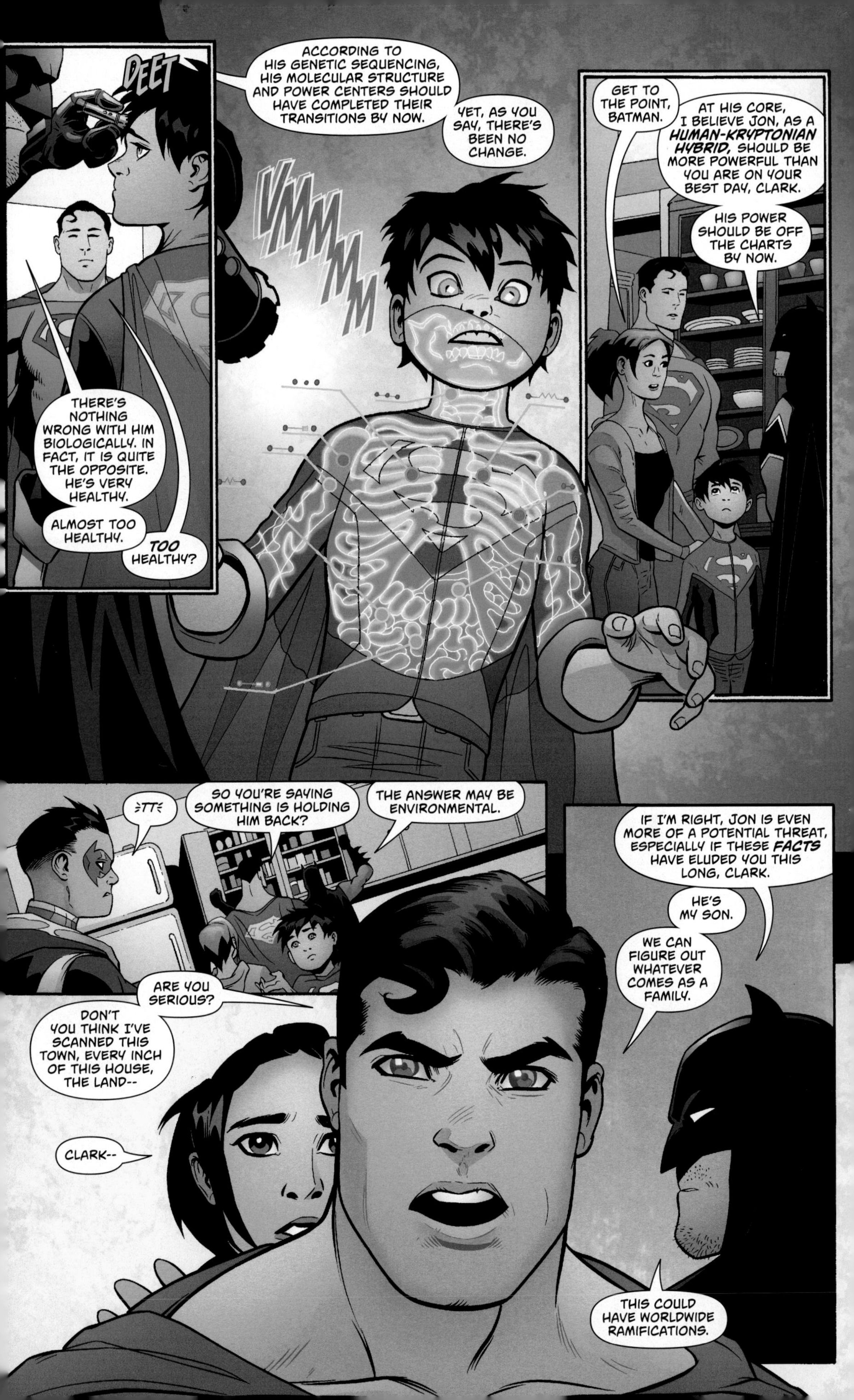
DEET
ACCORDING TO HIS GENETIC SEQUENCING, HIS MOLECULAR STRUCTURE AND POWER CENTERS SHOULD HAVE COMPLETED THEIR TRANSITIONS BY NOW.
YET, AS YOU SAY, THERE'S BEEN NO CHANGE.
THERE'S NOTHING WRONG WITH HIM BIOLOGICALLY. IN FACT, IT IS QUITE THE OPPOSITE. HE'S VERY HEALTHY.
ALMOST TOO HEALTHY.
TOO HEALTHY?
VMMMMM
GET TO THE POINT, BATMAN.
AT HIS CORE, I BELIEVE JON, AS A HUMAN-KRYPTONIAN HYBRID, SHOULD BE MORE POWERFUL THAN YOU ARE ON YOUR BEST DAY, CLARK.
HIS POWER SHOULD BE OFF THE CHARTS BY NOW.
TT
SO YOU'RE SAYING SOMETHING IS HOLDING HIM BACK?
THE ANSWER MAY BE ENVIRONMENTAL.
ARE YOU SERIOUS?
DON'T YOU THINK I'VE SCANNED THIS TOWN, EVERY INCH OF THIS HOUSE, THE LAND--
CLARK--
IF I'M RIGHT, JON IS EVEN MORE OF A POTENTIAL THREAT, ESPECIALLY IF THESE FACTS HAVE ELUDED YOU THIS LONG, CLARK.
HE'S MY SON.
WE CAN FIGURE OUT WHATEVER COMES AS A FAMILY.
THIS COULD HAVE WORLDWIDE RAMIFICATIONS.

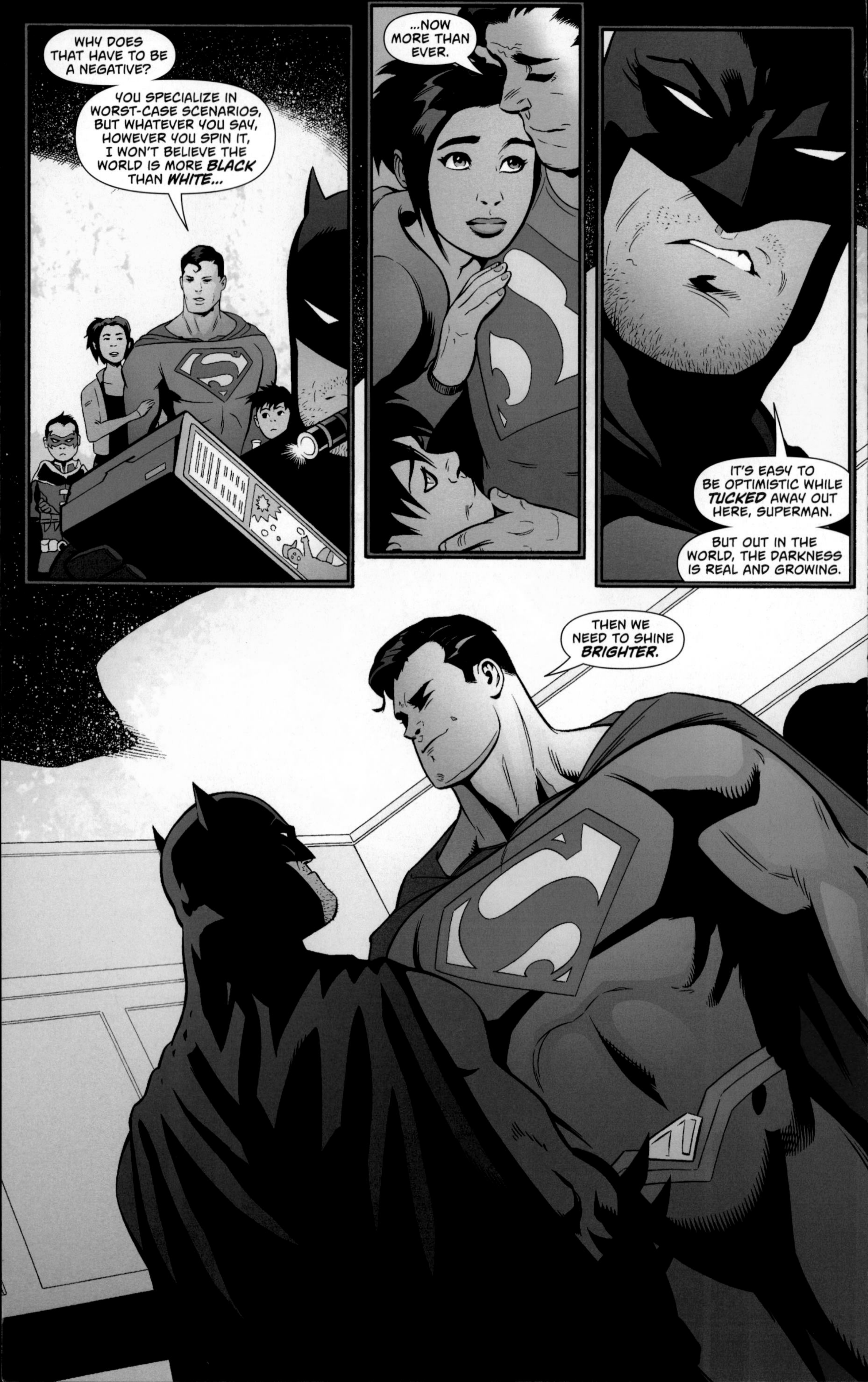
WHY DOES THAT HAVE TO BE A NEGATIVE?
YOU SPECIALIZE IN WORST-CASE SCENARIOS, BUT WHATEVER YOU SAY, HOWEVER YOU SPIN IT, I WON'T BELIEVE THE WORLD IS MORE BLACK THAN WHITE...
...NOW MORE THAN EVER.
IT'S EASY TO BE OPTIMISTIC WHILE TUCKED AWAY OUT HERE, SUPERMAN.
BUT OUT IN THE WORLD, THE DARKNESS IS REAL AND GROWING.
THEN WE NEED TO SHINE BRIGHTER.

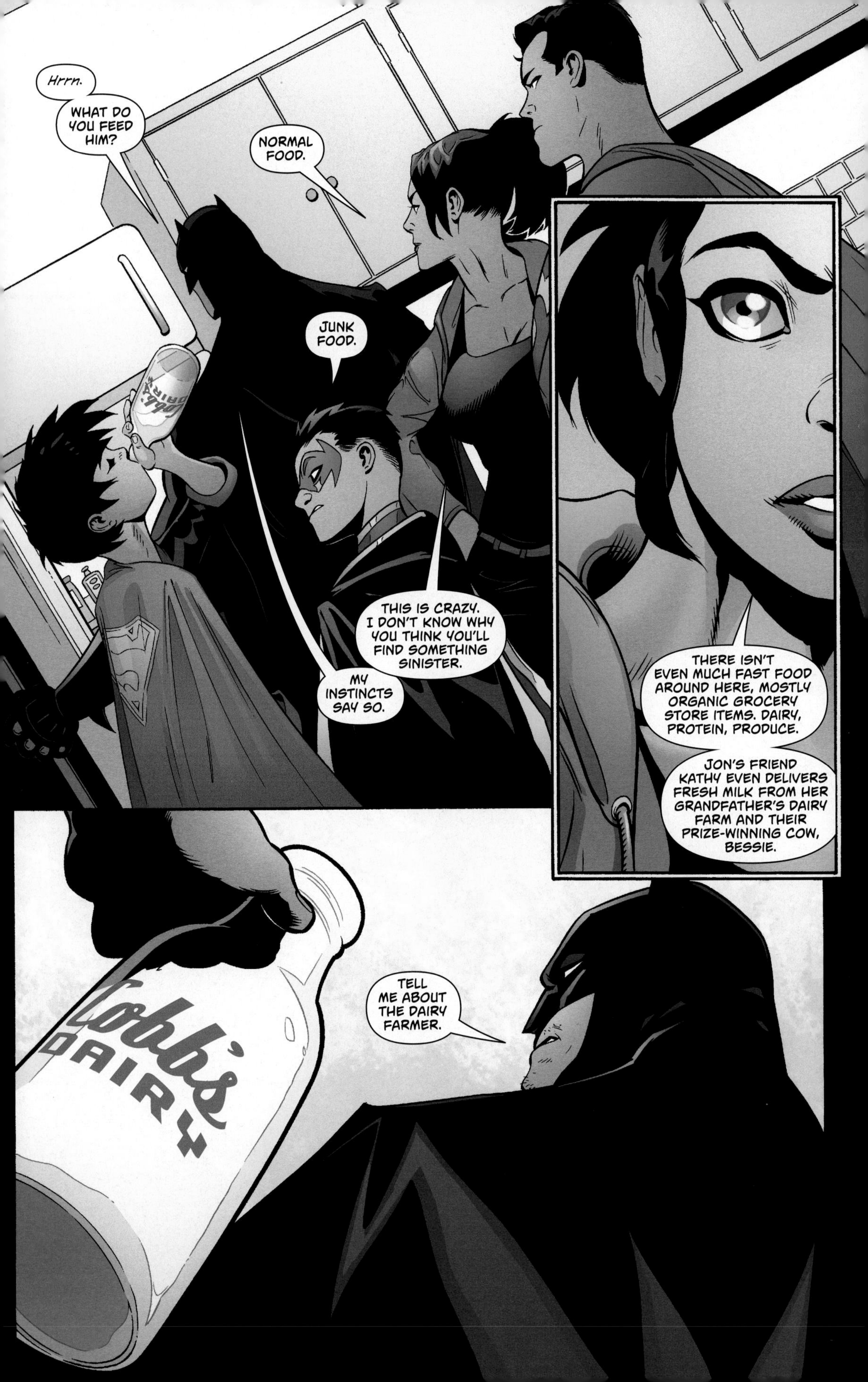
Hrrn.
WHAT DO YOU FEED HIM?
NORMAL FOOD.
JUNK FOOD.
THIS IS CRAZY. I DON'T KNOW WHY YOU THINK YOU'LL FIND SOMETHING SINISTER.
MY INSTINCTS SAY SO.
THERE ISN'T EVEN MUCH FAST FOOD AROUND HERE, MOSTLY ORGANIC GROCERY STORE ITEMS. DAIRY, PROTEIN, PRODUCE.
JON'S FRIEND KATHY EVEN DELIVERS FRESH MILK FROM HER GRANDFATHER'S DAIRY FARM AND THEIR PRIZE-WINNING COW, BESSIE.
Cobb's DAIRY
TELL ME ABOUT THE DAIRY FARMER.

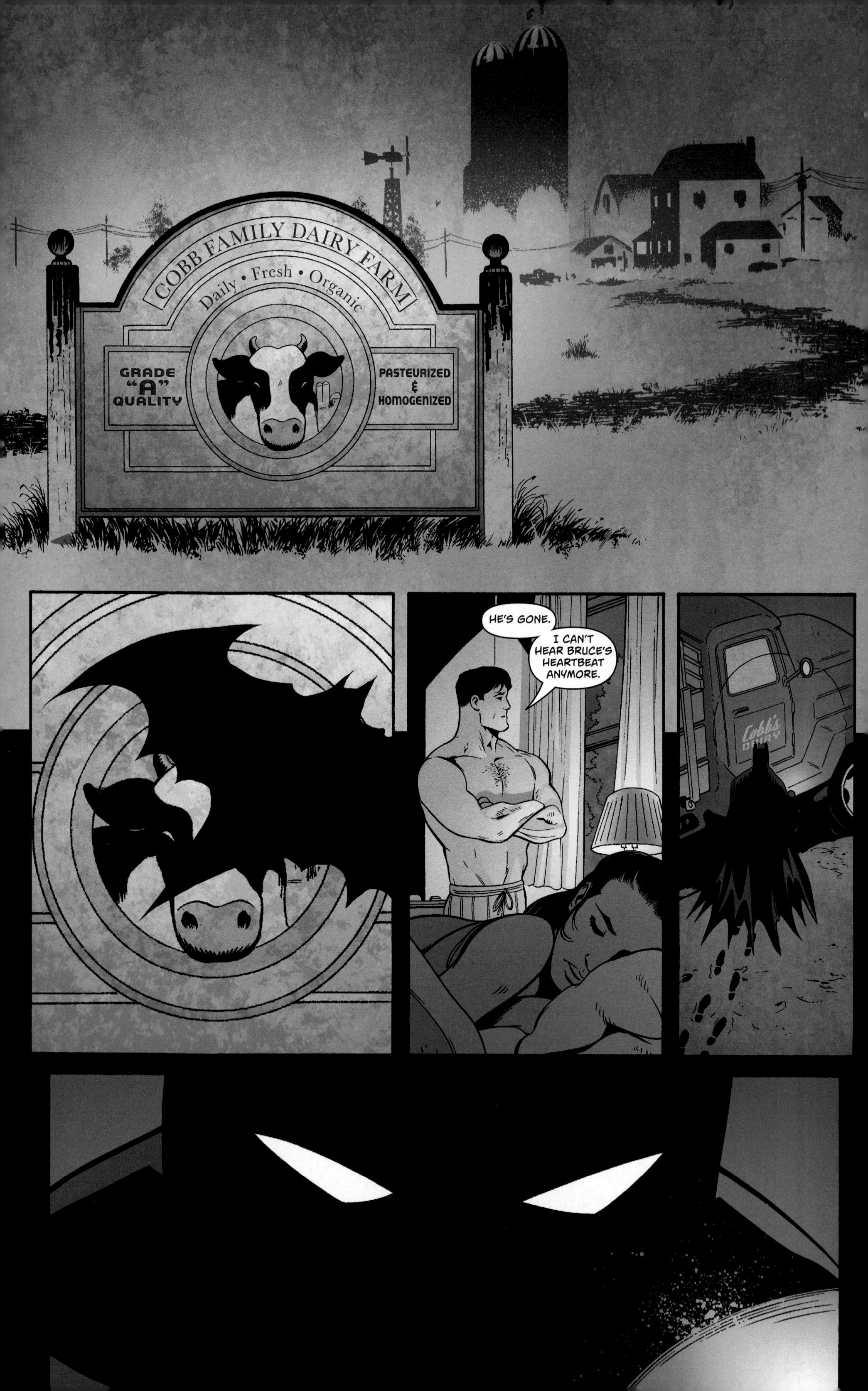
COBB FAMILY DAIRY FARM
Daily • Fresh • Organic
GRADE "A" QUALITY
PASTEURIZED & HOMOGENIZED
HE'S GONE.
I CAN'T HEAR BRUCE'S HEARTBEAT ANYMORE.
Cobb's DAIRY

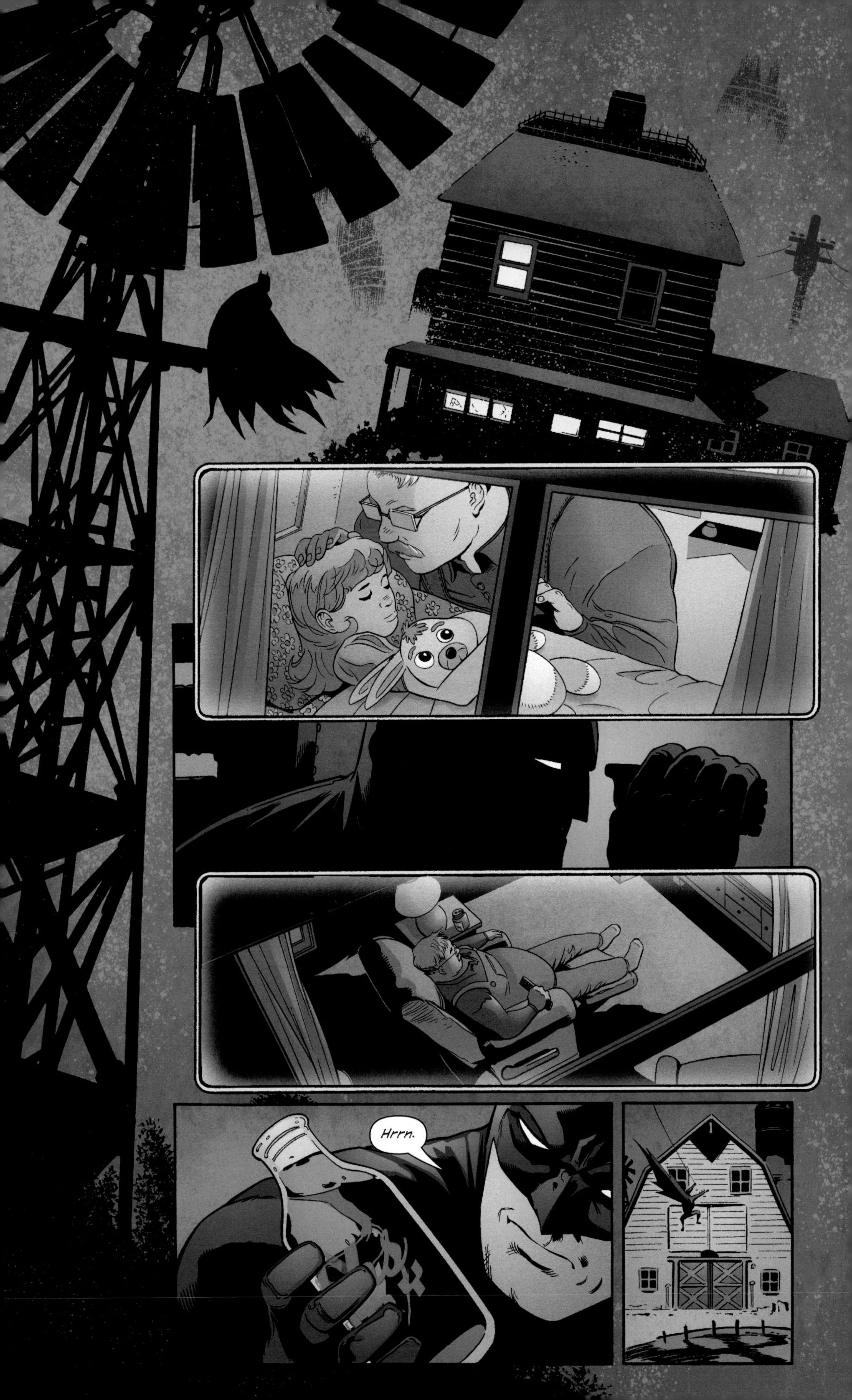
Hrrn.

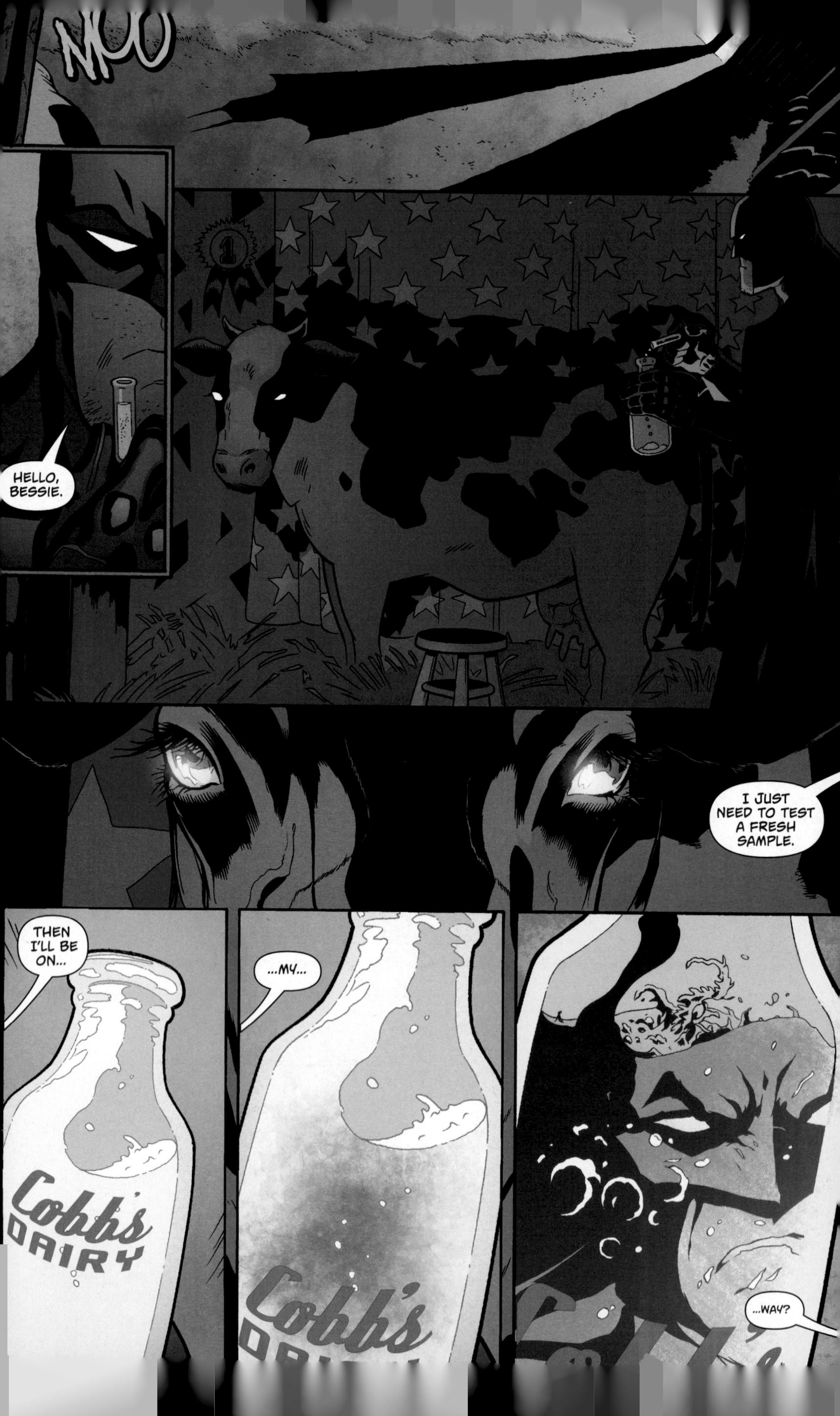
MOO
HELLO, BESSIE.
I JUST NEED TO TEST A FRESH SAMPLE.
THEN I'LL BE ON...
...MY...
Cobb's DAIRY
Cobb's
...WAY?

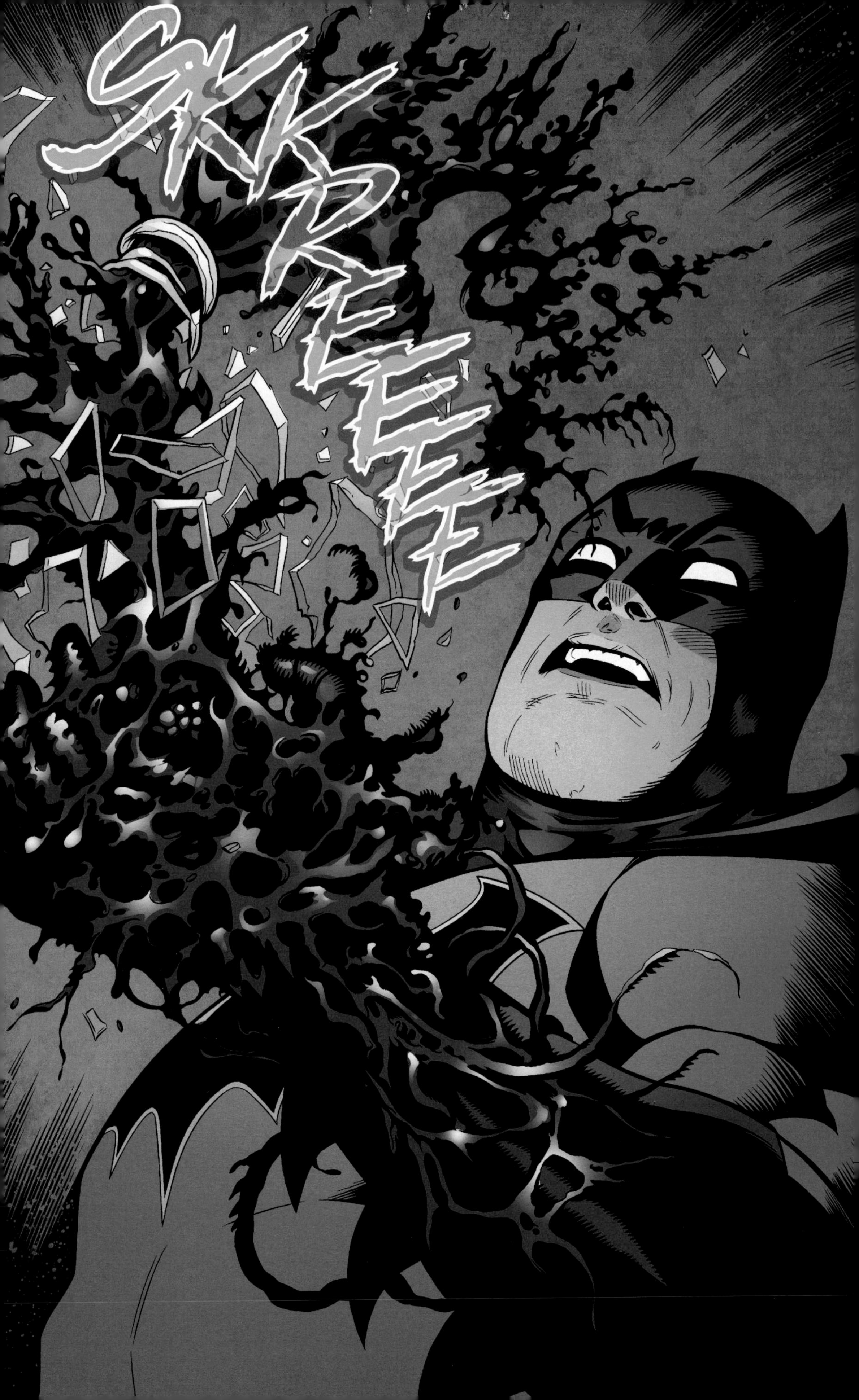
SKREEEEE

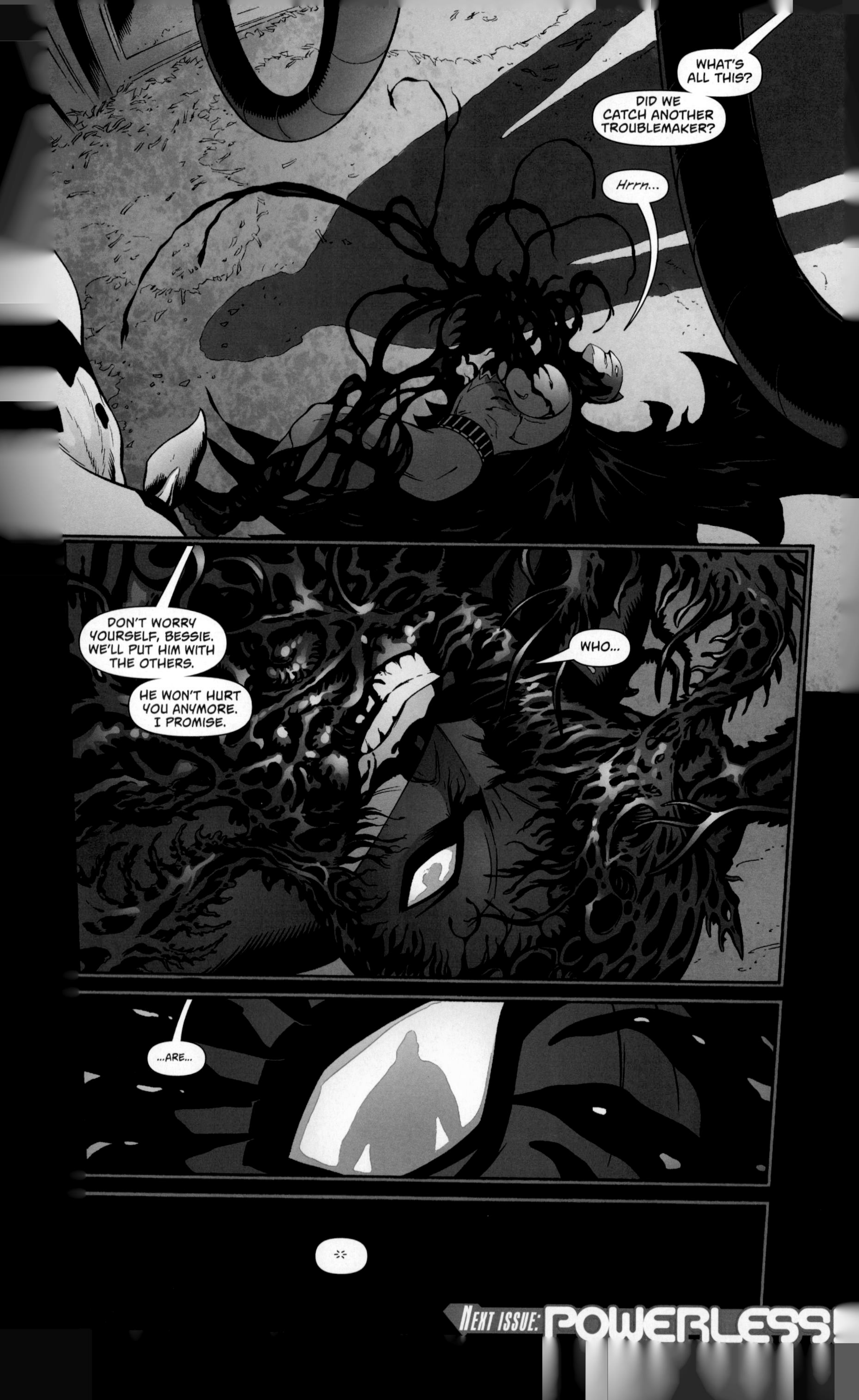
WHAT'S ALL THIS?
DID WE CATCH ANOTHER TROUBLEMAKER?
Hrrn...
DON'T WORRY YOURSELF, BESSIE. WE'LL PUT HIM WITH THE OTHERS.
HE WON'T HURT YOU ANYMORE. I PROMISE.
WHO...
...ARE...
NEXT ISSUE: POWERLESS!

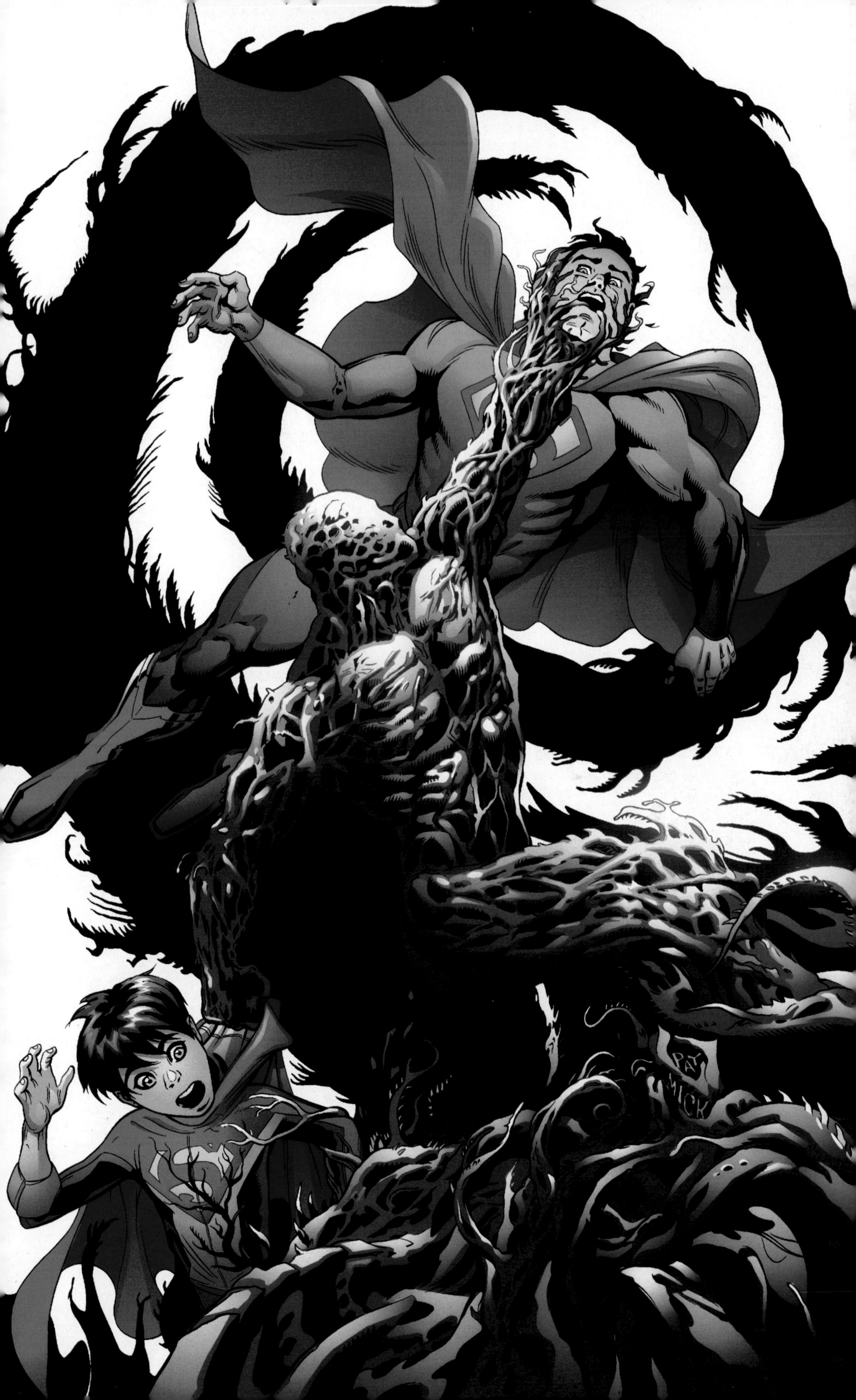
PAT
MICK

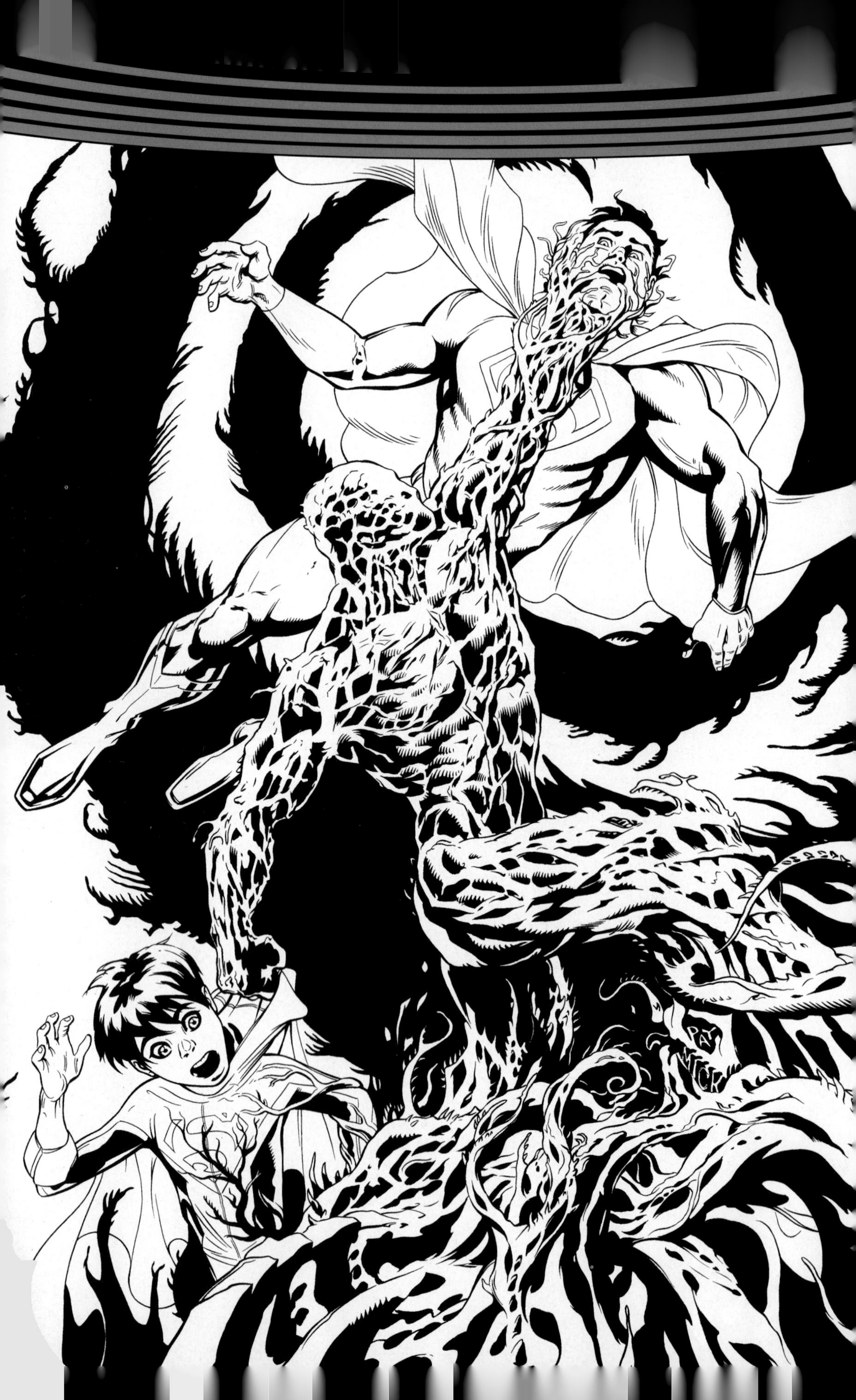

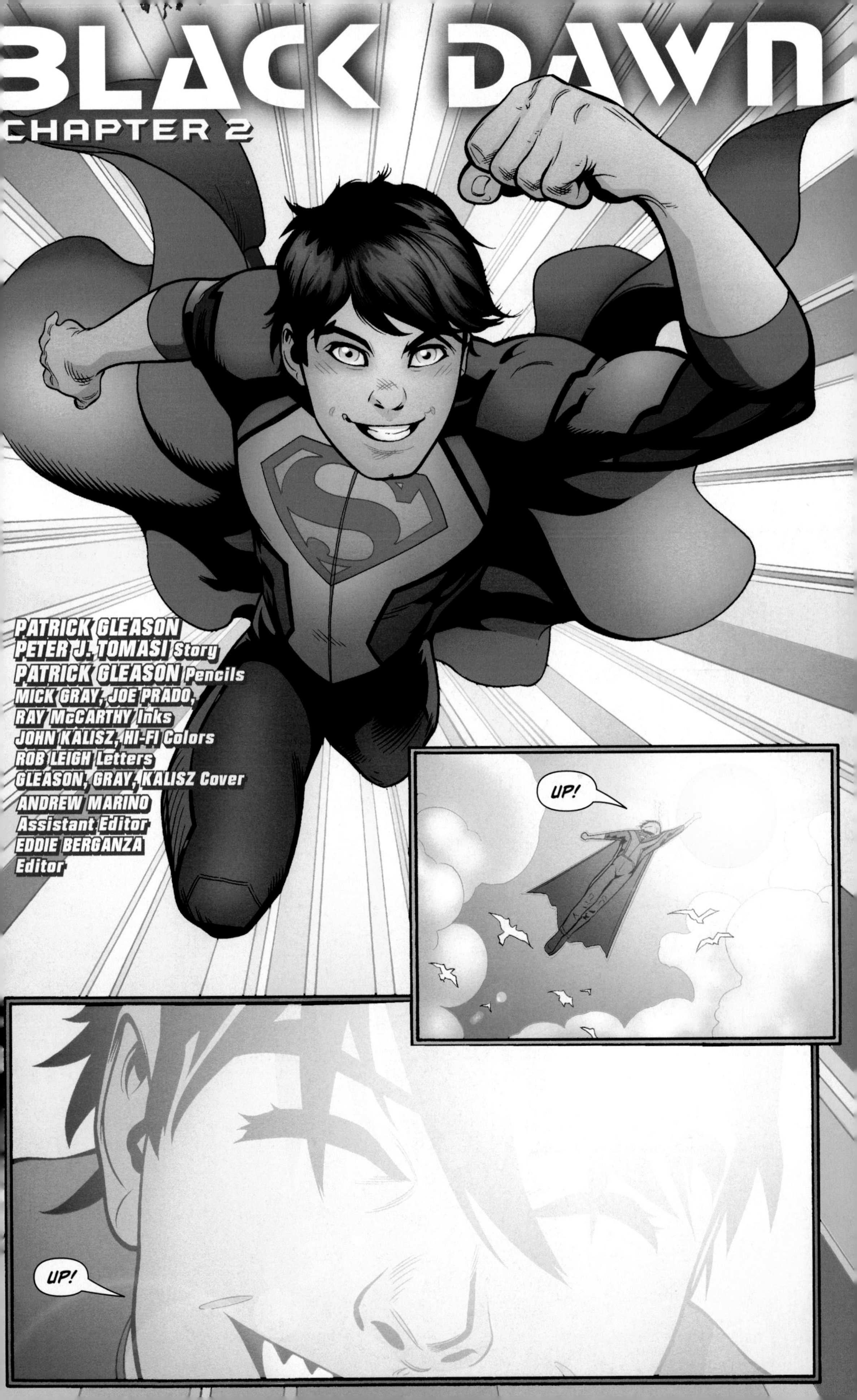
BLACK DAWN
CHAPTER 2
PATRICK GLEASON
PETER J. TOMASI Story
PATRICK GLEASON Pencils
MICK GRAY, JOE PRADO,
RAY McCARTHY Inks
JOHN KALISZ, HI-FI Colors
ROB LEIGH Letters
GLEASON, GRAY, KALISZ Cover
ANDREW MARINO
Assistant Editor
EDDIE BERGANZA
Editor
UP!
UP!

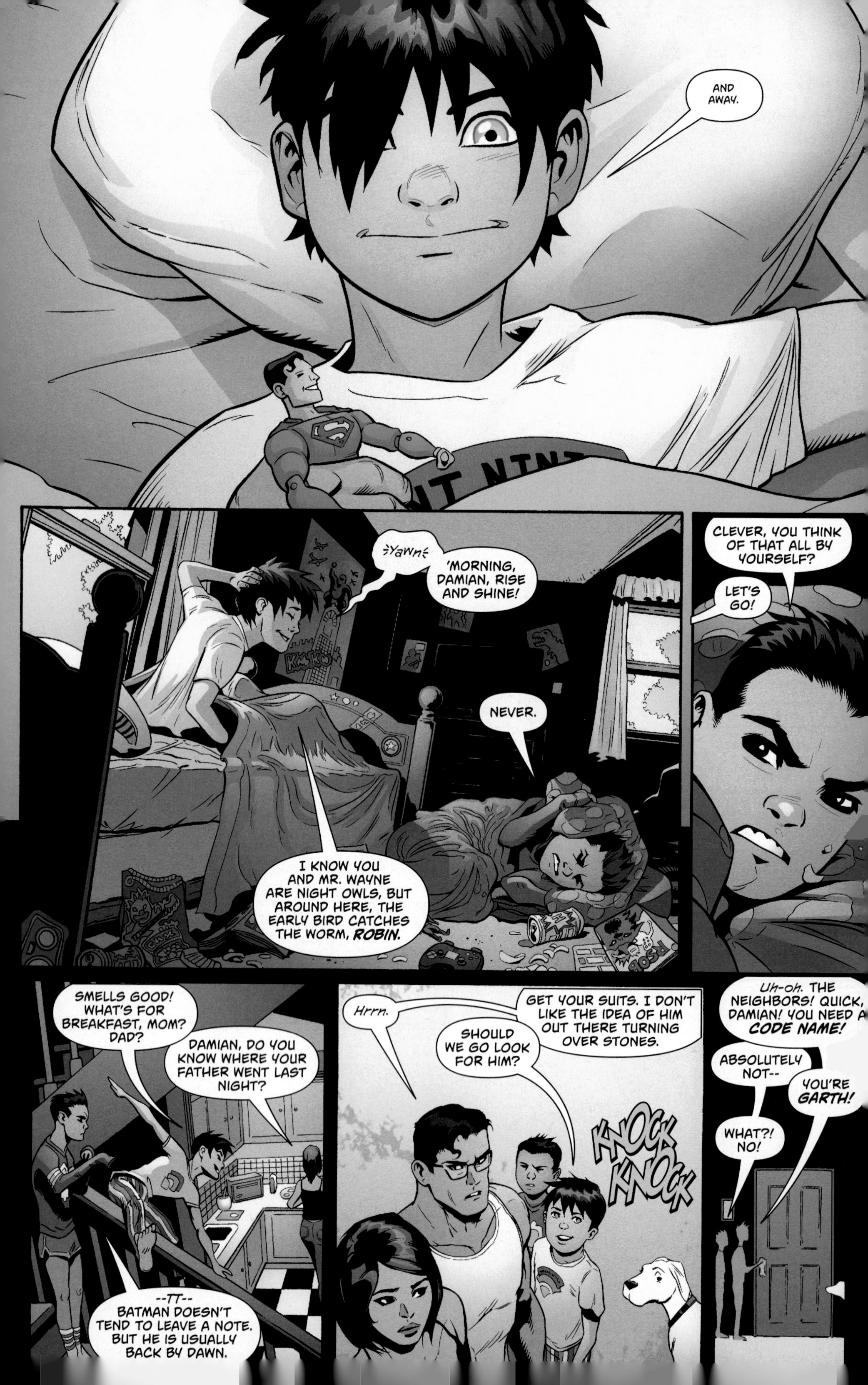
AND AWAY.
T NINT
Yawn
'MORNING, DAMIAN, RISE AND SHINE!
NEVER.
I KNOW YOU AND MR. WAYNE ARE NIGHT OWLS, BUT AROUND HERE, THE EARLY BIRD CATCHES THE WORM, ROBIN.
CLEVER, YOU THINK OF THAT ALL BY YOURSELF?
LET'S GO!
SMELLS GOOD! WHAT'S FOR BREAKFAST, MOM? DAD?
DAMIAN, DO YOU KNOW WHERE YOUR FATHER WENT LAST NIGHT?
--TT-- BATMAN DOESN'T TEND TO LEAVE A NOTE. BUT HE IS USUALLY BACK BY DAWN.
Hrrn.
GET YOUR SUITS. I DON'T LIKE THE IDEA OF HIM OUT THERE TURNING OVER STONES.
SHOULD WE GO LOOK FOR HIM?
KNOCK KNOCK
Uh-oh. THE NEIGHBORS! QUICK, DAMIAN! YOU NEED A CODE NAME!
ABSOLUTELY NOT--
YOU'RE GARTH!
WHAT?! NO!

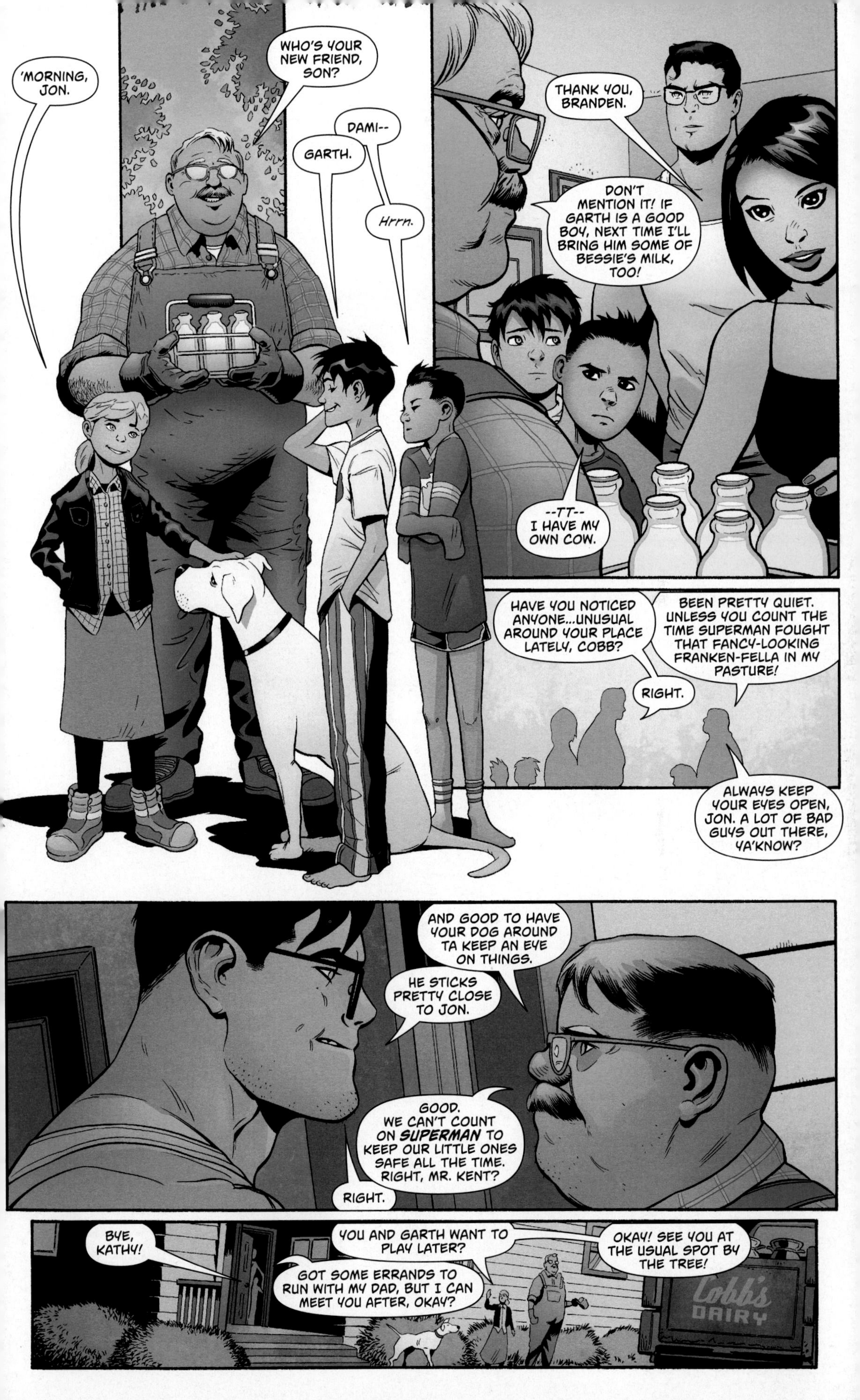

'MORNING, JON.
WHO'S YOUR NEW FRIEND, SON?
DAMI--
GARTH.
Hrrn.
THANK YOU, BRANDEN.
DON'T MENTION IT! IF GARTH IS A GOOD BOY, NEXT TIME I'LL BRING HIM SOME OF BESSIE'S MILK, TOO!
--TT-- I HAVE MY OWN COW.
HAVE YOU NOTICED ANYONE...UNUSUAL AROUND YOUR PLACE LATELY, COBB?
BEEN PRETTY QUIET. UNLESS YOU COUNT THE TIME SUPERMAN FOUGHT THAT FANCY-LOOKING FRANKEN-FELLA IN MY PASTURE!
RIGHT.
ALWAYS KEEP YOUR EYES OPEN, JON. A LOT OF BAD GUYS OUT THERE, YA'KNOW?
AND GOOD TO HAVE YOUR DOG AROUND TA KEEP AN EYE ON THINGS.
HE STICKS PRETTY CLOSE TO JON.
GOOD. WE CAN'T COUNT ON SUPERMAN TO KEEP OUR LITTLE ONES SAFE ALL THE TIME. RIGHT, MR. KENT?
RIGHT.
BYE, KATHY!
YOU AND GARTH WANT TO PLAY LATER?
GOT SOME ERRANDS TO RUN WITH MY DAD, BUT I CAN MEET YOU AFTER, OKAY?
OKAY! SEE YOU AT THE USUAL SPOT BY THE TREE!
Cobb's DAIRY

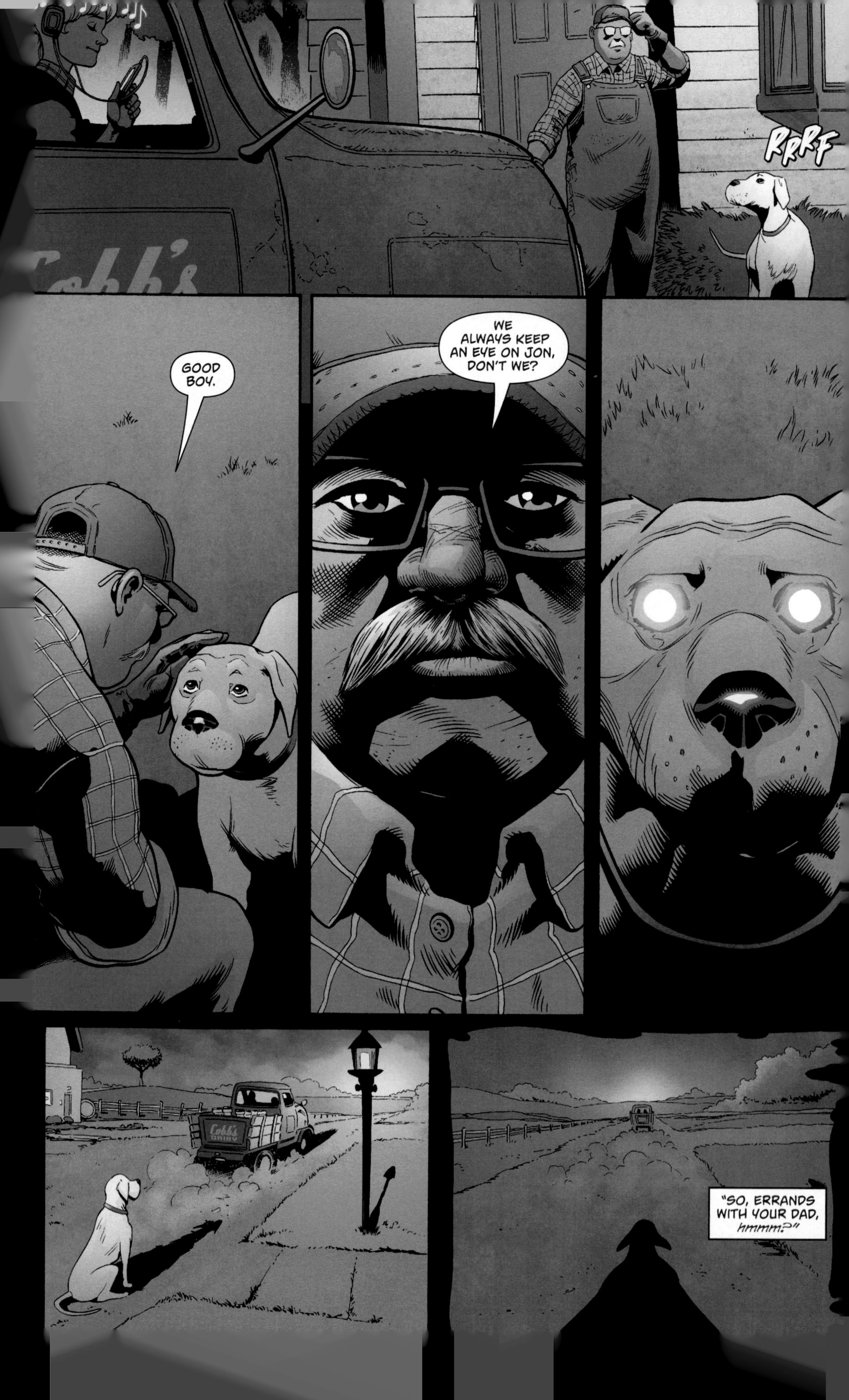
RRRF
GOOD BOY.
WE ALWAYS KEEP AN EYE ON JON, DON'T WE?
"SO, ERRANDS WITH YOUR DAD, *hmmm?*"

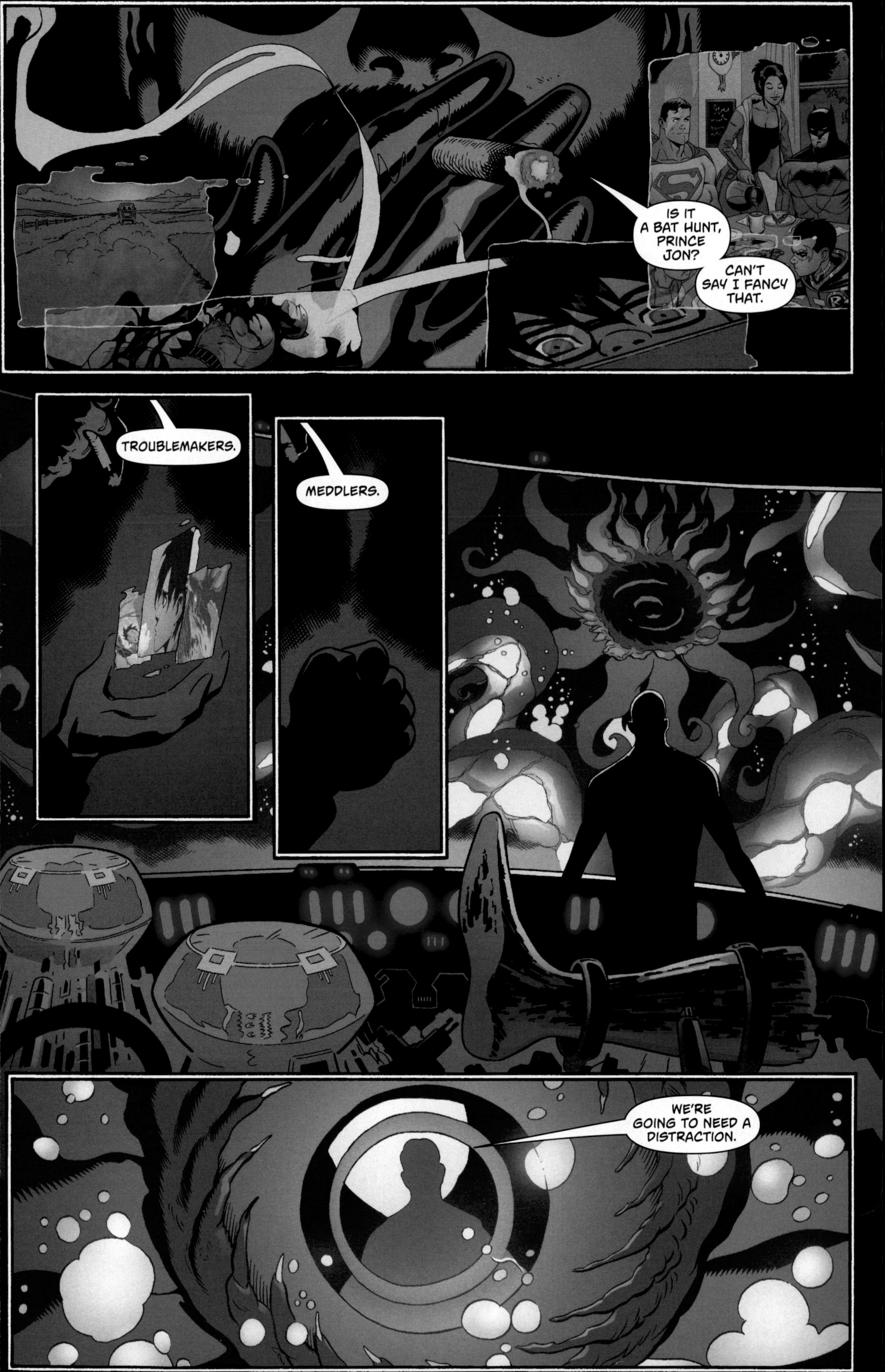
IS IT A BAT HUNT, PRINCE JON?
CAN'T SAY I FANCY THAT.
TROUBLEMAKERS.
MEDDLERS.
WE'RE GOING TO NEED A DISTRACTION.

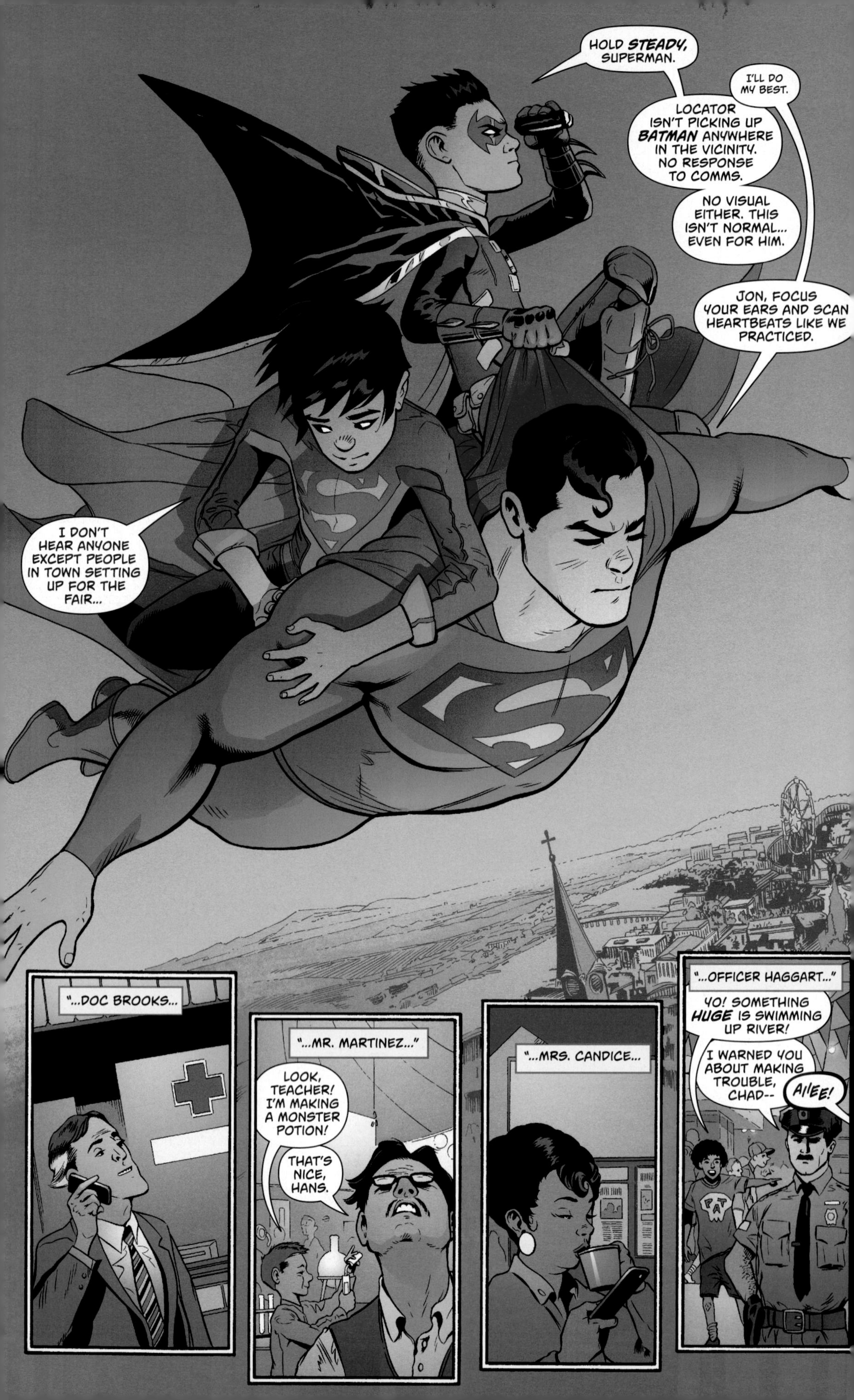

HOLD **STEADY,** SUPERMAN.
I'LL DO MY BEST.
LOCATOR ISN'T PICKING UP **BATMAN** ANYWHERE IN THE VICINITY. NO RESPONSE TO COMMS.
NO VISUAL EITHER. THIS ISN'T NORMAL... EVEN FOR HIM.
JON, FOCUS YOUR EARS AND SCAN HEARTBEATS LIKE WE PRACTICED.
I DON'T HEAR ANYONE EXCEPT PEOPLE IN TOWN SETTING UP FOR THE FAIR...
"...DOC BROOKS...
"...MR. MARTINEZ..."
LOOK, TEACHER! I'M MAKING A MONSTER POTION!
THAT'S NICE, HANS.
"...MRS. CANDICE...
"...OFFICER HAGGART..."
YO! SOMETHING **HUGE** IS SWIMMING UP RIVER!
I WARNED YOU ABOUT MAKING TROUBLE, CHAD--
AIIEE!

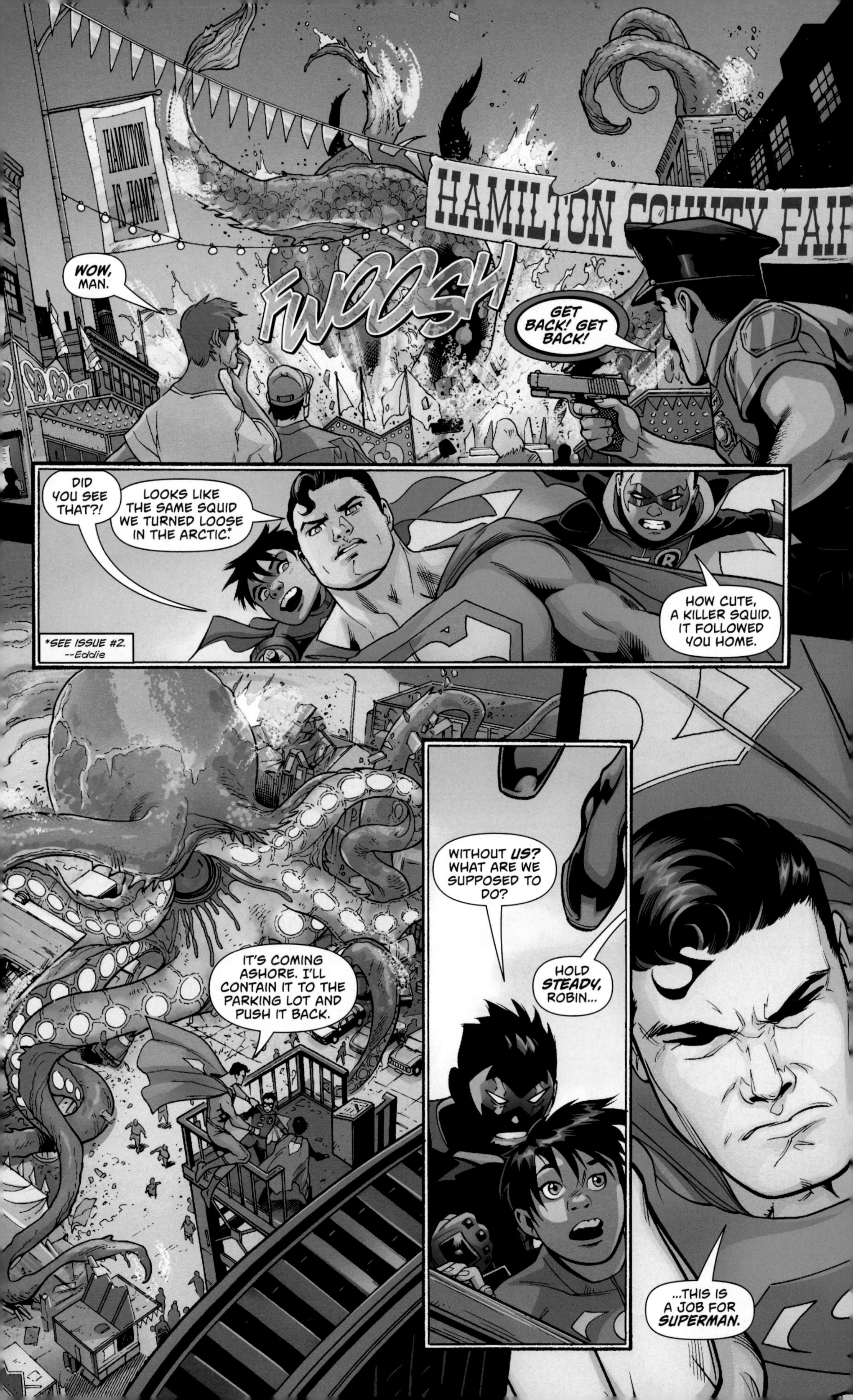
HAMILTON IS HOME
HAMILTON COUNTY FAIR
WOW, MAN.
FWOOSH
GET BACK! GET BACK!
DID YOU SEE THAT?!
LOOKS LIKE THE SAME SQUID WE TURNED LOOSE IN THE ARCTIC.*
HOW CUTE, A KILLER SQUID. IT FOLLOWED YOU HOME.
*SEE ISSUE #2. --Eddie
IT'S COMING ASHORE. I'LL CONTAIN IT TO THE PARKING LOT AND PUSH IT BACK.
WITHOUT US? WHAT ARE WE SUPPOSED TO DO?
HOLD STEADY, ROBIN...
...THIS IS A JOB FOR SUPERMAN.

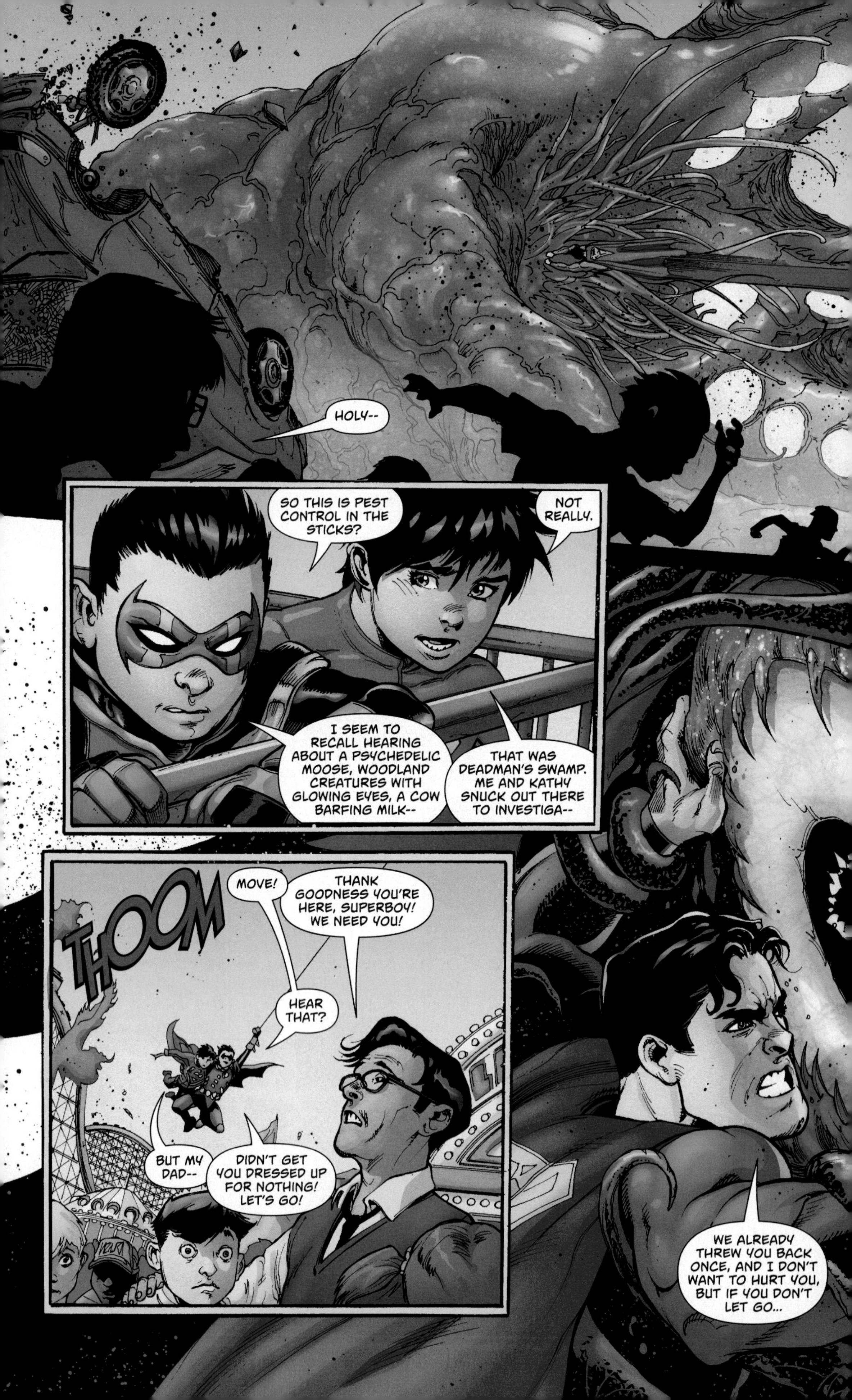
HOLY--
SO THIS IS PEST CONTROL IN THE STICKS?
NOT REALLY.
I SEEM TO RECALL HEARING ABOUT A PSYCHEDELIC MOOSE, WOODLAND CREATURES WITH GLOWING EYES, A COW BARFING MILK--
THAT WAS DEADMAN'S SWAMP. ME AND KATHY SNUCK OUT THERE TO INVESTIGA--
THOOM
MOVE!
THANK GOODNESS YOU'RE HERE, SUPERBOY! WE NEED YOU!
HEAR THAT?
BUT MY DAD--
DIDN'T GET YOU DRESSED UP FOR NOTHING! LET'S GO!
WE ALREADY THREW YOU BACK ONCE, AND I DON'T WANT TO HURT YOU, BUT IF YOU DON'T LET GO...

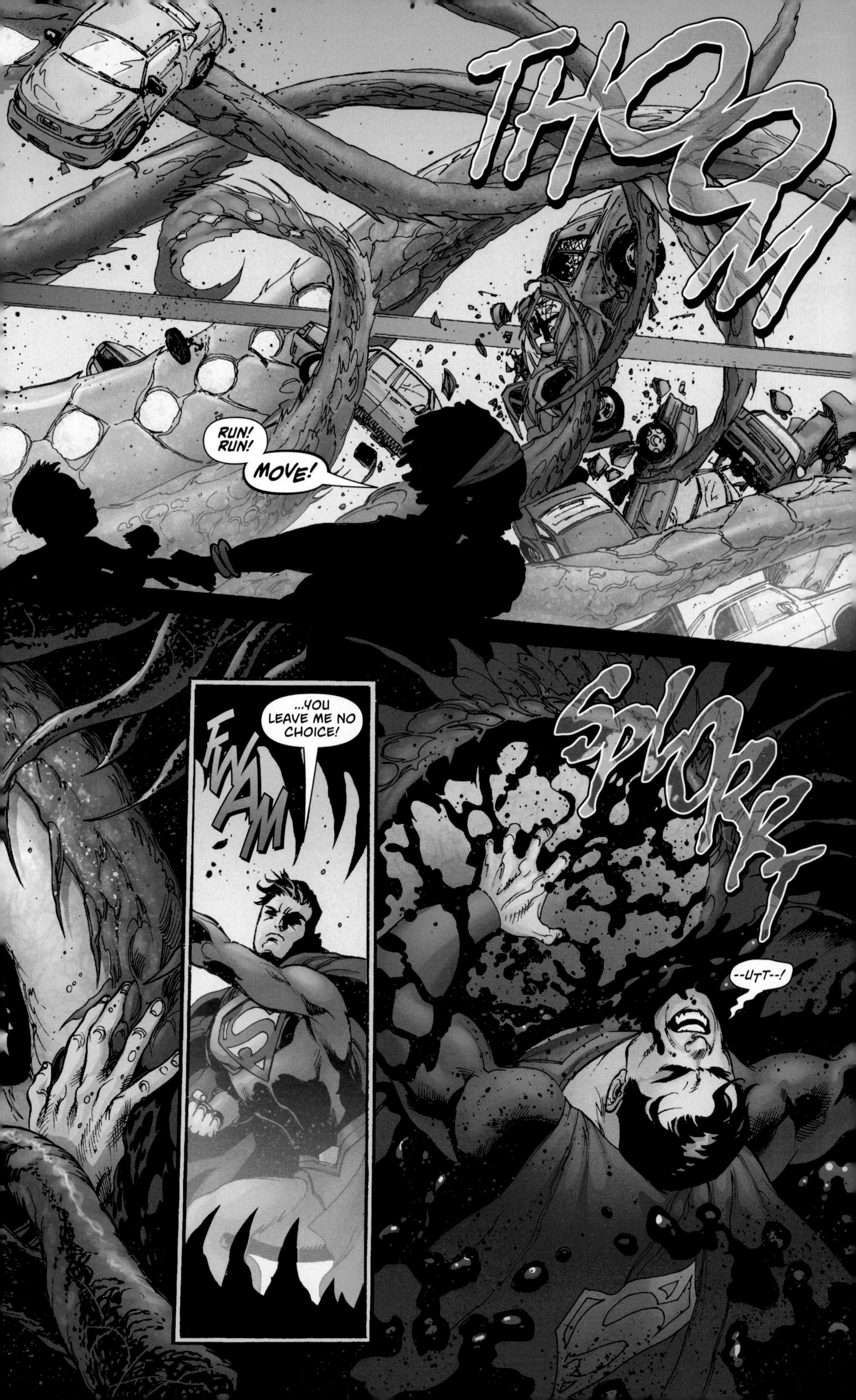
THOOM
RUN! RUN!
MOVE!
...YOU LEAVE ME NO CHOICE!
FWAM
SPLORRT
--UTT--!

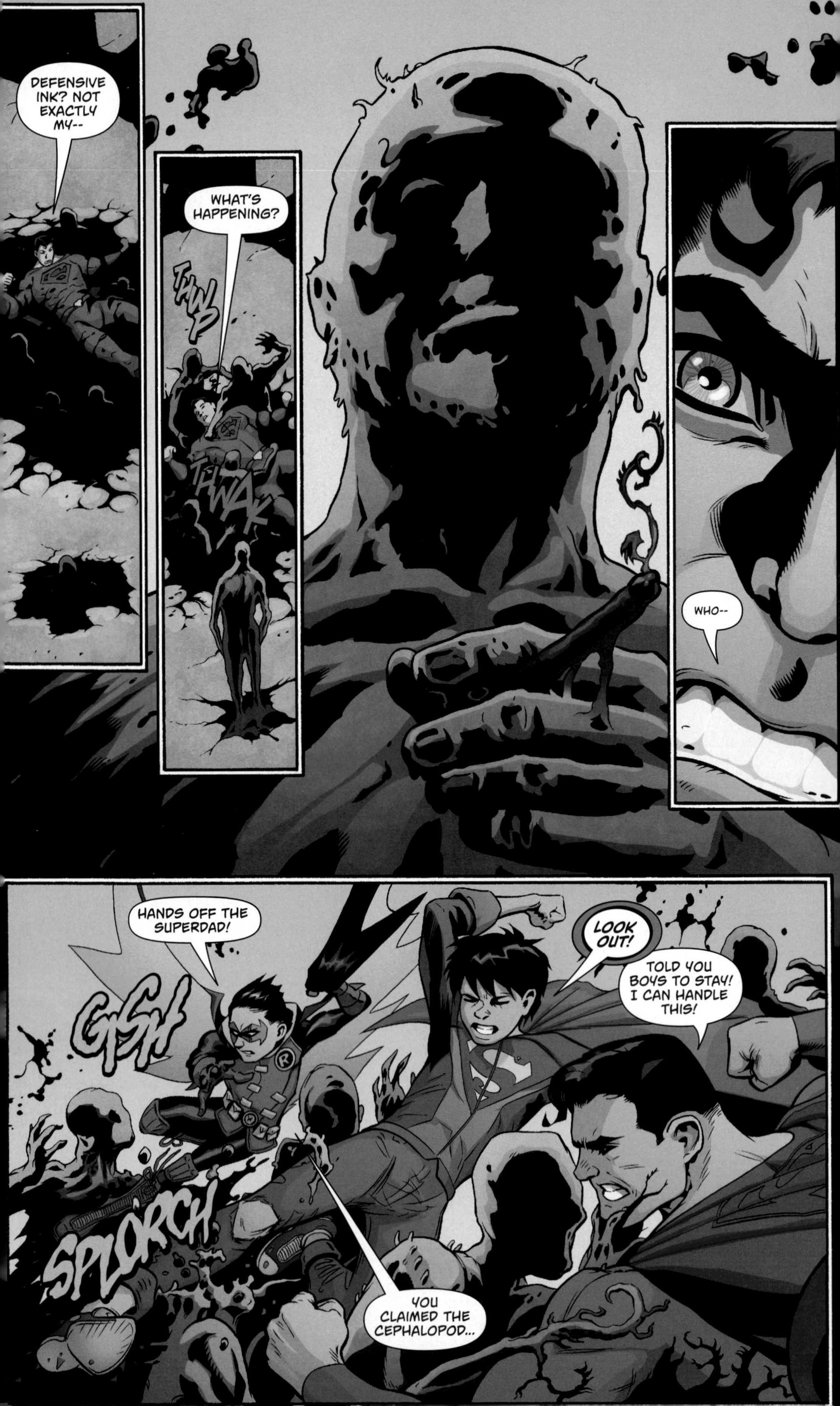
DEFENSIVE INK? NOT EXACTLY MY--
WHAT'S HAPPENING?
THWP
THWAK
WHO--
HANDS OFF THE SUPERDAD!
LOOK OUT!
TOLD YOU BOYS TO STAY! I CAN HANDLE THIS!
GISH
SPLORCH
YOU CLAIMED THE CEPHALOPOD...

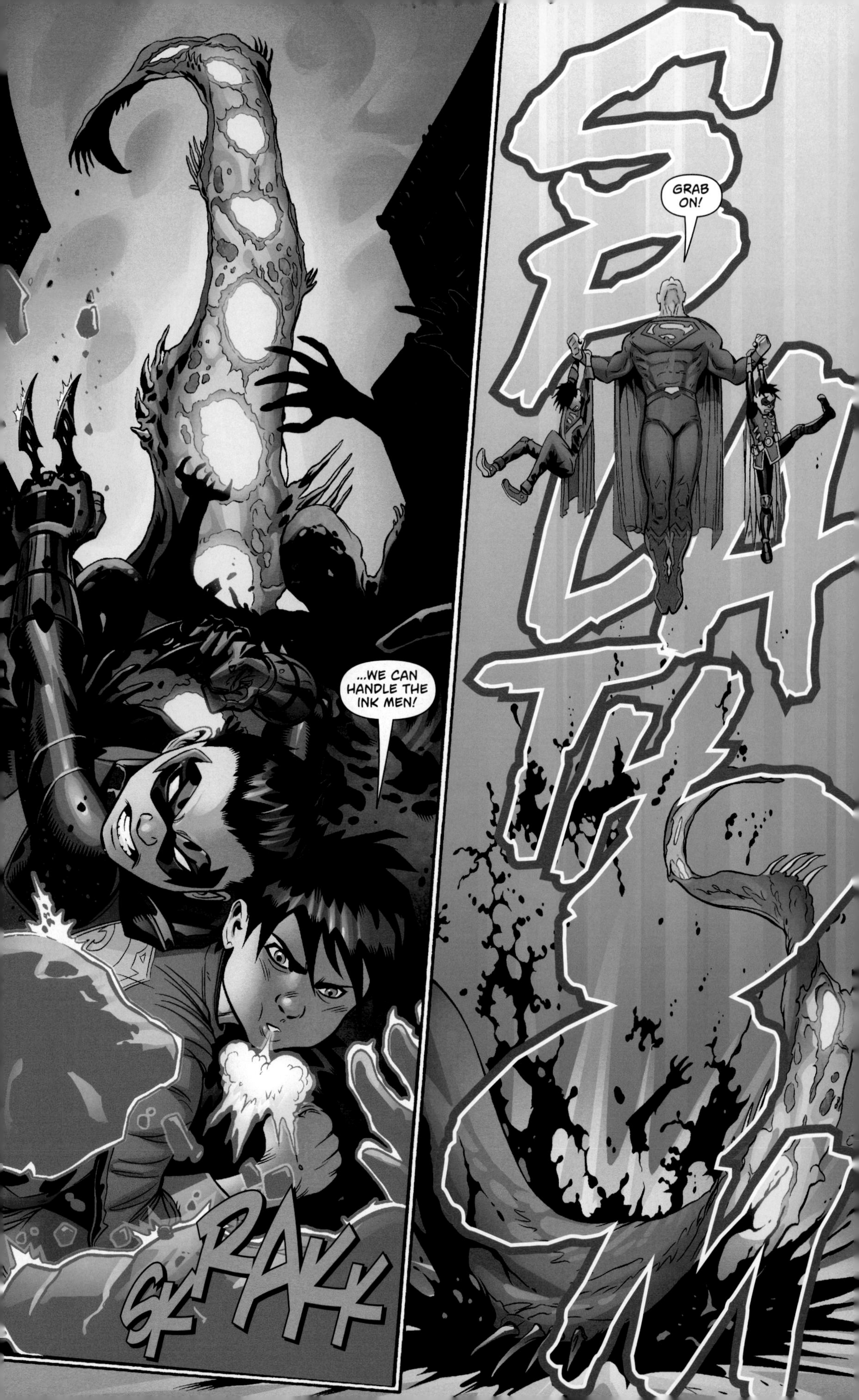
...WE CAN HANDLE THE INK MEN!
SKRAKK
GRAB ON!

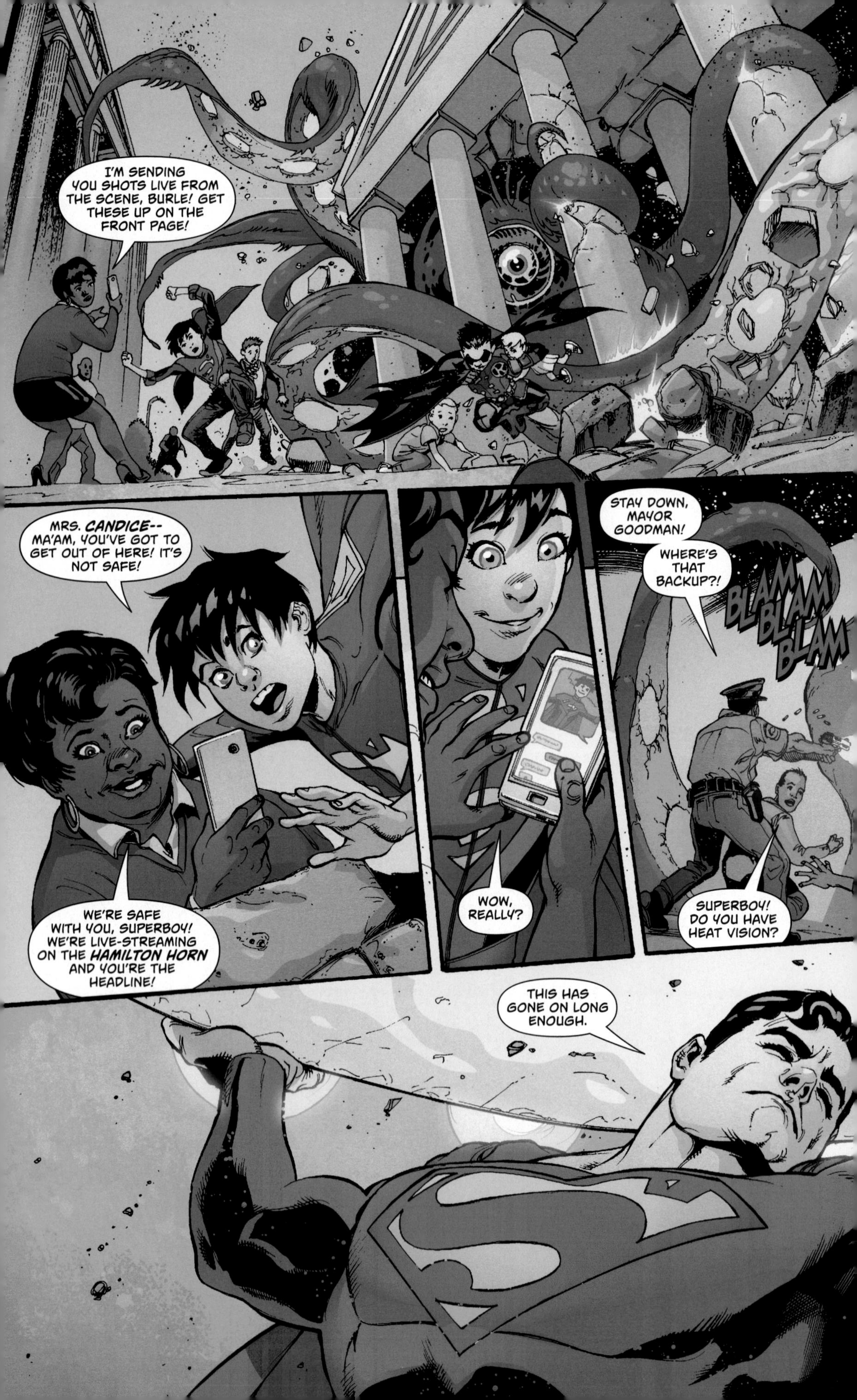
I'M SENDING YOU SHOTS LIVE FROM THE SCENE, BURLE! GET THESE UP ON THE FRONT PAGE!
MRS. CANDICE-- MA'AM, YOU'VE GOT TO GET OUT OF HERE! IT'S NOT SAFE!
WE'RE SAFE WITH YOU, SUPERBOY! WE'RE LIVE-STREAMING ON THE HAMILTON HORN AND YOU'RE THE HEADLINE!
WOW, REALLY?
STAY DOWN, MAYOR GOODMAN!
WHERE'S THAT BACKUP?!
BLAM BLAM BLAM
SUPERBOY! DO YOU HAVE HEAT VISION?
THIS HAS GONE ON LONG ENOUGH.

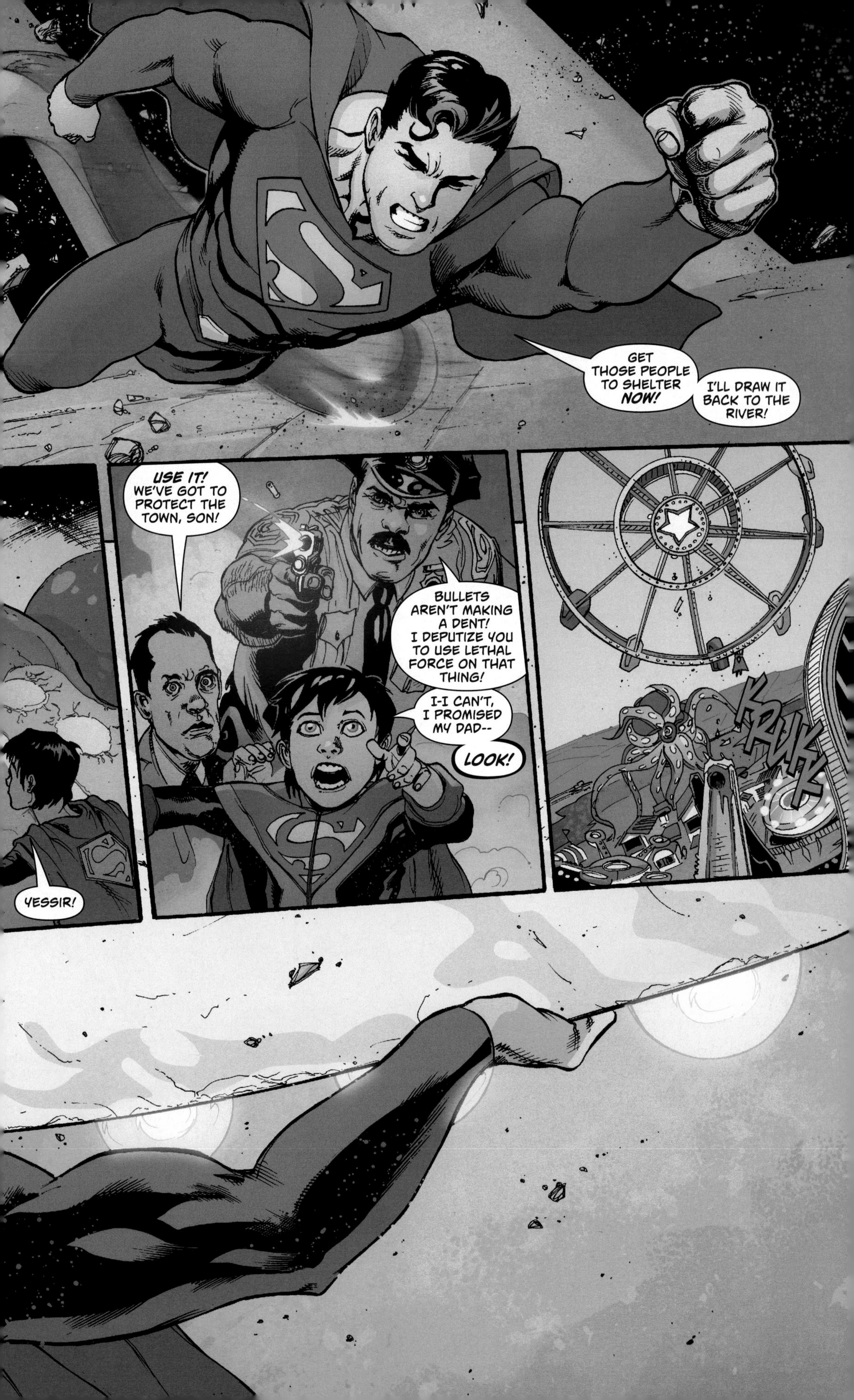
GET THOSE PEOPLE TO SHELTER NOW!
I'LL DRAW IT BACK TO THE RIVER!
YESSIR!
USE IT! WE'VE GOT TO PROTECT THE TOWN, SON!
BULLETS AREN'T MAKING A DENT! I DEPUTIZE YOU TO USE LETHAL FORCE ON THAT THING!
I-I CAN'T, I PROMISED MY DAD--
LOOK!
KRUKK

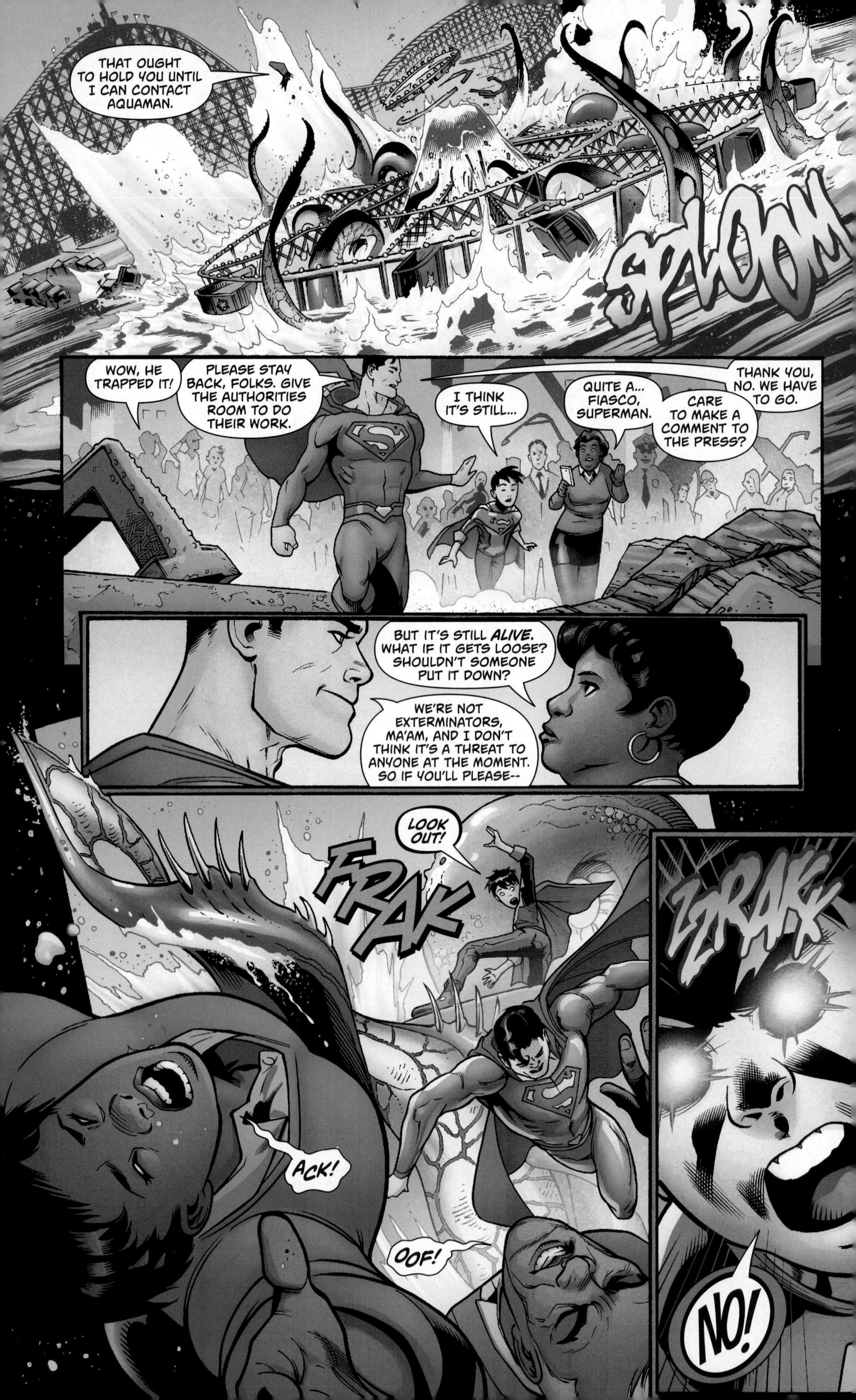
THAT OUGHT TO HOLD YOU UNTIL I CAN CONTACT AQUAMAN.
SPLOOM
WOW, HE TRAPPED IT!
PLEASE STAY BACK, FOLKS. GIVE THE AUTHORITIES ROOM TO DO THEIR WORK.
I THINK IT'S STILL...
QUITE A... FIASCO, SUPERMAN.
CARE TO MAKE A COMMENT TO THE PRESS?
THANK YOU, NO. WE HAVE TO GO.
BUT IT'S STILL ALIVE. WHAT IF IT GETS LOOSE? SHOULDN'T SOMEONE PUT IT DOWN?
WE'RE NOT EXTERMINATORS, MA'AM, AND I DON'T THINK IT'S A THREAT TO ANYONE AT THE MOMENT. SO IF YOU'LL PLEASE--
FRAK
LOOK OUT!
ACK!
OOF!
ZZRAKK
NO!

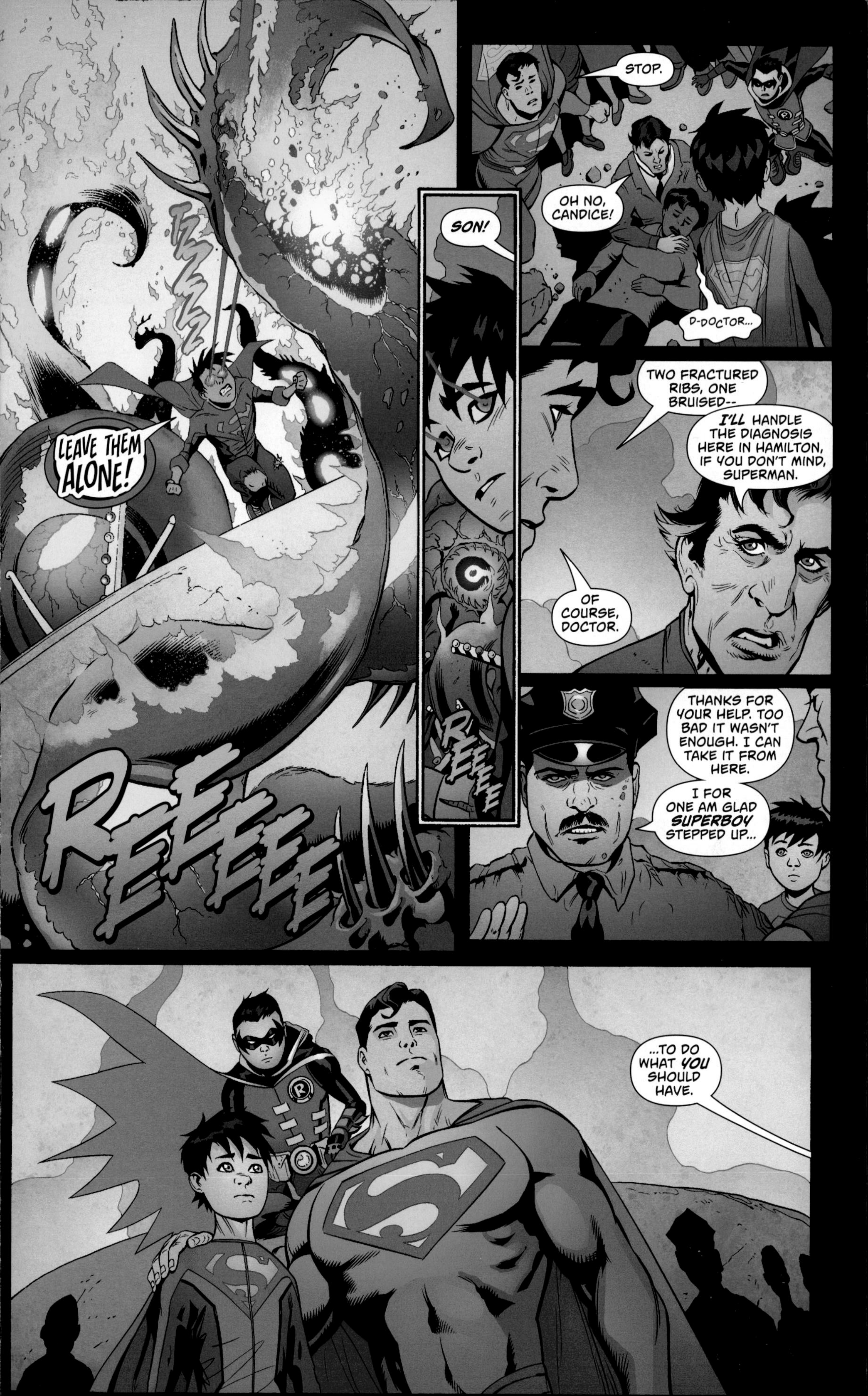
LEAVE THEM ALONE!
REEEEEE
SON!
REEEE
STOP.
OH NO, CANDICE!
D-DOCTOR...
TWO FRACTURED RIBS, ONE BRUISED--
I'LL HANDLE THE DIAGNOSIS HERE IN HAMILTON, IF YOU DON'T MIND, SUPERMAN.
OF COURSE, DOCTOR.
THANKS FOR YOUR HELP. TOO BAD IT WASN'T ENOUGH. I CAN TAKE IT FROM HERE.
I FOR ONE AM GLAD SUPERBOY STEPPED UP...
...TO DO WHAT YOU SHOULD HAVE.

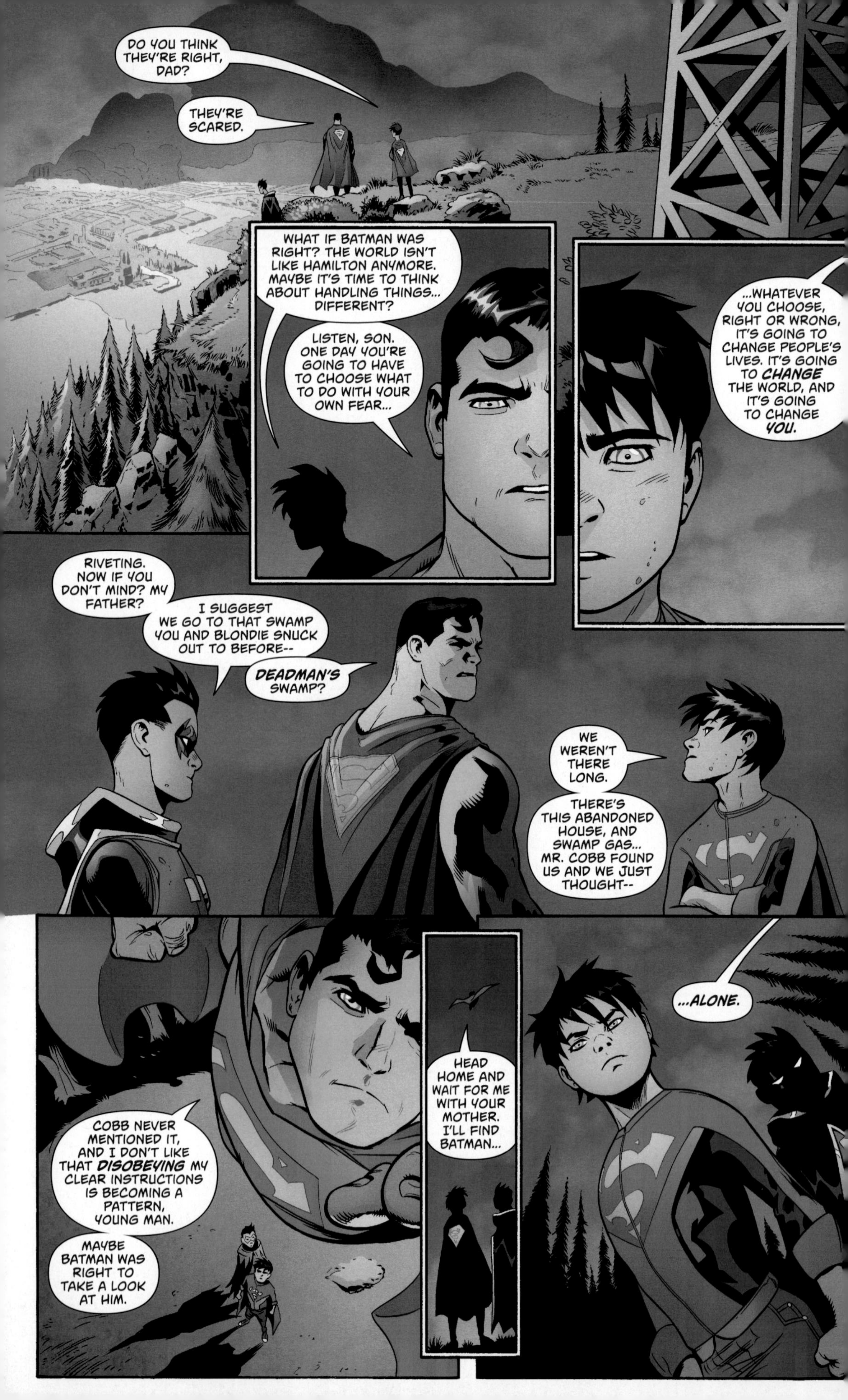
DO YOU THINK THEY'RE RIGHT, DAD?
THEY'RE SCARED.
WHAT IF BATMAN WAS RIGHT? THE WORLD ISN'T LIKE HAMILTON ANYMORE. MAYBE IT'S TIME TO THINK ABOUT HANDLING THINGS... DIFFERENT?
LISTEN, SON. ONE DAY YOU'RE GOING TO HAVE TO CHOOSE WHAT TO DO WITH YOUR OWN FEAR...
...WHATEVER YOU CHOOSE, RIGHT OR WRONG, IT'S GOING TO CHANGE PEOPLE'S LIVES. IT'S GOING TO CHANGE THE WORLD, AND IT'S GOING TO CHANGE YOU.
RIVETING. NOW IF YOU DON'T MIND? MY FATHER?
I SUGGEST WE GO TO THAT SWAMP YOU AND BLONDIE SNUCK OUT TO BEFORE--
DEADMAN'S SWAMP?
WE WEREN'T THERE LONG.
THERE'S THIS ABANDONED HOUSE, AND SWAMP GAS... MR. COBB FOUND US AND WE JUST THOUGHT--
COBB NEVER MENTIONED IT, AND I DON'T LIKE THAT DISOBEYING MY CLEAR INSTRUCTIONS IS BECOMING A PATTERN, YOUNG MAN.
MAYBE BATMAN WAS RIGHT TO TAKE A LOOK AT HIM.
HEAD HOME AND WAIT FOR ME WITH YOUR MOTHER. I'LL FIND BATMAN...
...ALONE.

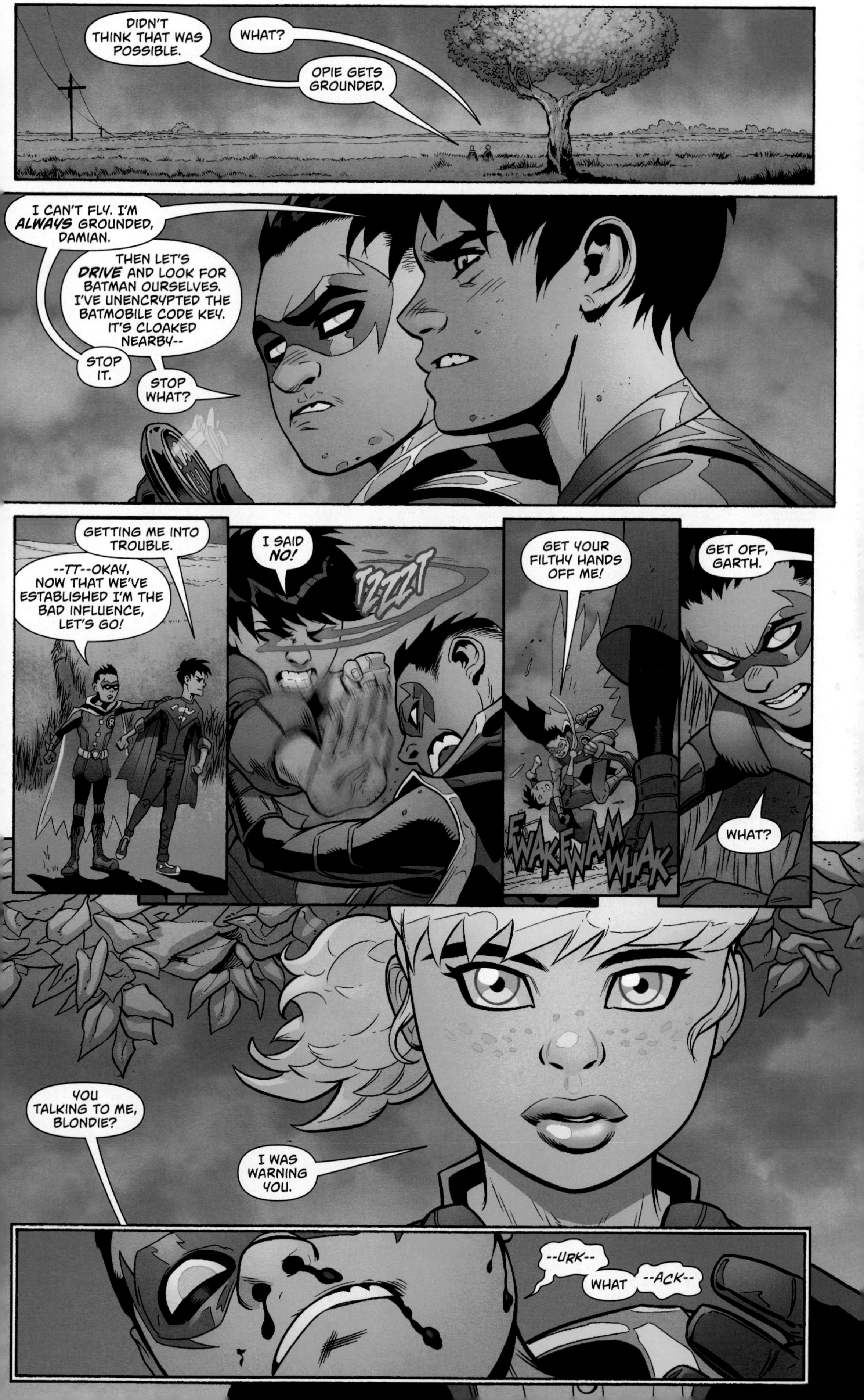
DIDN'T THINK THAT WAS POSSIBLE.
WHAT?
OPIE GETS GROUNDED.
I CAN'T FLY. I'M *ALWAYS* GROUNDED, DAMIAN.
THEN LET'S *DRIVE* AND LOOK FOR BATMAN OURSELVES. I'VE UNENCRYPTED THE BATMOBILE CODE KEY. IT'S CLOAKED NEARBY--
STOP IT.
STOP WHAT?
GETTING ME INTO TROUBLE.
--*TT*--OKAY, NOW THAT WE'VE ESTABLISHED I'M THE BAD INFLUENCE, LET'S GO!
I SAID *NO!*
TZZZT
GET YOUR FILTHY HANDS OFF ME!
FWAK FWAM WHAK
GET OFF, GARTH.
WHAT?
YOU TALKING TO ME, BLONDIE?
I WAS WARNING YOU.
--URK--
WHAT
--ACK--

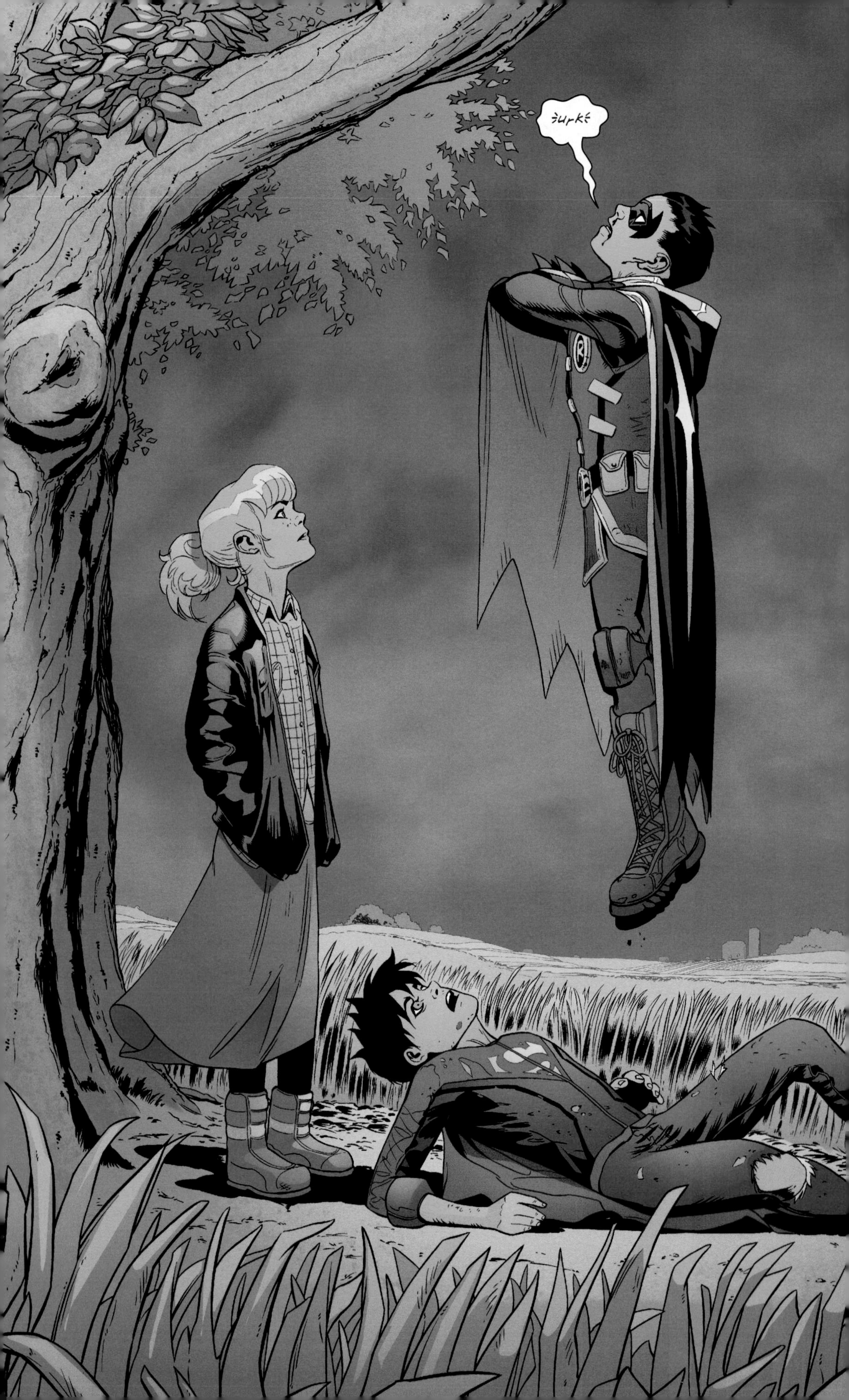
urk

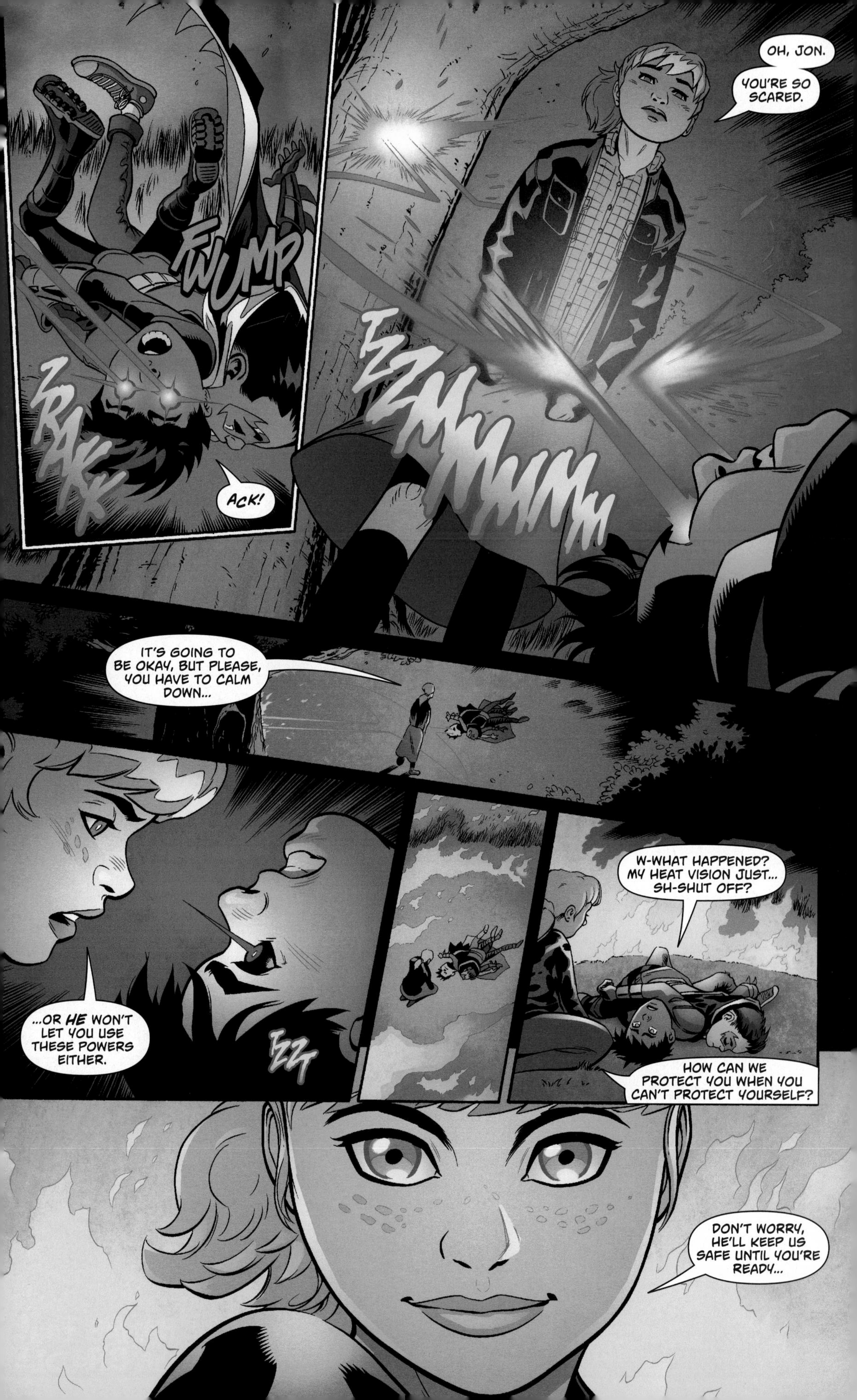
FWUMP
ZRAKK
ACK!
OH, JON.
YOU'RE SO SCARED.
IZZMMMMMM
IT'S GOING TO BE OKAY, BUT PLEASE, YOU HAVE TO CALM DOWN...
...OR HE WON'T LET YOU USE THESE POWERS EITHER.
IZZT
W-WHAT HAPPENED? MY HEAT VISION JUST... SH-SHUT OFF?
HOW CAN WE PROTECT YOU WHEN YOU CAN'T PROTECT YOURSELF?
DON'T WORRY, HE'LL KEEP US SAFE UNTIL YOU'RE READY...

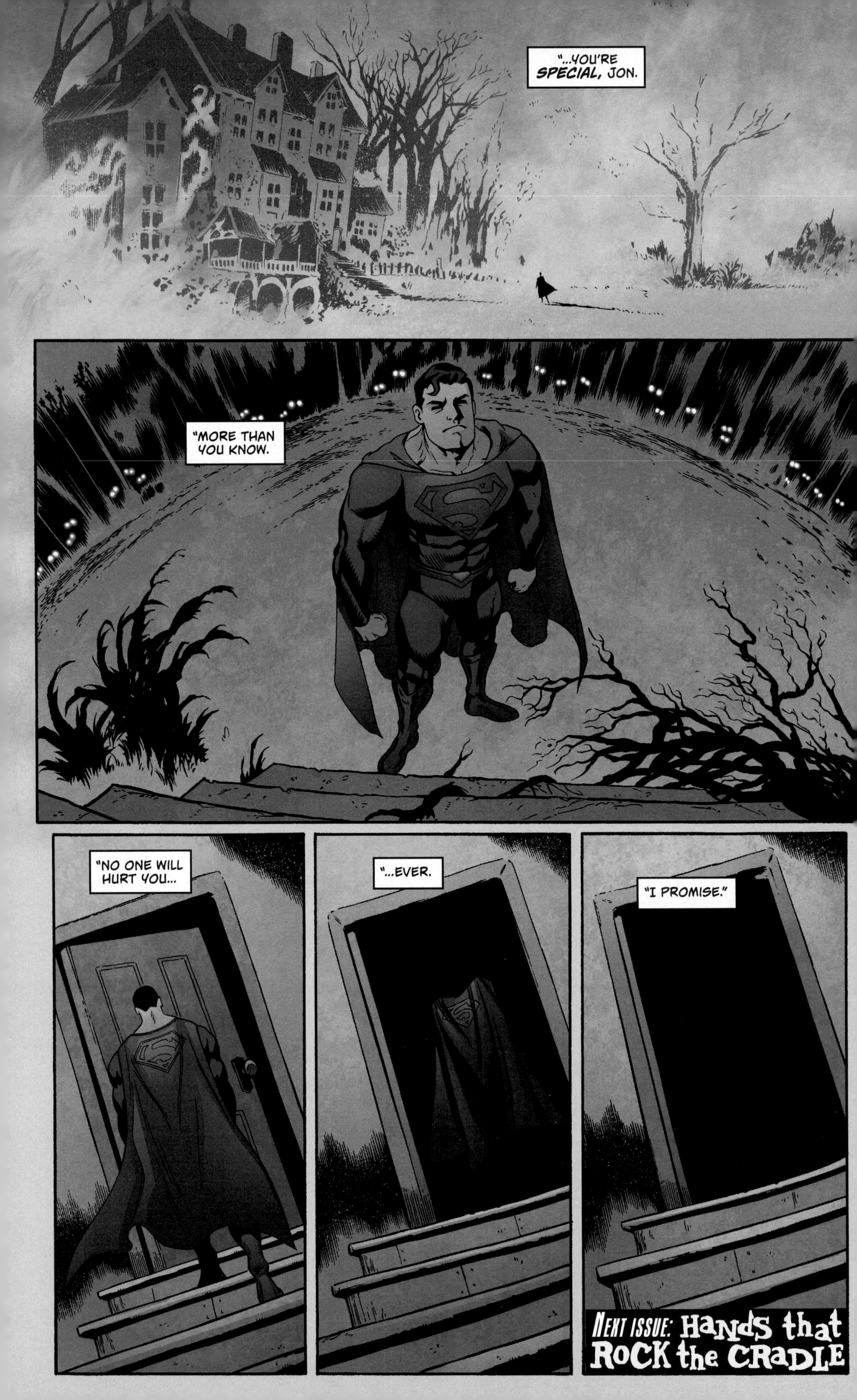
"...YOU'RE SPECIAL, JON.
"MORE THAN YOU KNOW.
"NO ONE WILL HURT YOU...
"...EVER.
"I PROMISE."
NEXT ISSUE: Hands that ROCK the CRADLE

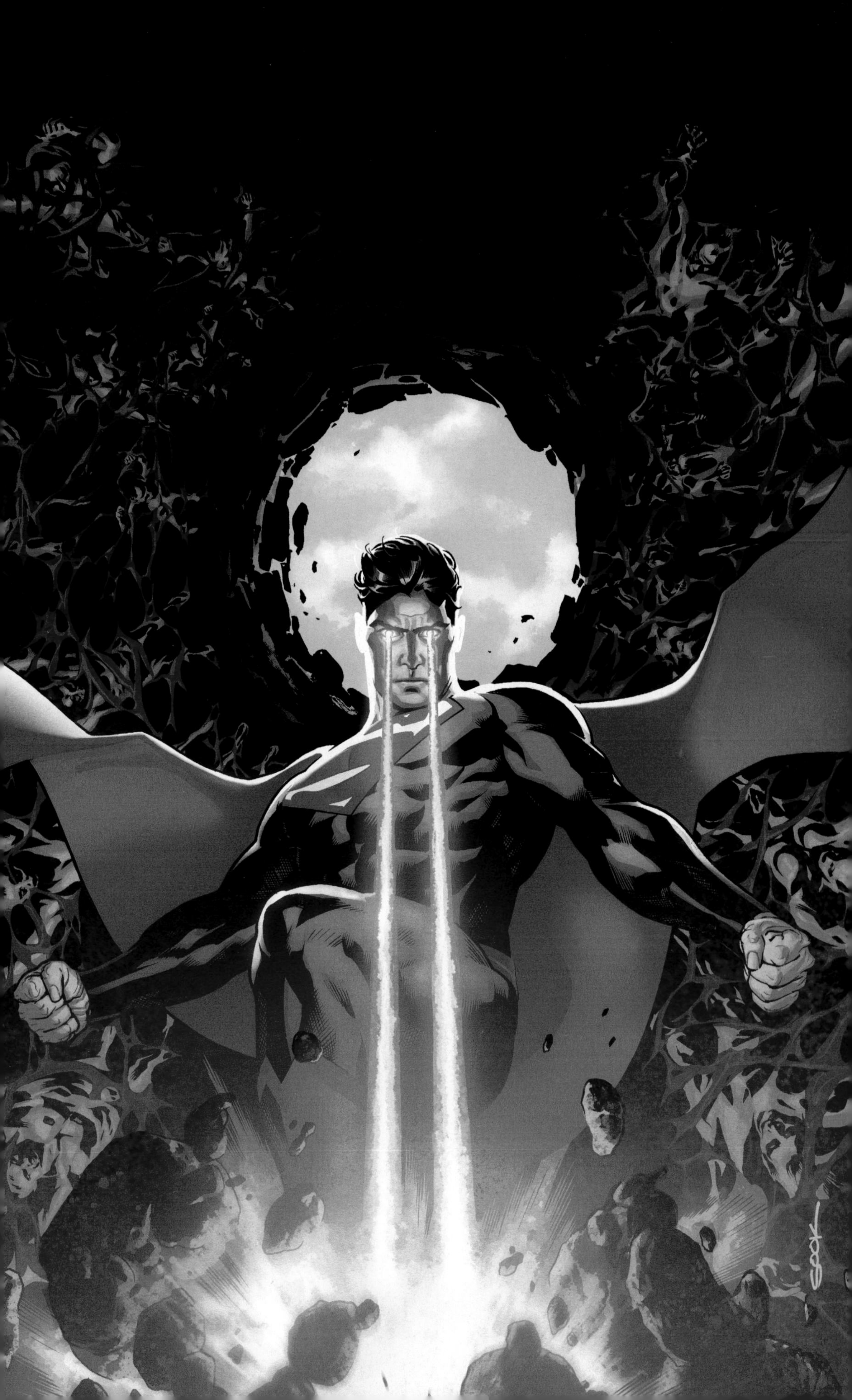

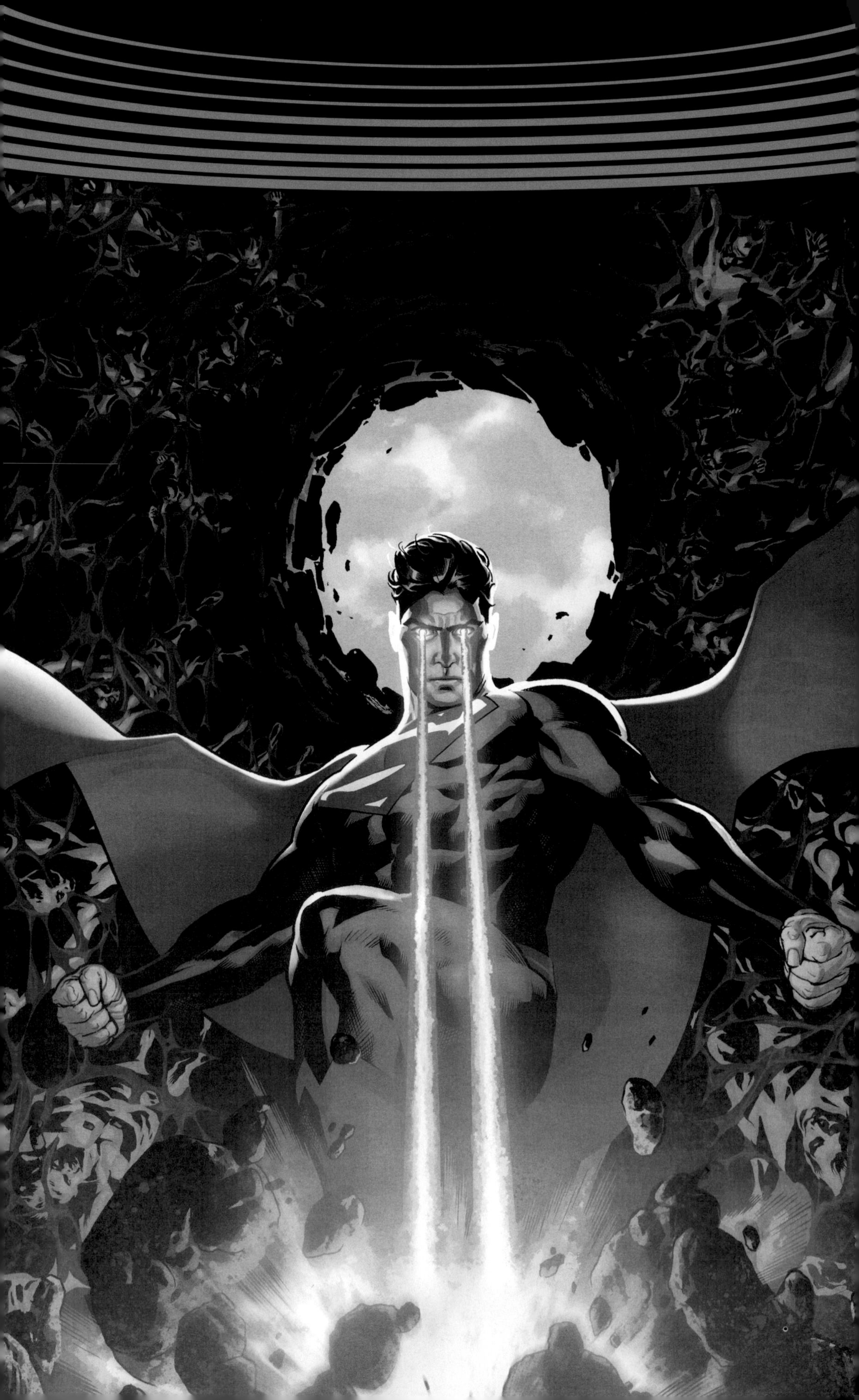

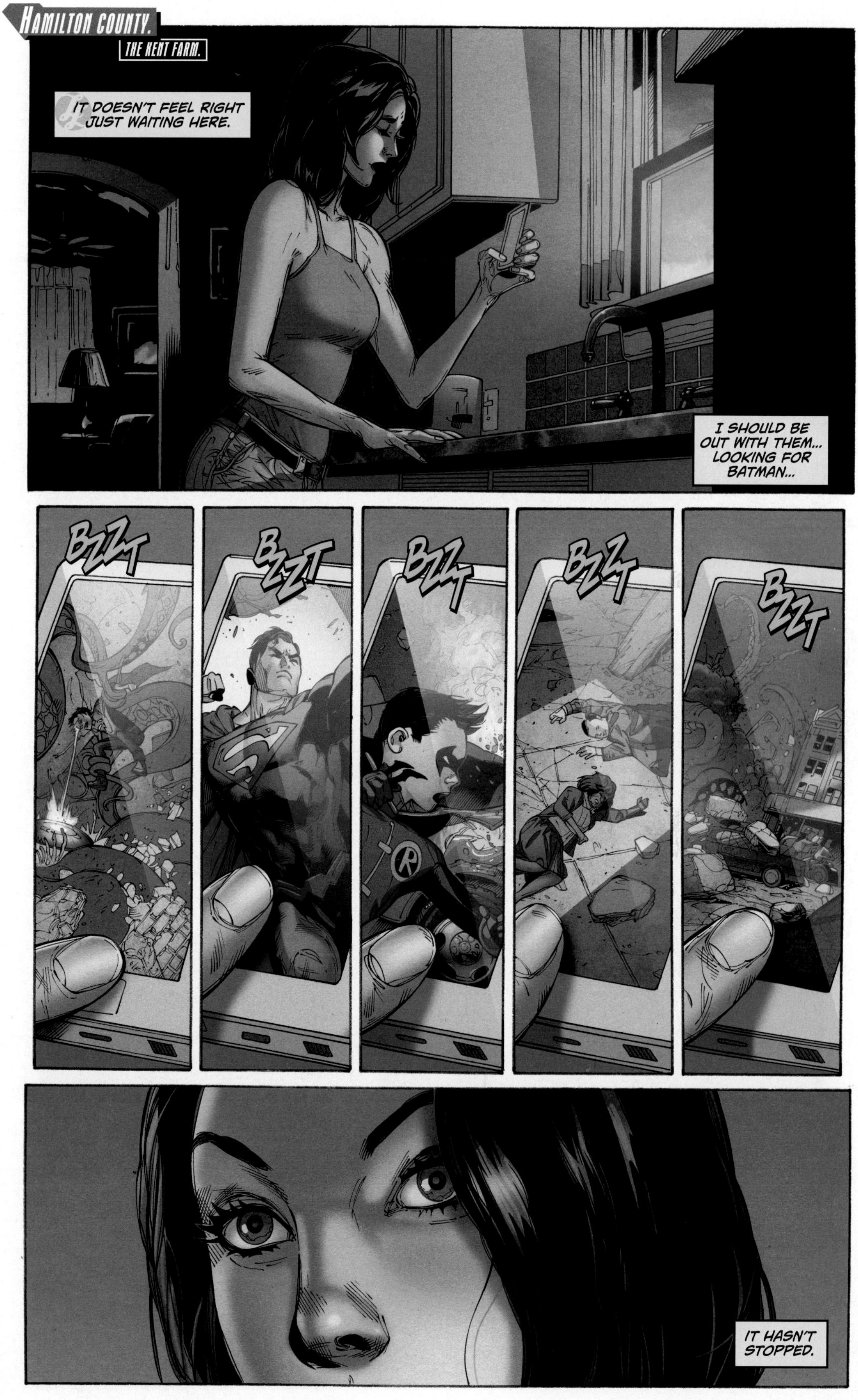

HAMILTON COUNTY.
THE KENT FARM.
IT DOESN'T FEEL RIGHT JUST WAITING HERE.
I SHOULD BE OUT WITH THEM... LOOKING FOR BATMAN...
BZZT
BZZT
BZZT
BZZT
BZZT
IT HASN'T STOPPED.

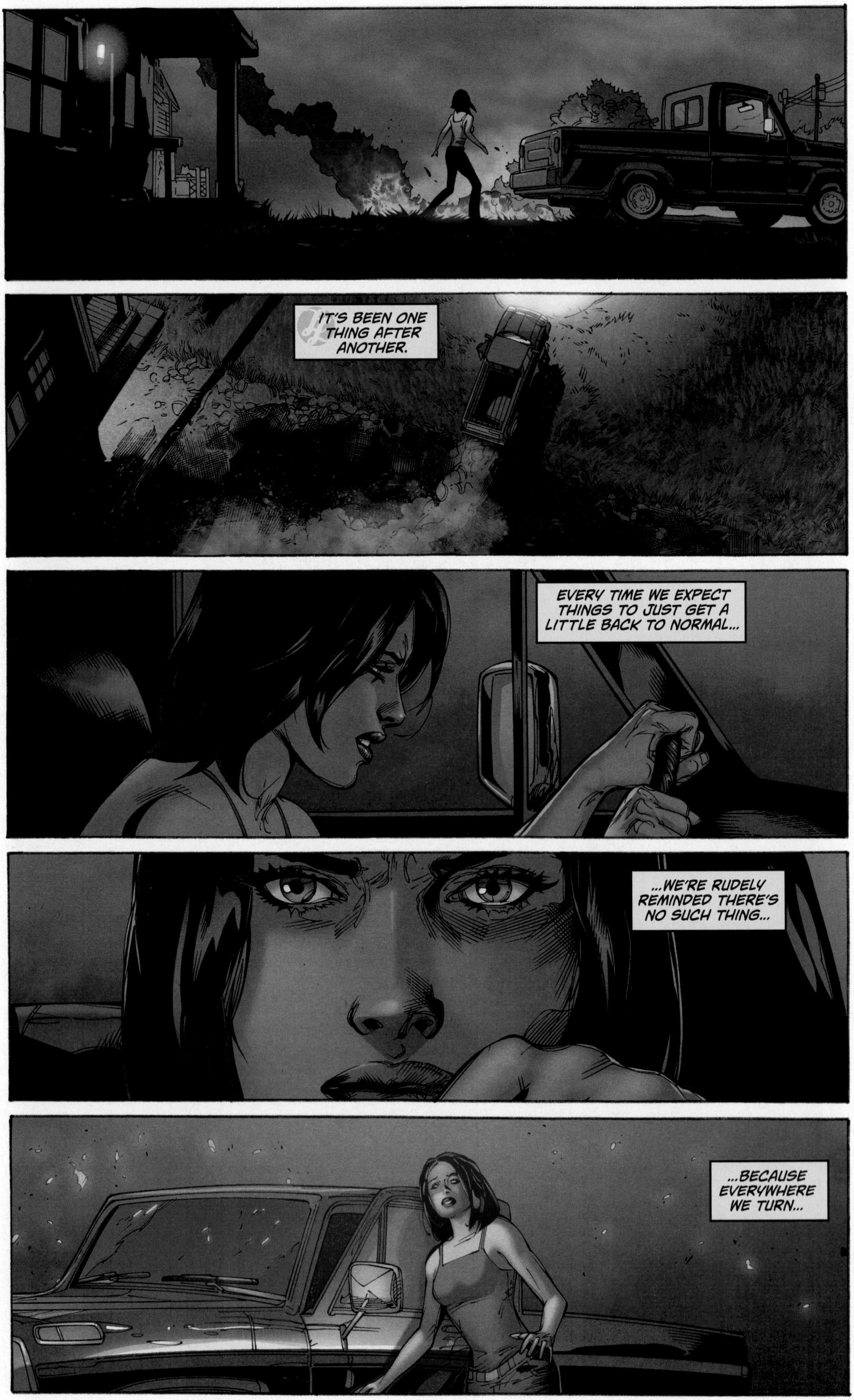
IT'S BEEN ONE THING AFTER ANOTHER.
EVERY TIME WE EXPECT THINGS TO JUST GET A LITTLE BACK TO NORMAL...
...WE'RE RUDELY REMINDED THERE'S NO SUCH THING...
...BECAUSE EVERYWHERE WE TURN...

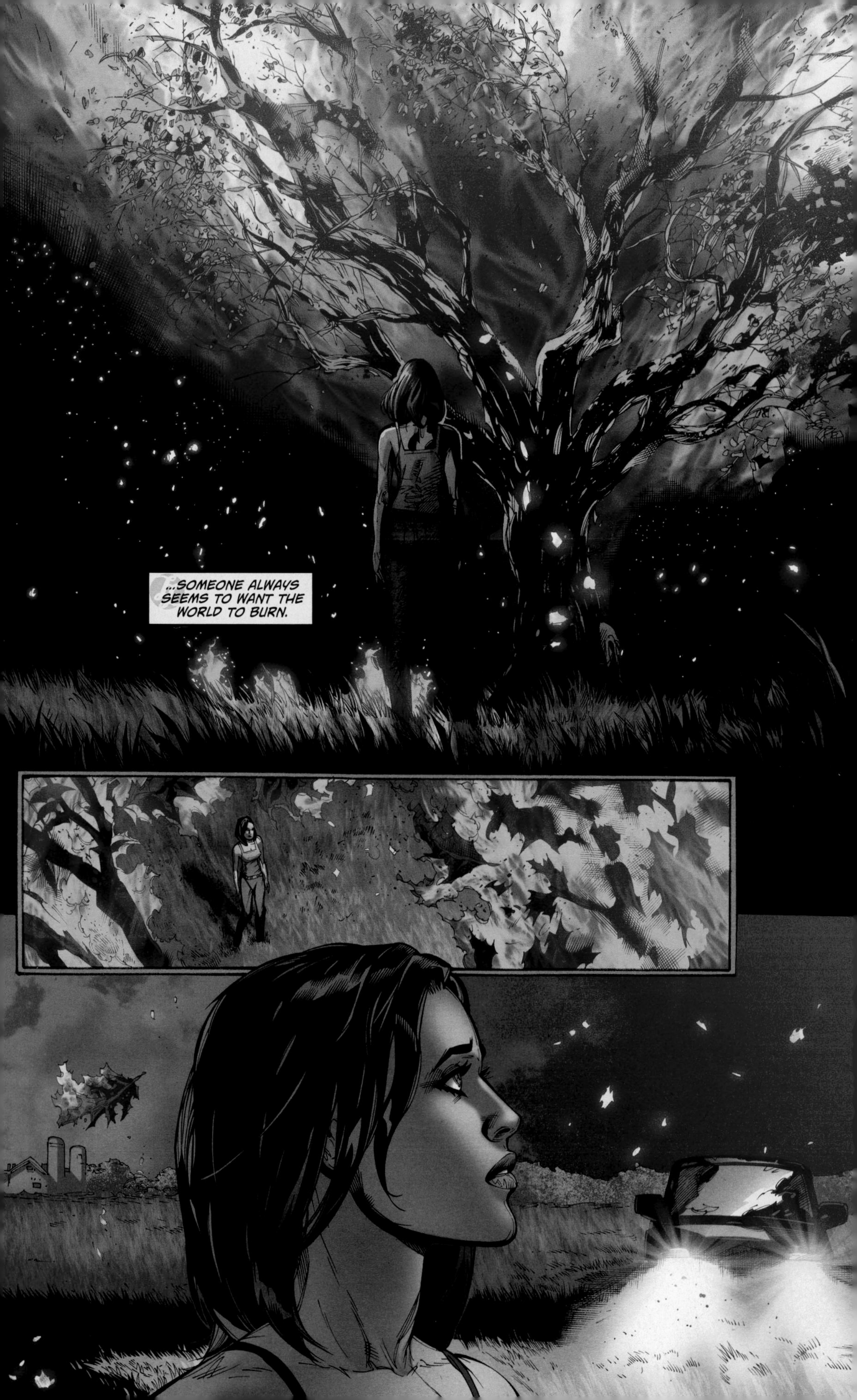
...SOMEONE ALWAYS SEEMS TO WANT THE WORLD TO BURN.

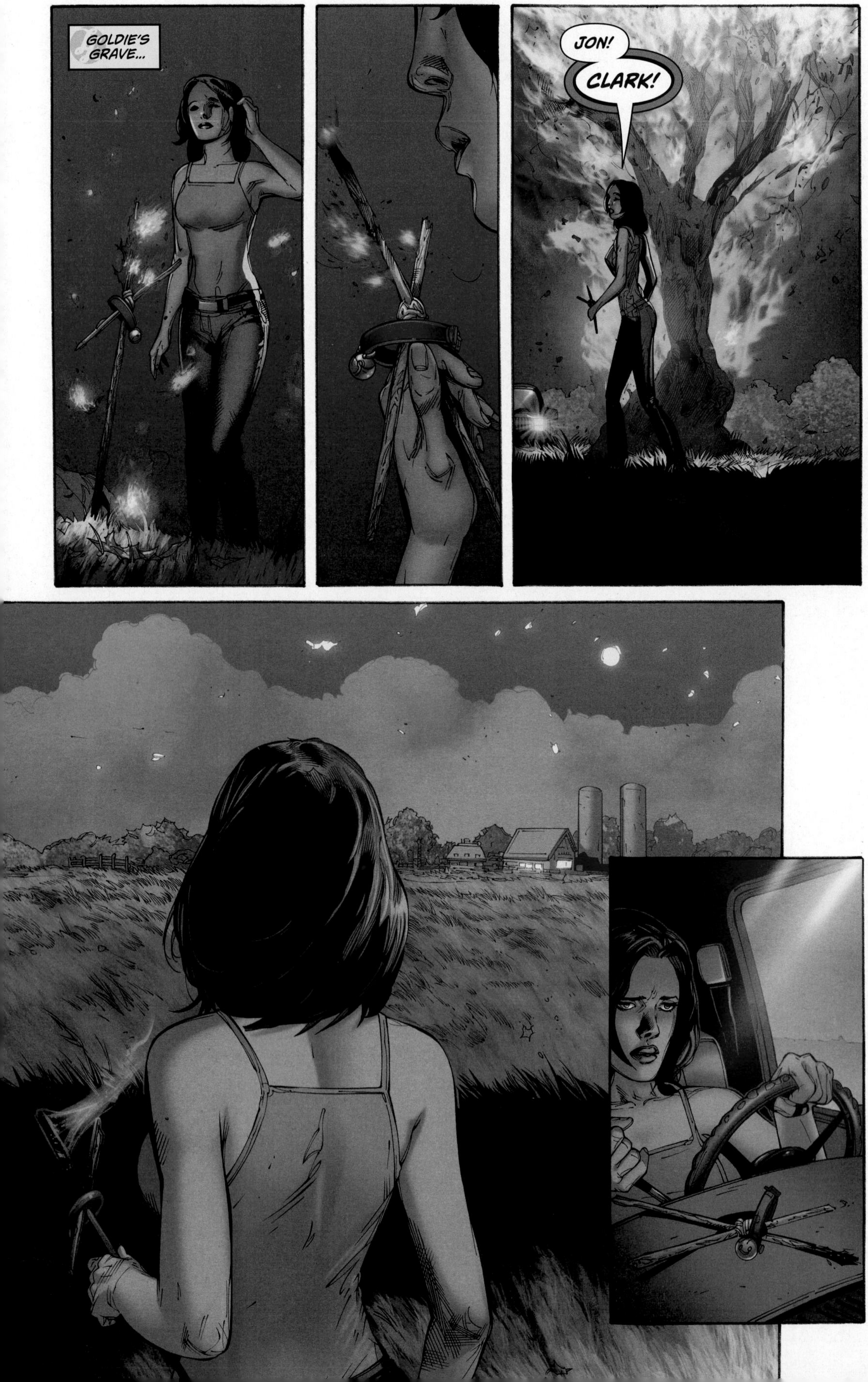
GOLDIE'S GRAVE...
JON!
CLARK!

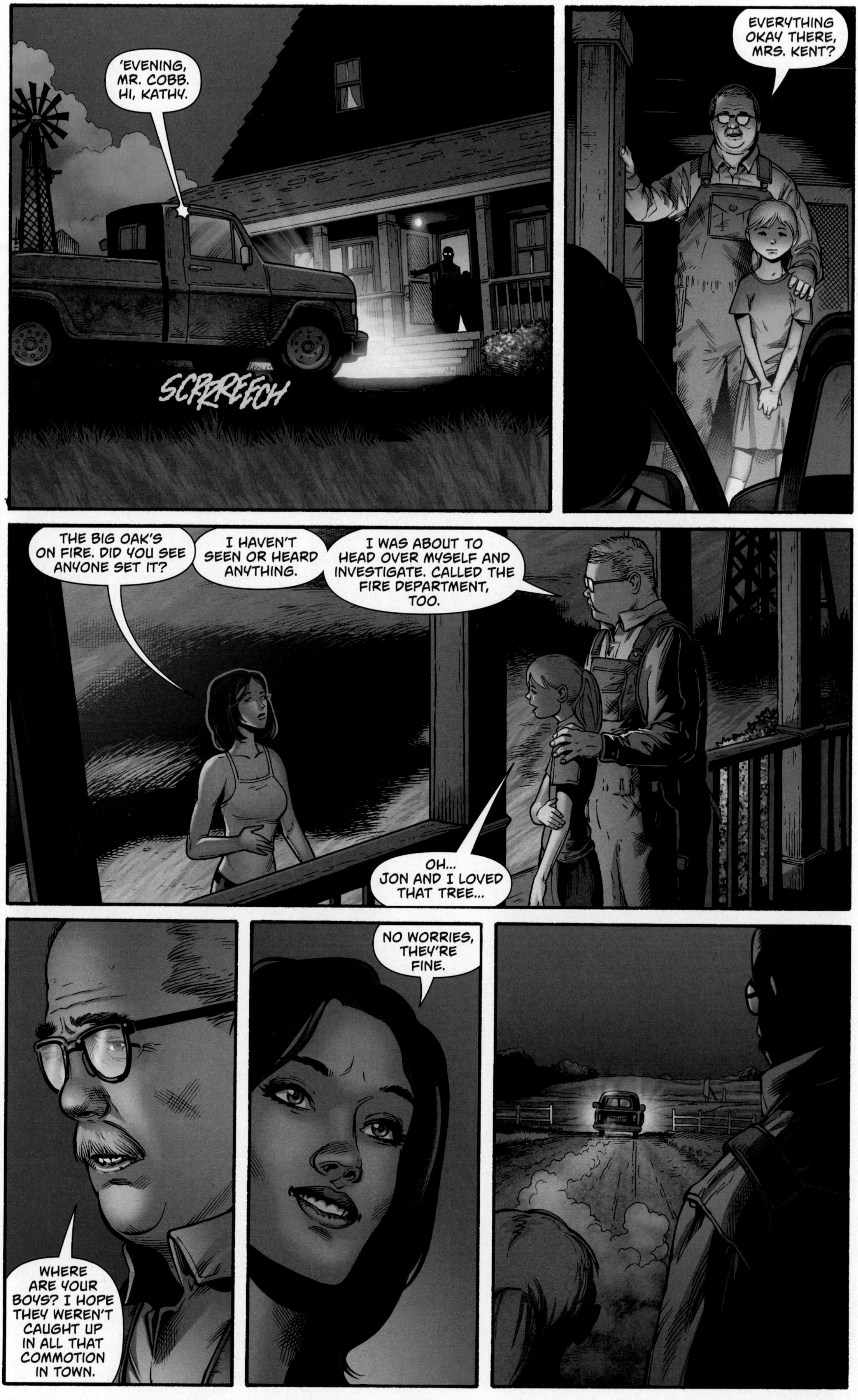
'EVENING, MR. COBB. HI, KATHY.
SCRREECH
EVERYTHING OKAY THERE, MRS. KENT?
THE BIG OAK'S ON FIRE. DID YOU SEE ANYONE SET IT?
I HAVEN'T SEEN OR HEARD ANYTHING.
I WAS ABOUT TO HEAD OVER MYSELF AND INVESTIGATE. CALLED THE FIRE DEPARTMENT, TOO.
OH... JON AND I LOVED THAT TREE...
WHERE ARE YOUR BOYS? I HOPE THEY WEREN'T CAUGHT UP IN ALL THAT COMMOTION IN TOWN.
NO WORRIES, THEY'RE FINE.

ALL RIGHT, RUNDOWN ON WHAT WE KNOW: **BATMAN** AND **ROBIN** COME TO THE HOUSE, WORRIED ABOUT JON...

BATMAN GOES OUT BY HIMSELF TO DIG AROUND...

POOF. BATS DISAPPEARS.

THIS GIANT **SQUID** ATTACKS THE TOWN.

CLARK, JON AND DAMIAN TAKE IT DOWN.

THEN, NOT A WORD FROM THEM.

POOF, JUST LIKE BATMAN, THEY'RE GONE AND--

CANDICE?

THE PICTURES I SAW OF HER...

HOW'S SHE ALREADY UP AND ABOUT AFTER GETTING INJURED?

SHE'S HEADING FOR THE TOWN HALL...

WHY'S SHE TAKING THE BACK DOOR?

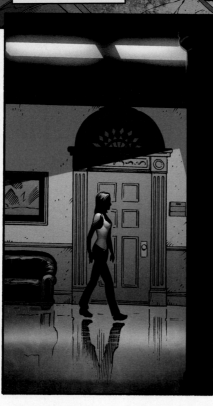

Hmm, LOWER LEVEL...

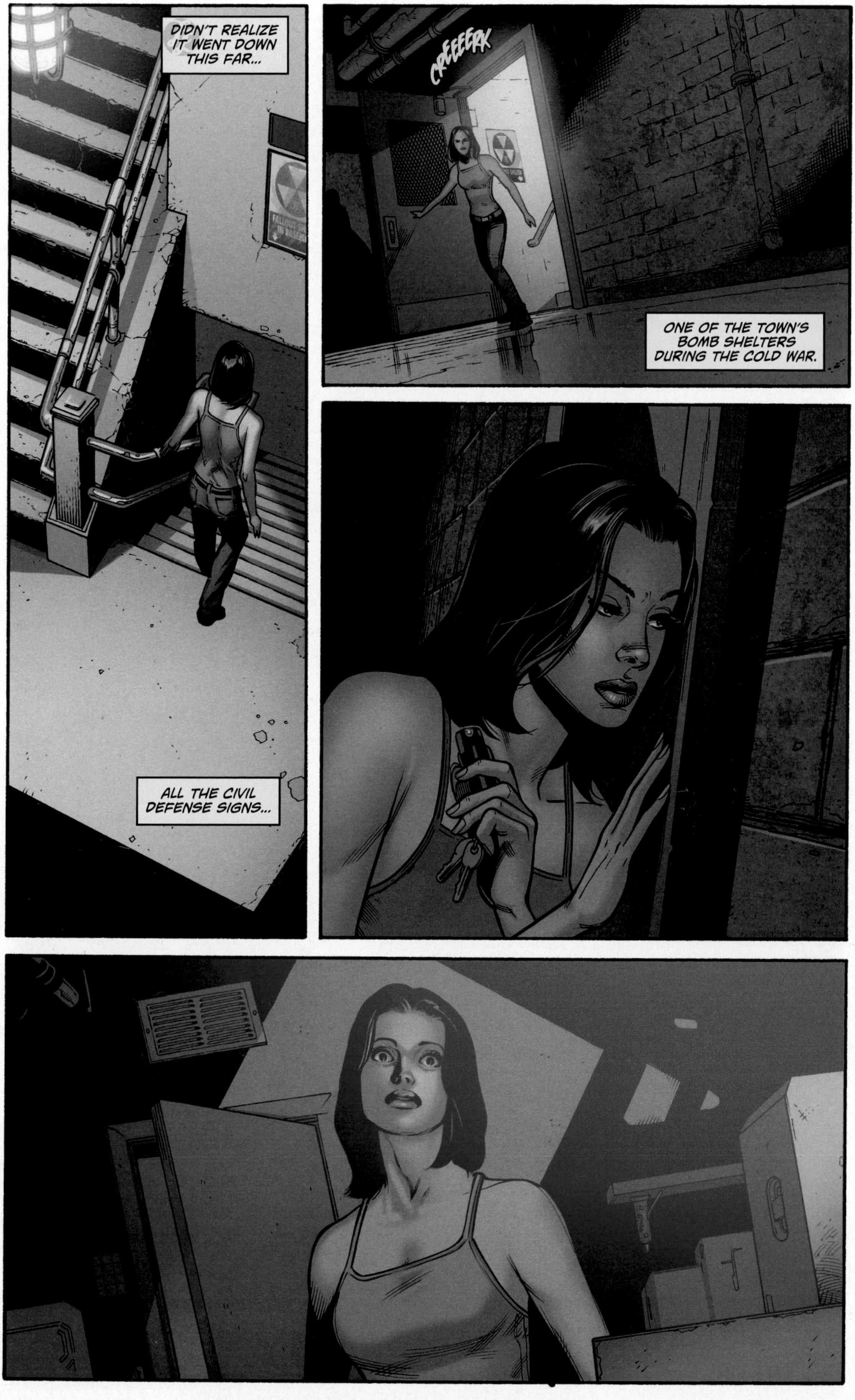
DIDN'T REALIZE IT WENT DOWN THIS FAR...
ALL THE CIVIL DEFENSE SIGNS...
CREEEERK
ONE OF THE TOWN'S BOMB SHELTERS DURING THE COLD WAR.

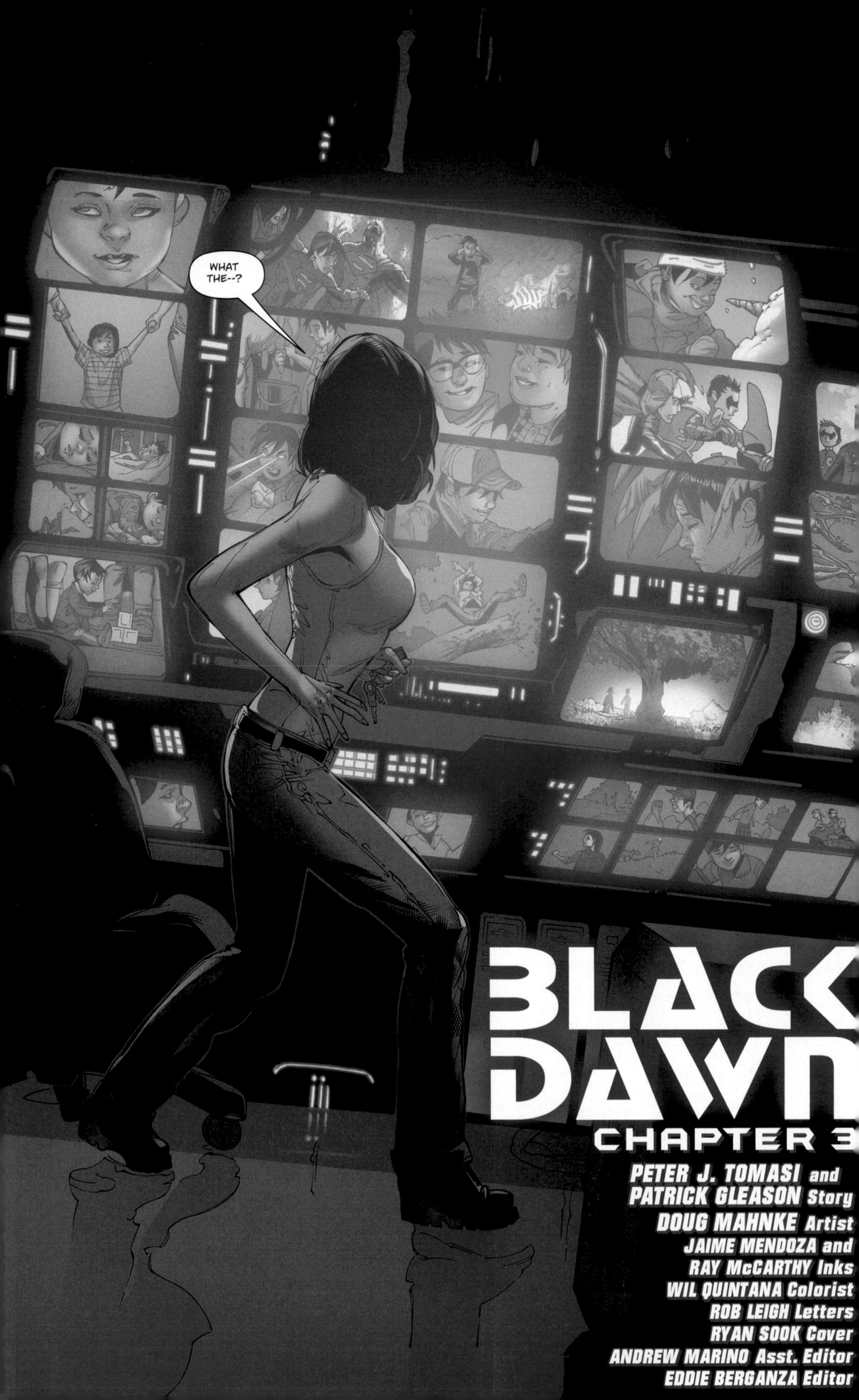
WHAT THE--?

BLACK DAWN
CHAPTER 3

PETER J. TOMASI and **PATRICK GLEASON** Story
DOUG MAHNKE Artist
JAIME MENDOZA and **RAY McCARTHY** Inks
WIL QUINTANA Colorist
ROB LEIGH Letters
RYAN SOOK Cover
ANDREW MARINO Asst. Editor
EDDIE BERGANZA Editor

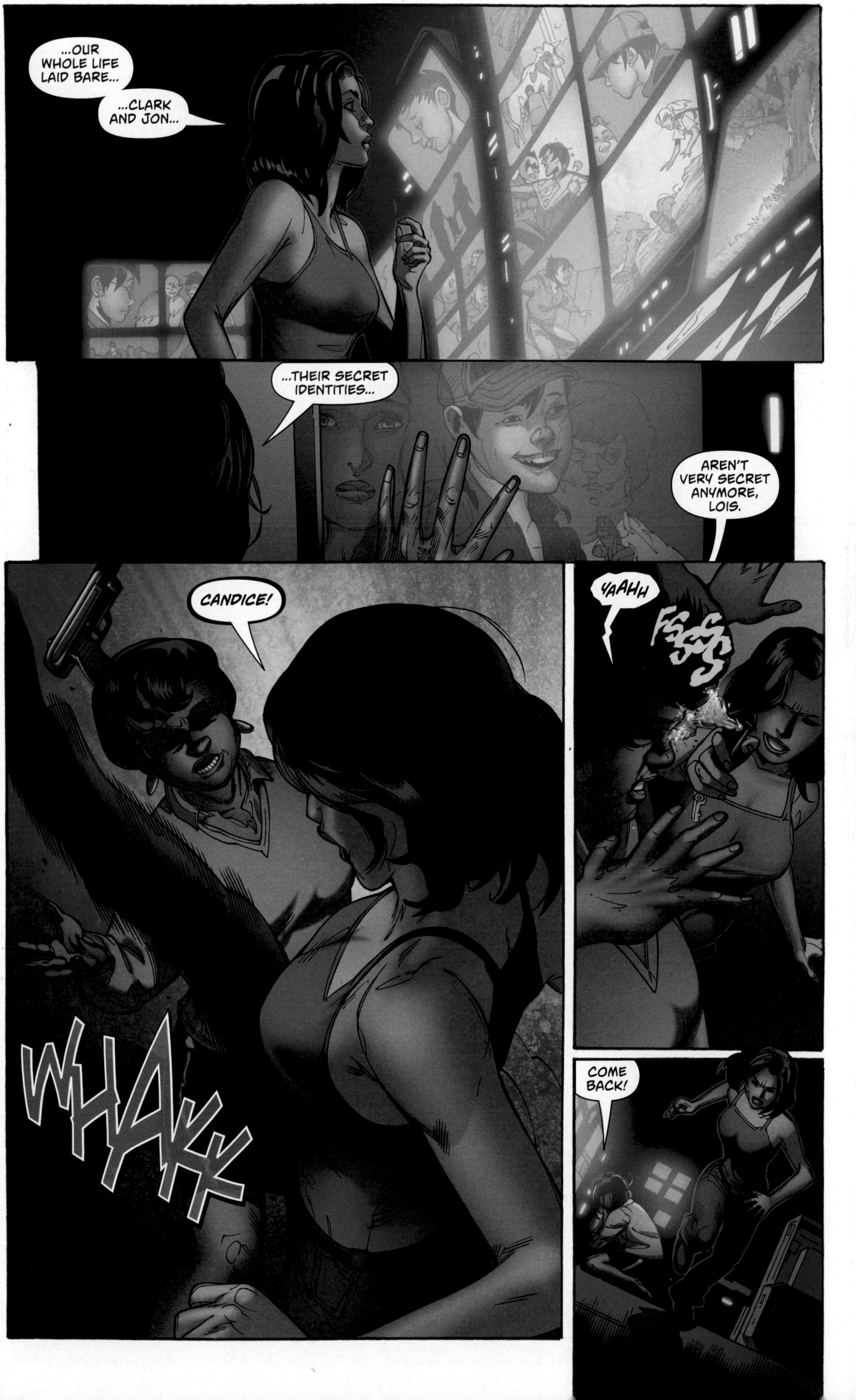
...OUR WHOLE LIFE LAID BARE...
...CLARK AND JON...
...THEIR SECRET IDENTITIES...
AREN'T VERY SECRET ANYMORE, LOIS.
CANDICE!
WHAKK
YAAHH
FSSSS
COME BACK!

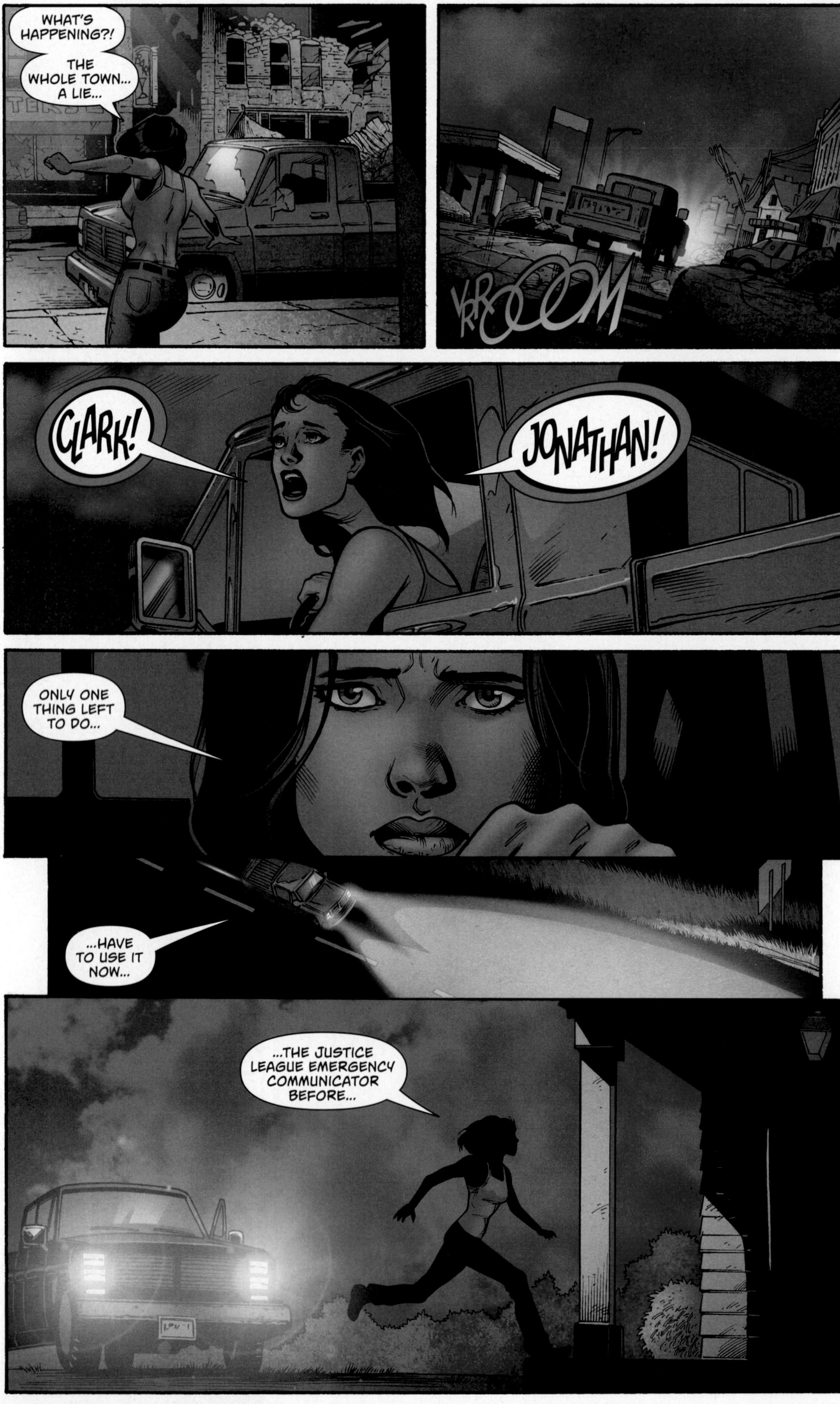
WHAT'S HAPPENING?!
THE WHOLE TOWN... A LIE...
VRROOOM
CLARK!
JONATHAN!
ONLY ONE THING LEFT TO DO...
...HAVE TO USE IT NOW...
...THE JUSTICE LEAGUE EMERGENCY COMMUNICATOR BEFORE...

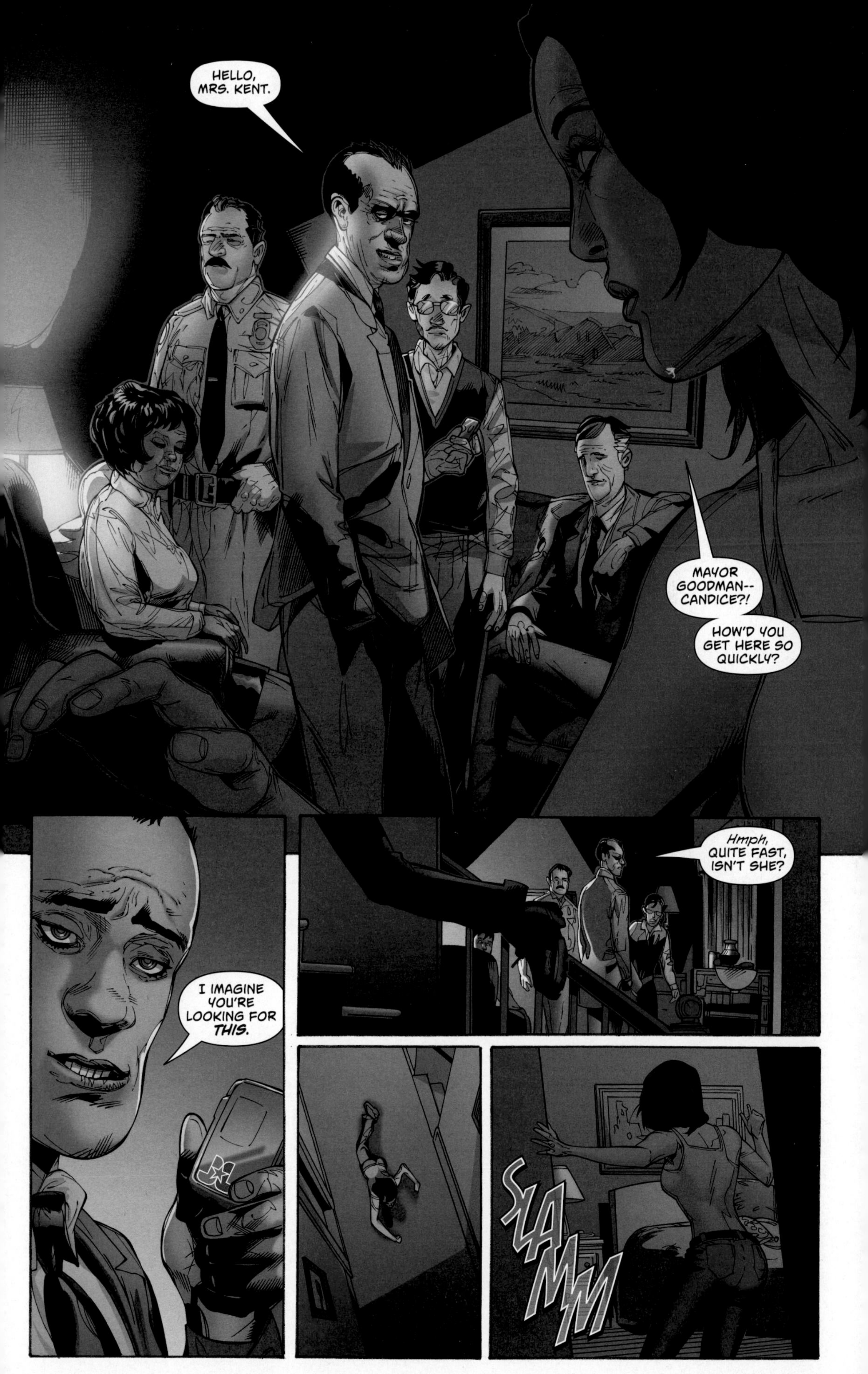
HELLO, MRS. KENT.
MAYOR GOODMAN-- CANDICE?!
HOW'D YOU GET HERE SO QUICKLY?
I IMAGINE YOU'RE LOOKING FOR *THIS*.
Hmph, QUITE FAST, ISN'T SHE?
SLAMM

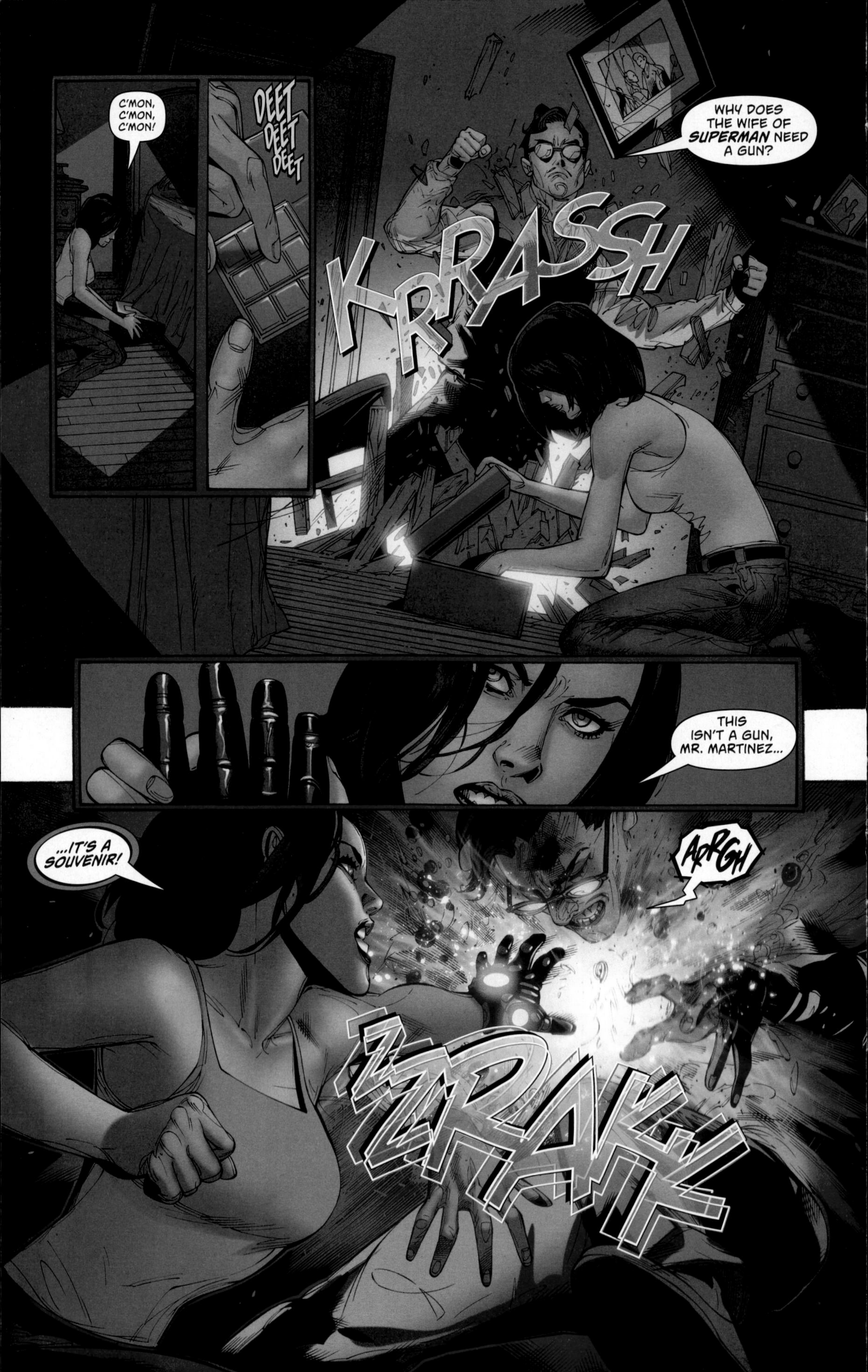
C'MON, C'MON, C'MON!
DEET DEET DEET
WHY DOES THE WIFE OF SUPERMAN NEED A GUN?
KRRASSH
THIS ISN'T A GUN, MR. MARTINEZ...
...IT'S A SOUVENIR!
ARRGH
ZZRAKK

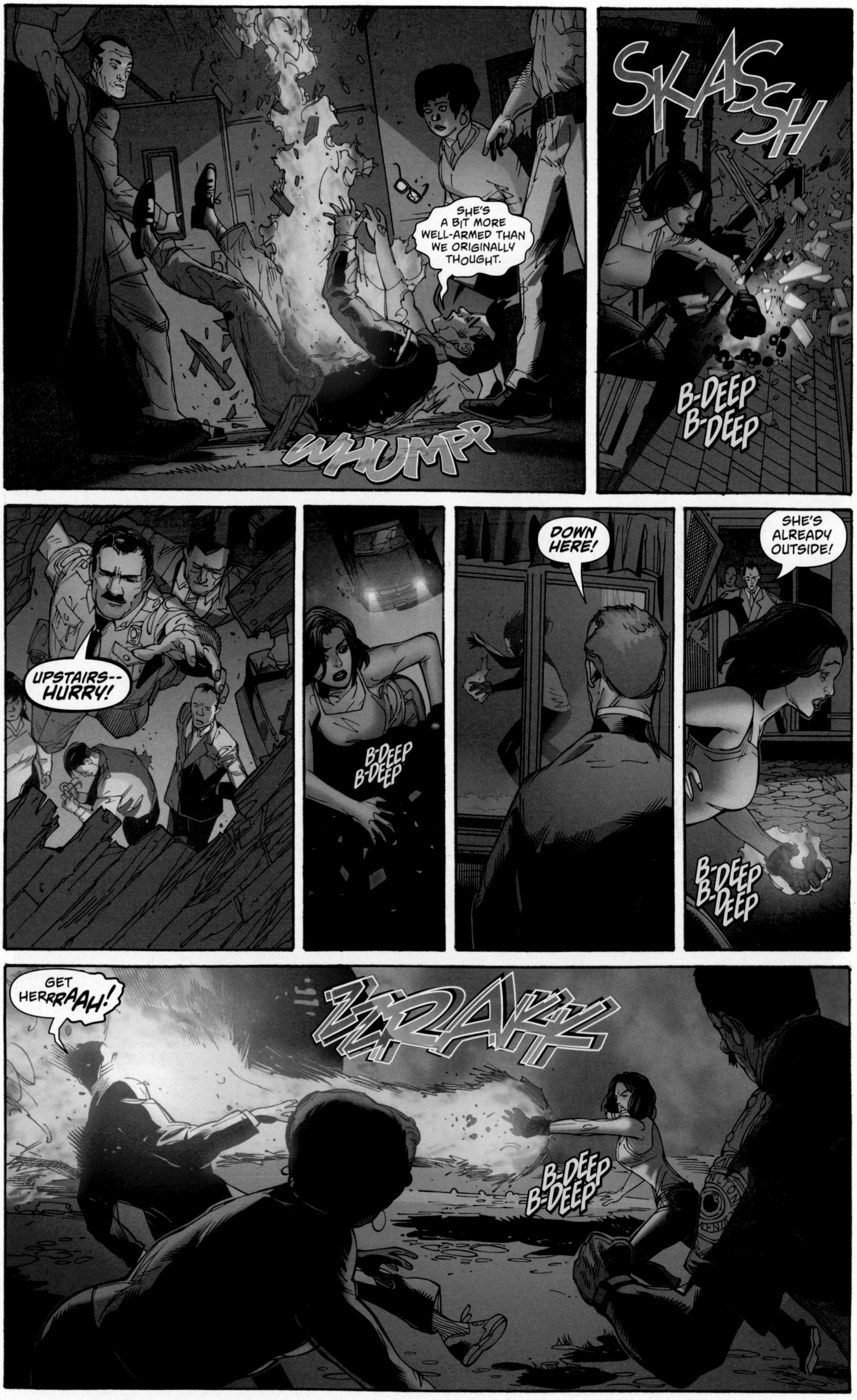
SHE'S A BIT MORE WELL-ARMED THAN WE ORIGINALLY THOUGHT.
WHUMPP
SKASSH
B-DEEP B-DEEP
UPSTAIRS-- HURRY!
B-DEEP B-DEEP
DOWN HERE!
SHE'S ALREADY OUTSIDE!
B-DEEP B-DEEP
GET HERRRAAH!
ZZRAKK
B-DEEP B-DEEP

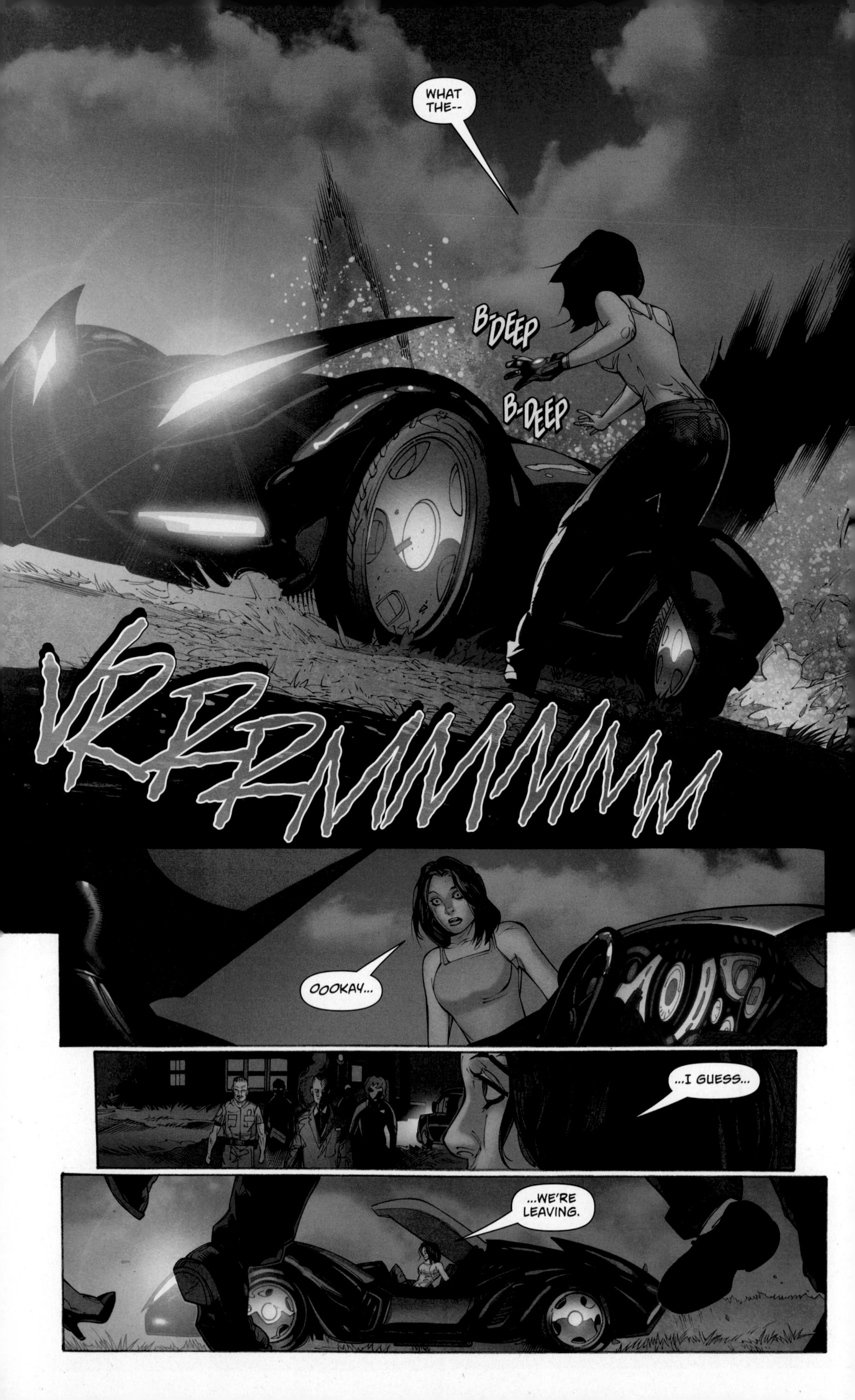

WHAT THE--
B-DEEP
B-DEEP
VRRRMMMMMM
OOOKAY...
...I GUESS...
...WE'RE LEAVING.

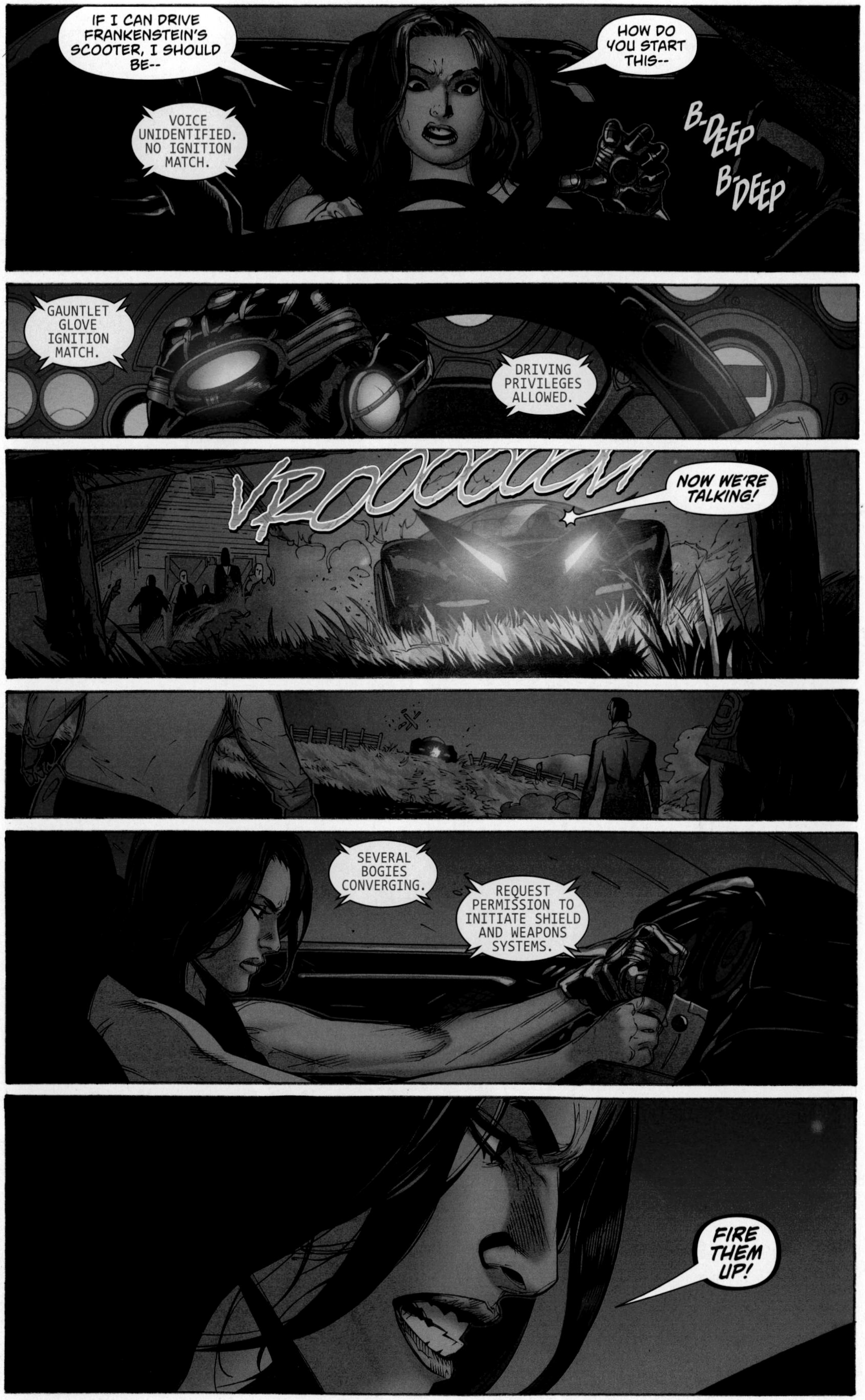
IF I CAN DRIVE FRANKENSTEIN'S SCOOTER, I SHOULD BE--
HOW DO YOU START THIS--
VOICE UNIDENTIFIED. NO IGNITION MATCH.
B-DEEP
B-DEEP
GAUNTLET GLOVE IGNITION MATCH.
DRIVING PRIVILEGES ALLOWED.
VROOOOOOM
NOW WE'RE TALKING!
SEVERAL BOGIES CONVERGING.
REQUEST PERMISSION TO INITIATE SHIELD AND WEAPONS SYSTEMS.
FIRE THEM UP!

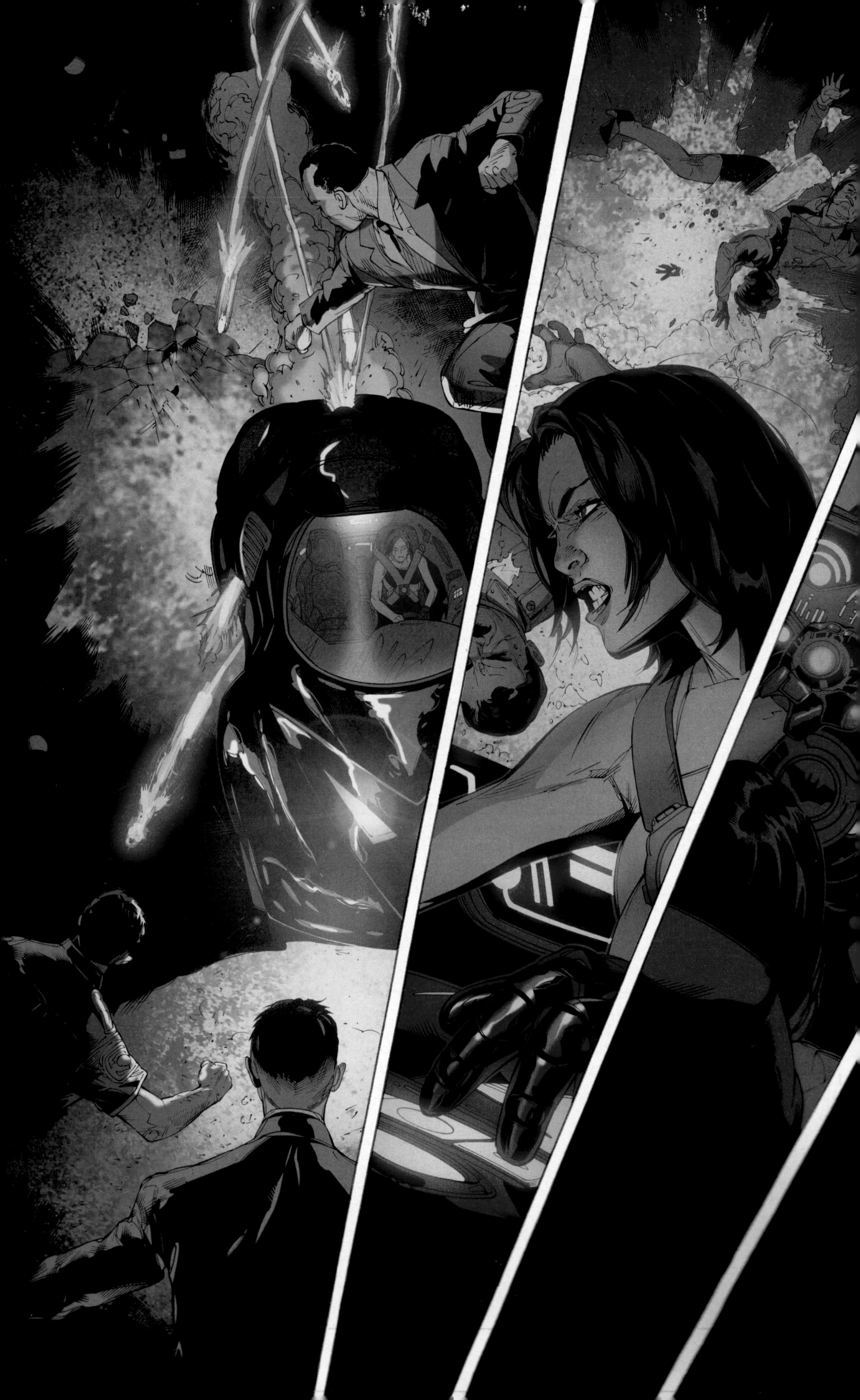

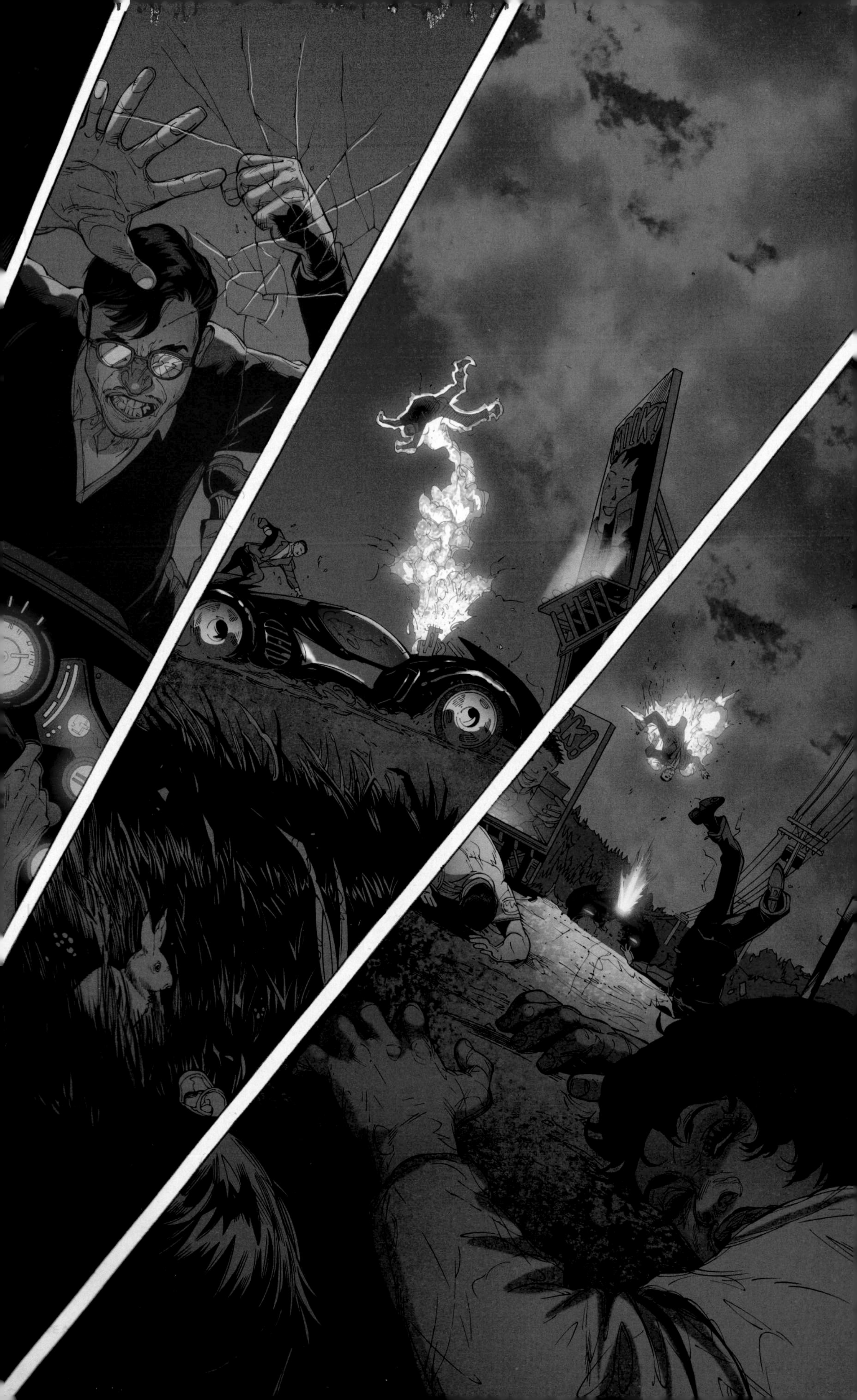

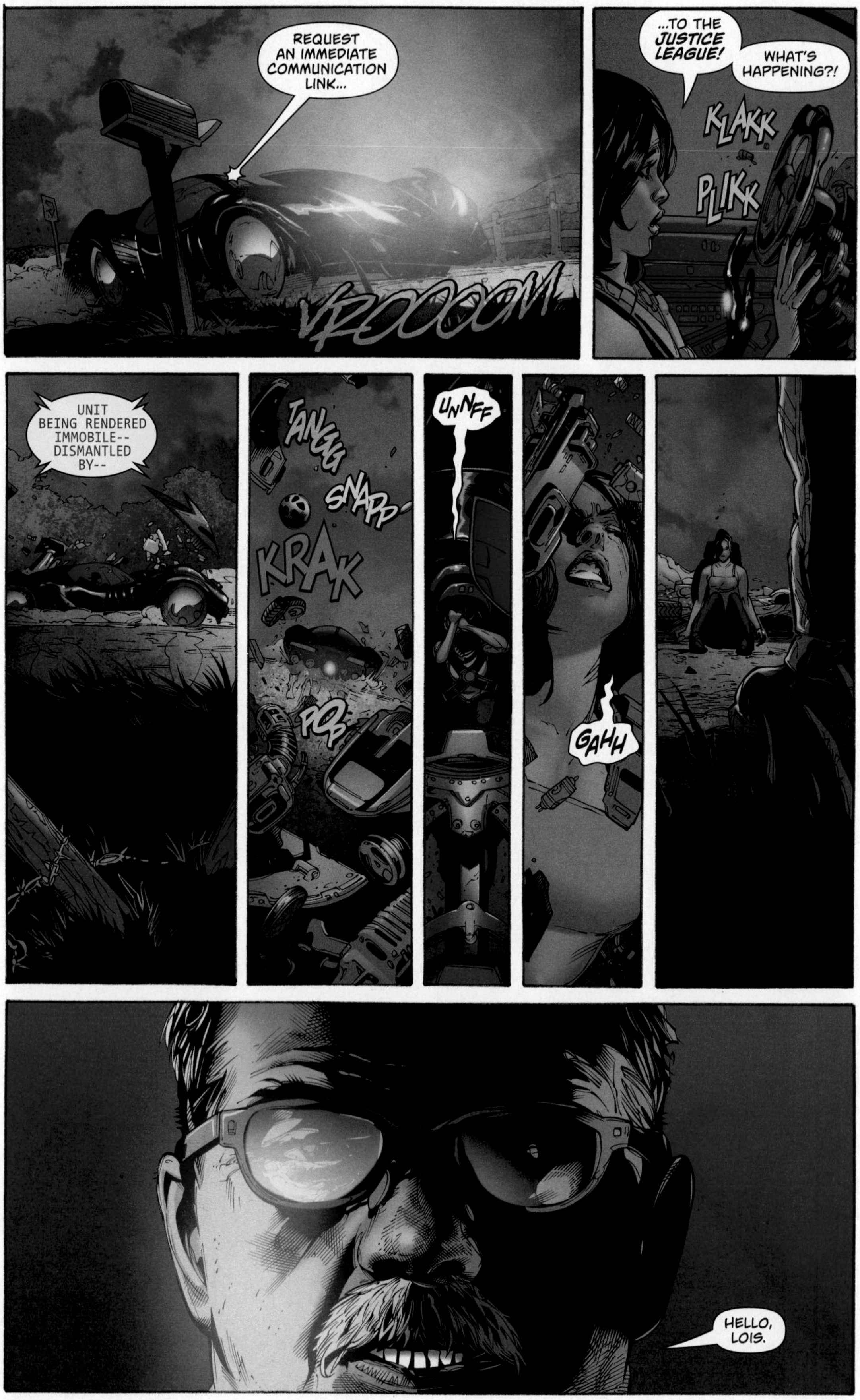
REQUEST AN IMMEDIATE COMMUNICATION LINK...
VROOOOOM
...TO THE JUSTICE LEAGUE!
WHAT'S HAPPENING?!
KLAKK
PLIKK
UNIT BEING RENDERED IMMOBILE-- DISMANTLED BY--
TANGG
SNAPP
KRAK
POP
UNNFF
GAHH
HELLO, LOIS.

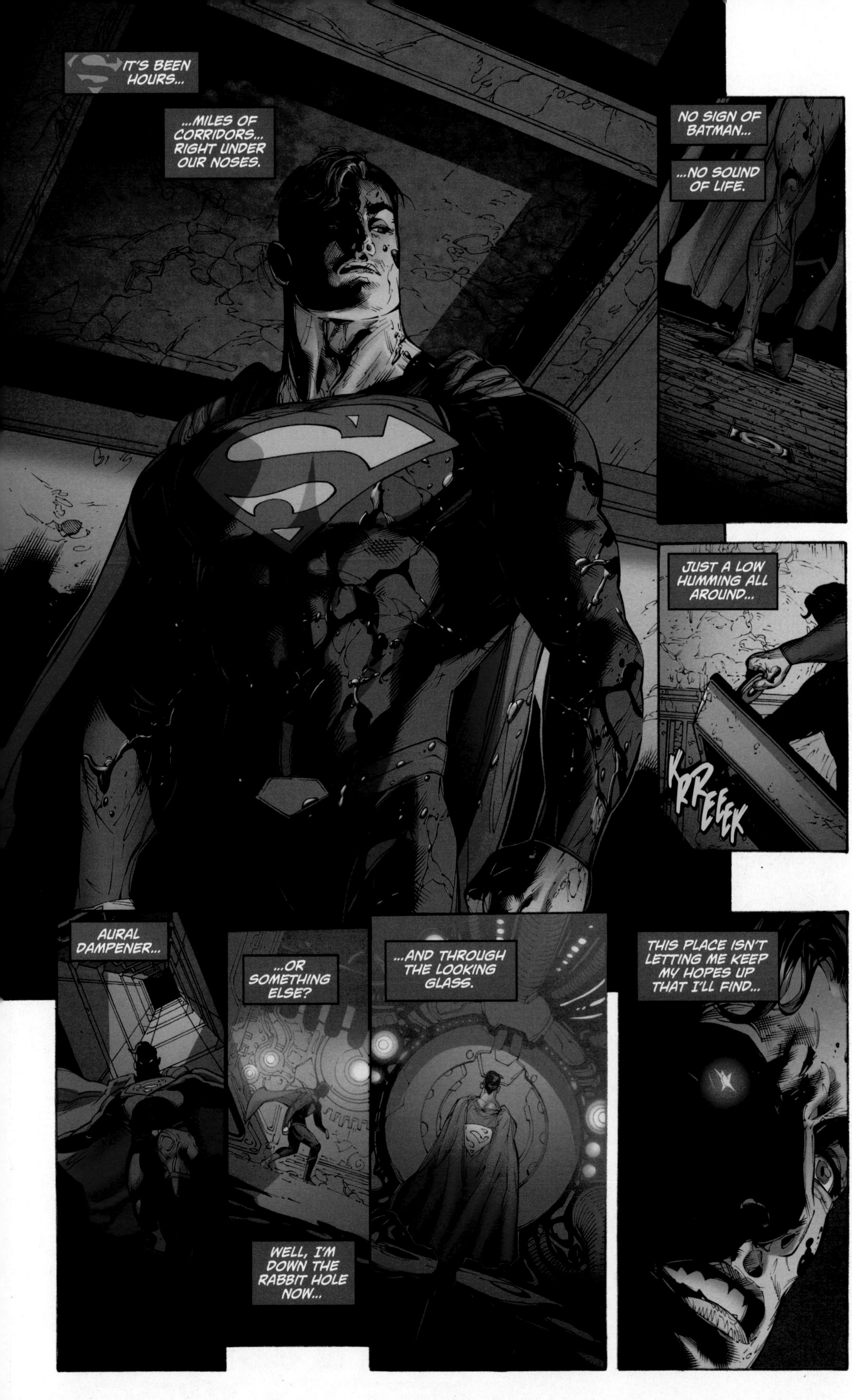
IT'S BEEN HOURS...
...MILES OF CORRIDORS... RIGHT UNDER OUR NOSES.
NO SIGN OF BATMAN...
...NO SOUND OF LIFE.
JUST A LOW HUMMING ALL AROUND...
KRREEEK
AURAL DAMPENER...
...OR SOMETHING ELSE?
WELL, I'M DOWN THE RABBIT HOLE NOW...
...AND THROUGH THE LOOKING GLASS.
THIS PLACE ISN'T LETTING ME KEEP MY HOPES UP THAT I'LL FIND...

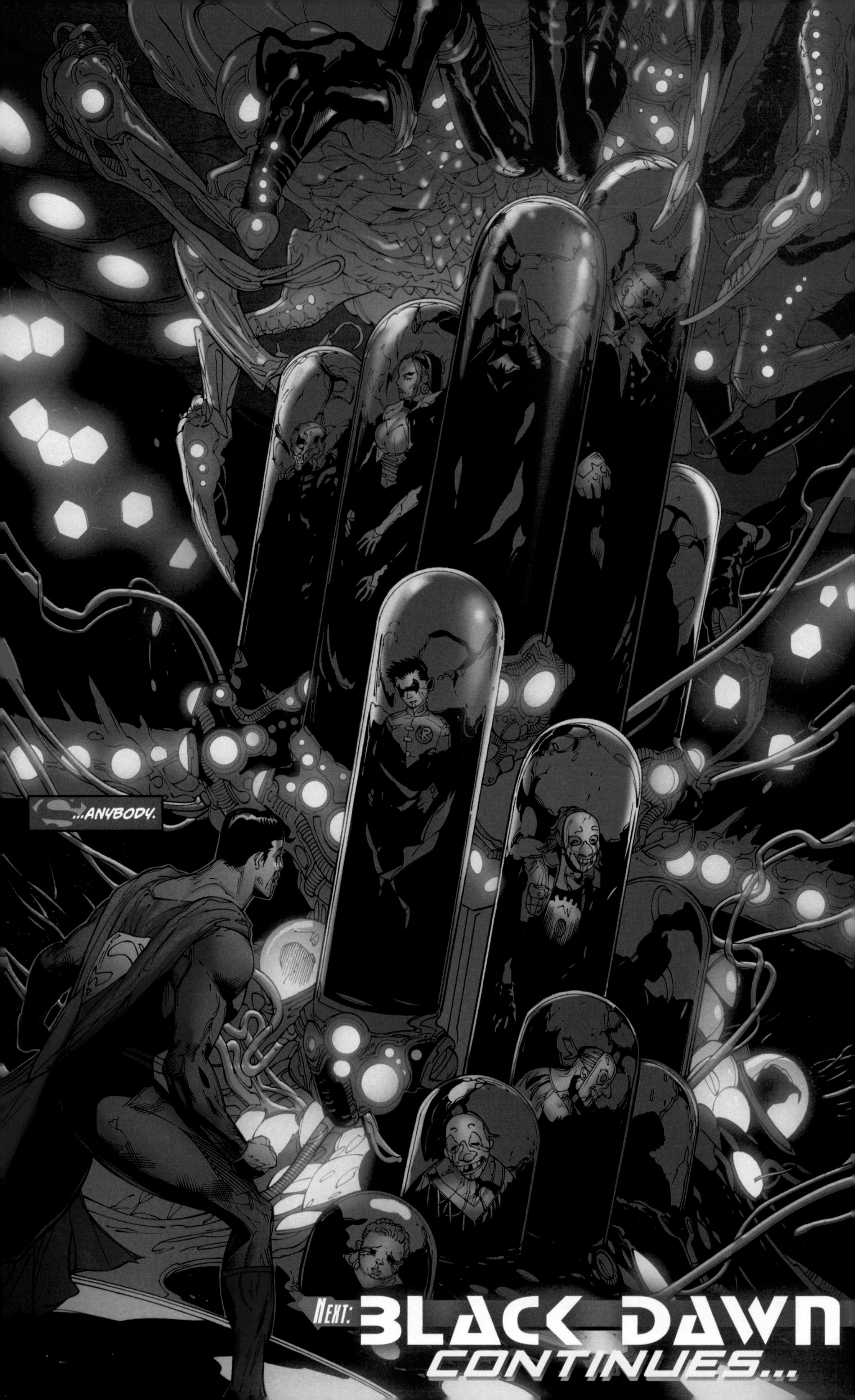
...ANYBODY.
NEXT: BLACK DAWN CONTINUES...

POWERLESS

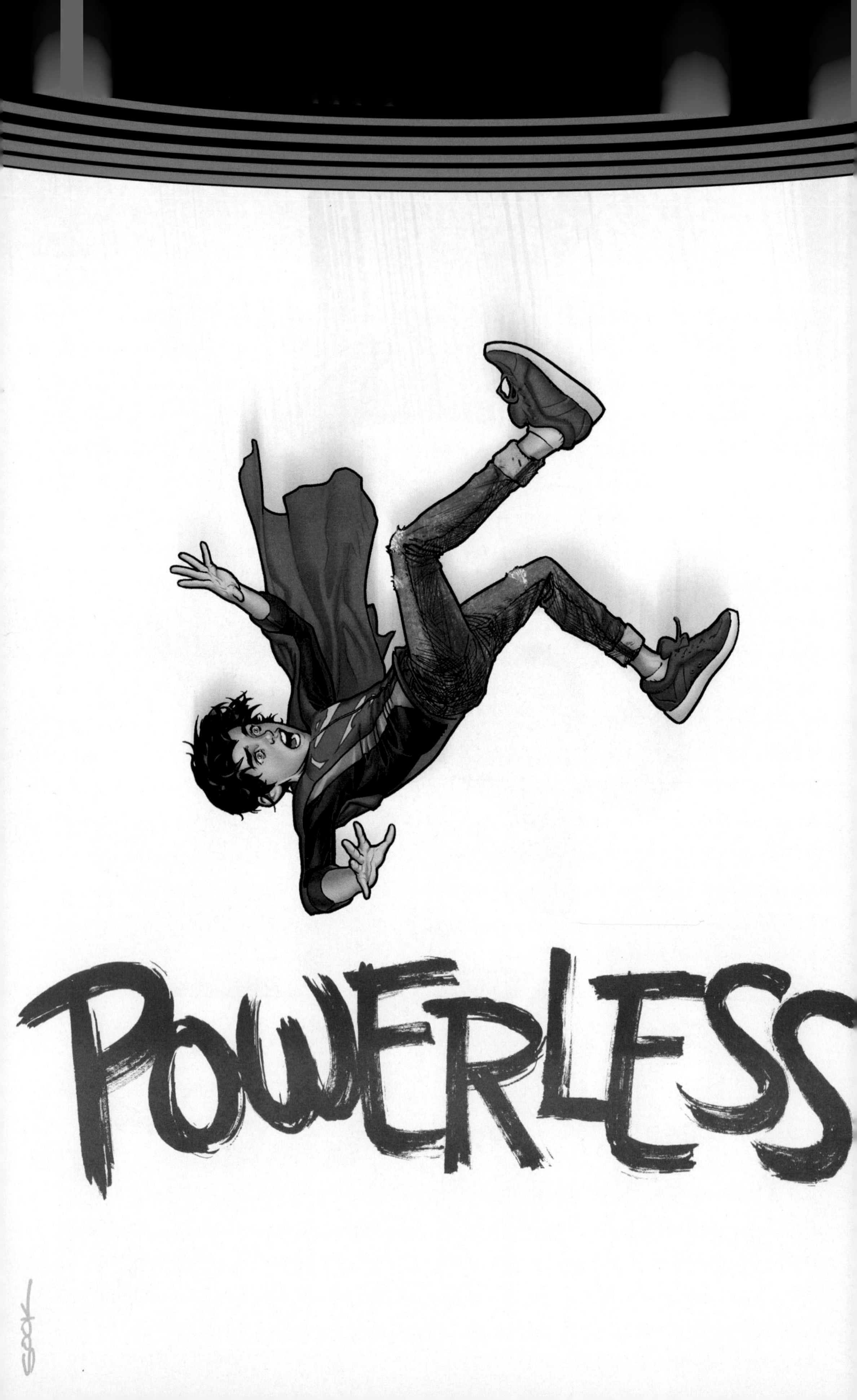
POWERLESS

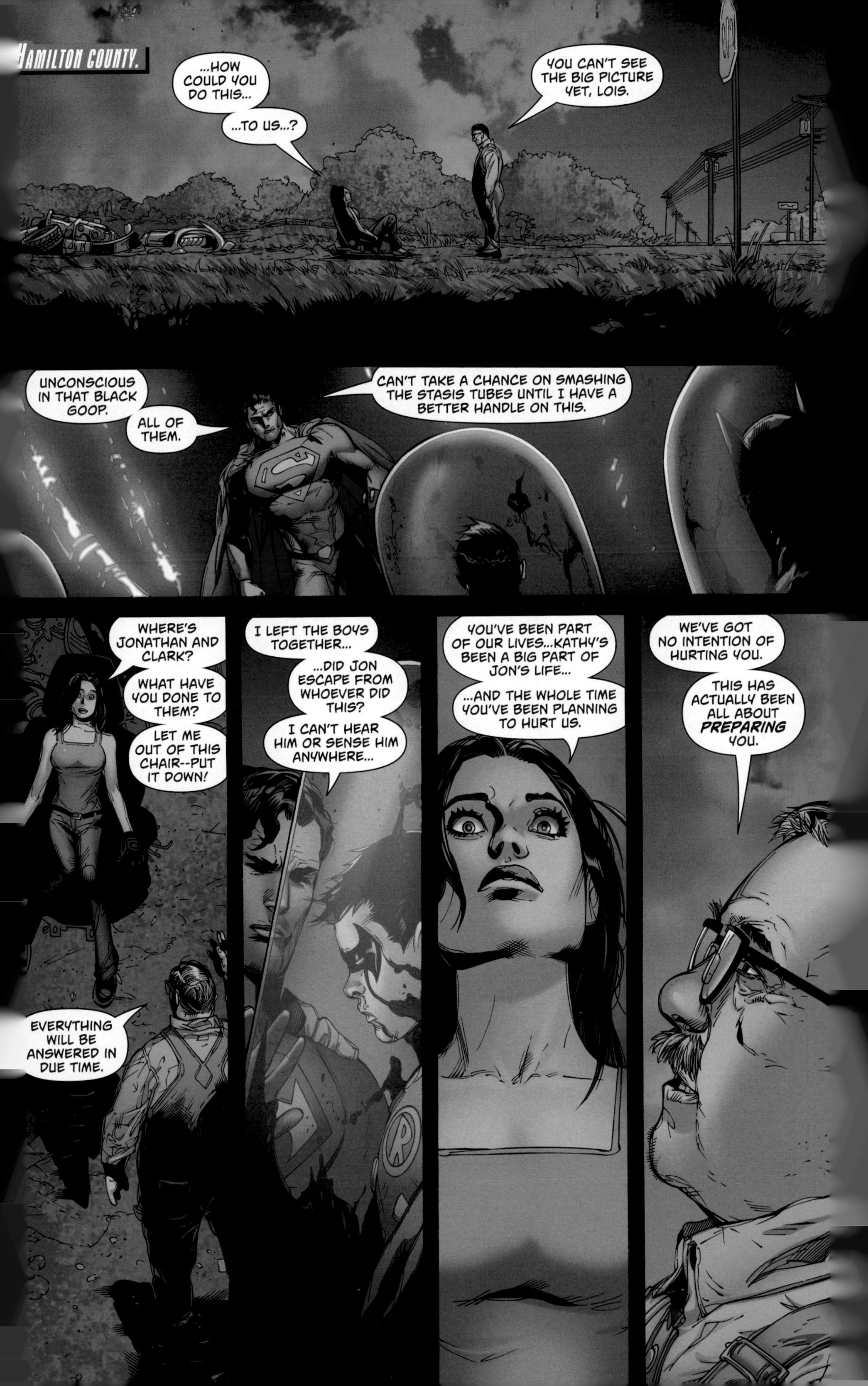
HAMILTON COUNTY.
...HOW COULD YOU DO THIS...
...TO US...?
YOU CAN'T SEE THE BIG PICTURE YET, LOIS.
UNCONSCIOUS IN THAT BLACK GOOP.
ALL OF THEM.
CAN'T TAKE A CHANCE ON SMASHING THE STASIS TUBES UNTIL I HAVE A BETTER HANDLE ON THIS.
WHERE'S JONATHAN AND CLARK?
WHAT HAVE YOU DONE TO THEM?
LET ME OUT OF THIS CHAIR--PUT IT DOWN!
EVERYTHING WILL BE ANSWERED IN DUE TIME.
I LEFT THE BOYS TOGETHER...
...DID JON ESCAPE FROM WHOEVER DID THIS?
I CAN'T HEAR HIM OR SENSE HIM ANYWHERE...
YOU'VE BEEN PART OF OUR LIVES...KATHY'S BEEN A BIG PART OF JON'S LIFE...
...AND THE WHOLE TIME YOU'VE BEEN PLANNING TO HURT US.
WE'VE GOT NO INTENTION OF HURTING YOU.
THIS HAS ACTUALLY BEEN ALL ABOUT *PREPARING* YOU.

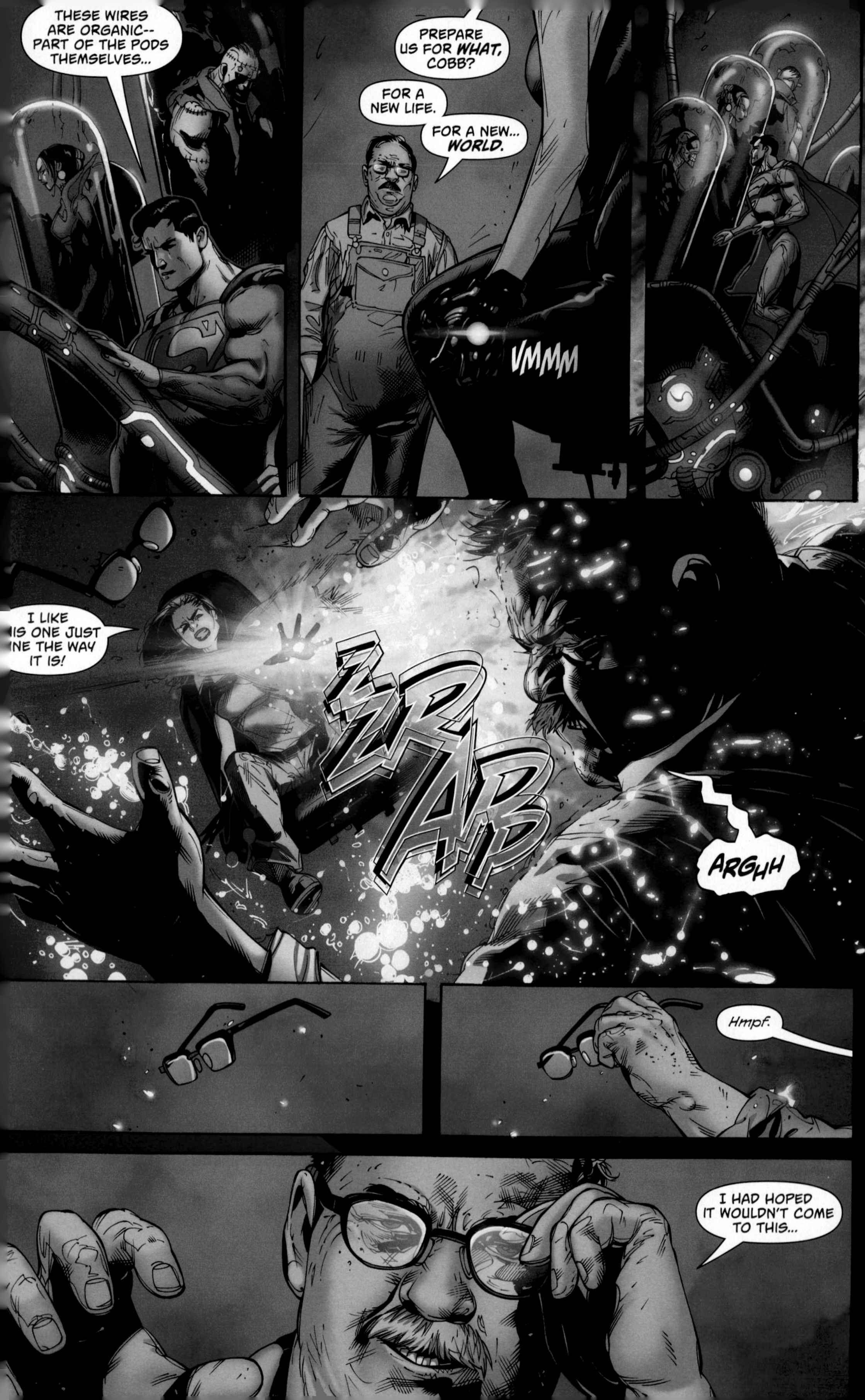
THESE WIRES ARE ORGANIC-- PART OF THE PODS THEMSELVES...
PREPARE US FOR WHAT, COBB?
FOR A NEW LIFE.
FOR A NEW... WORLD.
VMMM
I LIKE IS ONE JUST NE THE WAY IT IS!
ZZRAP
ARGHH
Hmpf.
I HAD HOPED IT WOULDN'T COME TO THIS...

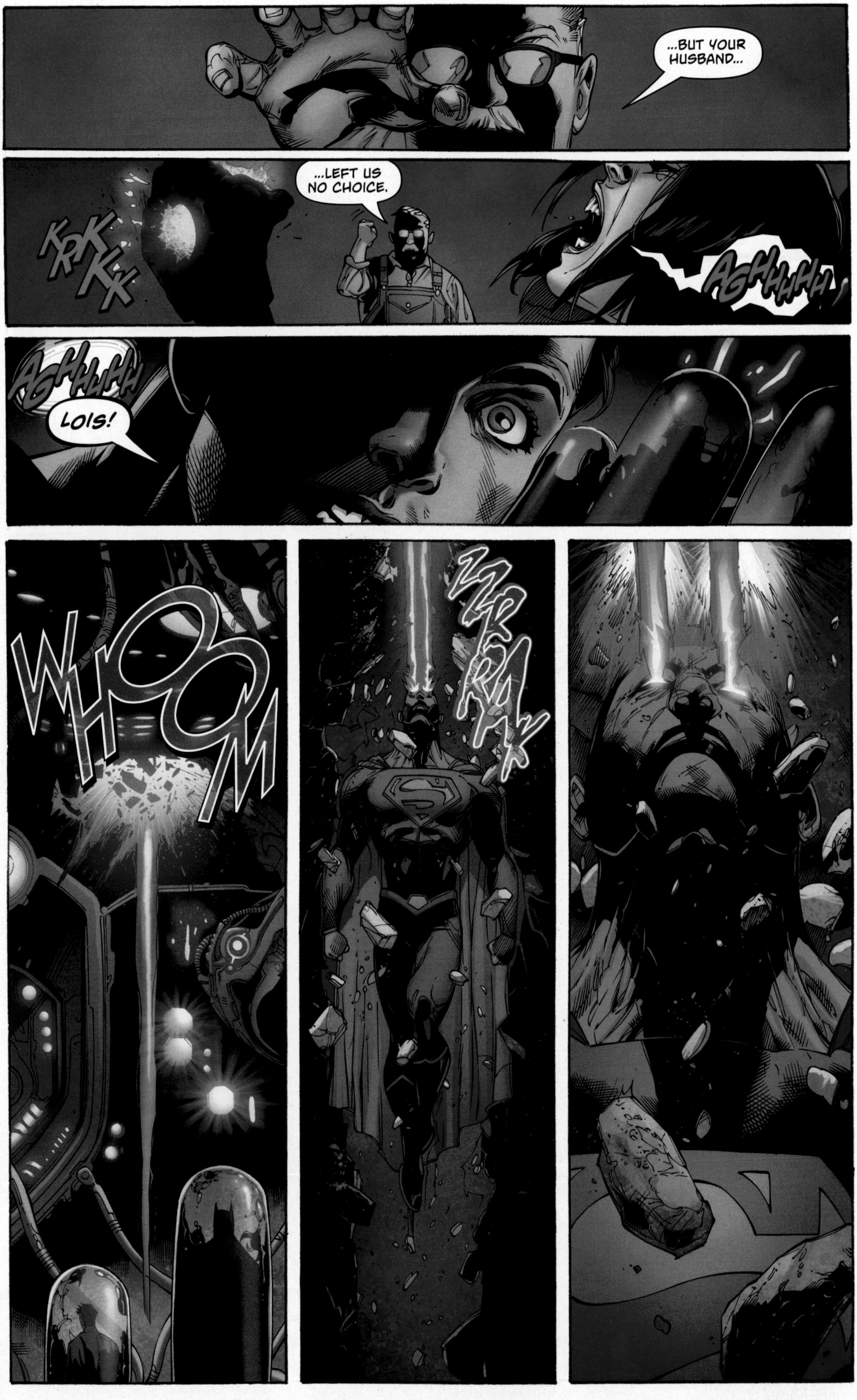
...BUT YOUR HUSBAND...
...LEFT US NO CHOICE.
KRKKK
AGHHHHH
AGHHHHH
LOIS!
WHOOM
ZZZRRAAK

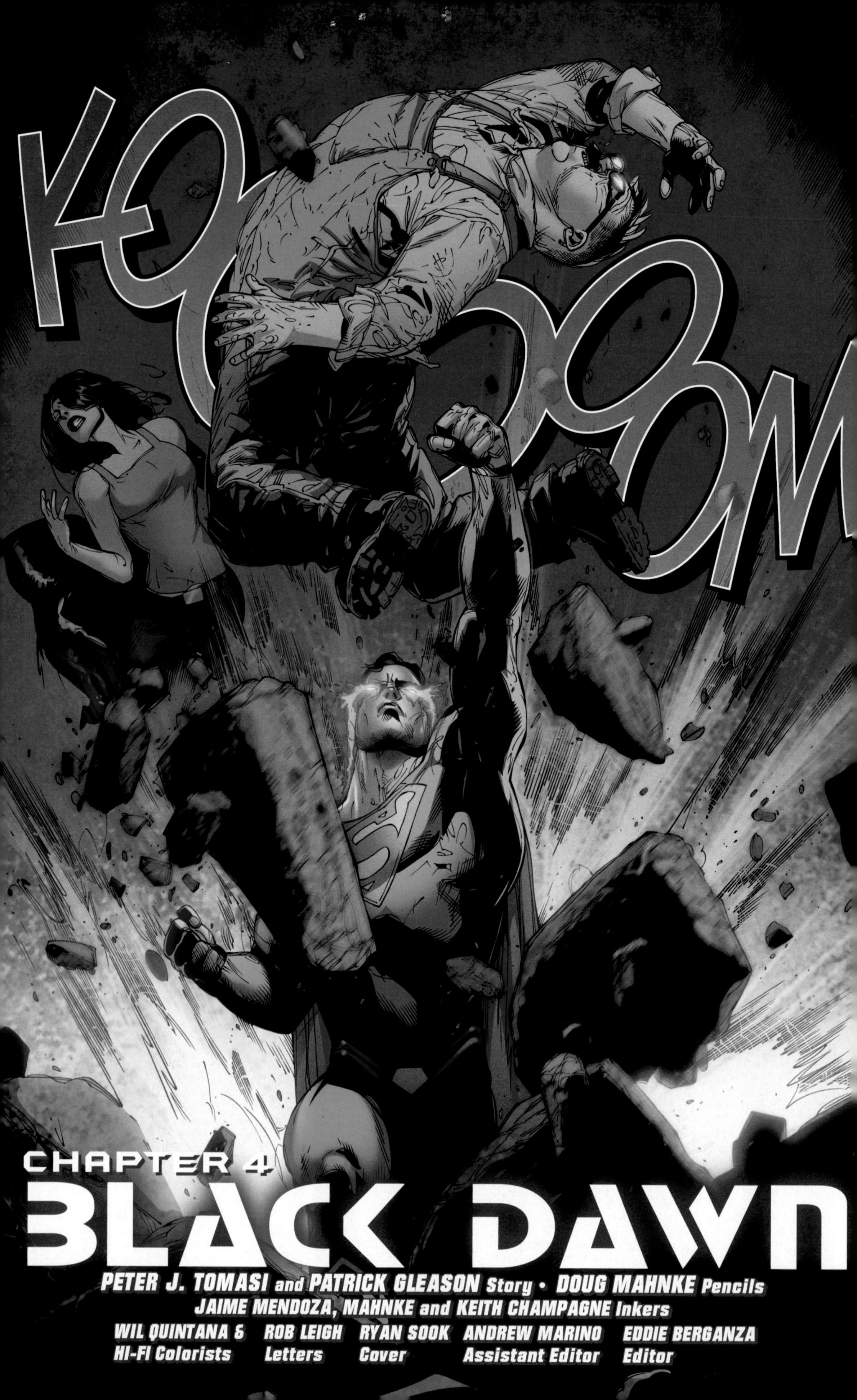

CHAPTER 4
BLACK DAWN

PETER J. TOMASI and **PATRICK GLEASON** Story • **DOUG MAHNKE** Pencils
JAIME MENDOZA, MAHNKE and **KEITH CHAMPAGNE** Inkers
WIL QUINTANA & HI-FI Colorists **ROB LEIGH** Letters **RYAN SOOK** Cover **ANDREW MARINO** Assistant Editor **EDDIE BERGANZA** Editor

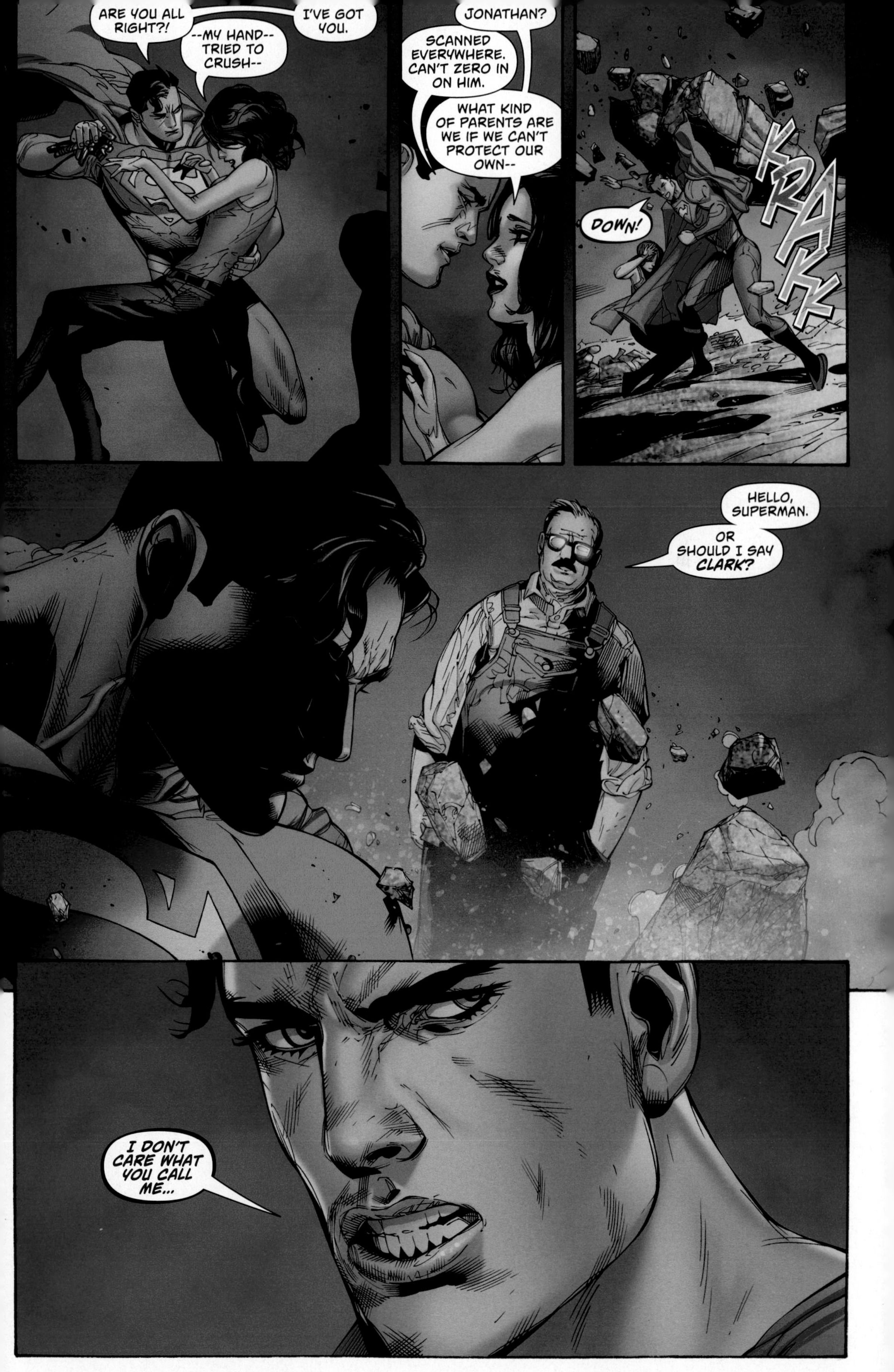
ARE YOU ALL RIGHT?!
I'VE GOT YOU.
--MY HAND--TRIED TO CRUSH--
JONATHAN?
SCANNED EVERYWHERE. CAN'T ZERO IN ON HIM.
WHAT KIND OF PARENTS ARE WE IF WE CAN'T PROTECT OUR OWN--
KRAKK
DOWN!
HELLO, SUPERMAN.
OR SHOULD I SAY CLARK?
I DON'T CARE WHAT YOU CALL ME...

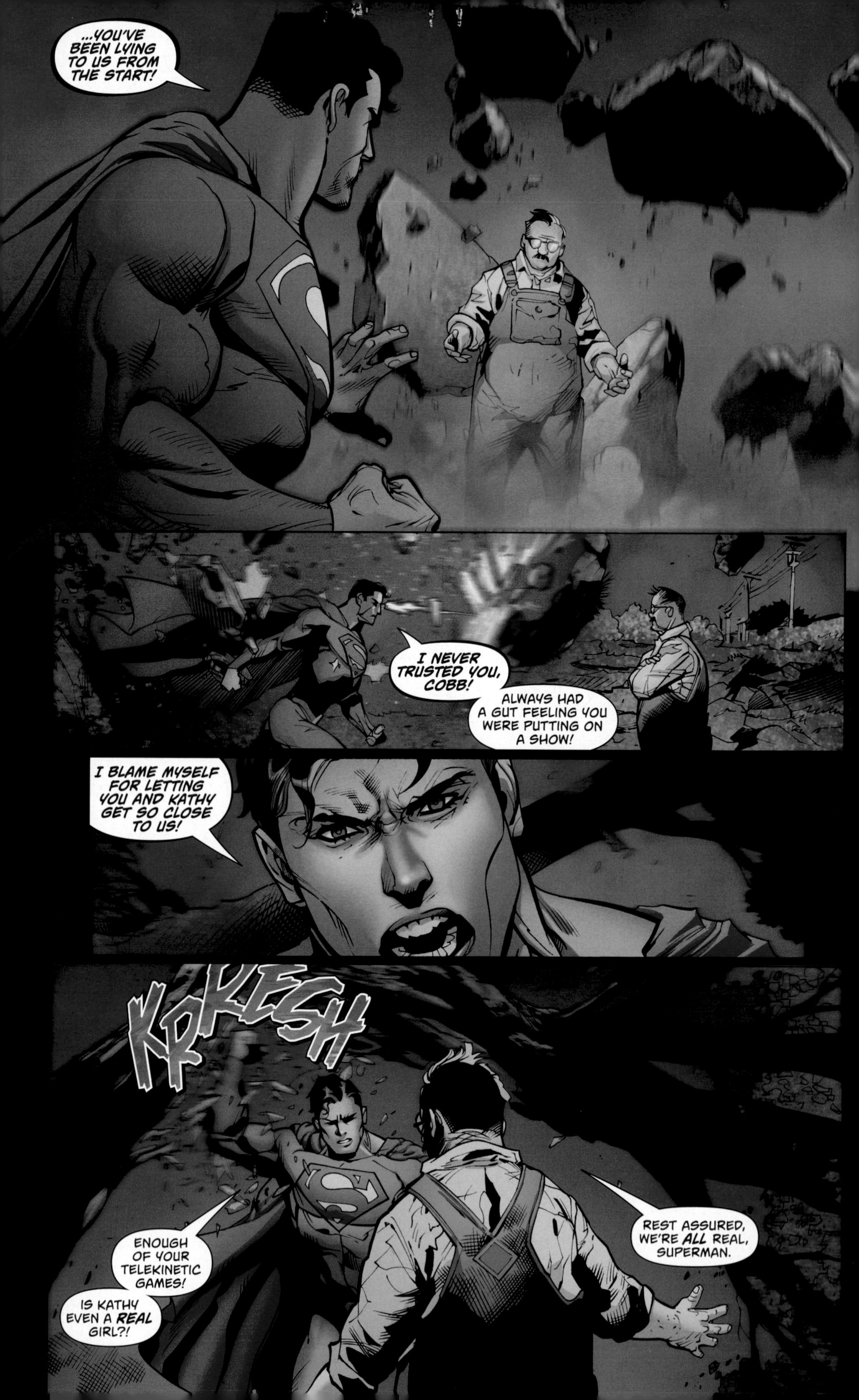
...YOU'VE BEEN LYING TO US FROM THE START!
I NEVER TRUSTED YOU, COBB!
ALWAYS HAD A GUT FEELING YOU WERE PUTTING ON A SHOW!
I BLAME MYSELF FOR LETTING YOU AND KATHY GET SO CLOSE TO US!
KRKESH
ENOUGH OF YOUR TELEKINETIC GAMES!
IS KATHY EVEN A REAL GIRL?!
REST ASSURED, WE'RE ALL REAL, SUPERMAN.

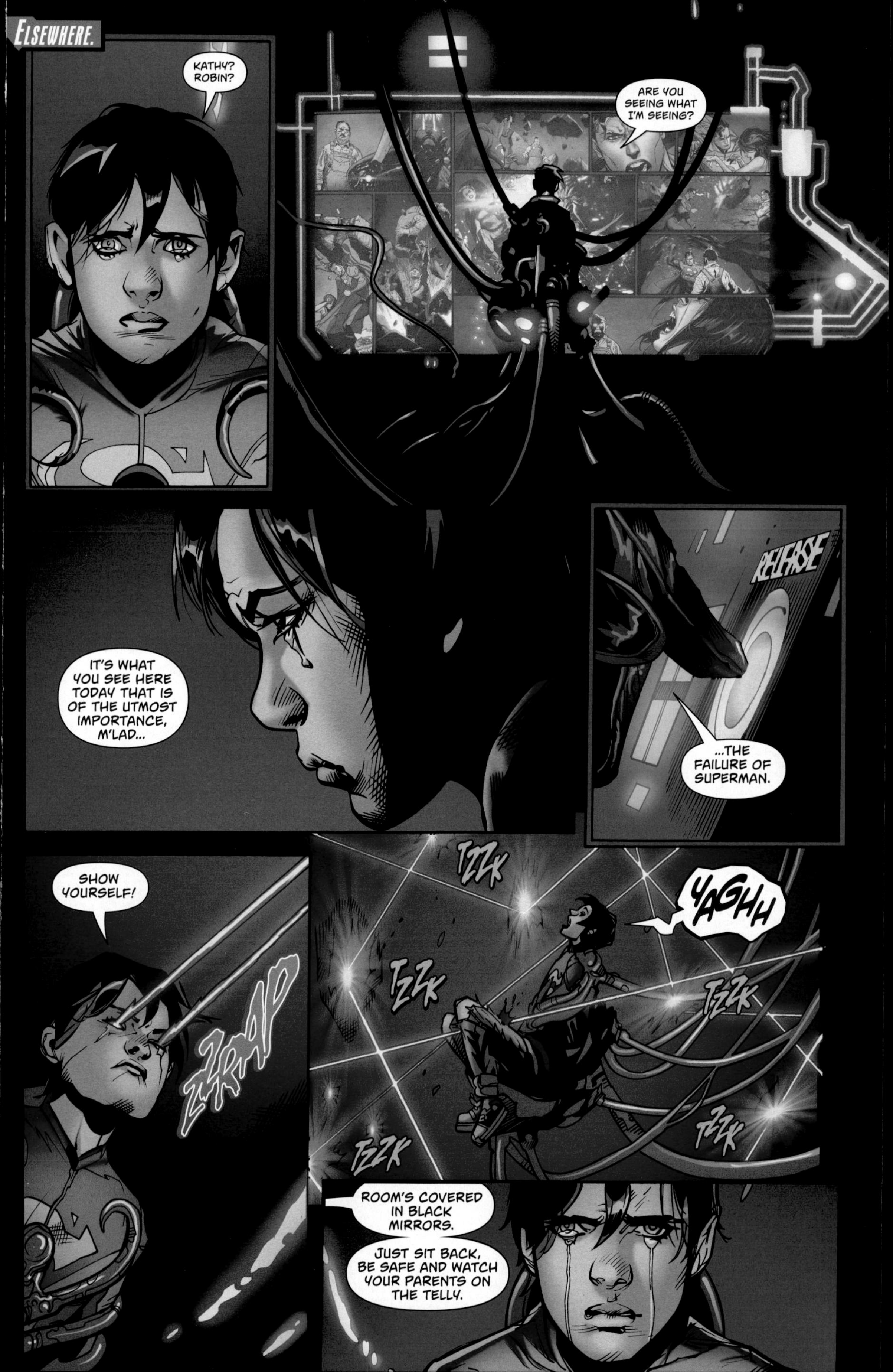
ELSEWHERE.
KATHY? ROBIN?
ARE YOU SEEING WHAT I'M SEEING?
IT'S WHAT YOU SEE HERE TODAY THAT IS OF THE UTMOST IMPORTANCE, M'LAD...
RELEASE
...THE FAILURE OF SUPERMAN.
SHOW YOURSELF!
ZZRRAP
TZZK
YAGHH
TZZK
TZZK
TZZK
TZZK
ROOM'S COVERED IN BLACK MIRRORS.
JUST SIT BACK, BE SAFE AND WATCH YOUR PARENTS ON THE TELLY.

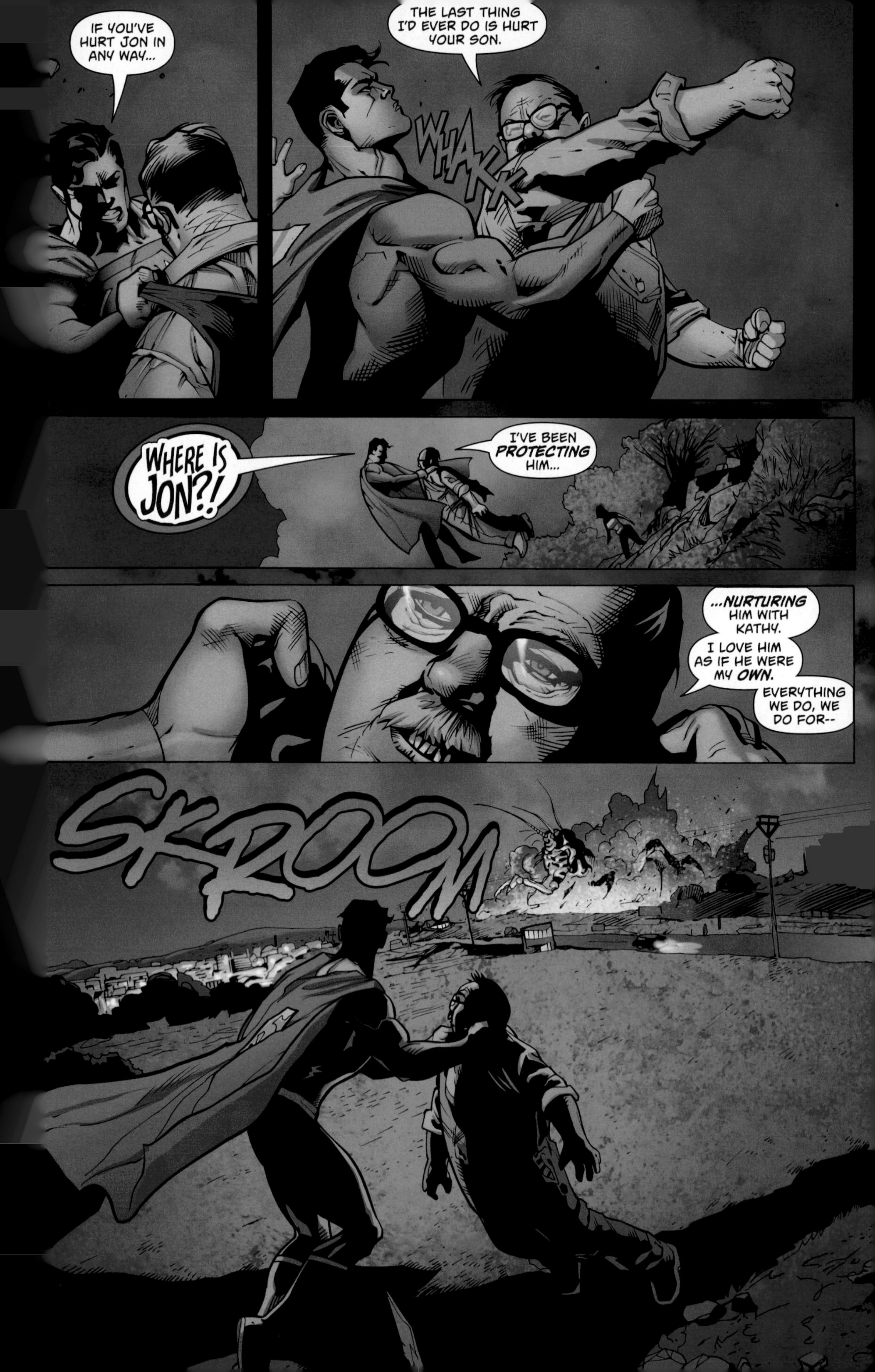
IF YOU'VE HURT JON IN ANY WAY...
THE LAST THING I'D EVER DO IS HURT YOUR SON.
WHAKK
WHERE IS JON?!
I'VE BEEN PROTECTING HIM...
...NURTURING HIM WITH KATHY.
I LOVE HIM AS IF HE WERE MY OWN.
EVERYTHING WE DO, WE DO FOR--
SKROOM

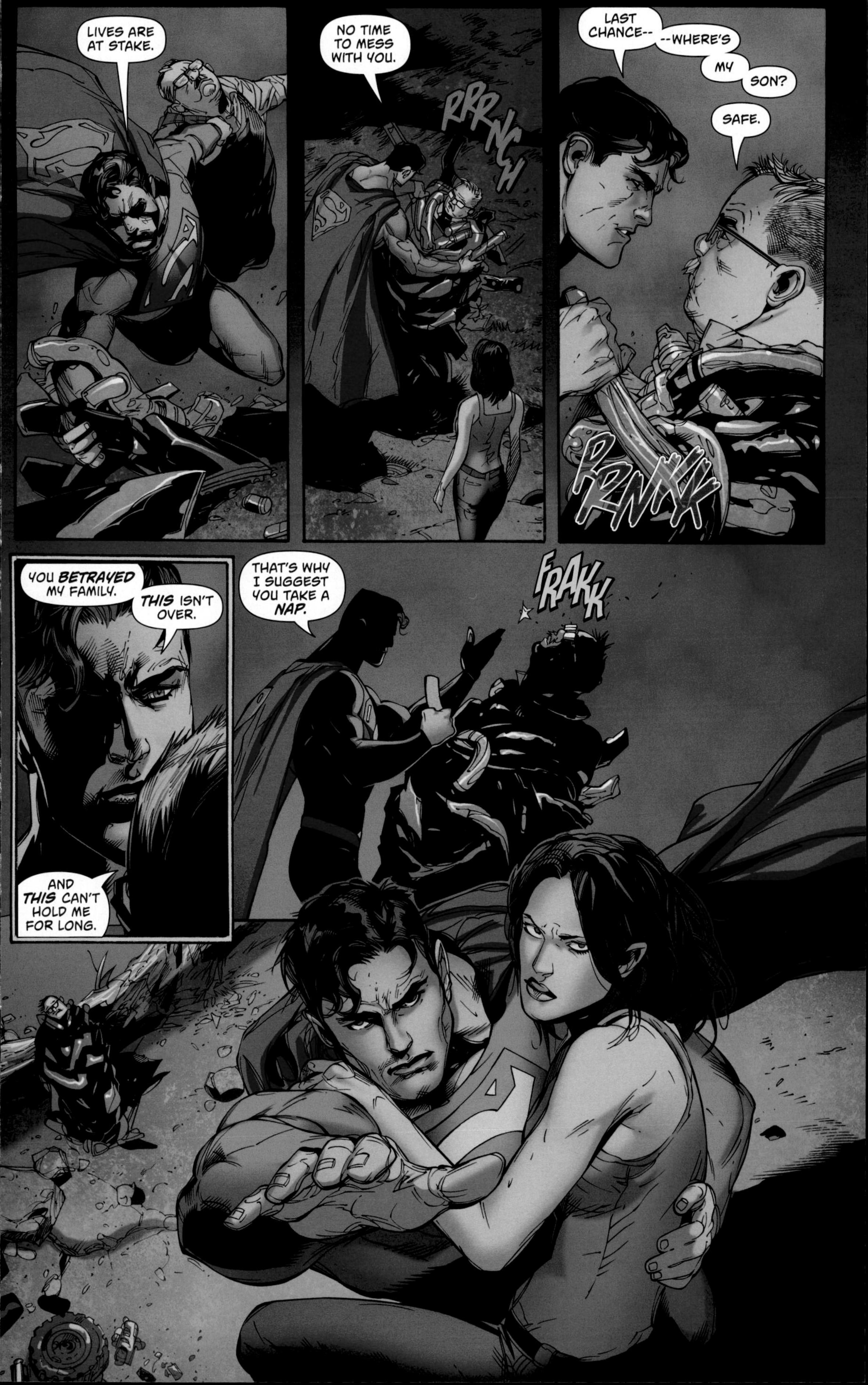
LIVES ARE AT STAKE.
NO TIME TO MESS WITH YOU.
RRRNCH
LAST CHANCE--
--WHERE'S
MY
SON?
SAFE.
PRNKK
YOU BETRAYED MY FAMILY.
THIS ISN'T OVER.
AND THIS CAN'T HOLD ME FOR LONG.
THAT'S WHY I SUGGEST YOU TAKE A NAP.
FRAKK

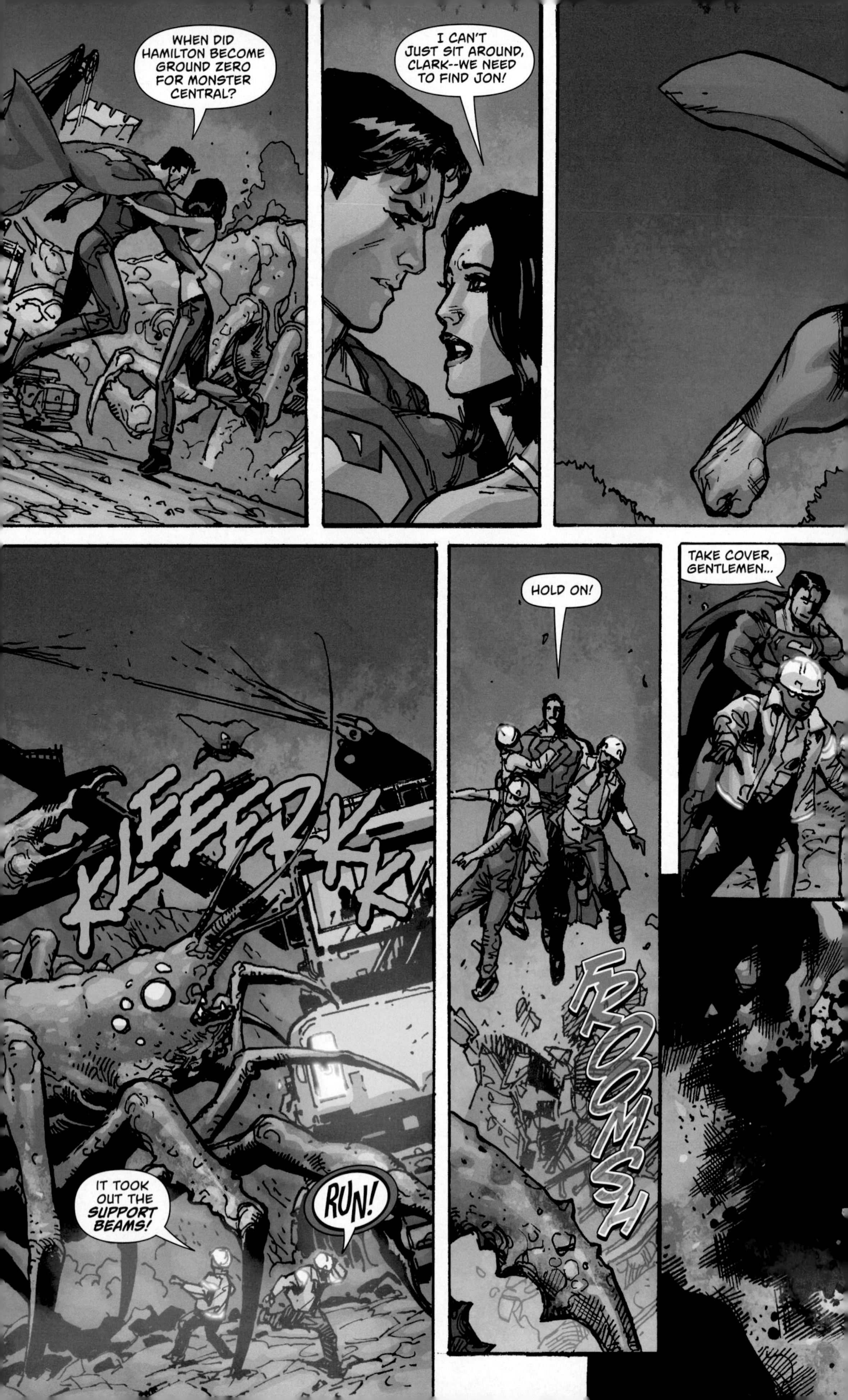
WHEN DID HAMILTON BECOME GROUND ZERO FOR MONSTER CENTRAL?
I CAN'T JUST SIT AROUND, CLARK--WE NEED TO FIND JON!
KLEEEDKKK
IT TOOK OUT THE SUPPORT BEAMS!
RUN!
HOLD ON!
FROOOMSH
TAKE COVER, GENTLEMEN...

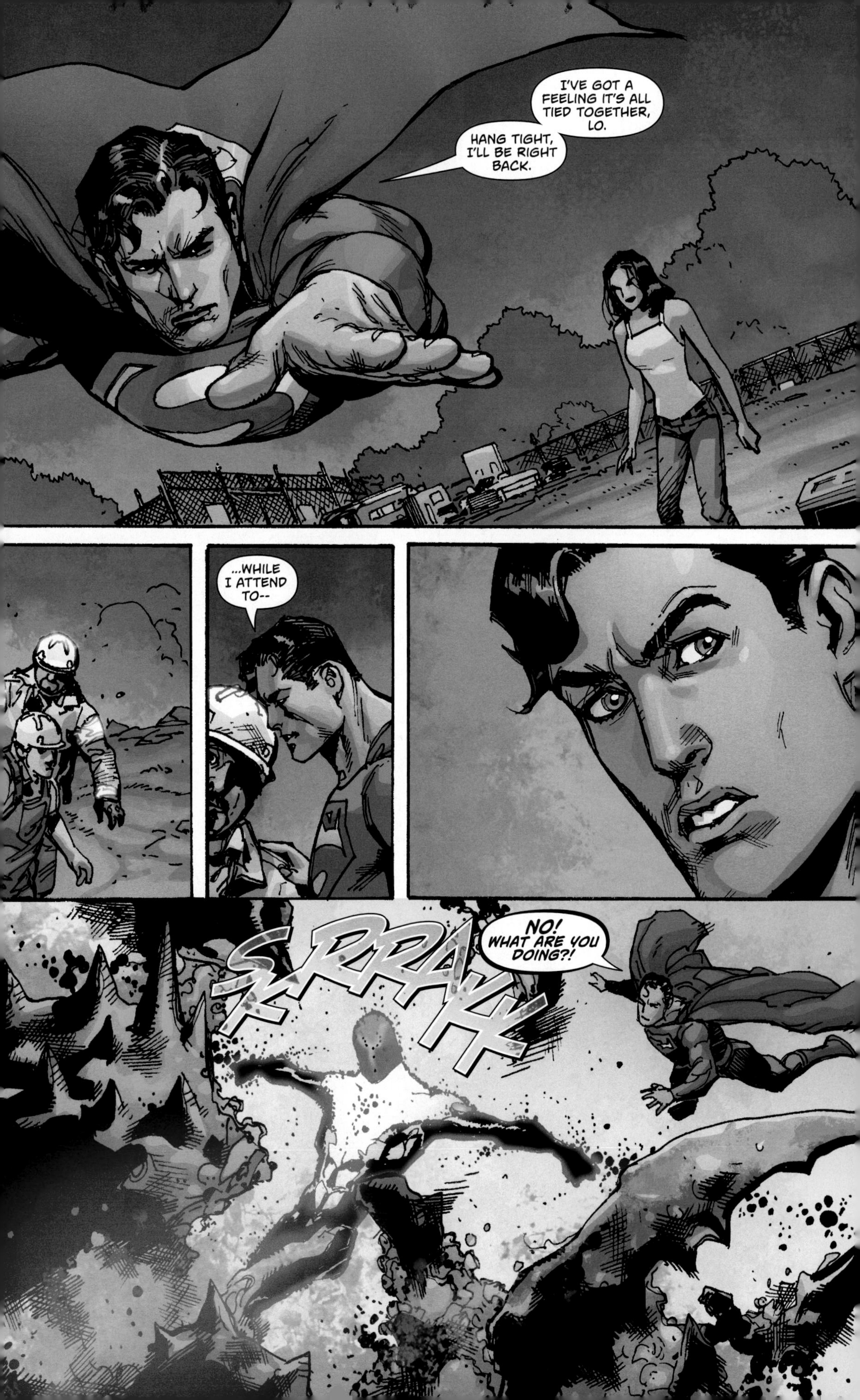
I'VE GOT A FEELING IT'S ALL TIED TOGETHER, LO.
HANG TIGHT, I'LL BE RIGHT BACK.
...WHILE I ATTEND TO--
SKRRAKK
NO! WHAT ARE YOU DOING?!

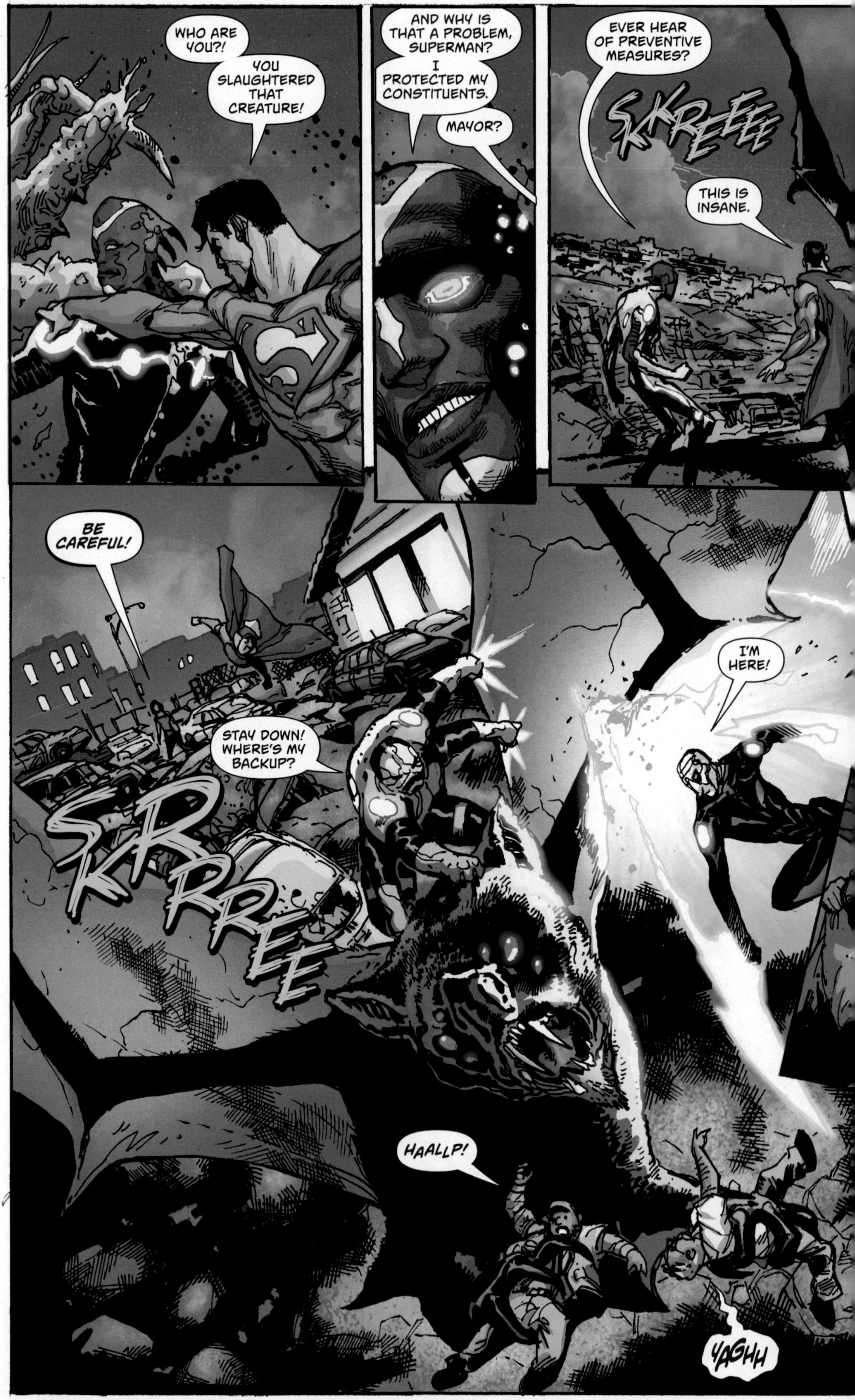

WHO ARE YOU?!
YOU SLAUGHTERED THAT CREATURE!
AND WHY IS THAT A PROBLEM, SUPERMAN?
I PROTECTED MY CONSTITUENTS.
MAYOR?
EVER HEAR OF PREVENTIVE MEASURES?
SKREEEEE
THIS IS INSANE.
BE CAREFUL!
STAY DOWN! WHERE'S MY BACKUP?
I'M HERE!
SKRRREE
HAALLP!
YAGHH

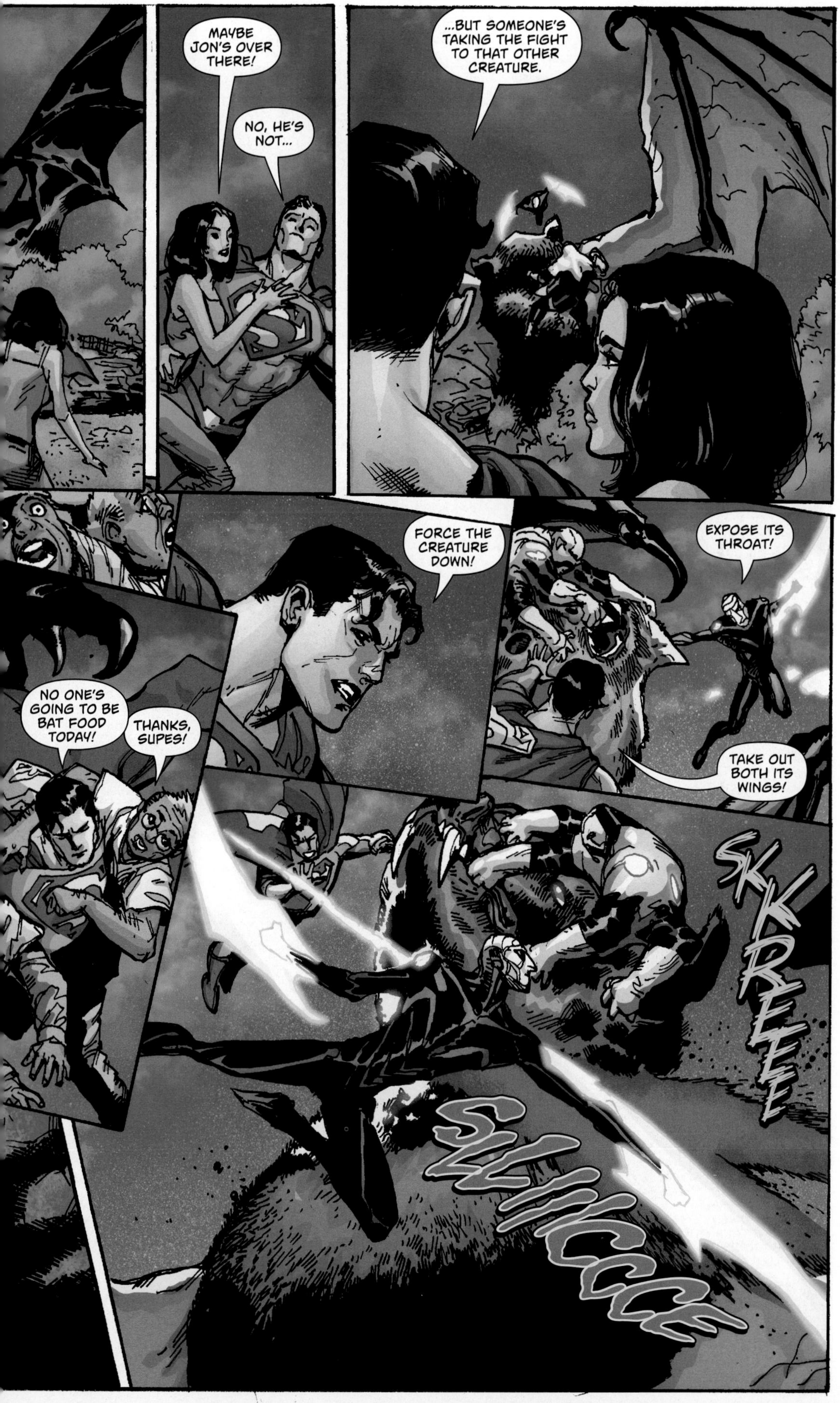
MAYBE JON'S OVER THERE!
NO, HE'S NOT...
...BUT SOMEONE'S TAKING THE FIGHT TO THAT OTHER CREATURE.
FORCE THE CREATURE DOWN!
EXPOSE ITS THROAT!
TAKE OUT BOTH ITS WINGS!
NO ONE'S GOING TO BE BAT FOOD TODAY!
THANKS, SUPES!
SKKREEEE
SWICCCE

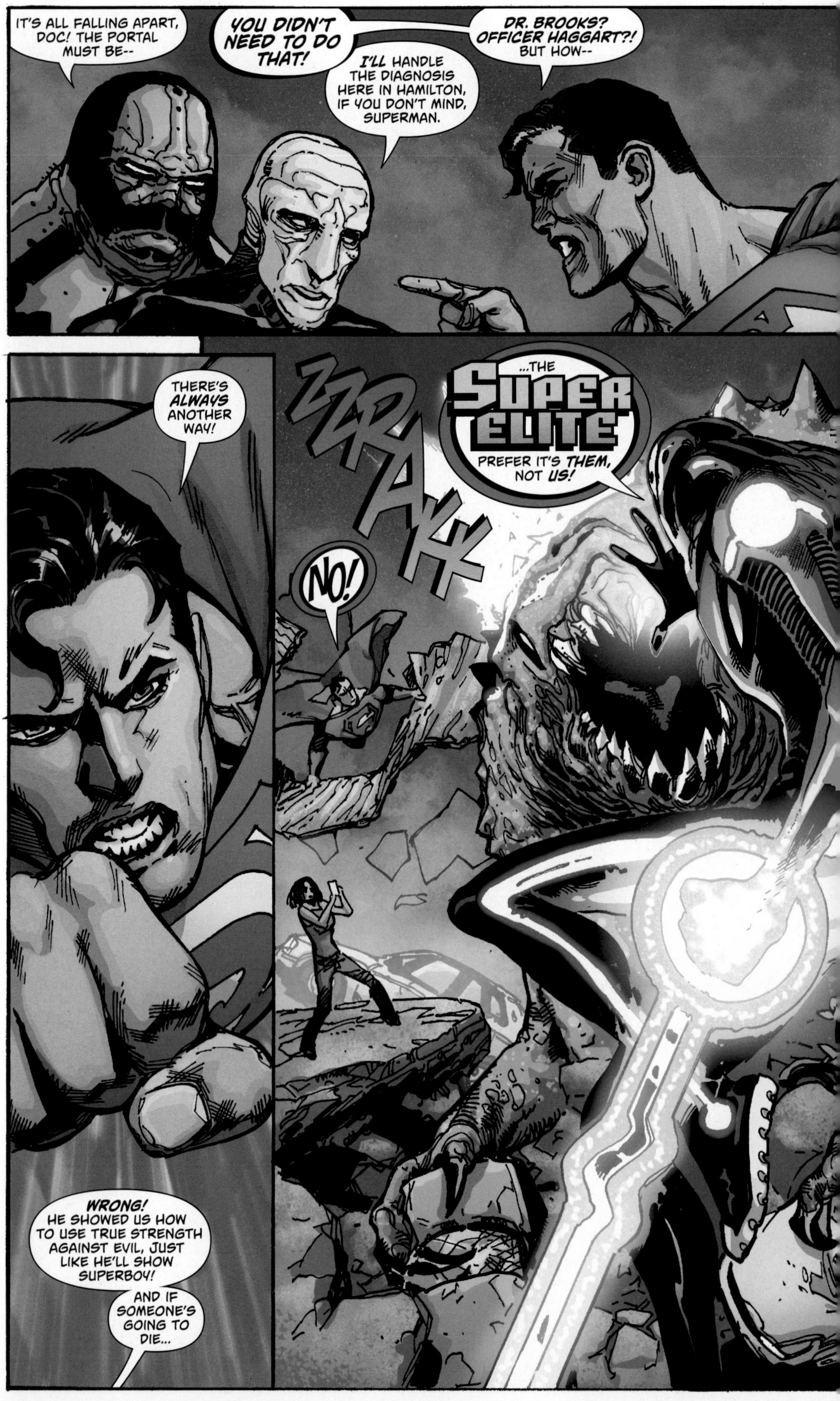
IT'S ALL FALLING APART, DOC! THE PORTAL MUST BE--
YOU DIDN'T NEED TO DO THAT!
I'LL HANDLE THE DIAGNOSIS HERE IN HAMILTON, IF YOU DON'T MIND, SUPERMAN.
DR. BROOKS? OFFICER HAGGART?! BUT HOW--
THERE'S ALWAYS ANOTHER WAY!
ZZRAKK
...THE SUPER ELITE PREFER IT'S THEM, NOT US!
NO!
WRONG! HE SHOWED US HOW TO USE TRUE STRENGTH AGAINST EVIL, JUST LIKE HE'LL SHOW SUPERBOY!
AND IF SOMEONE'S GOING TO DIE...

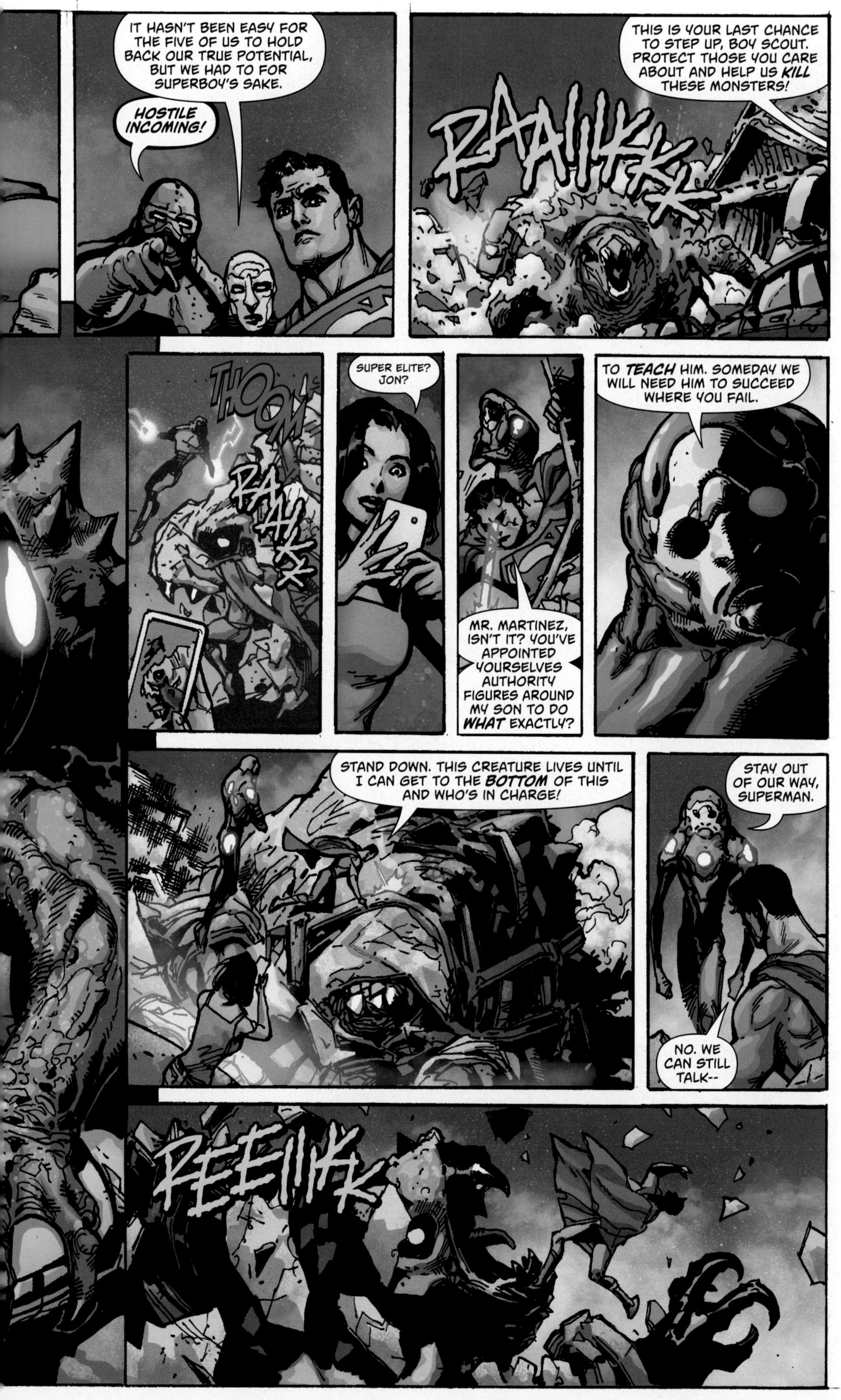
IT HASN'T BEEN EASY FOR THE FIVE OF US TO HOLD BACK OUR TRUE POTENTIAL, BUT WE HAD TO FOR SUPERBOY'S SAKE.
HOSTILE INCOMING!
THIS IS YOUR LAST CHANCE TO STEP UP, BOY SCOUT. PROTECT THOSE YOU CARE ABOUT AND HELP US KILL THESE MONSTERS!
RAAIIKKK
THOOM
RAAIKK
SUPER ELITE? JON?
MR. MARTINEZ, ISN'T IT? YOU'VE APPOINTED YOURSELVES AUTHORITY FIGURES AROUND MY SON TO DO WHAT EXACTLY?
TO TEACH HIM. SOMEDAY WE WILL NEED HIM TO SUCCEED WHERE YOU FAIL.
STAND DOWN. THIS CREATURE LIVES UNTIL I CAN GET TO THE BOTTOM OF THIS AND WHO'S IN CHARGE!
STAY OUT OF OUR WAY, SUPERMAN.
NO. WE CAN STILL TALK--
PEEIIIKK

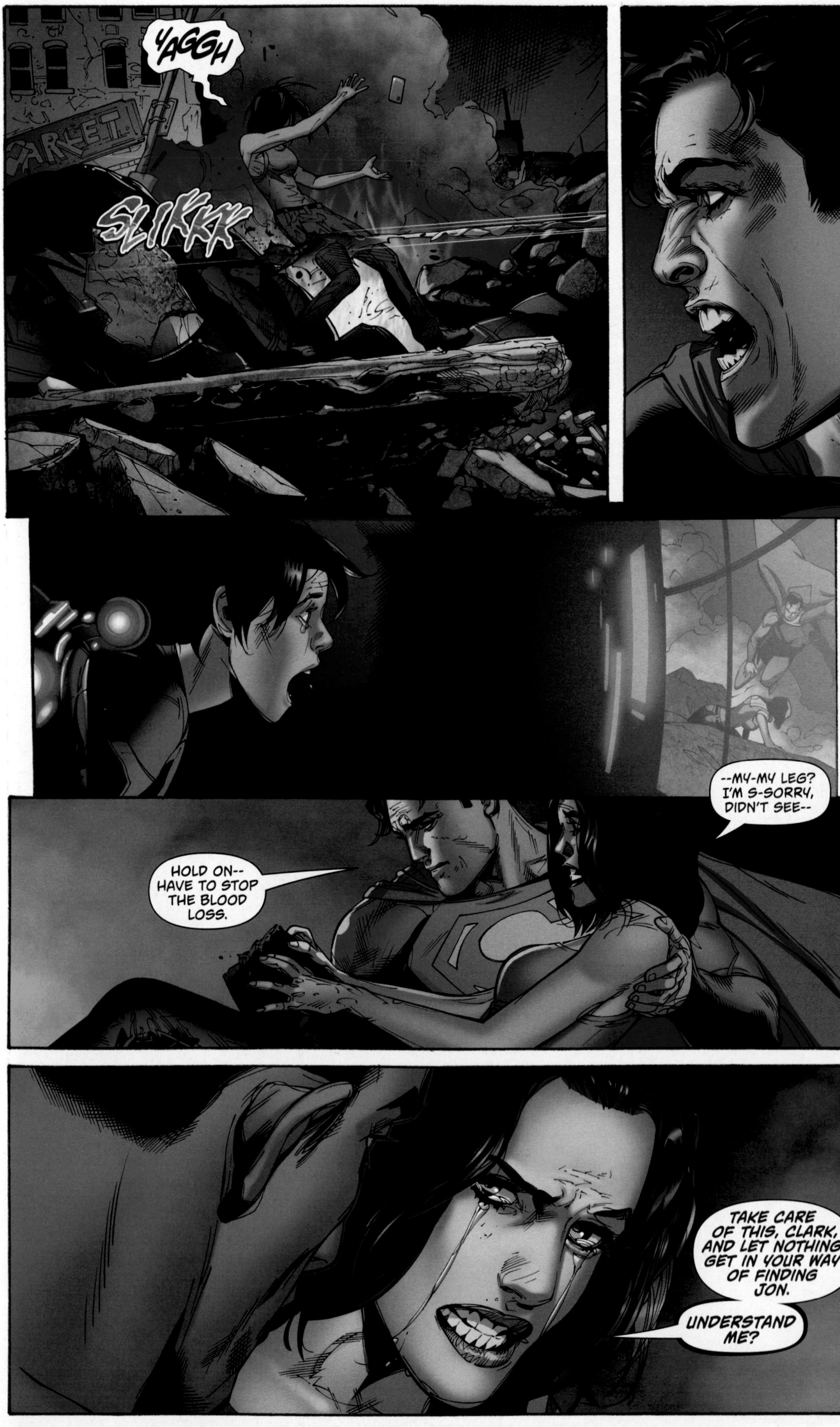
YAGGH
SLIKKK
--MY-MY LEG? I'M S-SORRY, DIDN'T SEE--
HOLD ON-- HAVE TO STOP THE BLOOD LOSS.
TAKE CARE OF THIS, CLARK, AND LET NOTHING GET IN YOUR WAY OF FINDING JON.
UNDERSTAND ME?

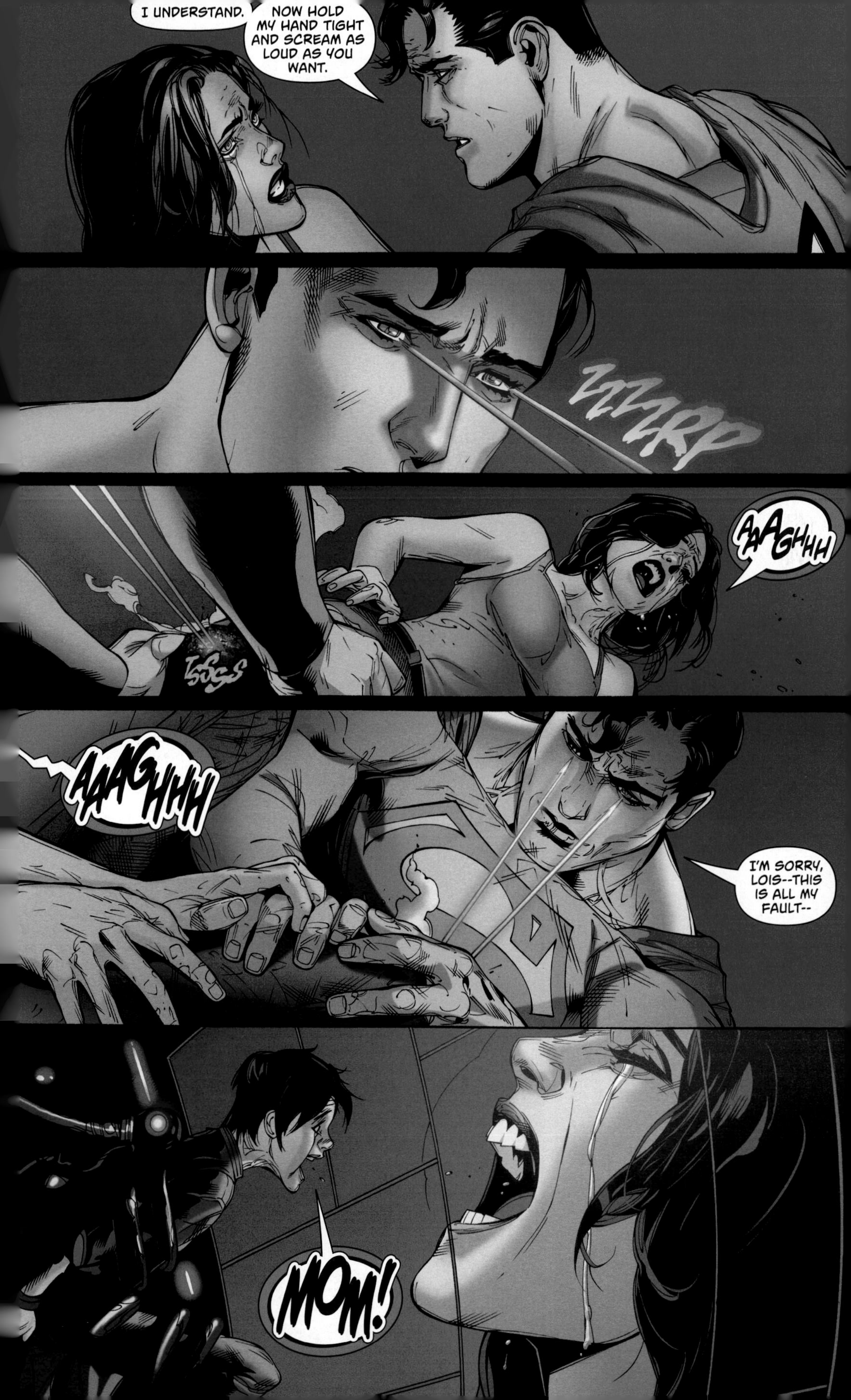
I UNDERSTAND.
NOW HOLD MY HAND TIGHT AND SCREAM AS LOUD AS YOU WANT.
ZZZMRP
AAAGHHH
TSSSS
AAAGHHH
I'M SORRY, LOIS--THIS IS ALL MY FAULT--
MOM!

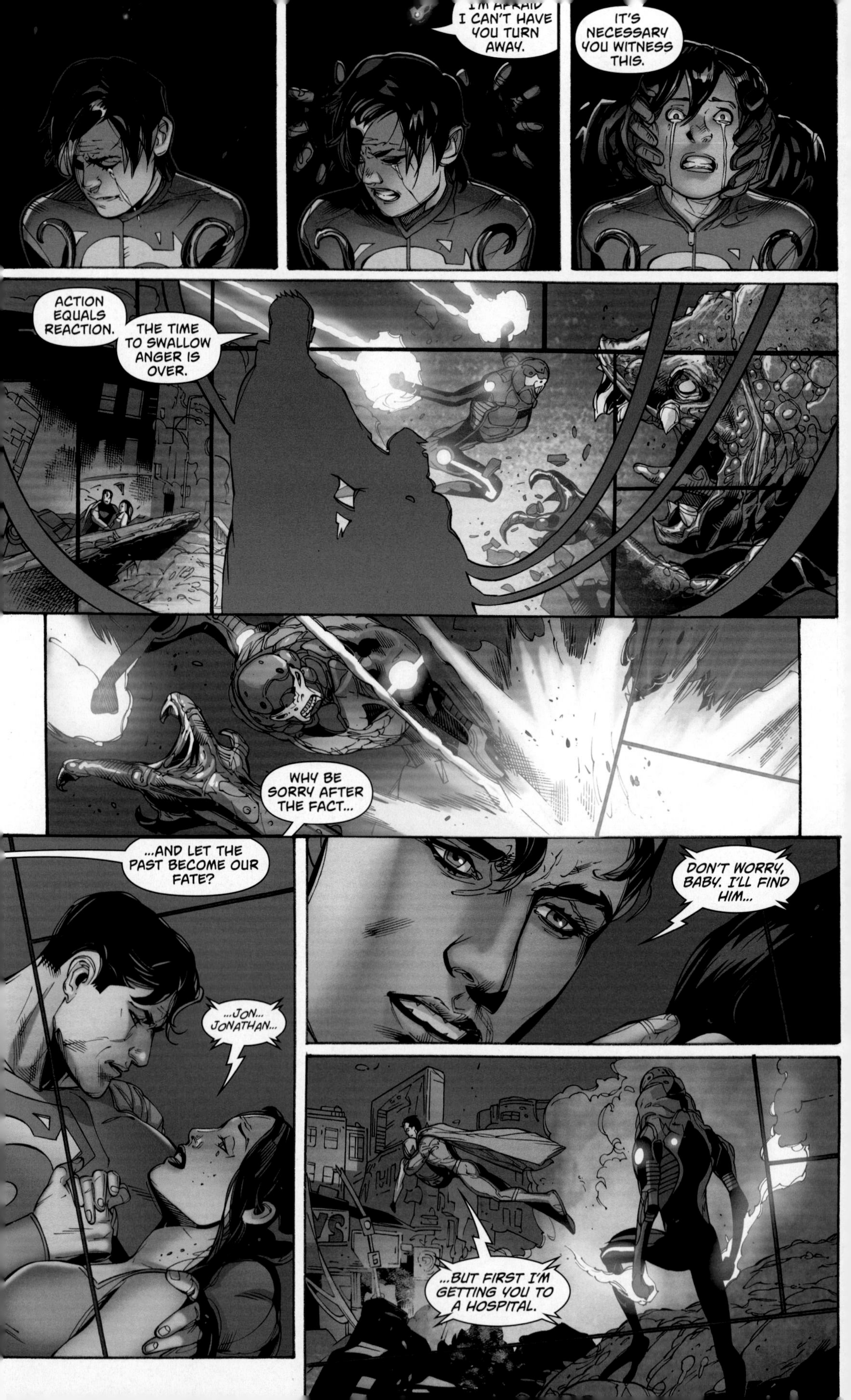
I'M AFRAID I CAN'T HAVE YOU TURN AWAY.
IT'S NECESSARY YOU WITNESS THIS.
ACTION EQUALS REACTION.
THE TIME TO SWALLOW ANGER IS OVER.
WHY BE SORRY AFTER THE FACT...
...AND LET THE PAST BECOME OUR FATE?
...JON... JONATHAN...
DON'T WORRY, BABY. I'LL FIND HIM...
...BUT FIRST I'M GETTING YOU TO A HOSPITAL.

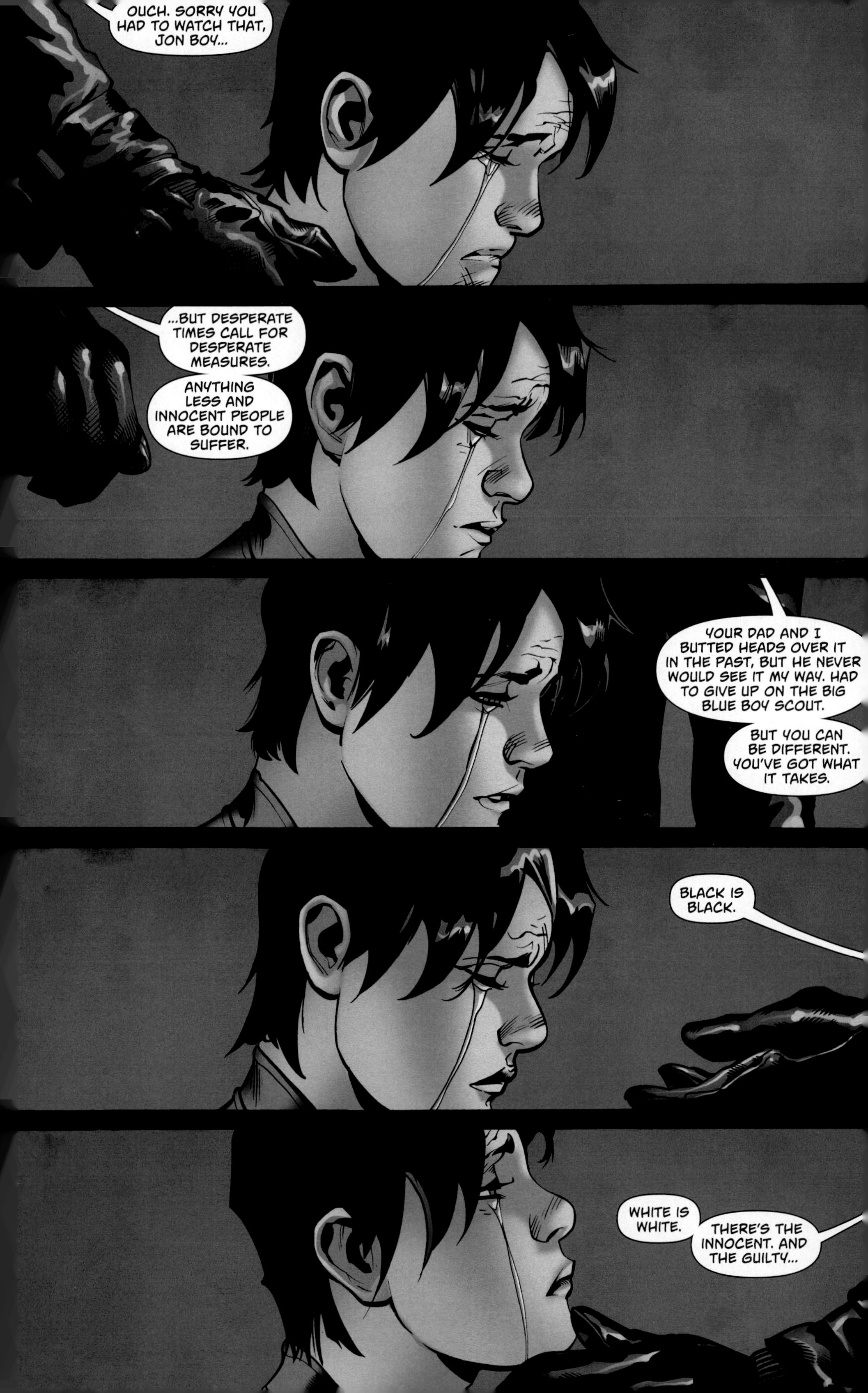
OUCH. SORRY YOU HAD TO WATCH THAT, JON BOY...
...BUT DESPERATE TIMES CALL FOR DESPERATE MEASURES.
ANYTHING LESS AND INNOCENT PEOPLE ARE BOUND TO SUFFER.
YOUR DAD AND I BUTTED HEADS OVER IT IN THE PAST, BUT HE NEVER WOULD SEE IT MY WAY. HAD TO GIVE UP ON THE BIG BLUE BOY SCOUT.
BUT YOU CAN BE DIFFERENT. YOU'VE GOT WHAT IT TAKES.
BLACK IS BLACK.
WHITE IS WHITE.
THERE'S THE INNOCENT. AND THE GUILTY...

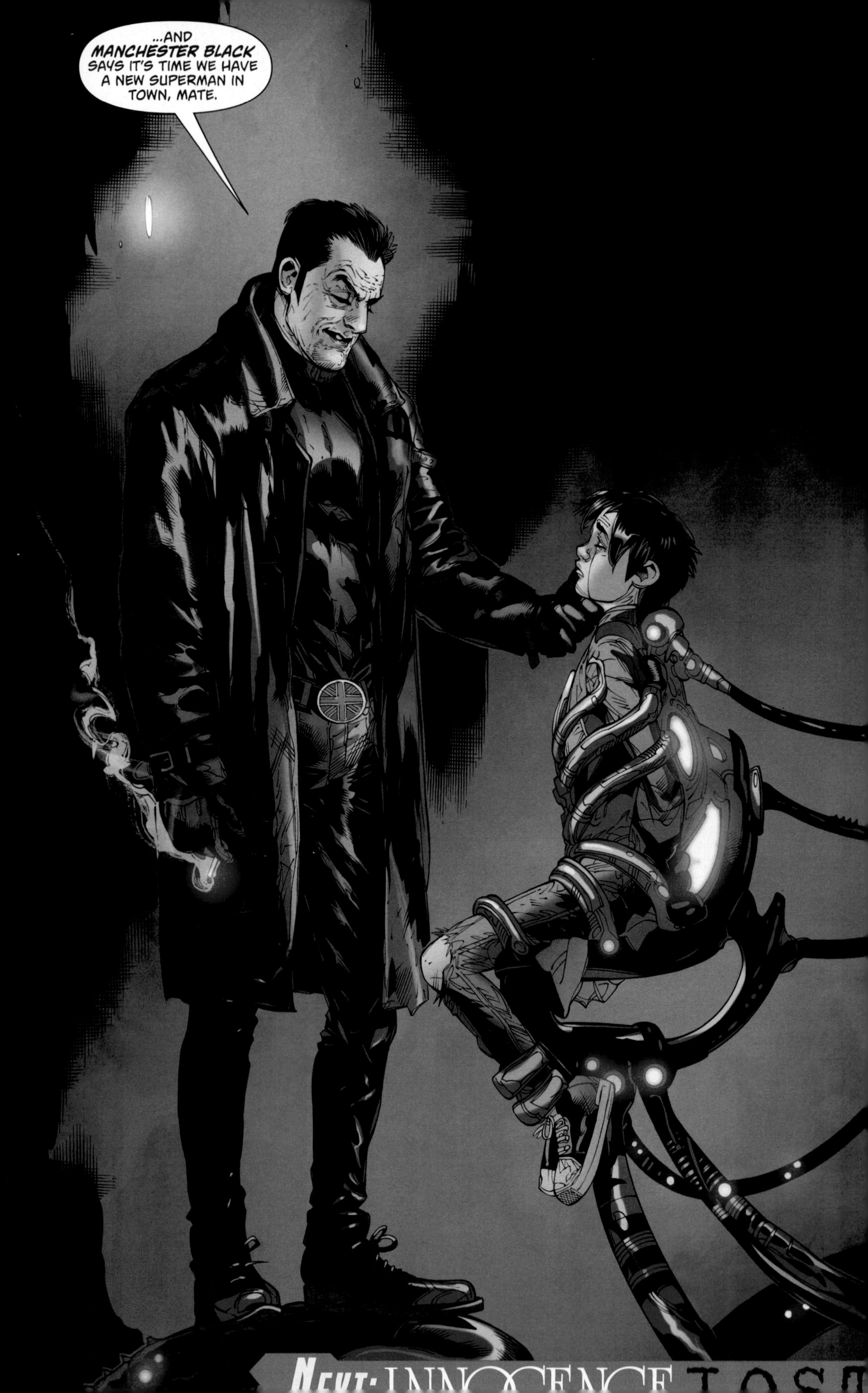
...AND MANCHESTER BLACK SAYS IT'S TIME WE HAVE A NEW SUPERMAN IN TOWN, MATE.

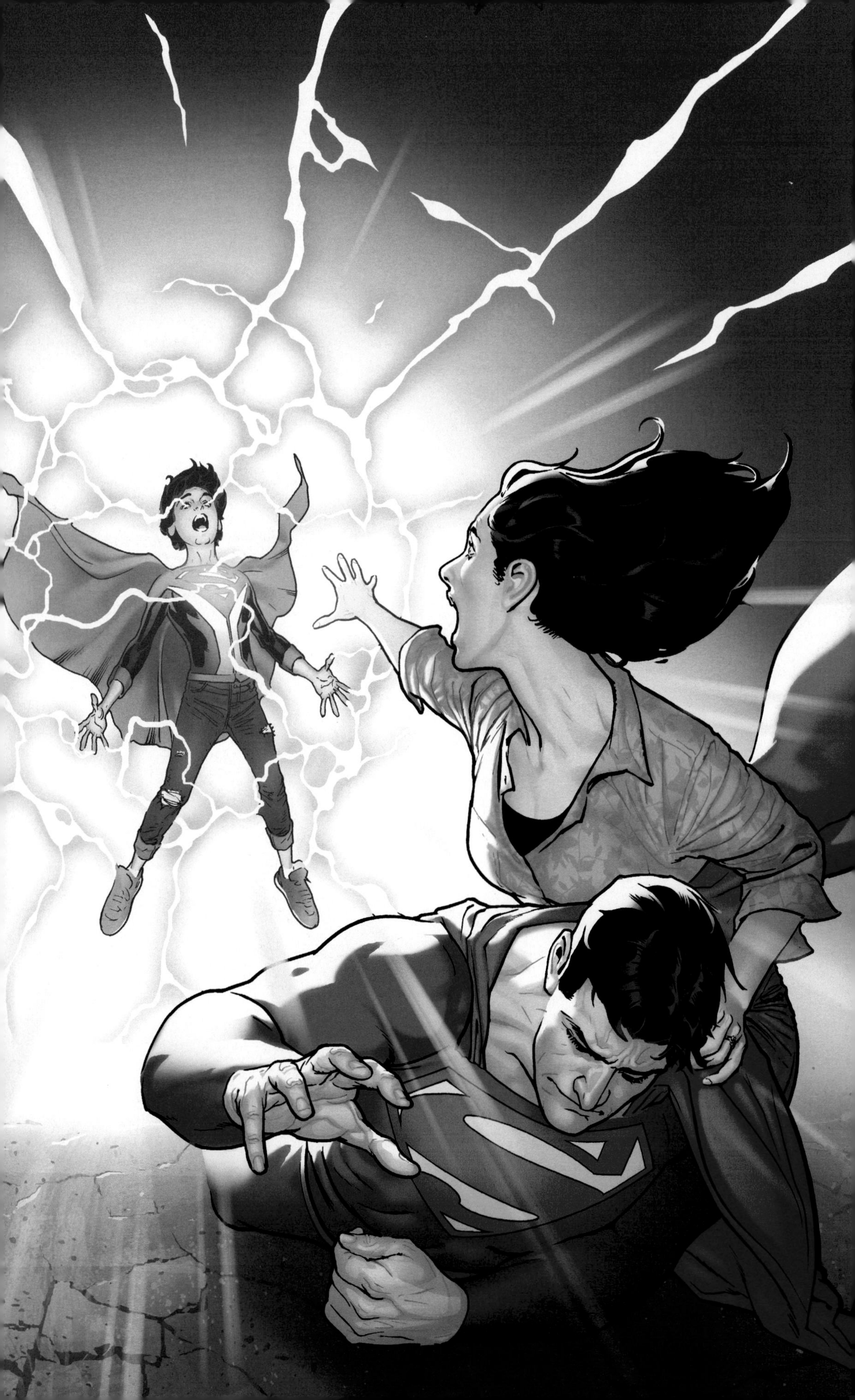

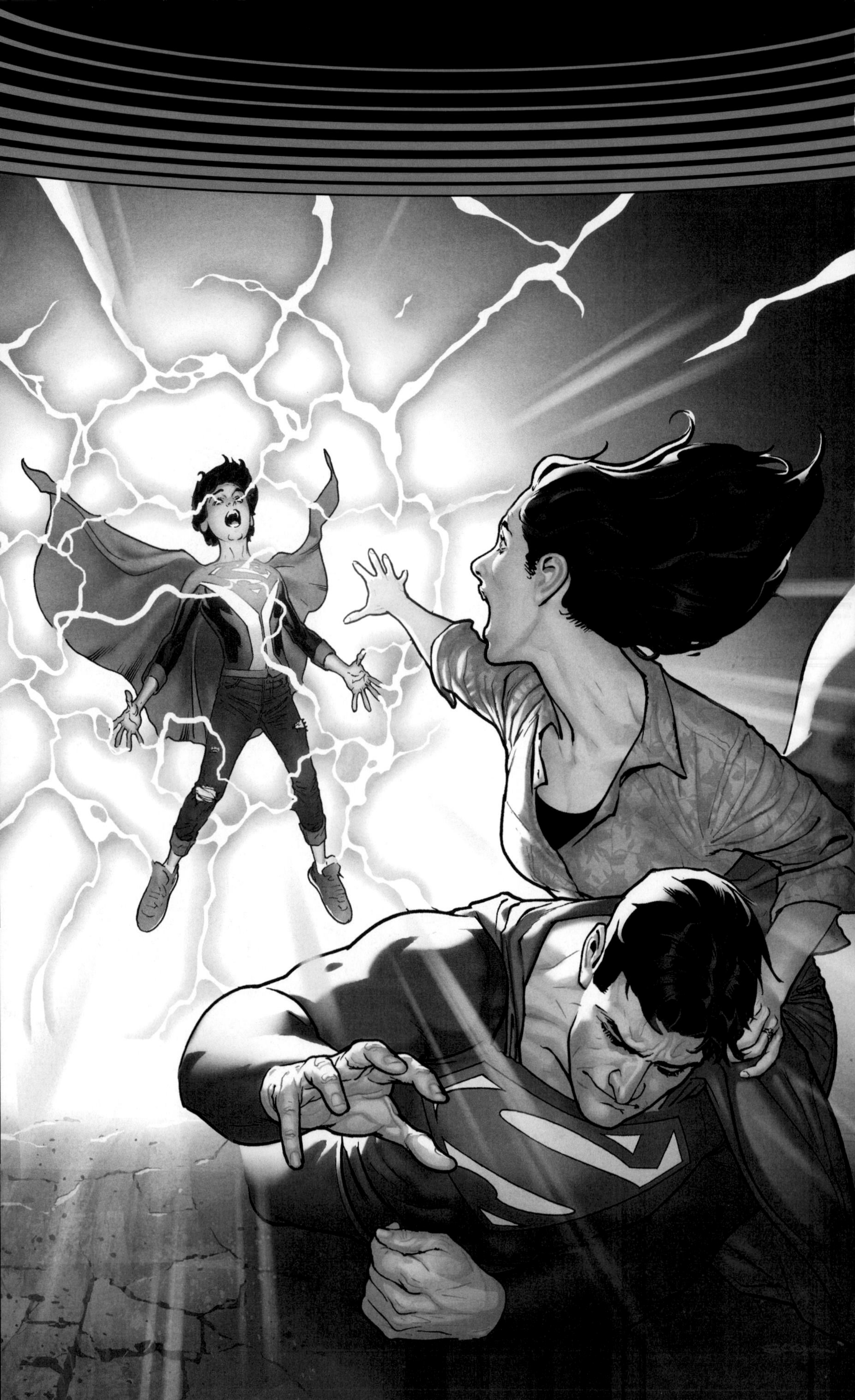

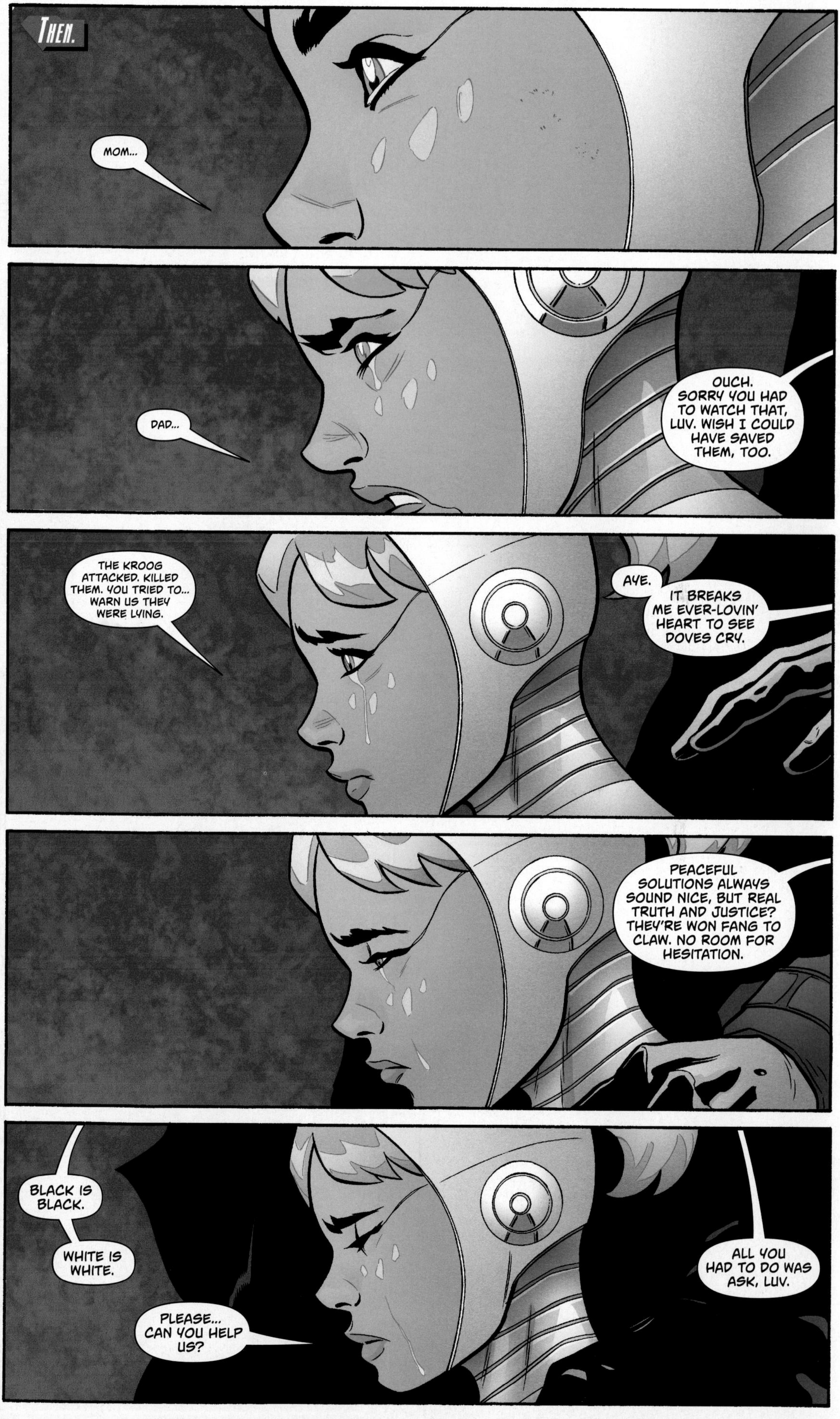
THEN.
MOM...
DAD...
OUCH. SORRY YOU HAD TO WATCH THAT, LUV. WISH I COULD HAVE SAVED THEM, TOO.
THE KROOG ATTACKED. KILLED THEM. YOU TRIED TO... WARN US THEY WERE LYING.
AYE.
IT BREAKS ME EVER-LOVIN' HEART TO SEE DOVES CRY.
PEACEFUL SOLUTIONS ALWAYS SOUND NICE, BUT REAL TRUTH AND JUSTICE? THEY'RE WON FANG TO CLAW. NO ROOM FOR HESITATION.
BLACK IS BLACK.
WHITE IS WHITE.
PLEASE... CAN YOU HELP US?
ALL YOU HAD TO DO WAS ASK, LUV.

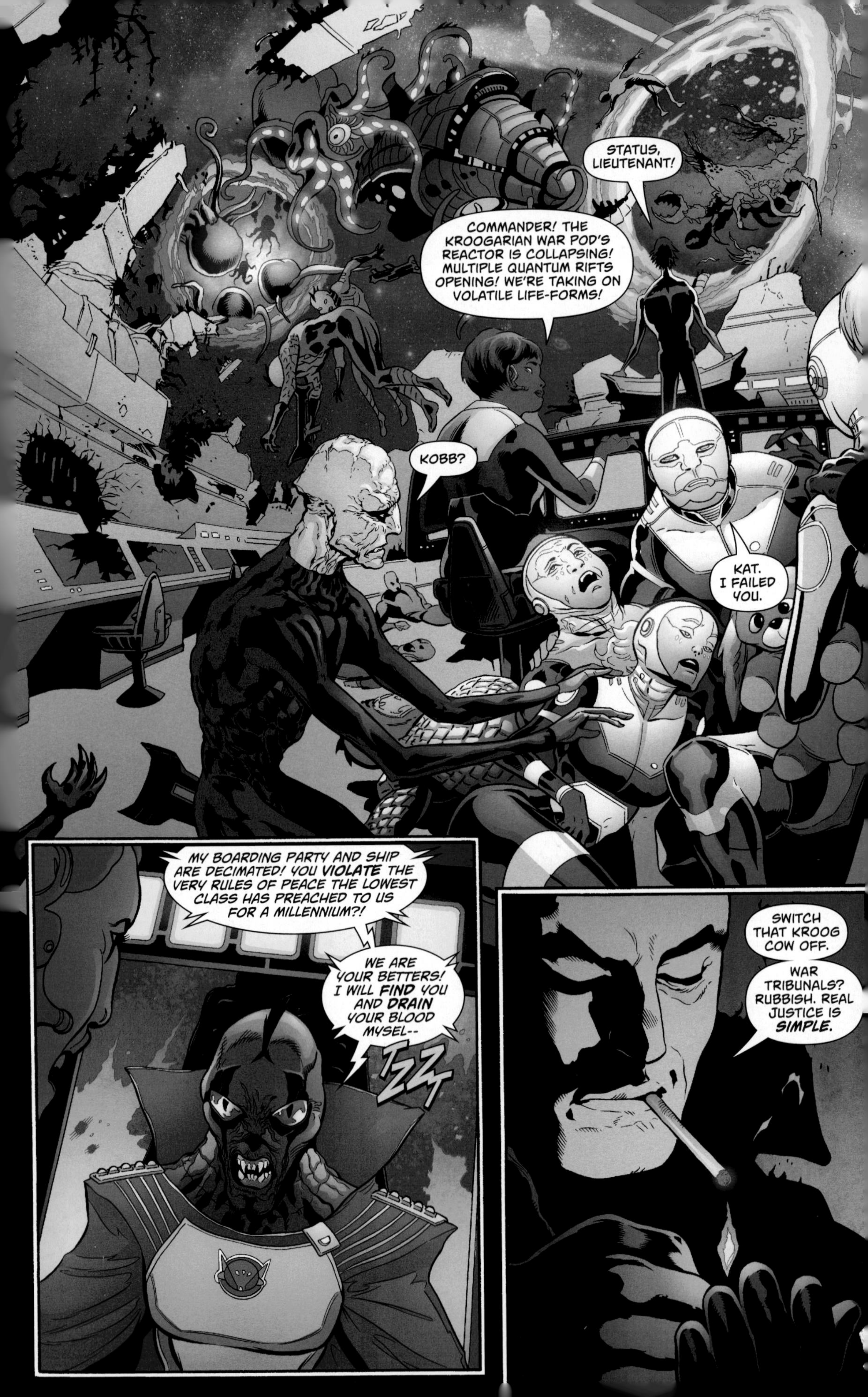
STATUS, LIEUTENANT!
COMMANDER! THE KROOGARIAN WAR POD'S REACTOR IS COLLAPSING! MULTIPLE QUANTUM RIFTS OPENING! WE'RE TAKING ON VOLATILE LIFE-FORMS!
KOBB?
KAT. I FAILED YOU.
MY BOARDING PARTY AND SHIP ARE DECIMATED! YOU VIOLATE THE VERY RULES OF PEACE THE LOWEST CLASS HAS PREACHED TO US FOR A MILLENNIUM?!
WE ARE YOUR BETTERS! I WILL FIND YOU AND DRAIN YOUR BLOOD MYSEL--
TZZT
SWITCH THAT KROOG COW OFF.
WAR TRIBUNALS? RUBBISH. REAL JUSTICE IS SIMPLE.

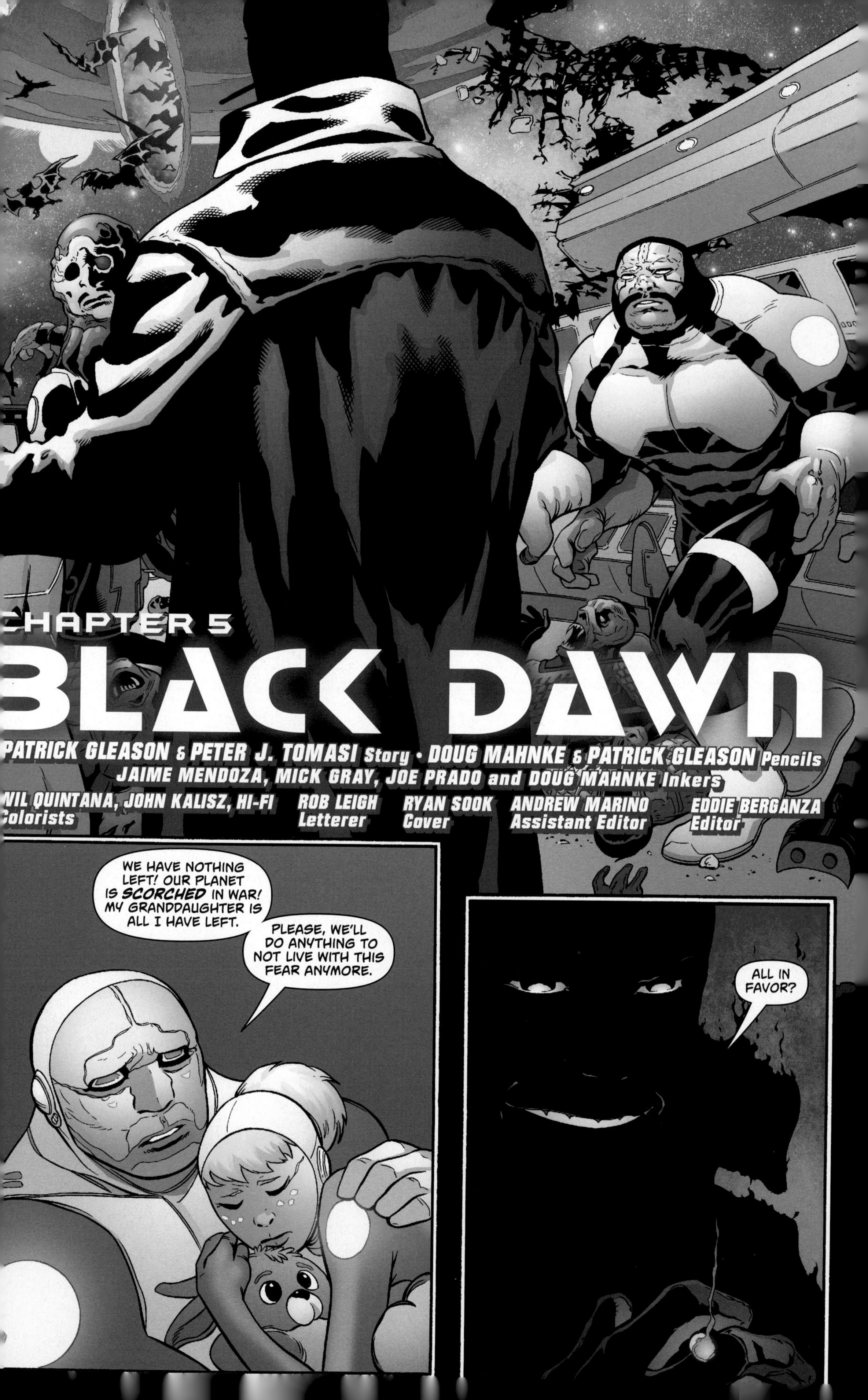
CHAPTER 5
BLACK DAWN
PATRICK GLEASON & PETER J. TOMASI Story • DOUG MAHNKE & PATRICK GLEASON Pencils
JAIME MENDOZA, MICK GRAY, JOE PRADO and DOUG MAHNKE Inkers
WIL QUINTANA, JOHN KALISZ, HI-FI Colorists
ROB LEIGH Letterer
RYAN SOOK Cover
ANDREW MARINO Assistant Editor
EDDIE BERGANZA Editor
WE HAVE NOTHING LEFT! OUR PLANET IS SCORCHED IN WAR! MY GRANDDAUGHTER IS ALL I HAVE LEFT.
PLEASE, WE'LL DO ANYTHING TO NOT LIVE WITH THIS FEAR ANYMORE.
ALL IN FAVOR?

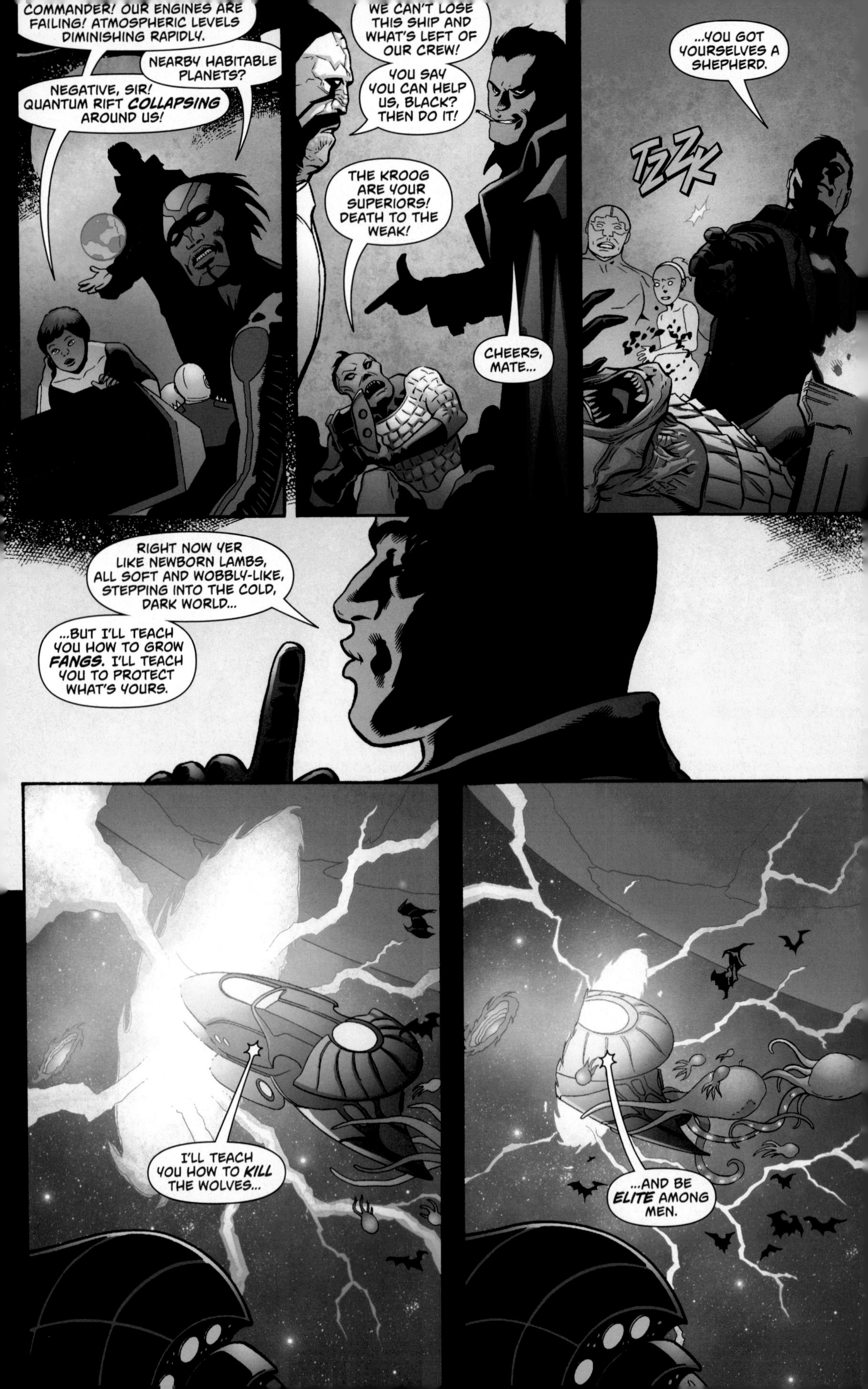
COMMANDER! OUR ENGINES ARE FAILING! ATMOSPHERIC LEVELS DIMINISHING RAPIDLY.
NEARBY HABITABLE PLANETS?
NEGATIVE, SIR! QUANTUM RIFT COLLAPSING AROUND US!
WE CAN'T LOSE THIS SHIP AND WHAT'S LEFT OF OUR CREW!
YOU SAY YOU CAN HELP US, BLACK? THEN DO IT!
THE KROOG ARE YOUR SUPERIORS! DEATH TO THE WEAK!
CHEERS, MATE...
...YOU GOT YOURSELVES A SHEPHERD.
TZZK
RIGHT NOW YER LIKE NEWBORN LAMBS, ALL SOFT AND WOBBLY-LIKE, STEPPING INTO THE COLD, DARK WORLD...
...BUT I'LL TEACH YOU HOW TO GROW FANGS. I'LL TEACH YOU TO PROTECT WHAT'S YOURS.
I'LL TEACH YOU HOW TO KILL THE WOLVES...
...AND BE ELITE AMONG MEN.

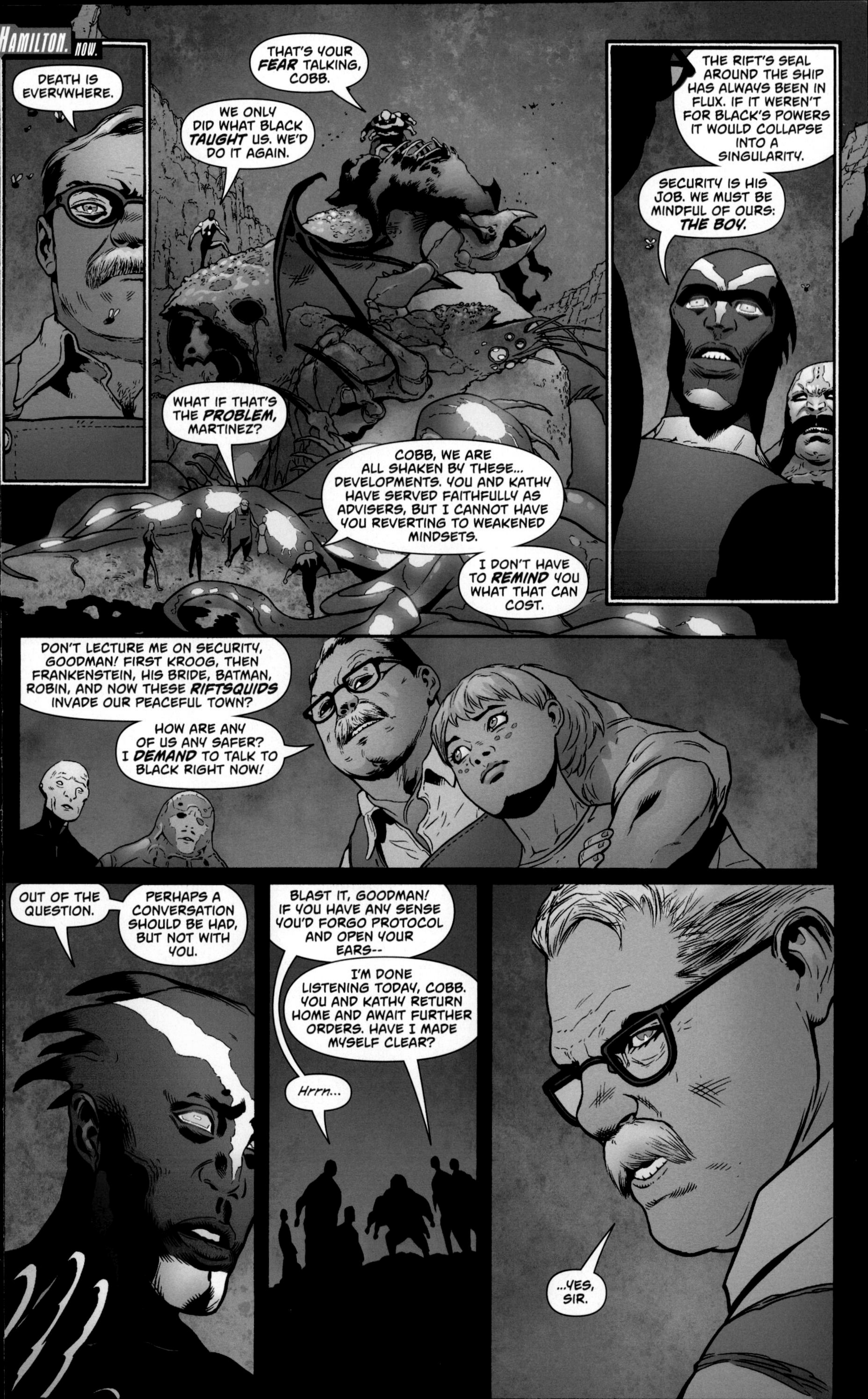
HAMILTON. NOW.
DEATH IS EVERYWHERE.
THAT'S YOUR FEAR TALKING, COBB.
WE ONLY DID WHAT BLACK TAUGHT US. WE'D DO IT AGAIN.
THE RIFT'S SEAL AROUND THE SHIP HAS ALWAYS BEEN IN FLUX. IF IT WEREN'T FOR BLACK'S POWERS IT WOULD COLLAPSE INTO A SINGULARITY.
SECURITY IS HIS JOB. WE MUST BE MINDFUL OF OURS: THE BOY.
WHAT IF THAT'S THE PROBLEM, MARTINEZ?
COBB, WE ARE ALL SHAKEN BY THESE... DEVELOPMENTS. YOU AND KATHY HAVE SERVED FAITHFULLY AS ADVISERS, BUT I CANNOT HAVE YOU REVERTING TO WEAKENED MINDSETS.
I DON'T HAVE TO REMIND YOU WHAT THAT CAN COST.
DON'T LECTURE ME ON SECURITY, GOODMAN! FIRST KROOG, THEN FRANKENSTEIN, HIS BRIDE, BATMAN, ROBIN, AND NOW THESE RIFTSQUIDS INVADE OUR PEACEFUL TOWN?
HOW ARE ANY OF US ANY SAFER? I DEMAND TO TALK TO BLACK RIGHT NOW!
OUT OF THE QUESTION.
PERHAPS A CONVERSATION SHOULD BE HAD, BUT NOT WITH YOU.
BLAST IT, GOODMAN! IF YOU HAVE ANY SENSE YOU'D FORGO PROTOCOL AND OPEN YOUR EARS--
I'M DONE LISTENING TODAY, COBB. YOU AND KATHY RETURN HOME AND AWAIT FURTHER ORDERS. HAVE I MADE MYSELF CLEAR?
Hrrn...
...YES, SIR.

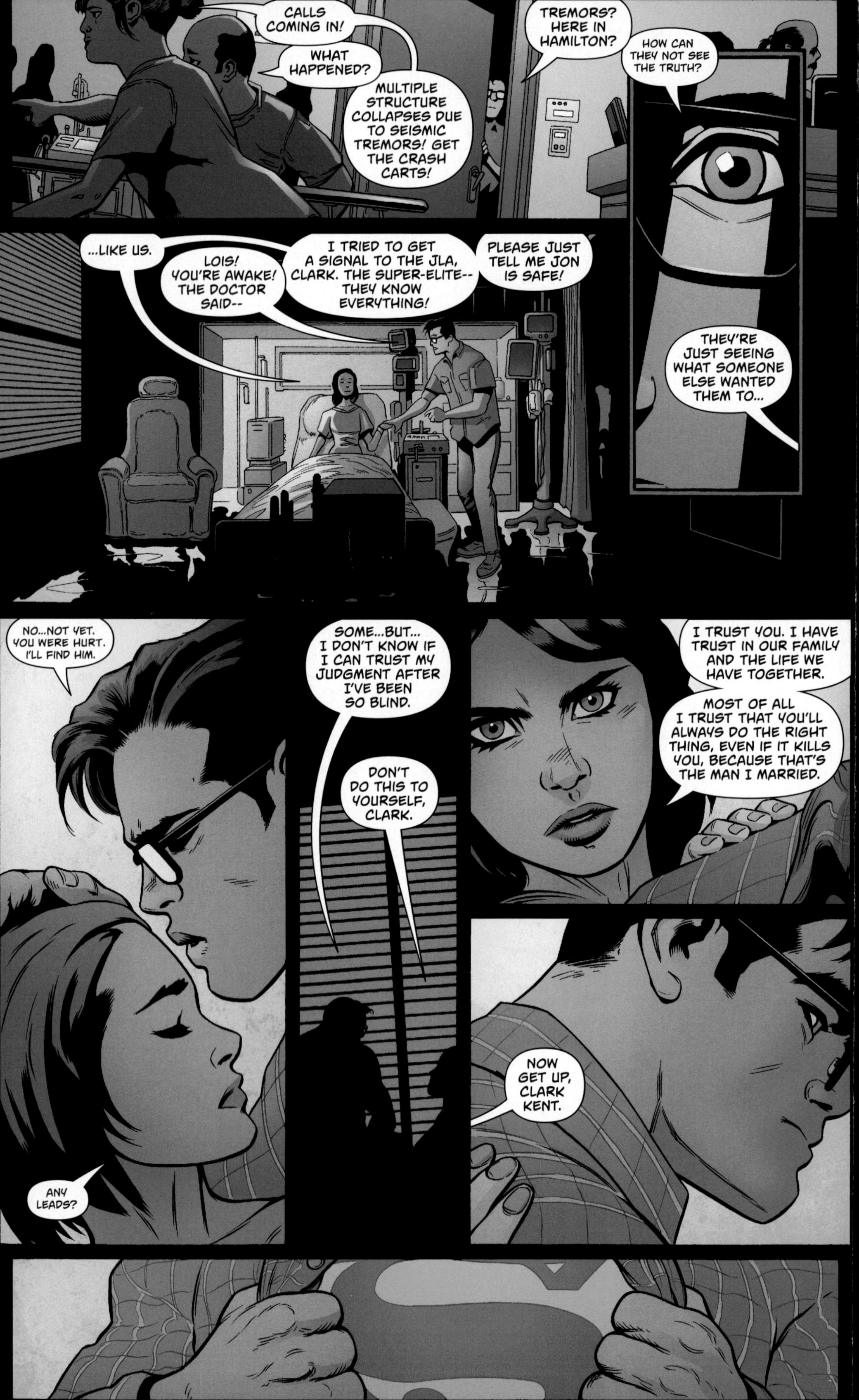
CALLS COMING IN!
WHAT HAPPENED?
MULTIPLE STRUCTURE COLLAPSES DUE TO SEISMIC TREMORS! GET THE CRASH CARTS!
TREMORS? HERE IN HAMILTON?
HOW CAN THEY NOT SEE THE TRUTH?
THEY'RE JUST SEEING WHAT SOMEONE ELSE WANTED THEM TO...
...LIKE US.
LOIS! YOU'RE AWAKE! THE DOCTOR SAID--
I TRIED TO GET A SIGNAL TO THE JLA, CLARK. THE SUPER-ELITE-- THEY KNOW EVERYTHING!
PLEASE JUST TELL ME JON IS SAFE!
NO...NOT YET. YOU WERE HURT. I'LL FIND HIM.
ANY LEADS?
SOME...BUT... I DON'T KNOW IF I CAN TRUST MY JUDGMENT AFTER I'VE BEEN SO BLIND.
DON'T DO THIS TO YOURSELF, CLARK.
I TRUST YOU. I HAVE TRUST IN OUR FAMILY AND THE LIFE WE HAVE TOGETHER.
MOST OF ALL I TRUST THAT YOU'LL ALWAYS DO THE RIGHT THING, EVEN IF IT KILLS YOU, BECAUSE THAT'S THE MAN I MARRIED.
NOW GET UP, CLARK KENT.

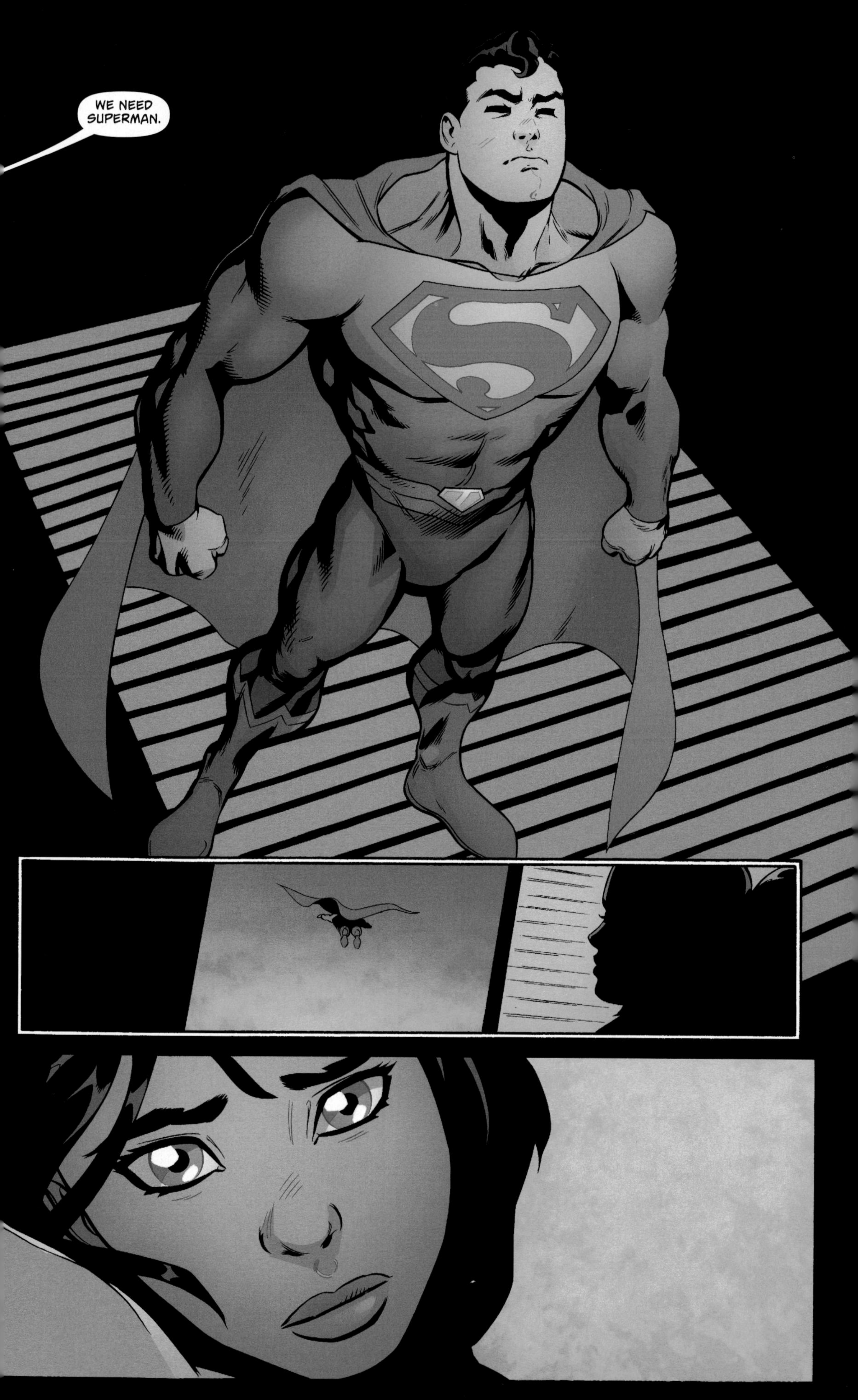
WE NEED SUPERMAN.

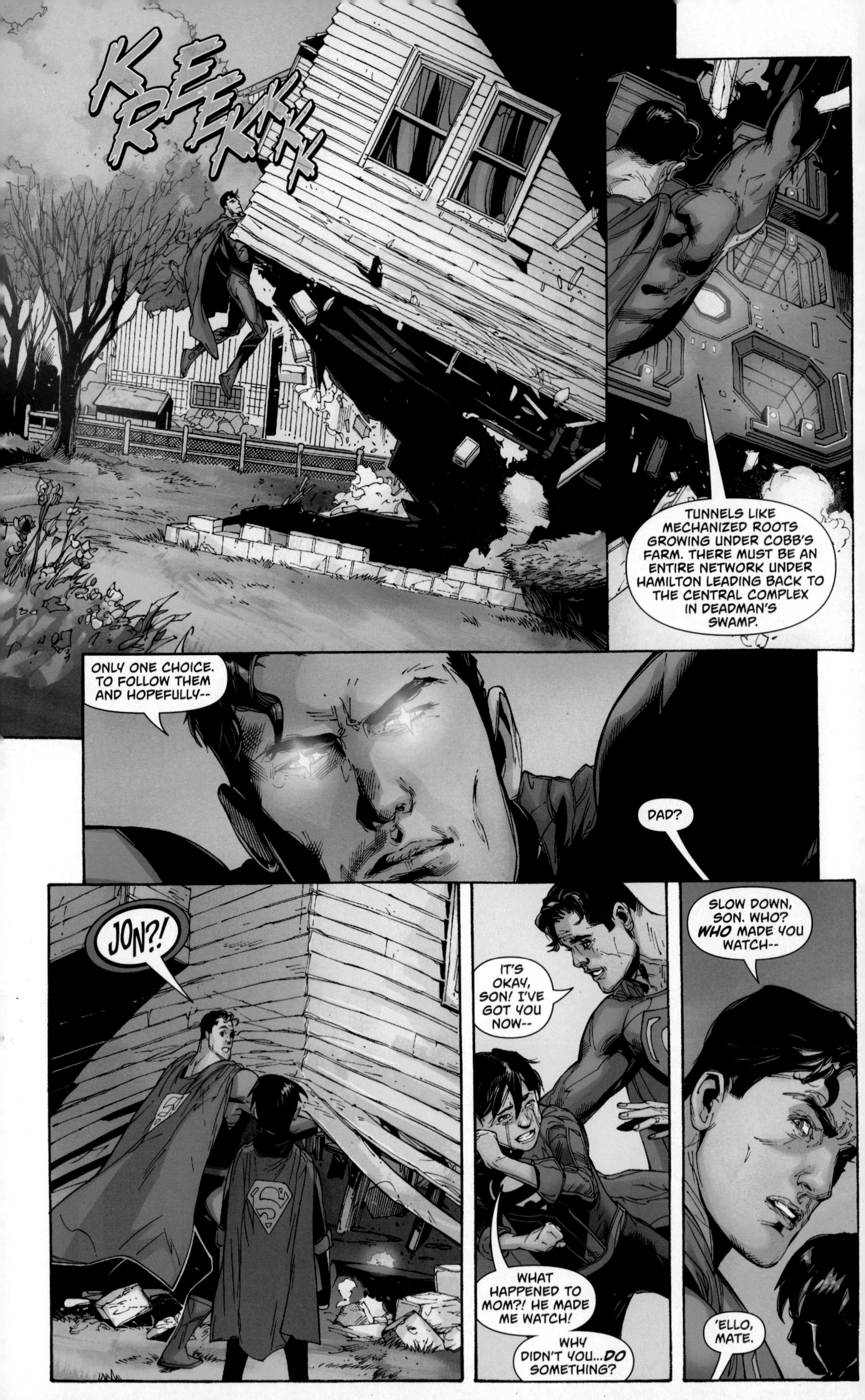
KREEKKK
TUNNELS LIKE MECHANIZED ROOTS GROWING UNDER COBB'S FARM. THERE MUST BE AN ENTIRE NETWORK UNDER HAMILTON LEADING BACK TO THE CENTRAL COMPLEX IN DEADMAN'S SWAMP.
ONLY ONE CHOICE. TO FOLLOW THEM AND HOPEFULLY--
DAD?
JON?!
IT'S OKAY, SON! I'VE GOT YOU NOW--
WHAT HAPPENED TO MOM?! HE MADE ME WATCH!
WHY DIDN'T YOU...DO SOMETHING?
SLOW DOWN, SON. WHO? WHO MADE YOU WATCH--
'ELLO, MATE.

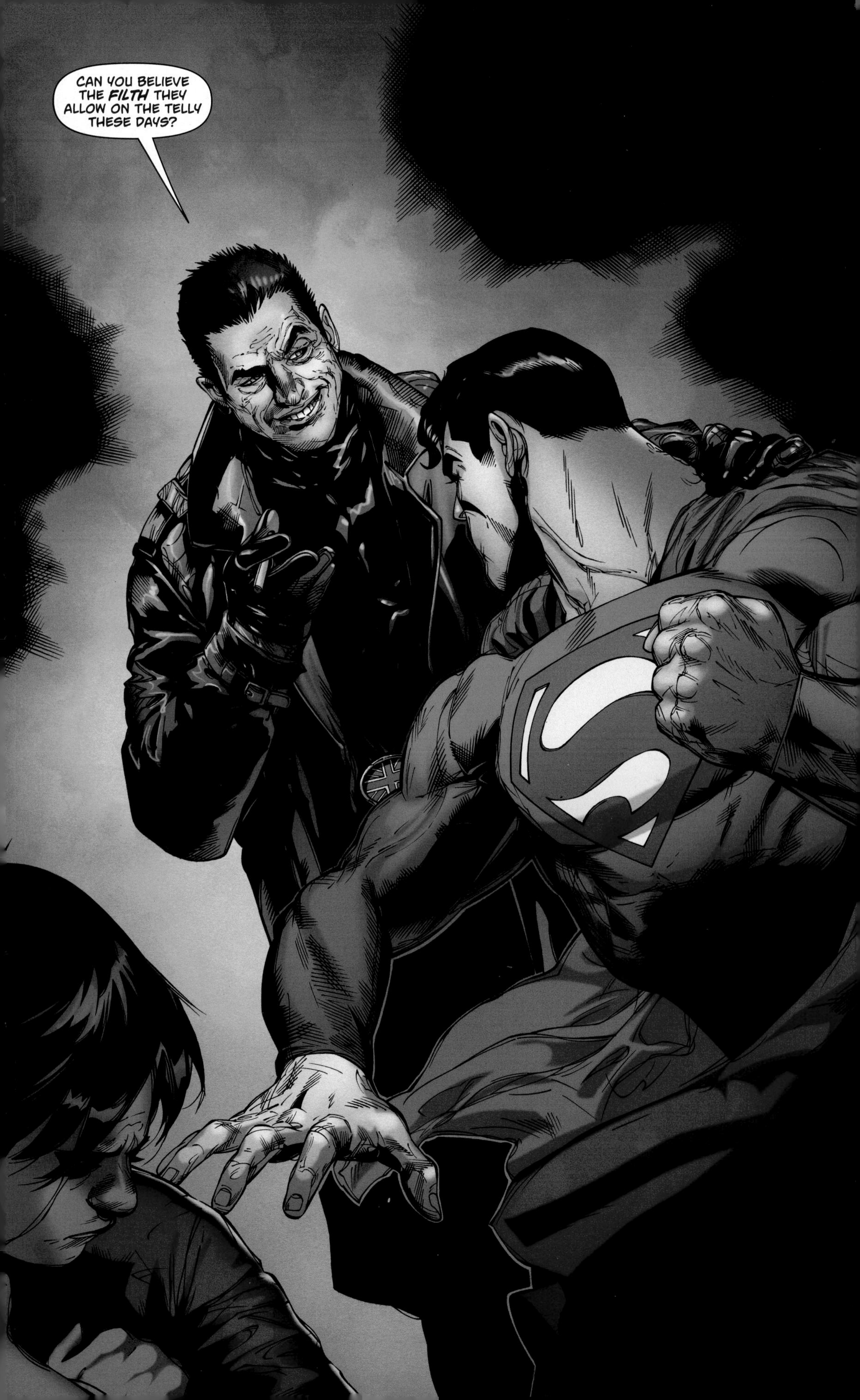
CAN YOU BELIEVE THE FILTH THEY ALLOW ON THE TELLY THESE DAYS?

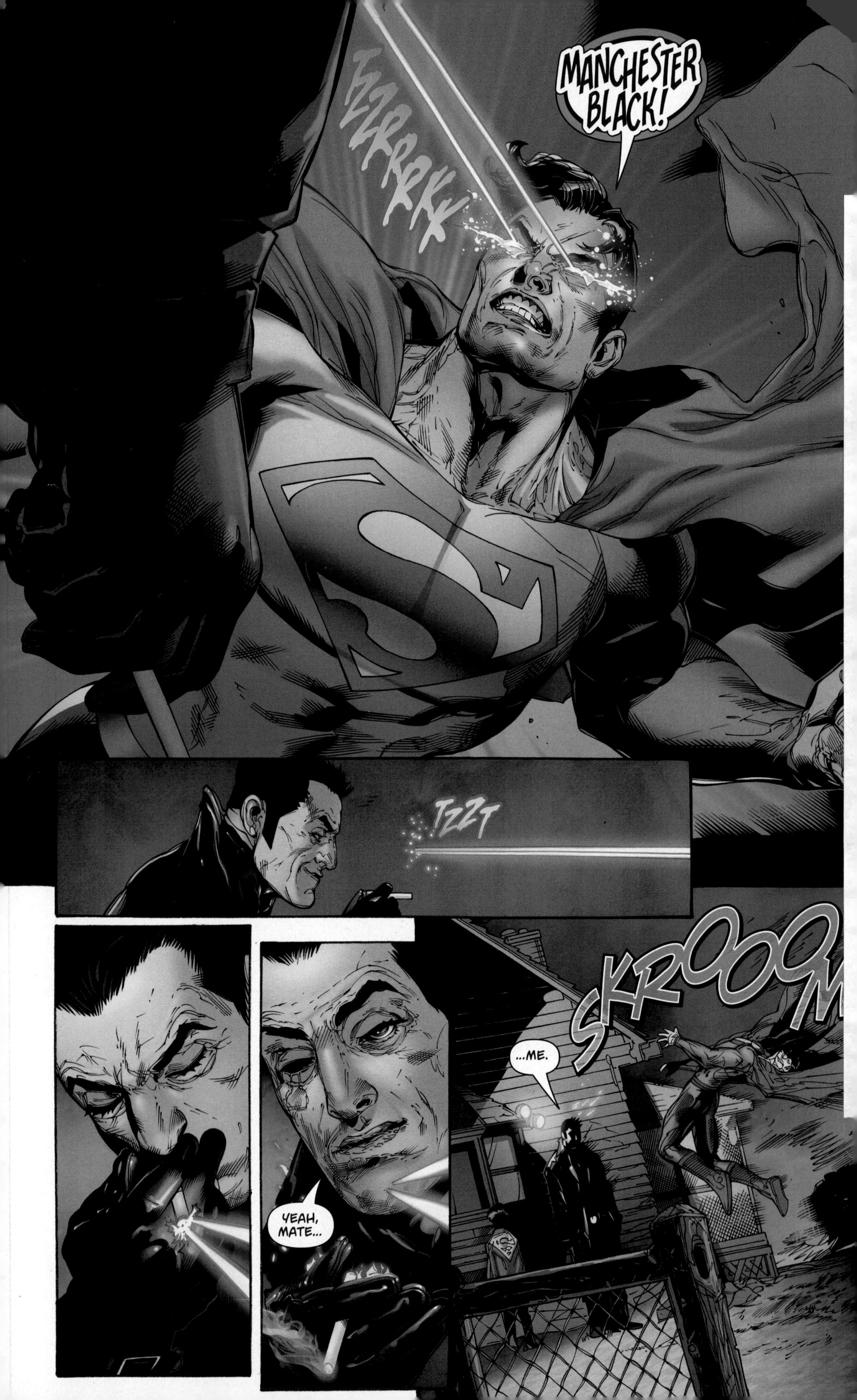

ZZZRRKK
MANCHESTER BLACK!
TZZT
YEAH, MATE...
...ME.
SKROOOM

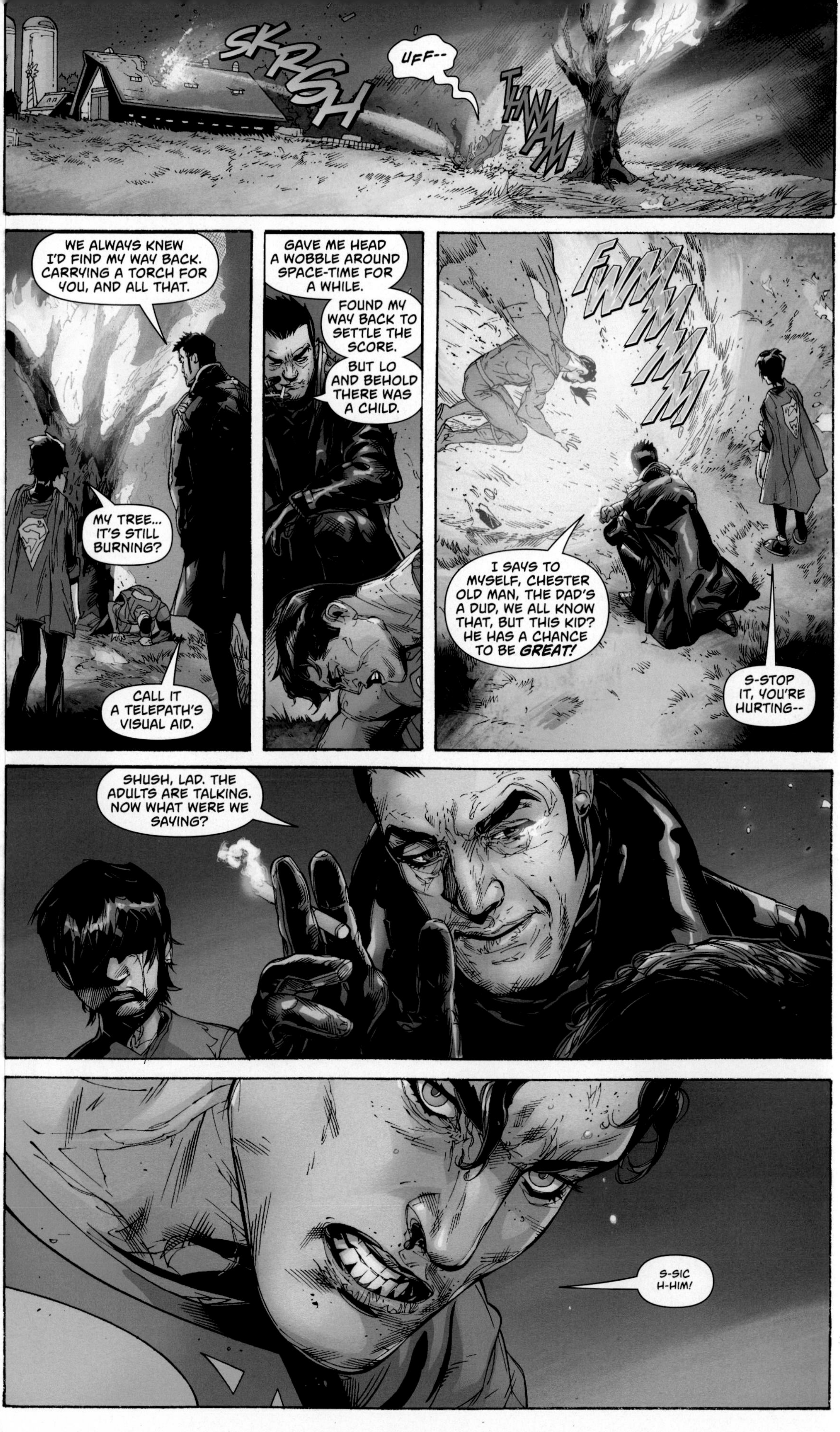

SKRSH
UFF--
THWAM
WE ALWAYS KNEW I'D FIND MY WAY BACK. CARRYING A TORCH FOR YOU, AND ALL THAT.
MY TREE... IT'S STILL BURNING?
CALL IT A TELEPATH'S VISUAL AID.
GAVE ME HEAD A WOBBLE AROUND SPACE-TIME FOR A WHILE.
FOUND MY WAY BACK TO SETTLE THE SCORE.
BUT LO AND BEHOLD THERE WAS A CHILD.
FWMMMMM
I SAYS TO MYSELF, CHESTER OLD MAN, THE DAD'S A DUD, WE ALL KNOW THAT, BUT THIS KID? HE HAS A CHANCE TO BE *GREAT!*
S-STOP IT, YOU'RE HURTING--
SHUSH, LAD. THE ADULTS ARE TALKING. NOW WHAT WERE WE SAYING?
S-SIC H-HIM!

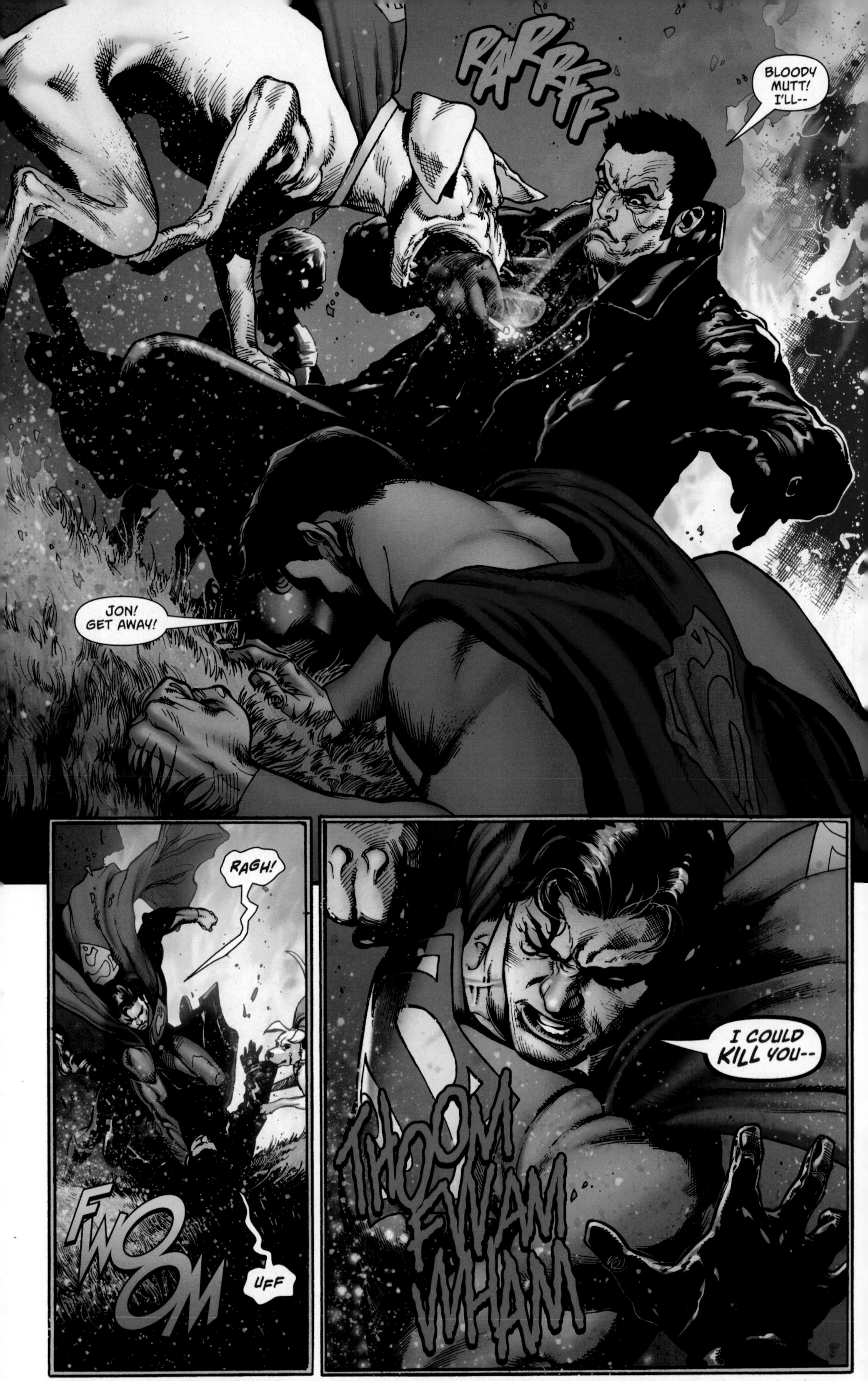
RARRFF
BLOODY MUTT! I'LL--
JON! GET AWAY!
RAGH!
FWOOM
UFF
I COULD KILL YOU--
THOOM
FWAM
WHAM

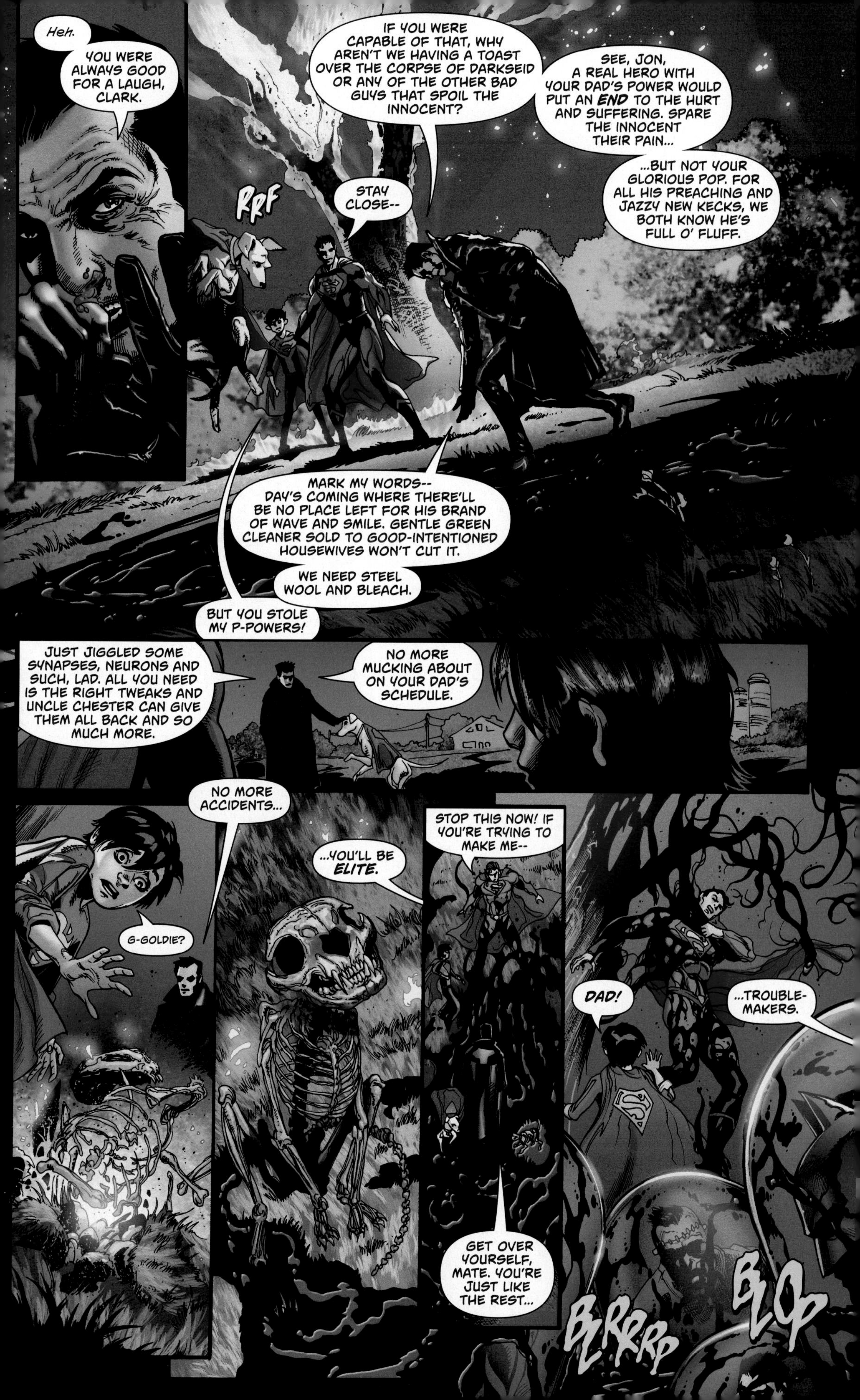
Heh.
YOU WERE ALWAYS GOOD FOR A LAUGH, CLARK.
IF YOU WERE CAPABLE OF THAT, WHY AREN'T WE HAVING A TOAST OVER THE CORPSE OF DARKSEID OR ANY OF THE OTHER BAD GUYS THAT SPOIL THE INNOCENT?
SEE, JON, A REAL HERO WITH YOUR DAD'S POWER WOULD PUT AN END TO THE HURT AND SUFFERING. SPARE THE INNOCENT THEIR PAIN...
...BUT NOT YOUR GLORIOUS POP. FOR ALL HIS PREACHING AND JAZZY NEW KECKS, WE BOTH KNOW HE'S FULL O' FLUFF.
RRF
STAY CLOSE--
MARK MY WORDS-- DAY'S COMING WHERE THERE'LL BE NO PLACE LEFT FOR HIS BRAND OF WAVE AND SMILE. GENTLE GREEN CLEANER SOLD TO GOOD-INTENTIONED HOUSEWIVES WON'T CUT IT.
WE NEED STEEL WOOL AND BLEACH.
BUT YOU STOLE MY P-POWERS!
JUST JIGGLED SOME SYNAPSES, NEURONS AND SUCH, LAD. ALL YOU NEED IS THE RIGHT TWEAKS AND UNCLE CHESTER CAN GIVE THEM ALL BACK AND SO MUCH MORE.
NO MORE MUCKING ABOUT ON YOUR DAD'S SCHEDULE.
NO MORE ACCIDENTS...
G-GOLDIE?
...YOU'LL BE ELITE.
STOP THIS NOW! IF YOU'RE TRYING TO MAKE ME--
GET OVER YOURSELF, MATE. YOU'RE JUST LIKE THE REST...
DAD!
...TROUBLE-MAKERS.
BZRRRRP
BLOP

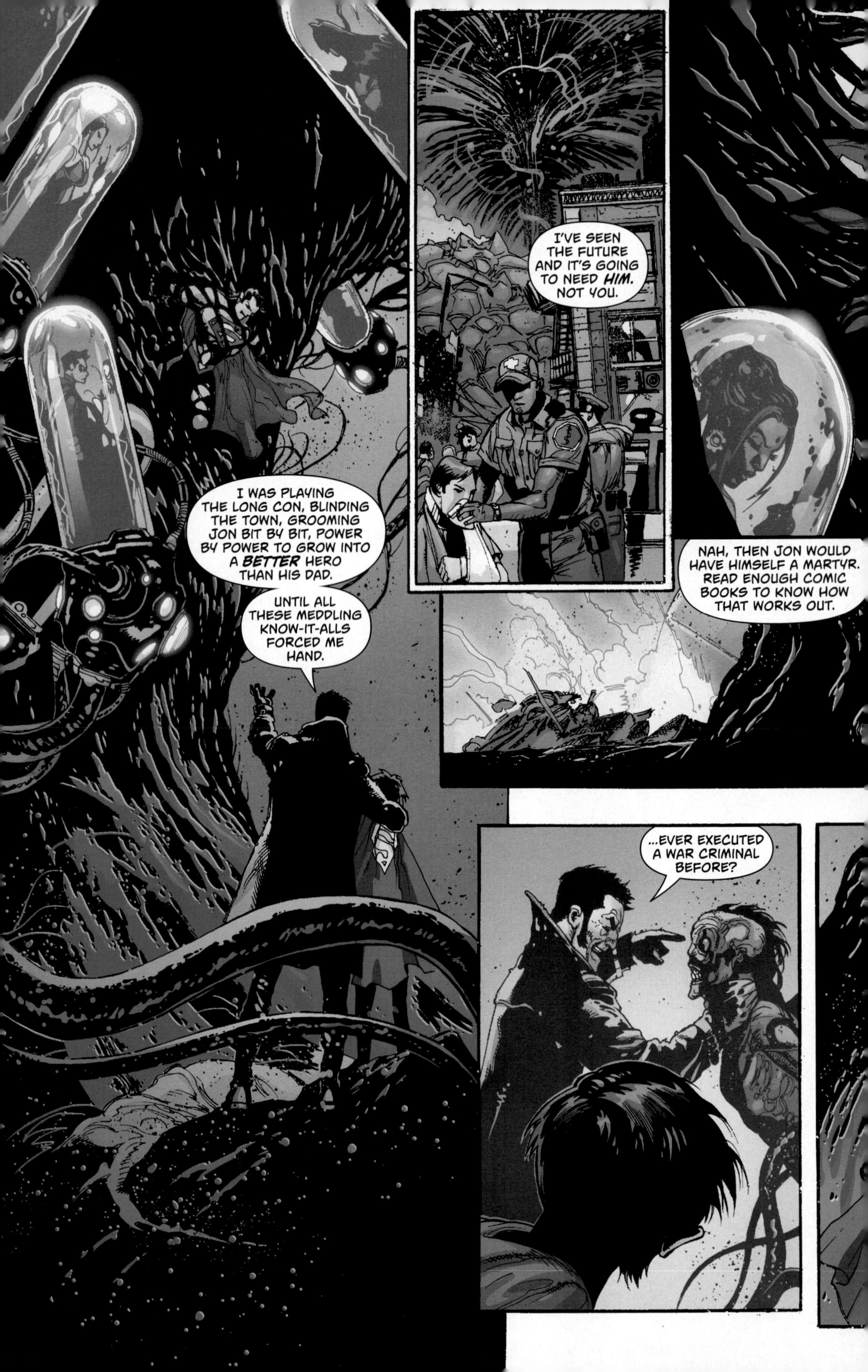
I WAS PLAYING THE LONG CON, BLINDING THE TOWN, GROOMING JON BIT BY BIT, POWER BY POWER TO GROW INTO A BETTER HERO THAN HIS DAD.
UNTIL ALL THESE MEDDLING KNOW-IT-ALLS FORCED ME HAND.
I'VE SEEN THE FUTURE AND IT'S GOING TO NEED HIM. NOT YOU.
NAH, THEN JON WOULD HAVE HIMSELF A MARTYR. READ ENOUGH COMIC BOOKS TO KNOW HOW THAT WORKS OUT.
...EVER EXECUTED A WAR CRIMINAL BEFORE?

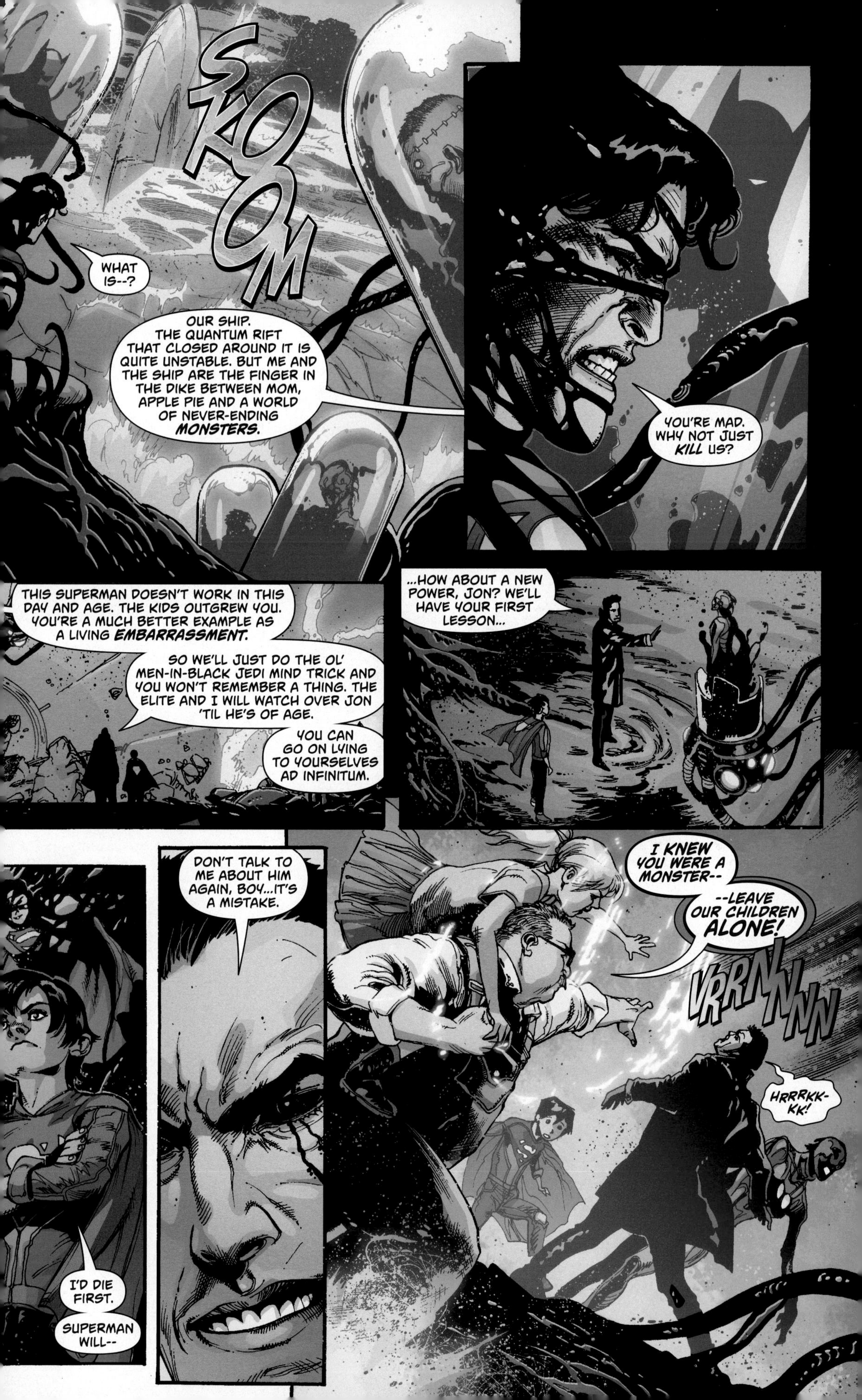
SKOOM
WHAT IS--?
OUR SHIP. THE QUANTUM RIFT THAT CLOSED AROUND IT IS QUITE UNSTABLE. BUT ME AND THE SHIP ARE THE FINGER IN THE DIKE BETWEEN MOM, APPLE PIE AND A WORLD OF NEVER-ENDING MONSTERS.
YOU'RE MAD. WHY NOT JUST KILL US?
THIS SUPERMAN DOESN'T WORK IN THIS DAY AND AGE. THE KIDS OUTGREW YOU. YOU'RE A MUCH BETTER EXAMPLE AS A LIVING EMBARRASSMENT.
SO WE'LL JUST DO THE OL' MEN-IN-BLACK JEDI MIND TRICK AND YOU WON'T REMEMBER A THING. THE ELITE AND I WILL WATCH OVER JON 'TIL HE'S OF AGE.
YOU CAN GO ON LYING TO YOURSELVES AD INFINITUM.
...HOW ABOUT A NEW POWER, JON? WE'LL HAVE YOUR FIRST LESSON...
I'D DIE FIRST.
SUPERMAN WILL--
DON'T TALK TO ME ABOUT HIM AGAIN, BOY...IT'S A MISTAKE.
I KNEW YOU WERE A MONSTER--
--LEAVE OUR CHILDREN ALONE!
VRRNNNNN
HRRRKK-KK!

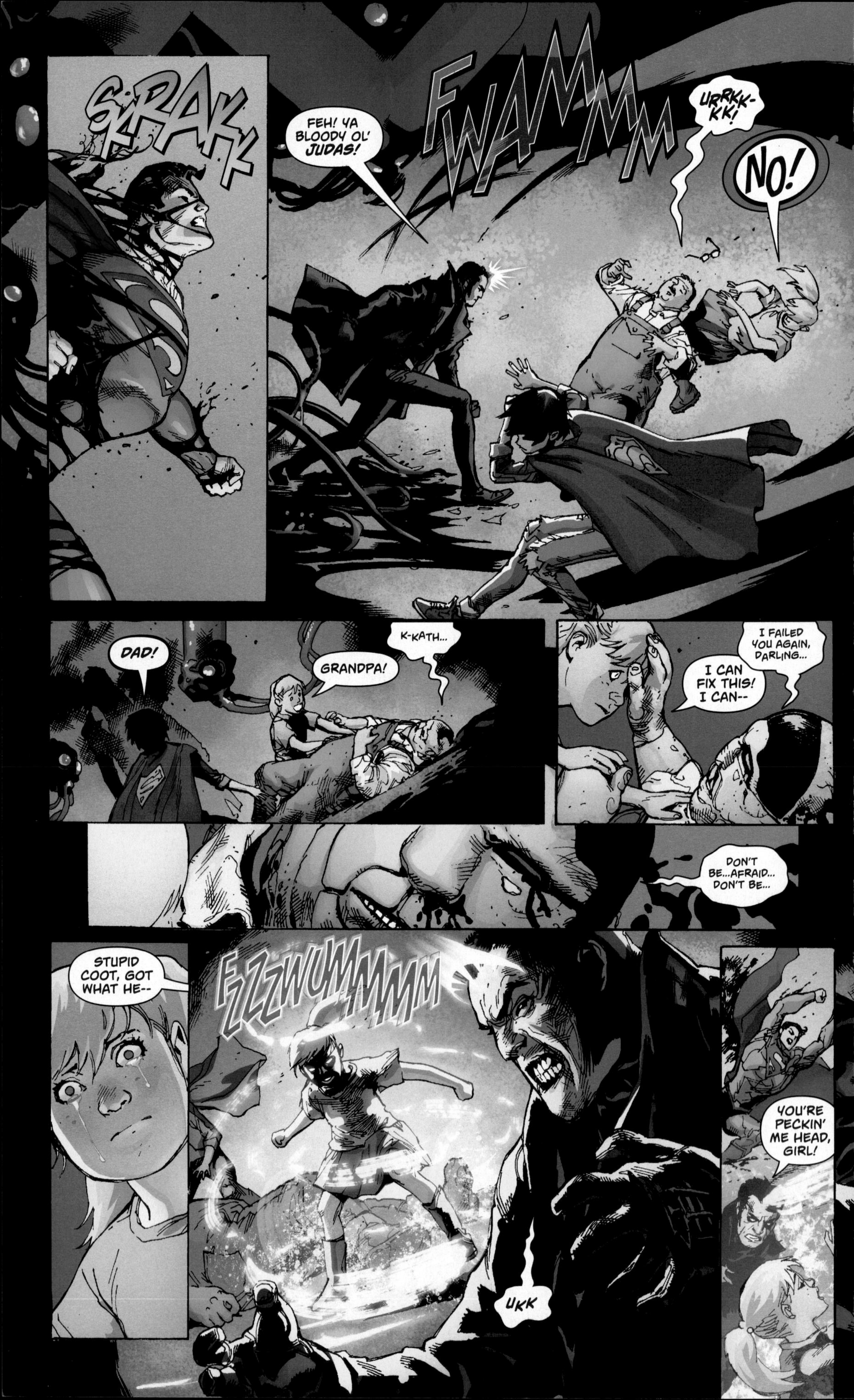
SKRAKK
FEH! YA BLOODY OL' JUDAS!
FWAMMMM
URRKK-KK!
NO!
DAD!
GRANDPA!
K-KATH...
I FAILED YOU AGAIN, DARLING...
I CAN FIX THIS! I CAN--
DON'T BE...AFRAID... DON'T BE...
STUPID COOT, GOT WHAT HE--
FZZZWUMMMMM
UKK
YOU'RE PECKIN' ME HEAD, GIRL!

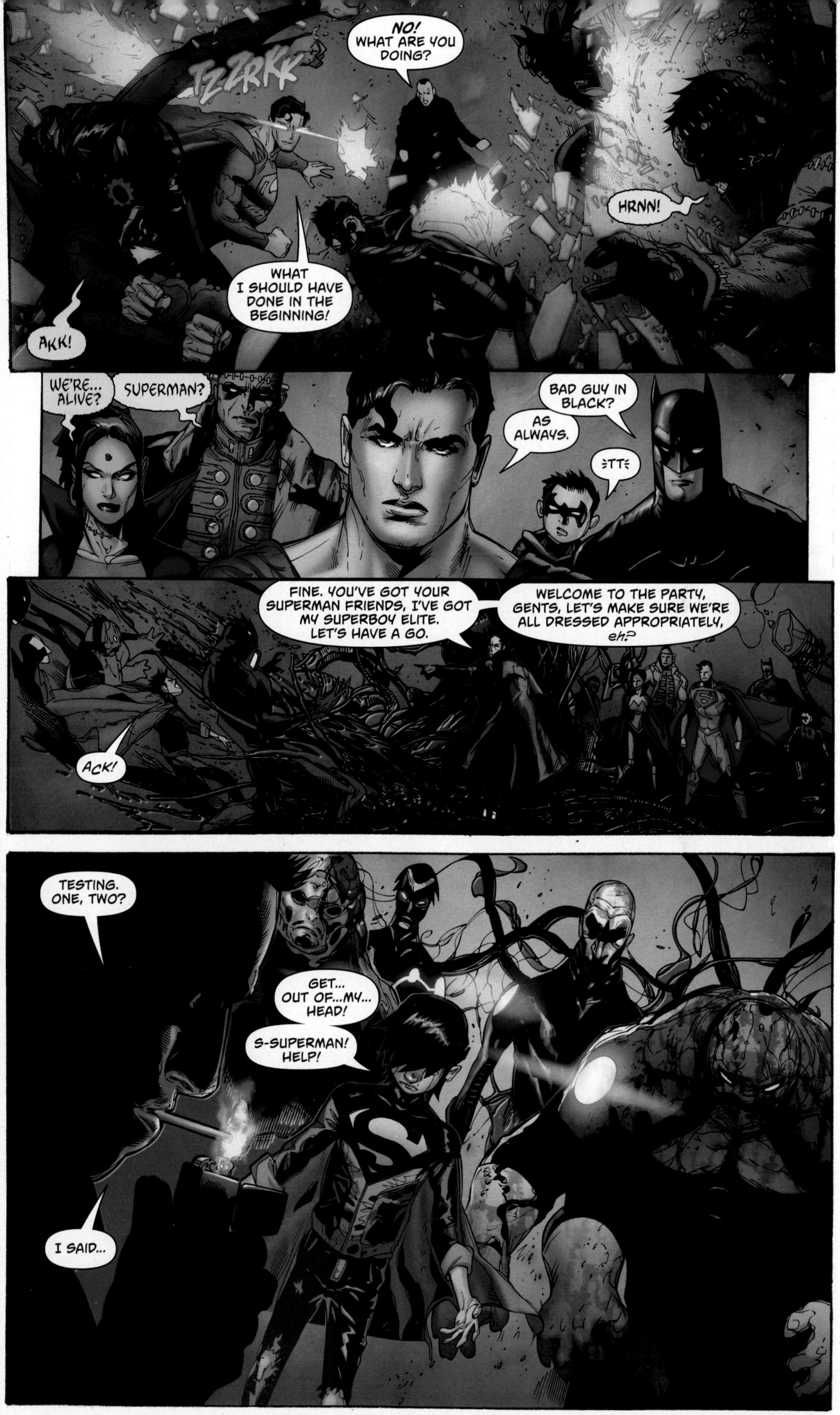
TZZRKK
NO! WHAT ARE YOU DOING?
WHAT I SHOULD HAVE DONE IN THE BEGINNING!
HRNN!
AKK!
WE'RE... ALIVE?
SUPERMAN?
BAD GUY IN BLACK?
AS ALWAYS.
TT
FINE. YOU'VE GOT YOUR SUPERMAN FRIENDS, I'VE GOT MY SUPERBOY ELITE. LET'S HAVE A GO.
WELCOME TO THE PARTY, GENTS, LET'S MAKE SURE WE'RE ALL DRESSED APPROPRIATELY, eh?
ACK!
TESTING. ONE, TWO?
GET... OUT OF...MY... HEAD!
S-SUPERMAN! HELP!
I SAID...

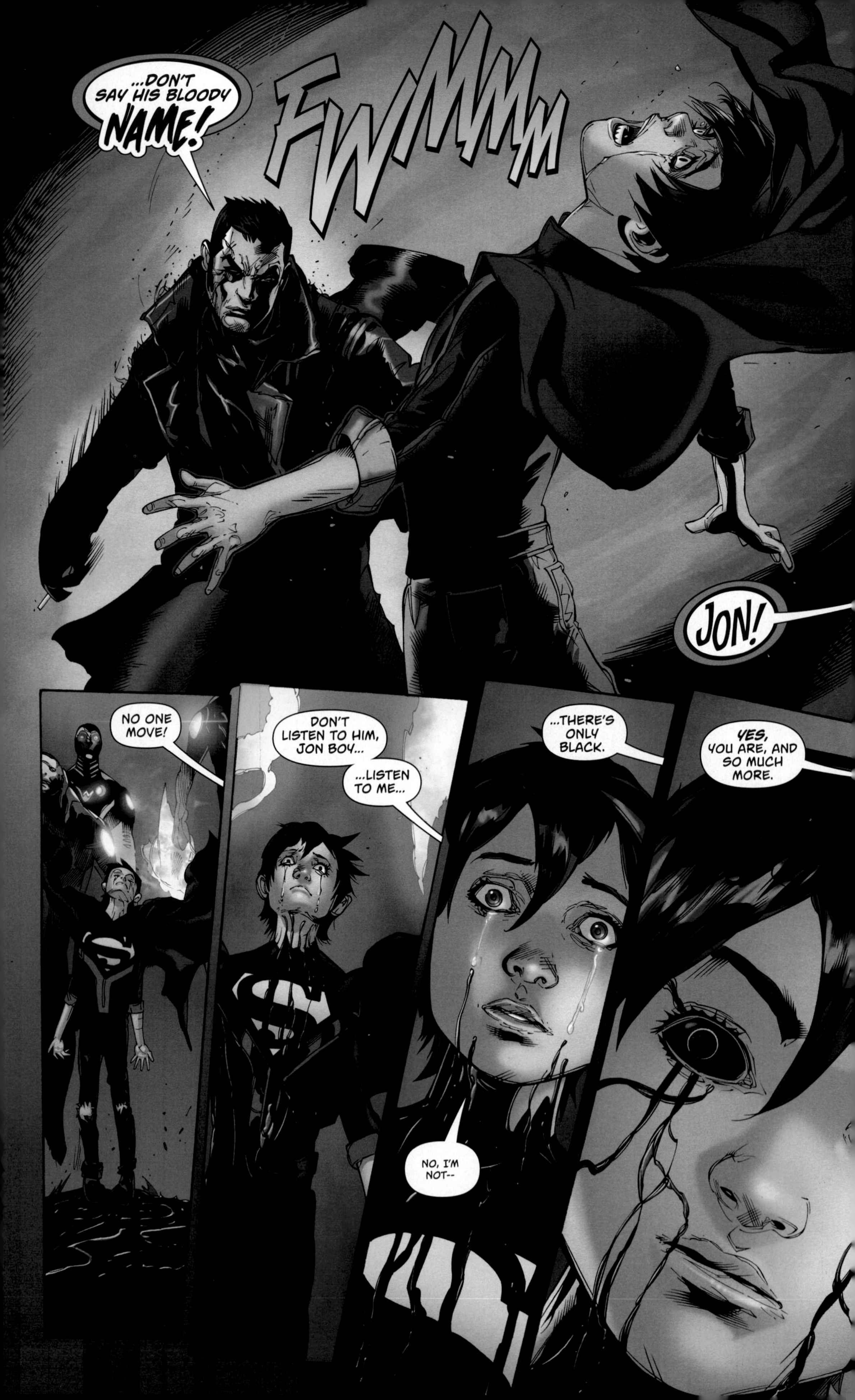
...DON'T SAY HIS BLOODY NAME!
FWMMM
JON!
NO ONE MOVE!
DON'T LISTEN TO HIM, JON BOY...
...LISTEN TO ME...
...THERE'S ONLY BLACK.
NO, I'M NOT--
YES, YOU ARE, AND SO MUCH MORE.

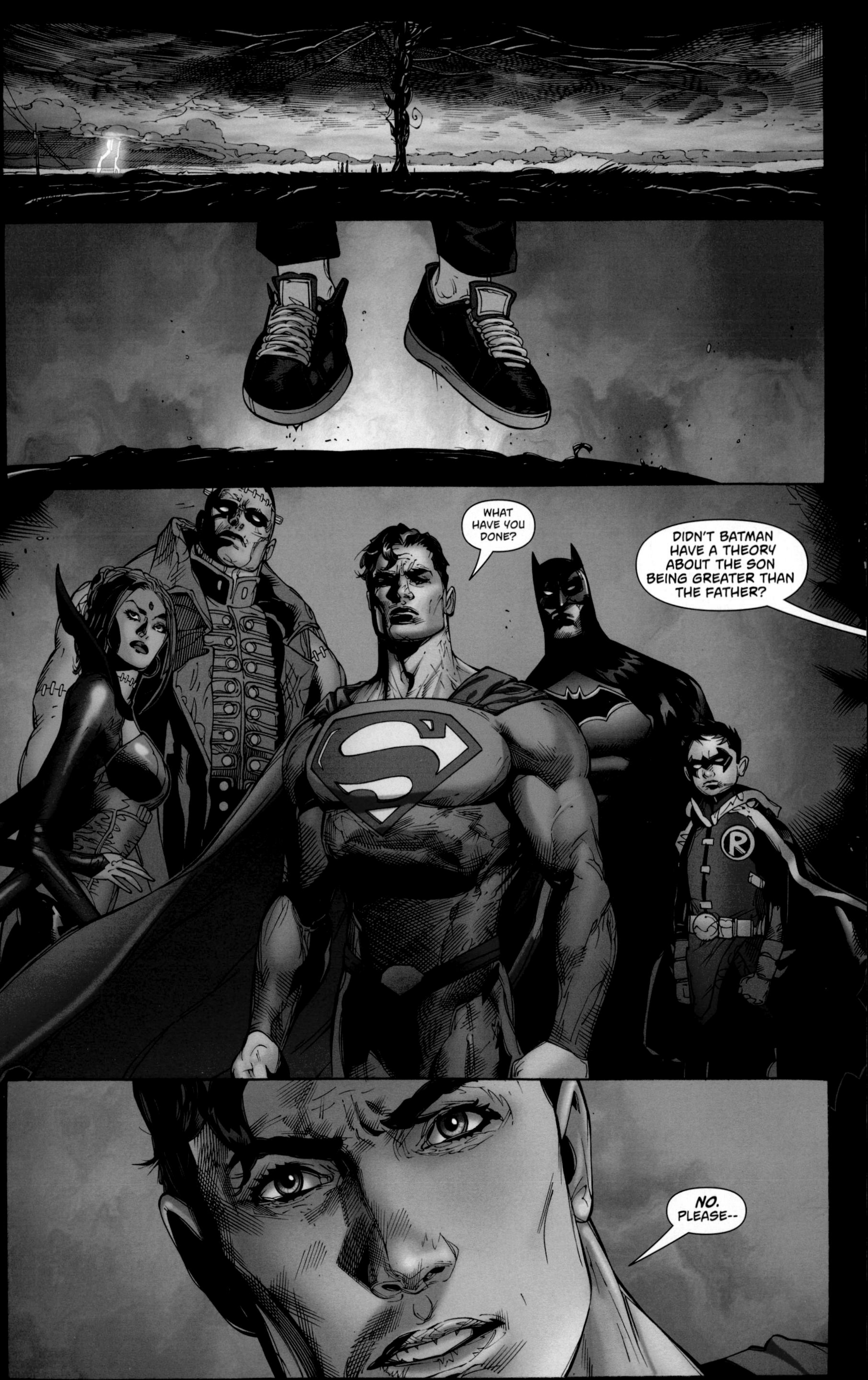
WHAT HAVE YOU DONE?
DIDN'T BATMAN HAVE A THEORY ABOUT THE SON BEING GREATER THAN THE FATHER?
NO. PLEASE--

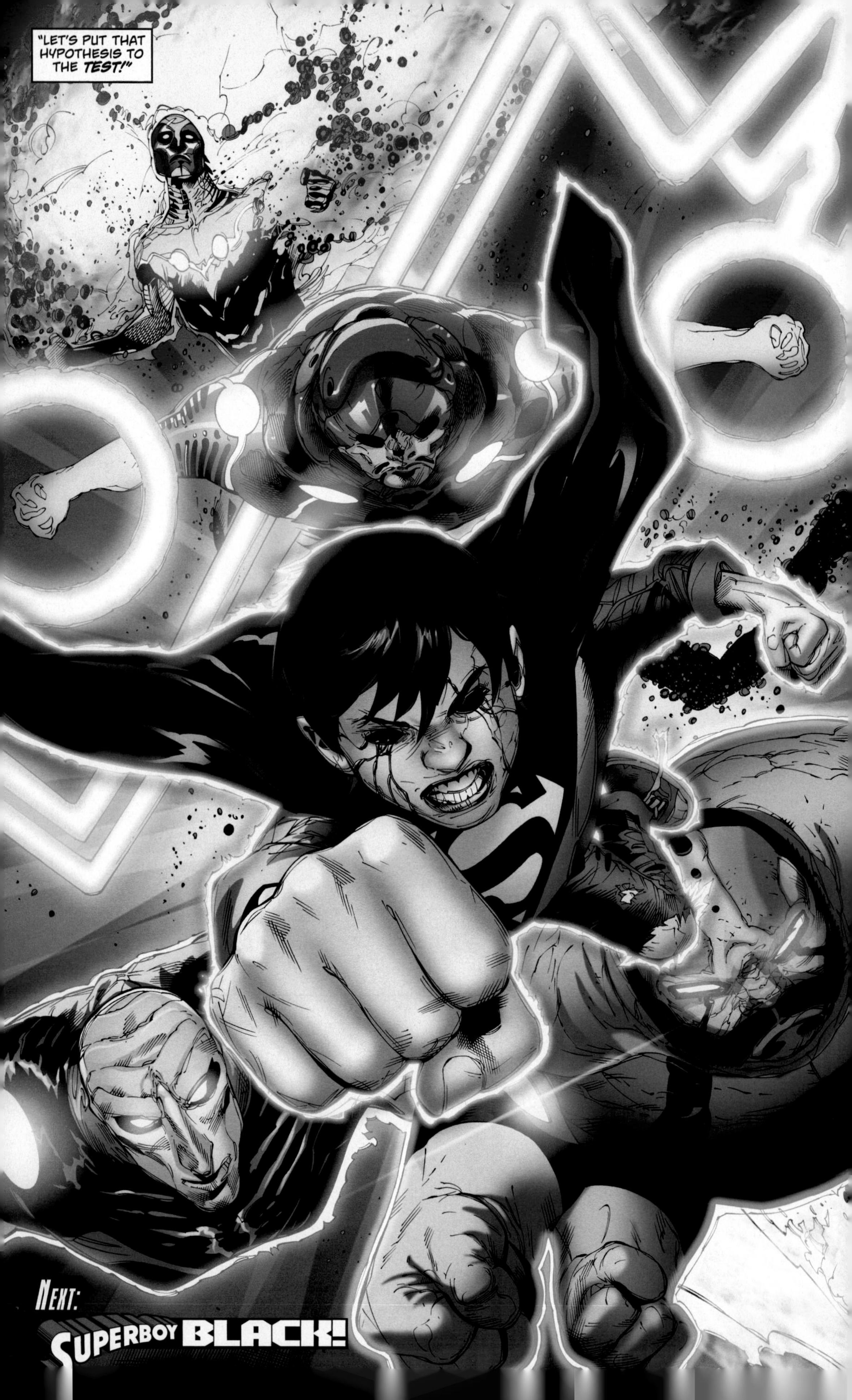
"LET'S PUT THAT HYPOTHESIS TO THE TEST!"
NEXT:
SUPERBOY BLACK!

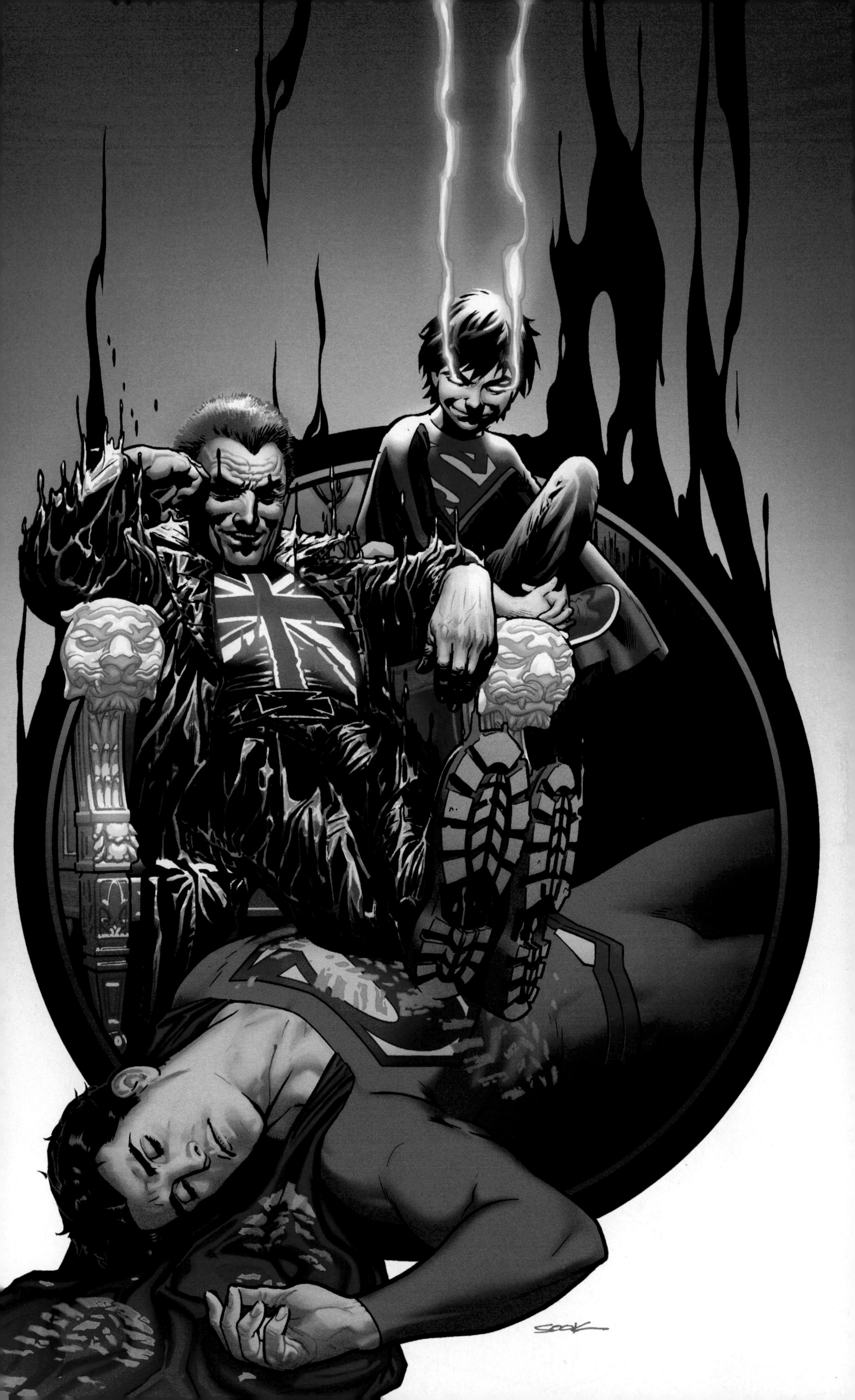

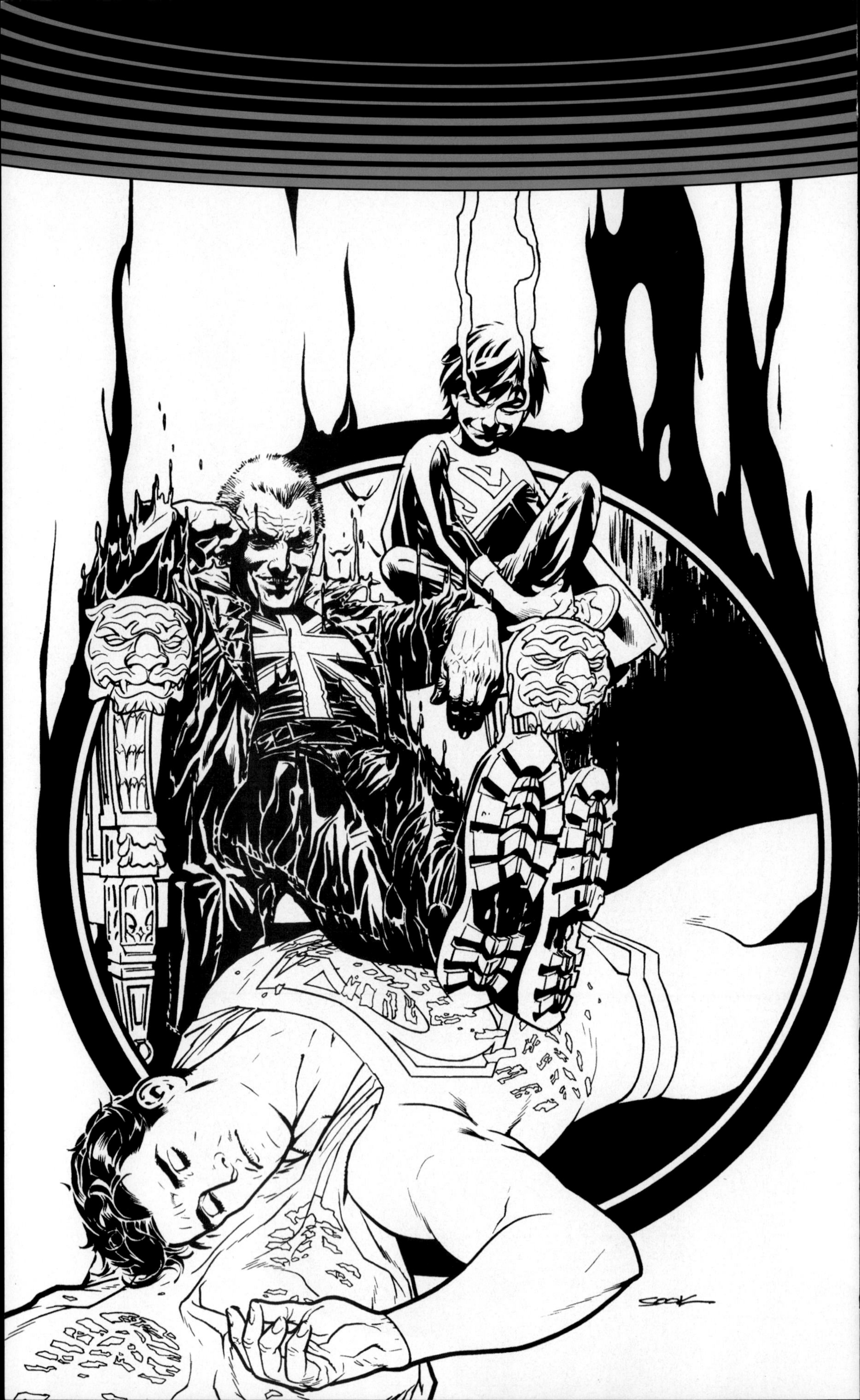

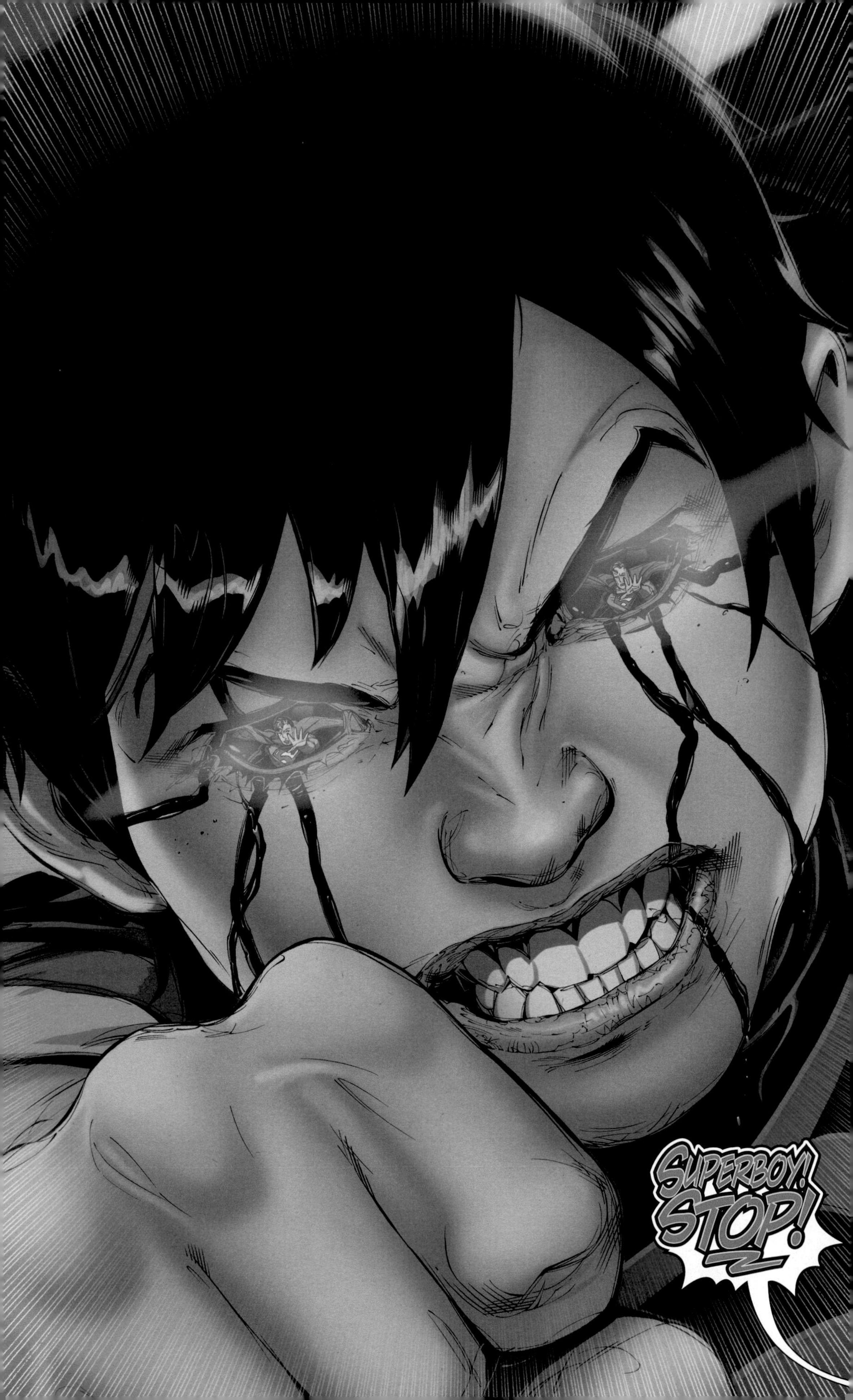
SUPERBOY! STOP!

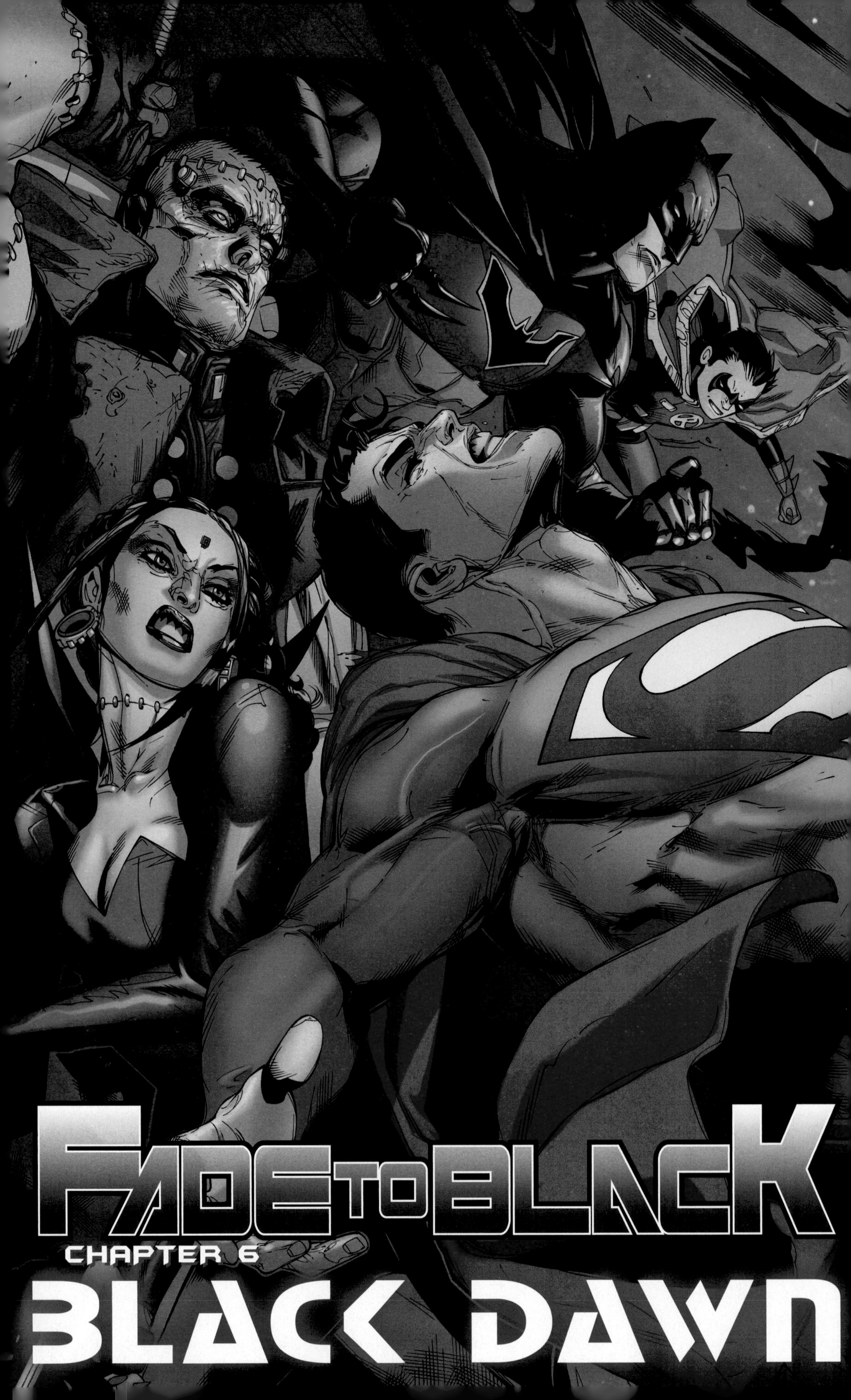
FADE TO BLACK
CHAPTER 6
BLACK DAWN

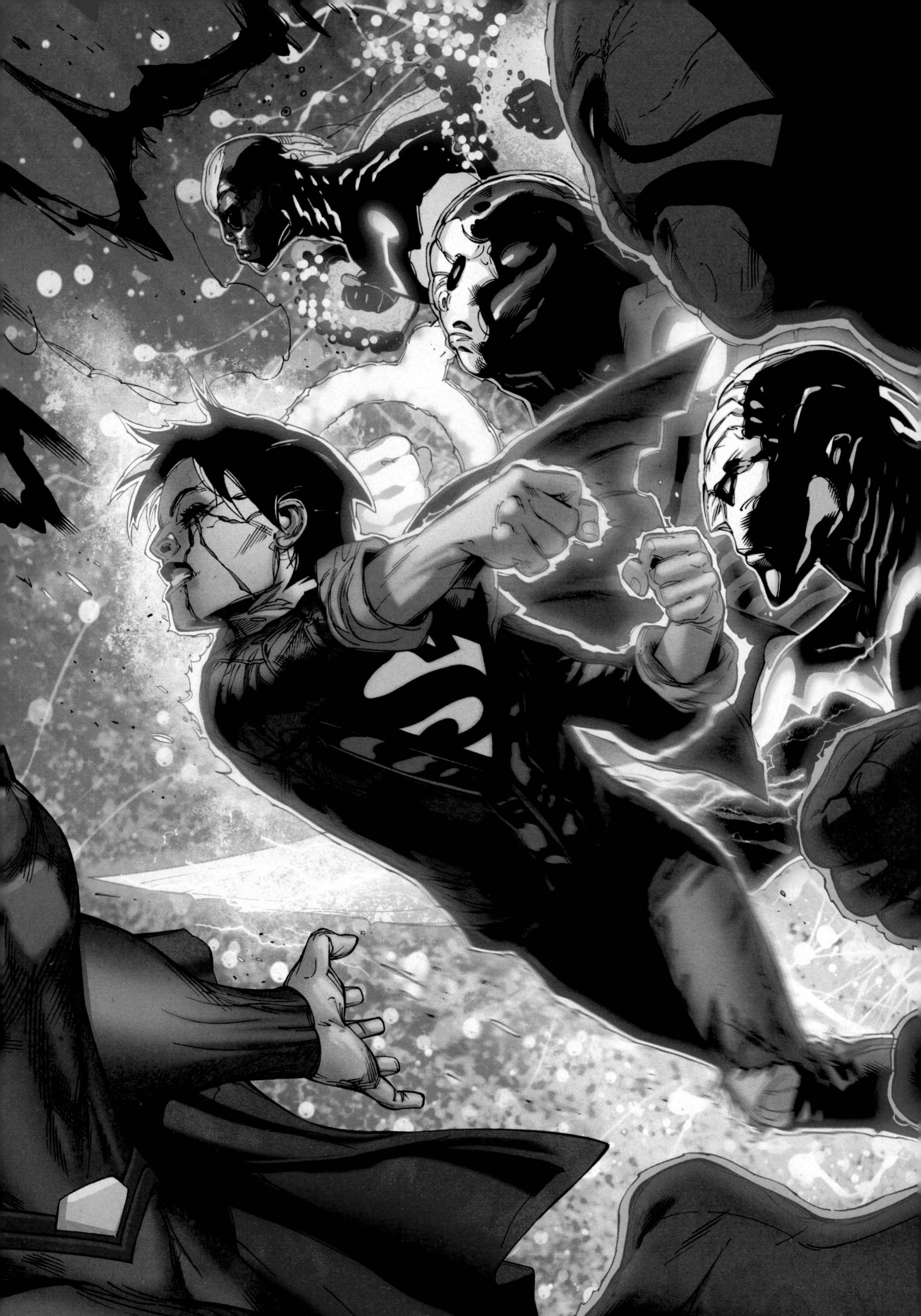

PATRICK GLEASON & PETER J. TOMASI Story • **DOUG MAHNKE & PATRICK GLEASON** Pencils
JAIME MENDOZA, MICK GRAY, JOE PRADO, RAY McCARTHY, SCOTT HANNA & MATT SANTORELLI Inkers
WIL QUINTANA & JOHN KALISZ Colorists · **DAVE SHARPE** Letterer · **RYAN SOOK** Cover · **ANDREW MARINO** Assistant Editor · **EDDIE BERGANZA** Editor

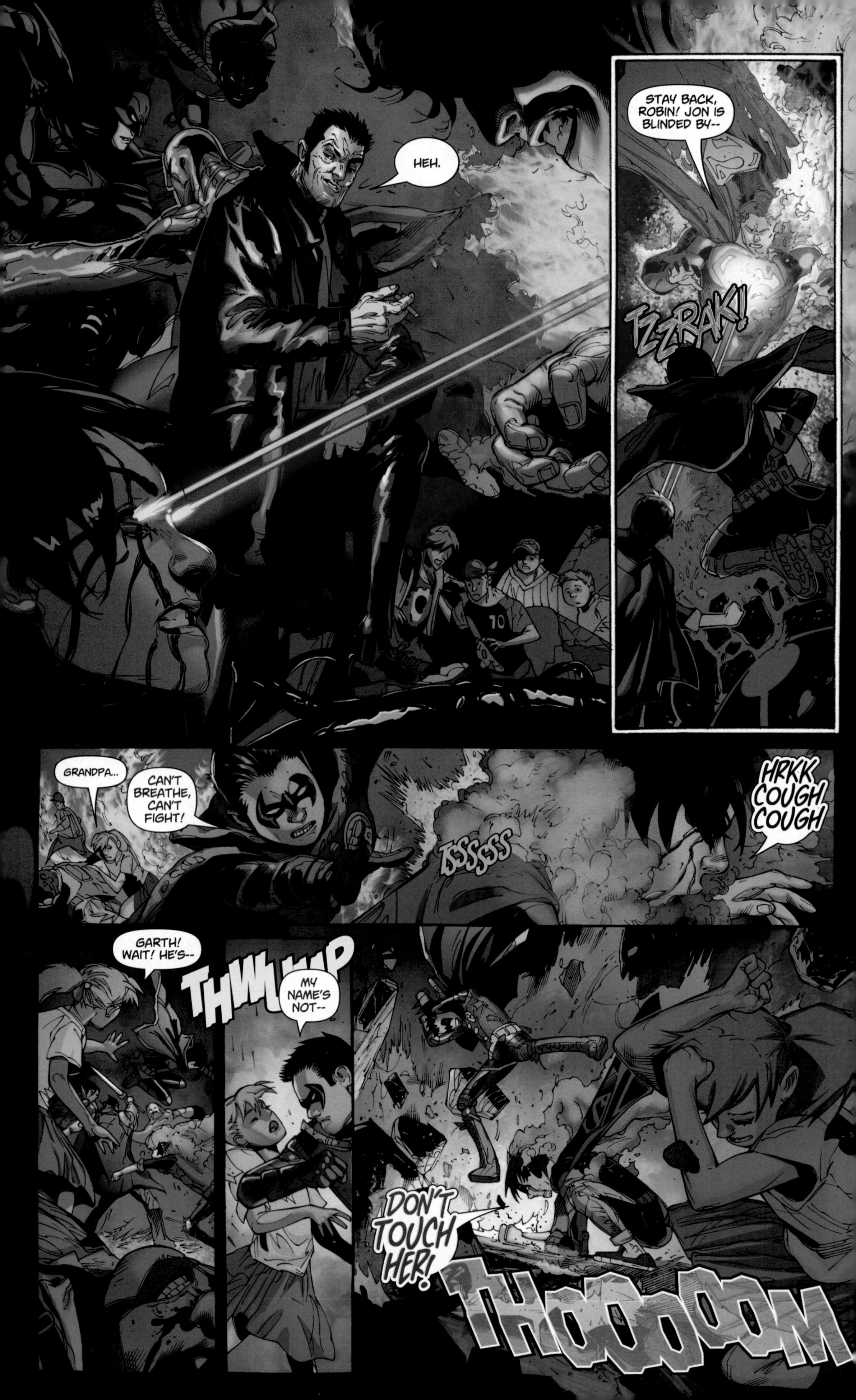
HEH.
STAY BACK, ROBIN! JON IS BLINDED BY--
TZZRAK!
GRANDPA...
CAN'T BREATHE, CAN'T FIGHT!
TSSSSSS
HRKK COUGH COUGH
GARTH! WAIT! HE'S--
THWUMP
MY NAME'S NOT--
DON'T TOUCH HER!
THOOOOOM

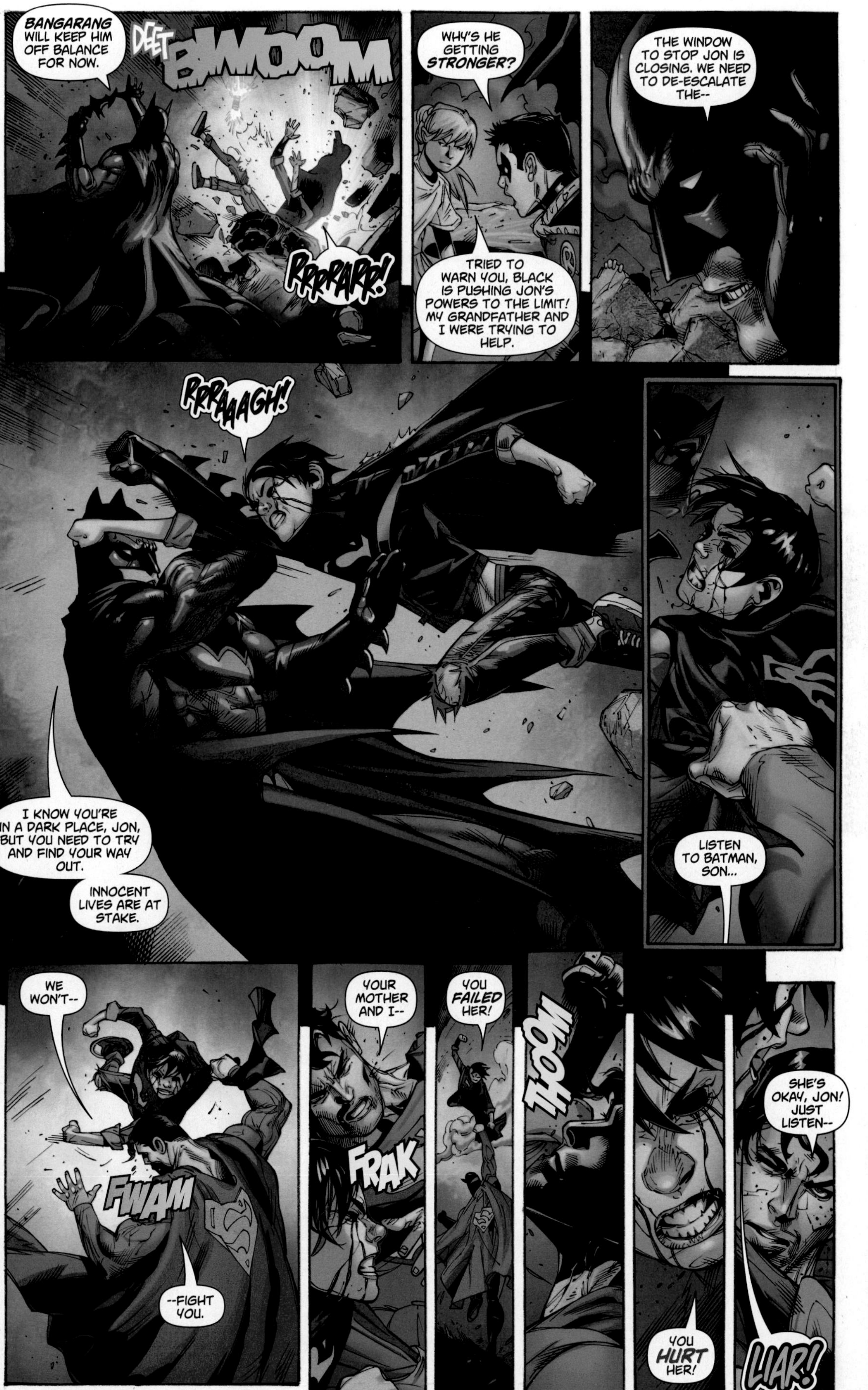
BANGARANG WILL KEEP HIM OFF BALANCE FOR NOW.
DEET
BWOOM
RRRRARR!
WHY'S HE GETTING STRONGER?
TRIED TO WARN YOU, BLACK IS PUSHING JON'S POWERS TO THE LIMIT! MY GRANDFATHER AND I WERE TRYING TO HELP.
THE WINDOW TO STOP JON IS CLOSING. WE NEED TO DE-ESCALATE THE--
RRRAAAGH!
I KNOW YOU'RE IN A DARK PLACE, JON, BUT YOU NEED TO TRY AND FIND YOUR WAY OUT.
INNOCENT LIVES ARE AT STAKE.
LISTEN TO BATMAN, SON...
WE WON'T--
FWAM
--FIGHT YOU.
YOUR MOTHER AND I--
FRAK
YOU FAILED HER!
THOOM
YOU HURT HER!
SHE'S OKAY, JON! JUST LISTEN--
LIAR!

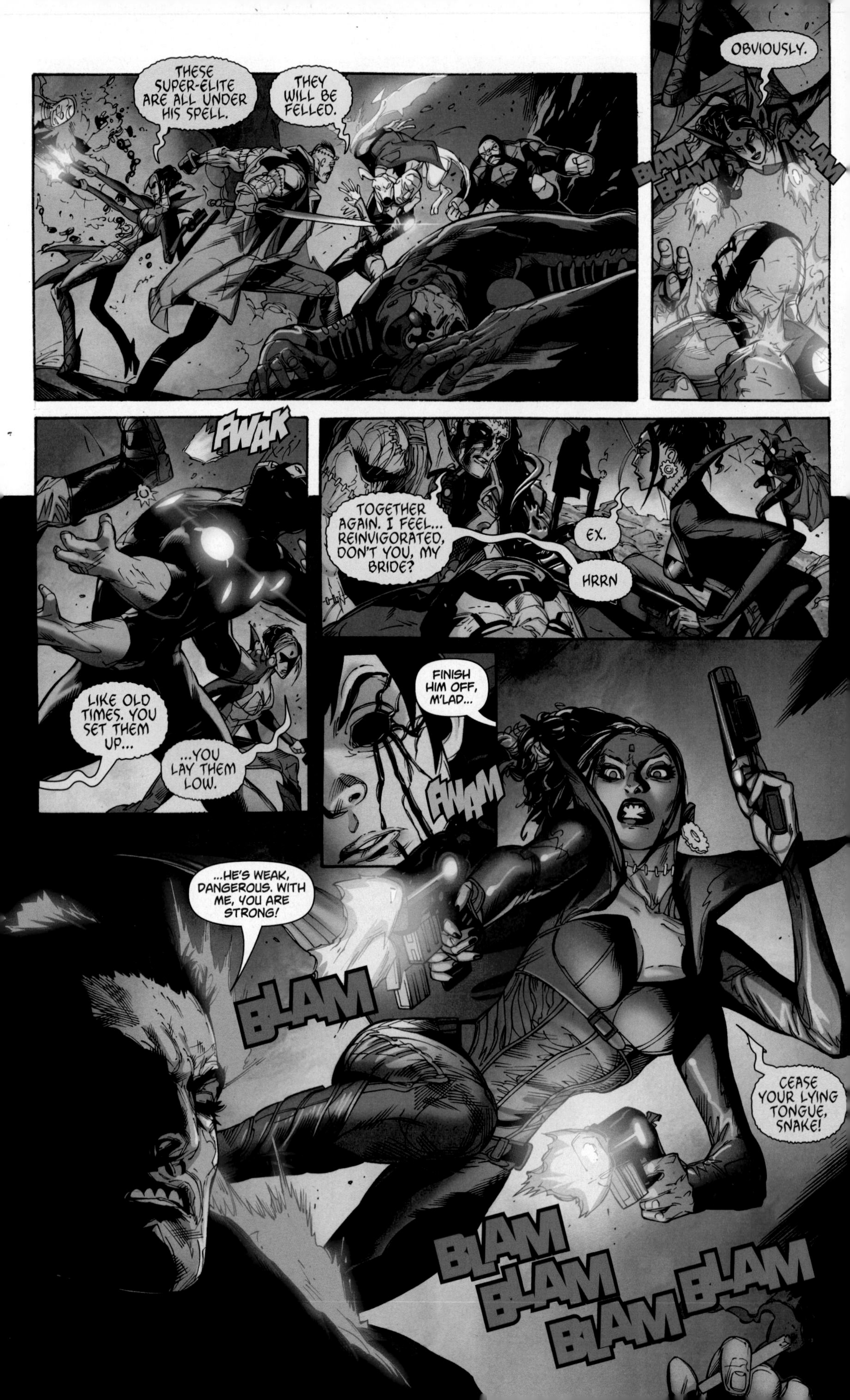
THESE SUPER-ELITE ARE ALL UNDER HIS SPELL.
THEY WILL BE FELLED.
OBVIOUSLY.
BLAM BLAM BLAM
FWAK
TOGETHER AGAIN. I FEEL... REINVIGORATED, DON'T YOU, MY BRIDE?
EX.
HRRN
LIKE OLD TIMES. YOU SET THEM UP...
...YOU LAY THEM LOW.
FINISH HIM OFF, M'LAD...
FWAM
...HE'S WEAK, DANGEROUS. WITH ME, YOU ARE STRONG!
BLAM
CEASE YOUR LYING TONGUE, SNAKE!
BLAM BLAM BLAM BLAM

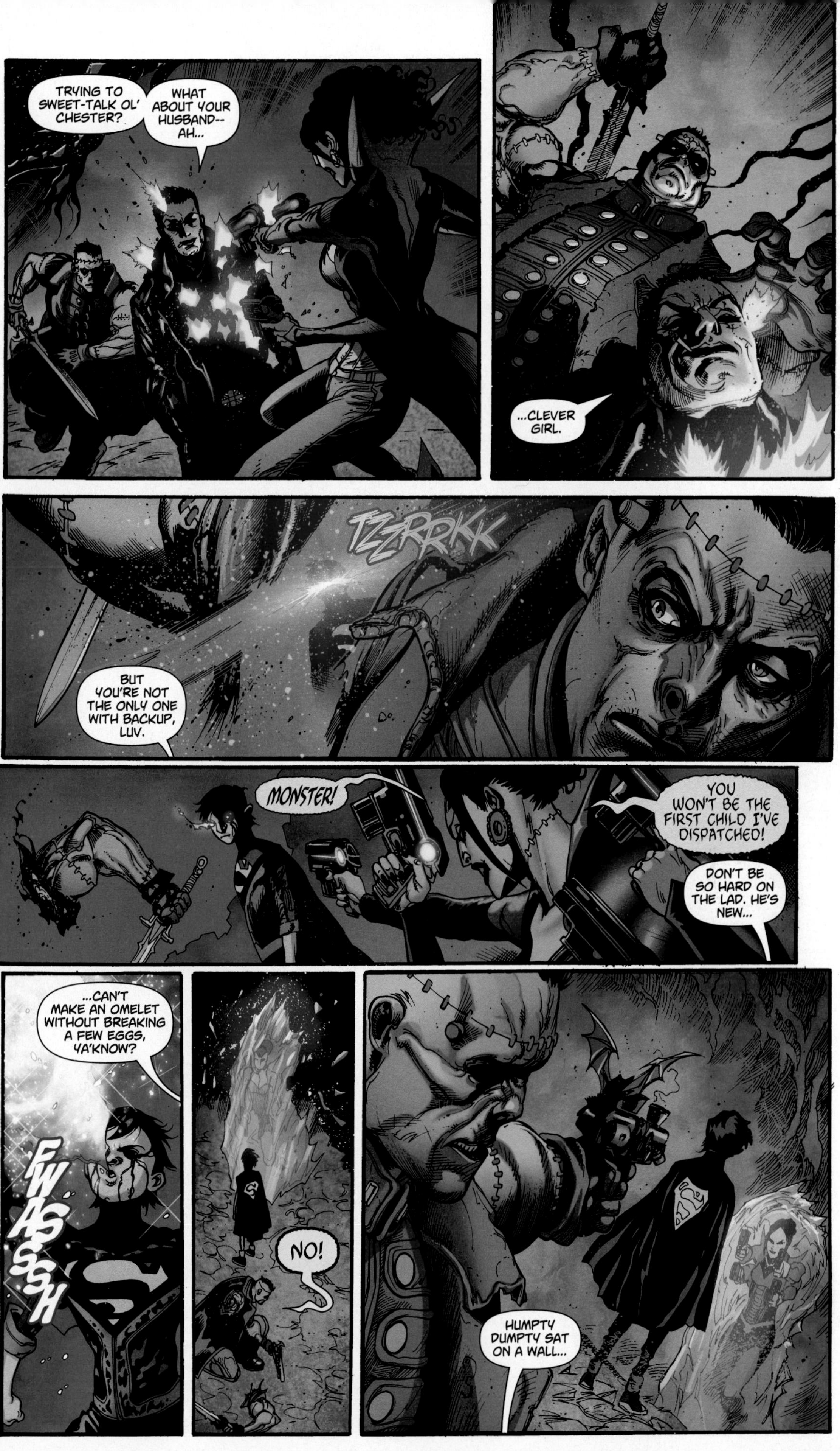
TRYING TO SWEET-TALK OL' CHESTER?
WHAT ABOUT YOUR HUSBAND-- AH...
...CLEVER GIRL.
TZZRRKK
BUT YOU'RE NOT THE ONLY ONE WITH BACKUP, LUV.
MONSTER!
YOU WON'T BE THE FIRST CHILD I'VE DISPATCHED!
DON'T BE SO HARD ON THE LAD. HE'S NEW...
...CAN'T MAKE AN OMELET WITHOUT BREAKING A FEW EGGS, YA'KNOW?
FWASSSH
NO!
HUMPTY DUMPTY SAT ON A WALL...

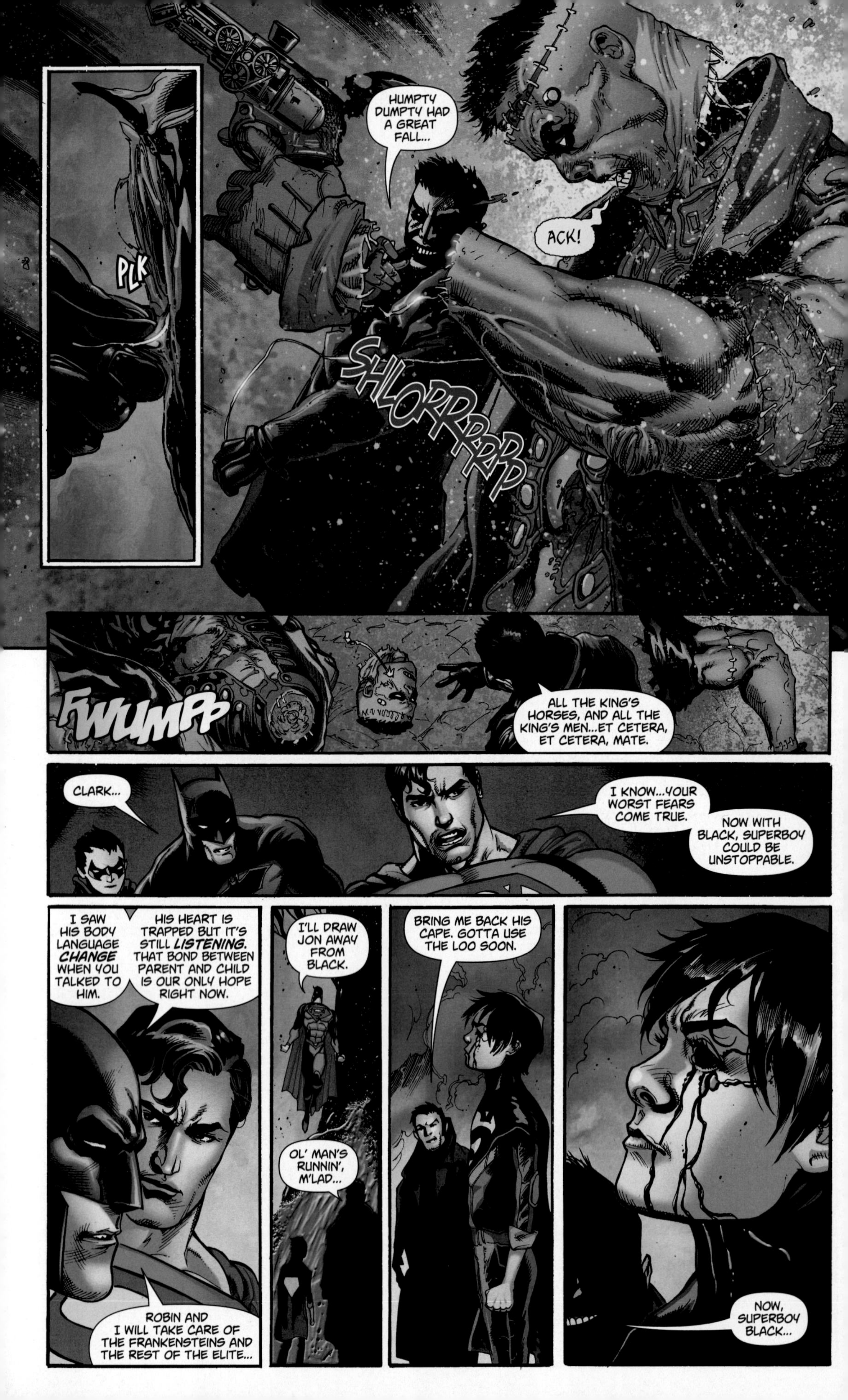
HUMPTY DUMPTY HAD A GREAT FALL...
PLK
ACK!
SHLORRRRRP
FWUMPP
ALL THE KING'S HORSES, AND ALL THE KING'S MEN...ET CETERA, ET CETERA, MATE.
CLARK...
I KNOW...YOUR WORST FEARS COME TRUE.
NOW WITH BLACK, SUPERBOY COULD BE UNSTOPPABLE.
I SAW HIS BODY LANGUAGE CHANGE WHEN YOU TALKED TO HIM.
HIS HEART IS TRAPPED BUT IT'S STILL LISTENING. THAT BOND BETWEEN PARENT AND CHILD IS OUR ONLY HOPE RIGHT NOW.
ROBIN AND I WILL TAKE CARE OF THE FRANKENSTEINS AND THE REST OF THE ELITE...
I'LL DRAW JON AWAY FROM BLACK.
OL' MAN'S RUNNIN', M'LAD...
BRING ME BACK HIS CAPE. GOTTA USE THE LOO SOON.
NOW, SUPERBOY BLACK...

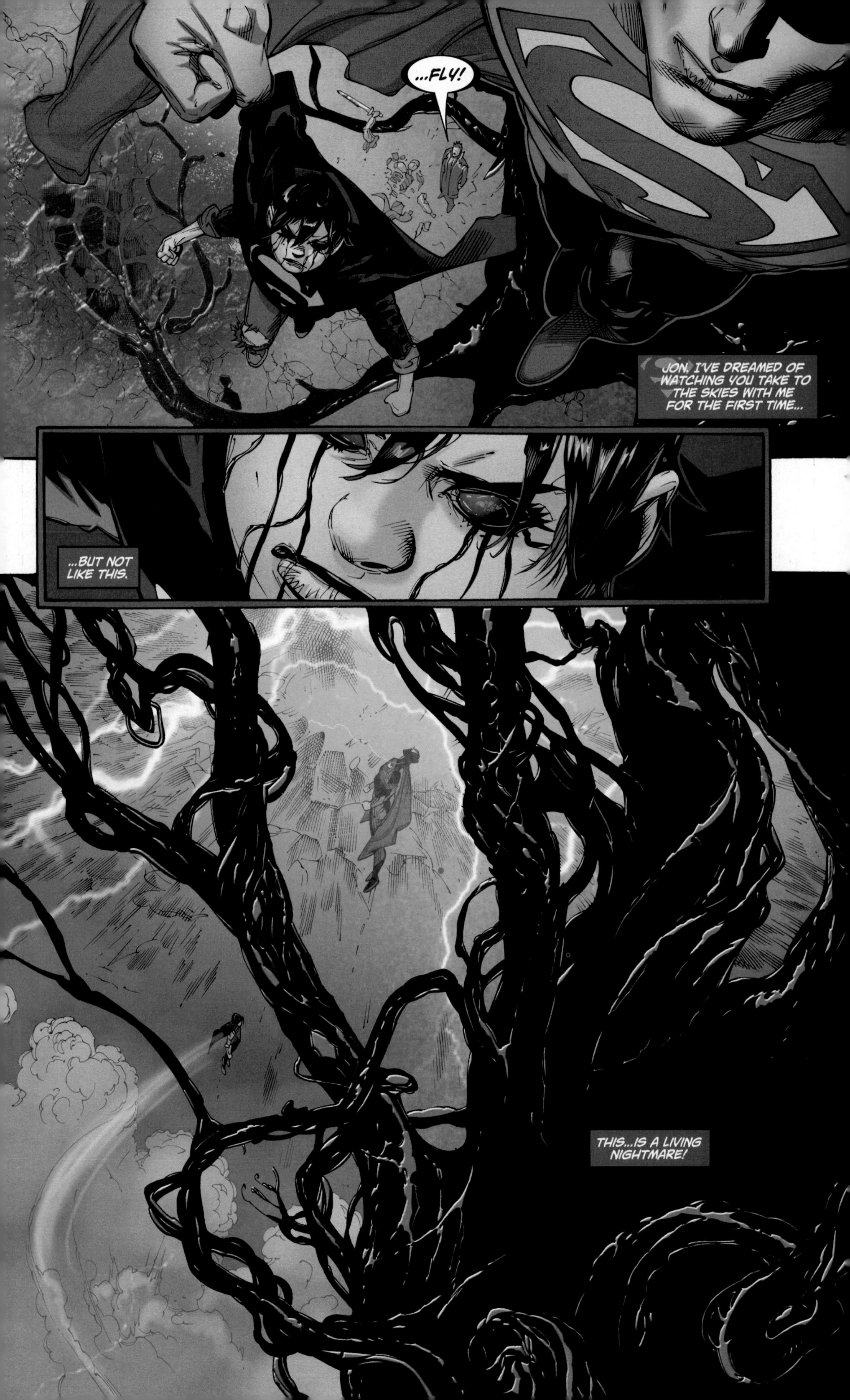
...FLY!
JON, I'VE DREAMED OF WATCHING YOU TAKE TO THE SKIES WITH ME FOR THE FIRST TIME...
...BUT NOT LIKE THIS.
THIS...IS A LIVING NIGHTMARE!

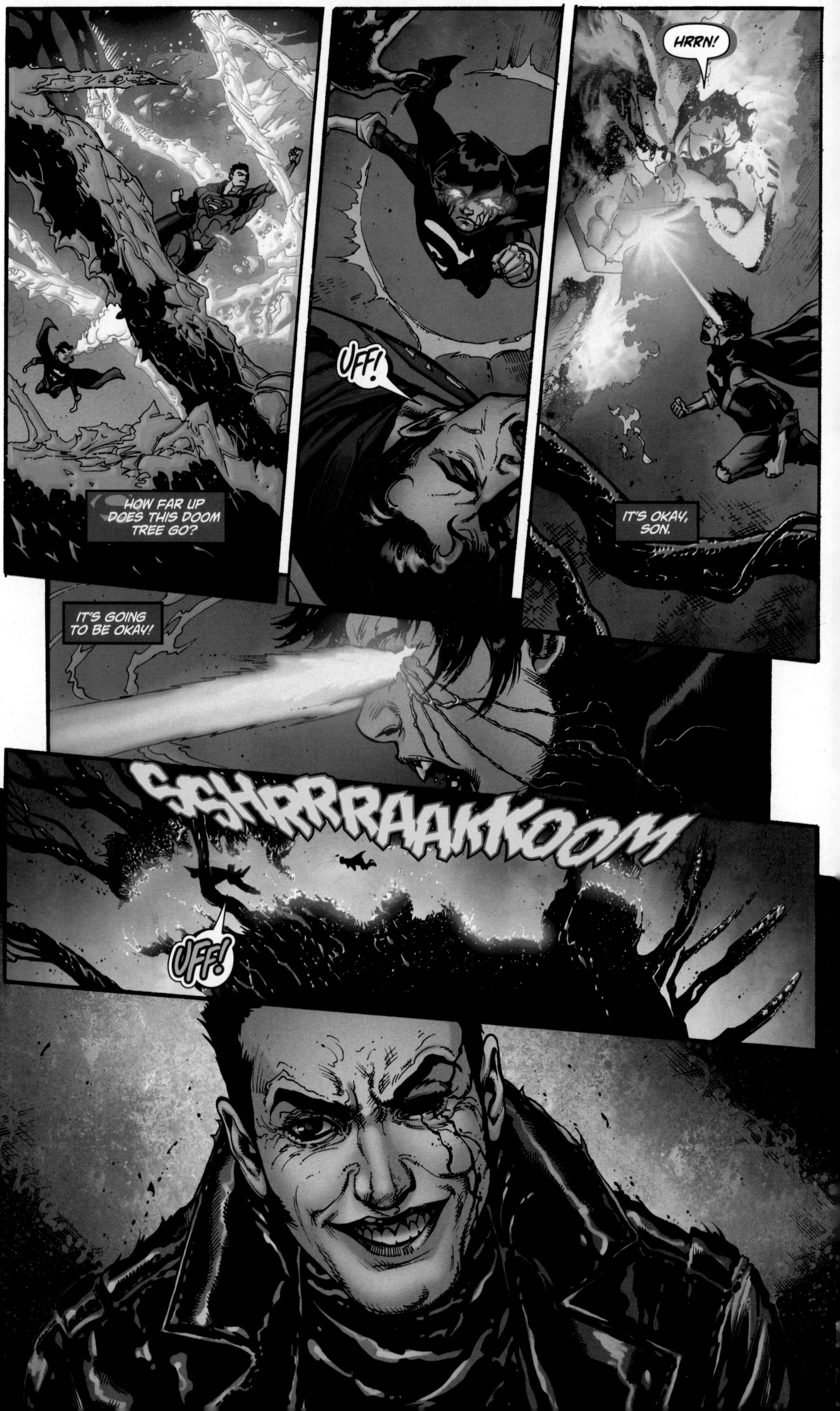
HOW FAR UP DOES THIS DOOM TREE GO?
UFF!
HRRN!
IT'S OKAY, SON.
IT'S GOING TO BE OKAY!
SSHRRRAAKKOOM
UFF!

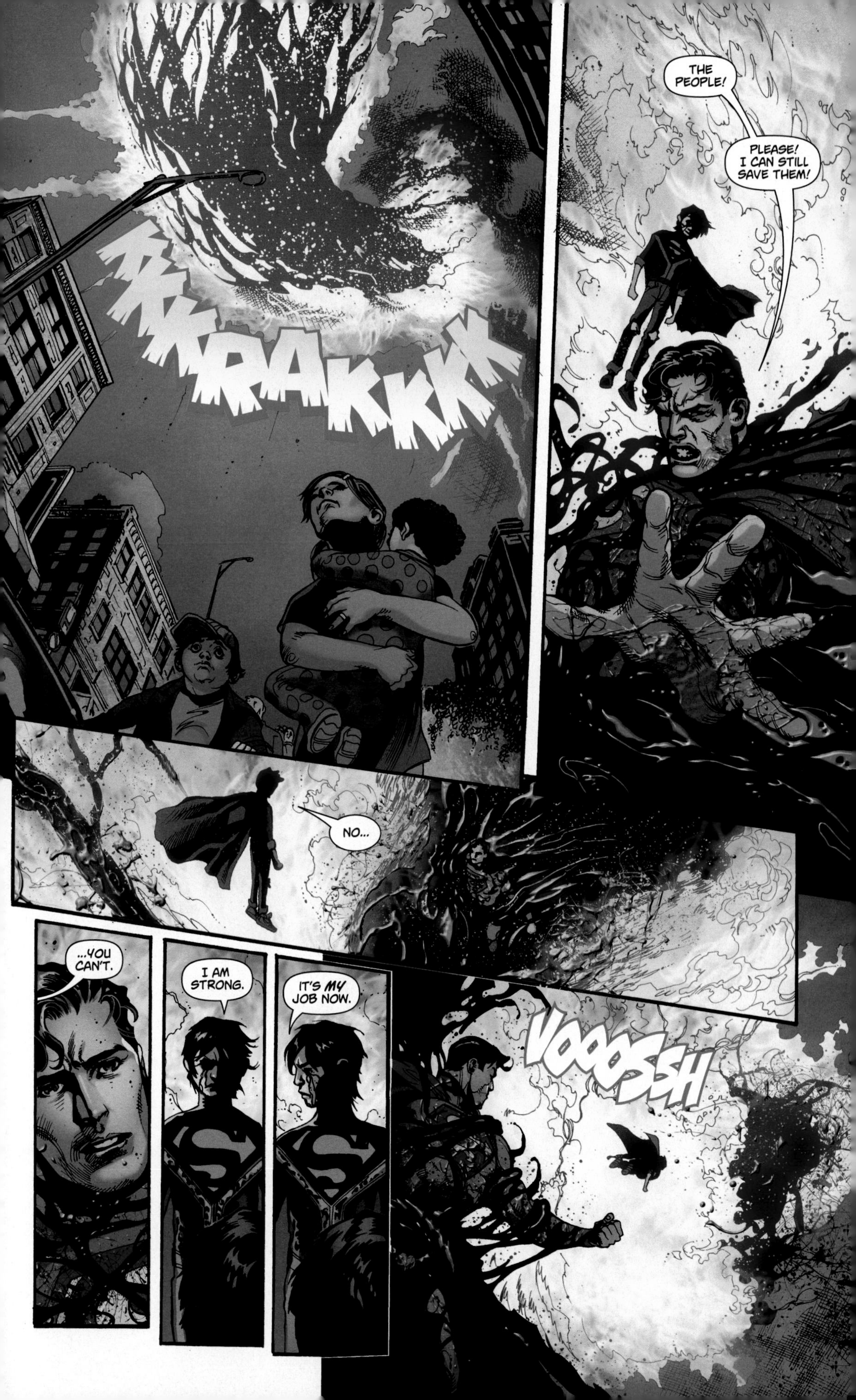
KKRAKKK
THE PEOPLE!
PLEASE! I CAN STILL SAVE THEM!
NO...
...YOU CAN'T.
I AM STRONG.
IT'S MY JOB NOW.
VOOOSSH

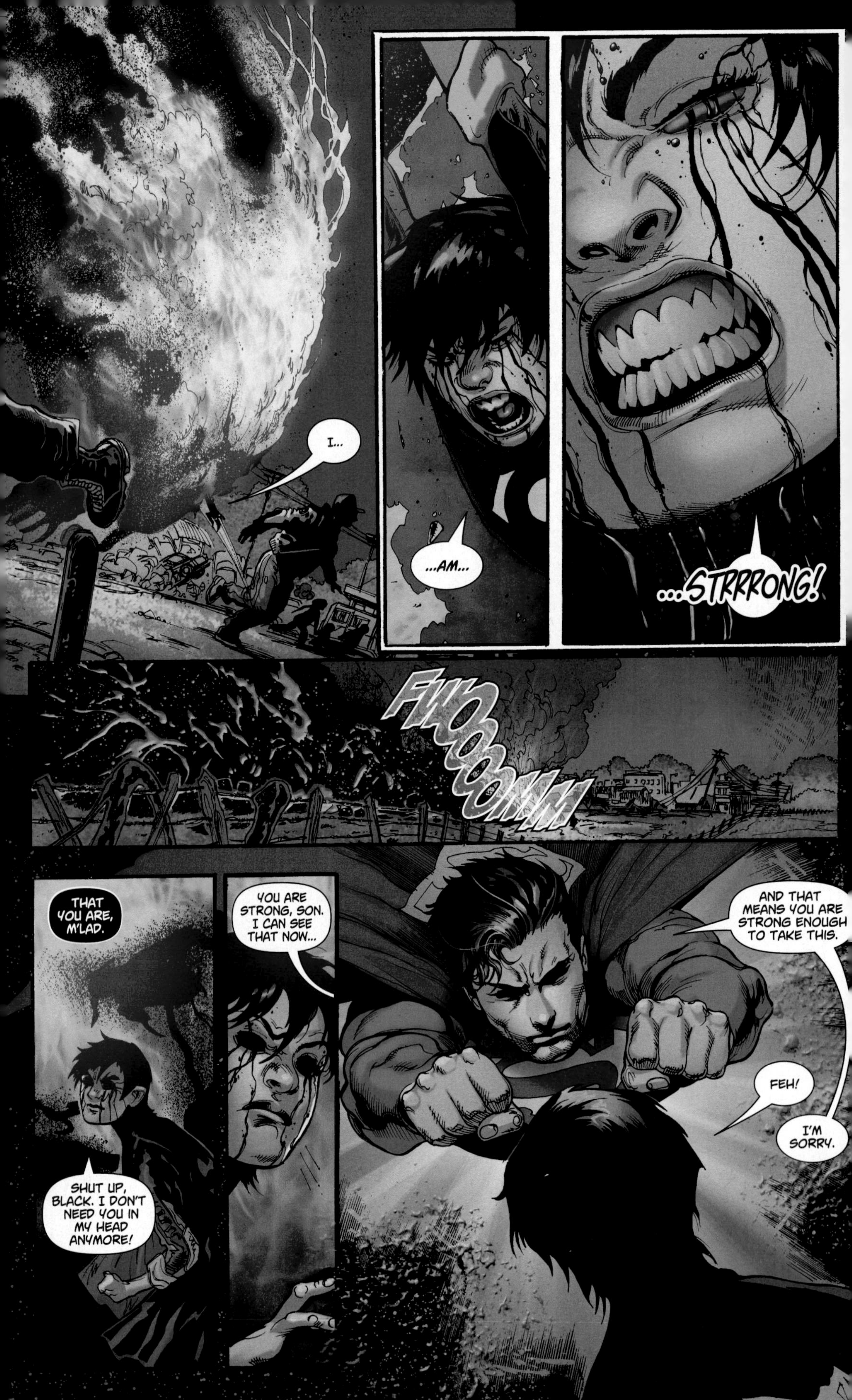
I...
...AM...
...STRRRONG!
FWOOOOMM
THAT YOU ARE, M'LAD.
SHUT UP, BLACK. I DON'T NEED YOU IN MY HEAD ANYMORE!
YOU ARE STRONG, SON. I CAN SEE THAT NOW...
AND THAT MEANS YOU ARE STRONG ENOUGH TO TAKE THIS.
FEH!
I'M SORRY.

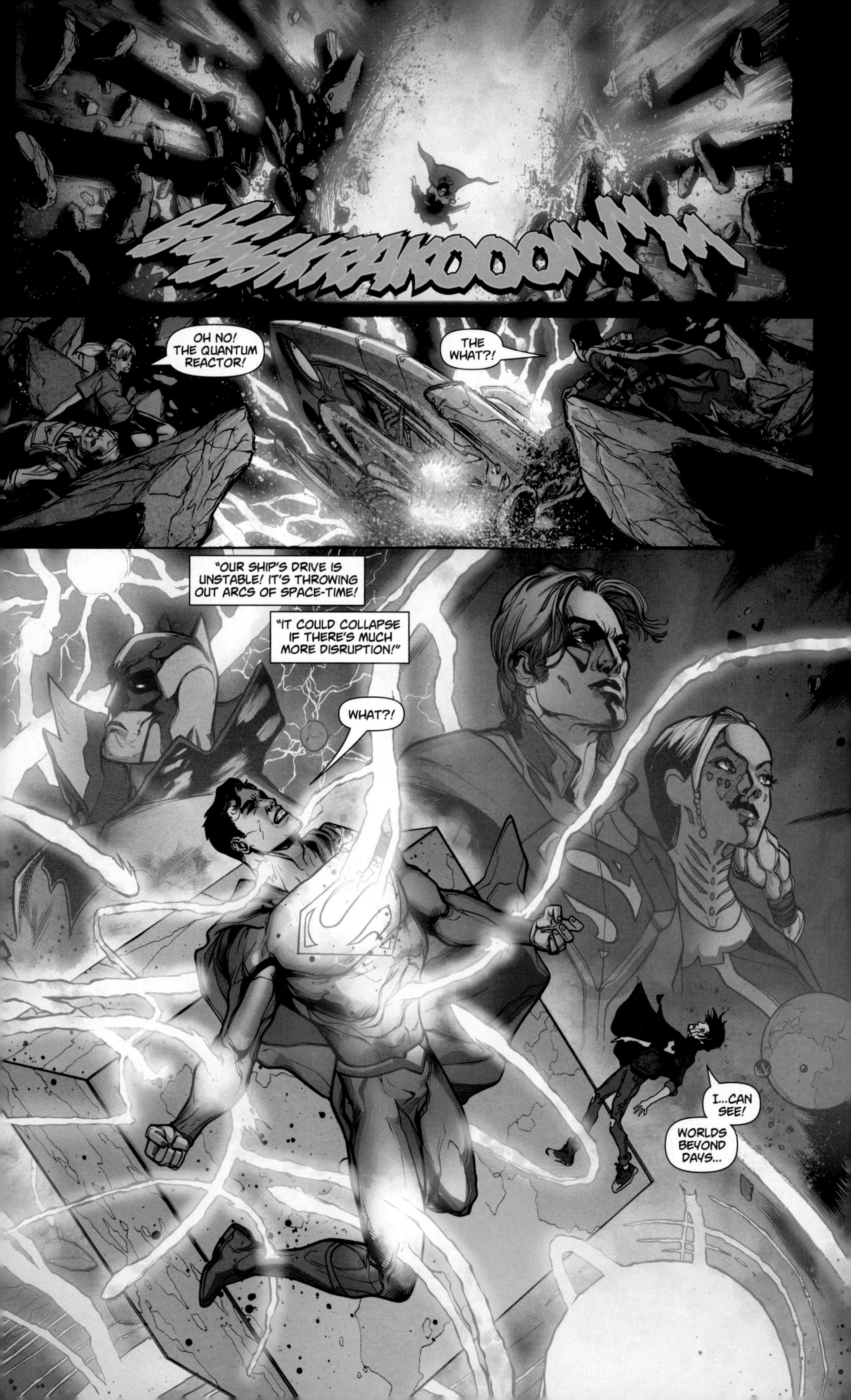
SSSSKRRAKOOOOMMM
OH NO! THE QUANTUM REACTOR!
THE WHAT?!
"OUR SHIP'S DRIVE IS UNSTABLE! IT'S THROWING OUT ARCS OF SPACE-TIME!
"IT COULD COLLAPSE IF THERE'S MUCH MORE DISRUPTION!"
WHAT?!
I...CAN SEE!
WORLDS BEYOND DAYS...

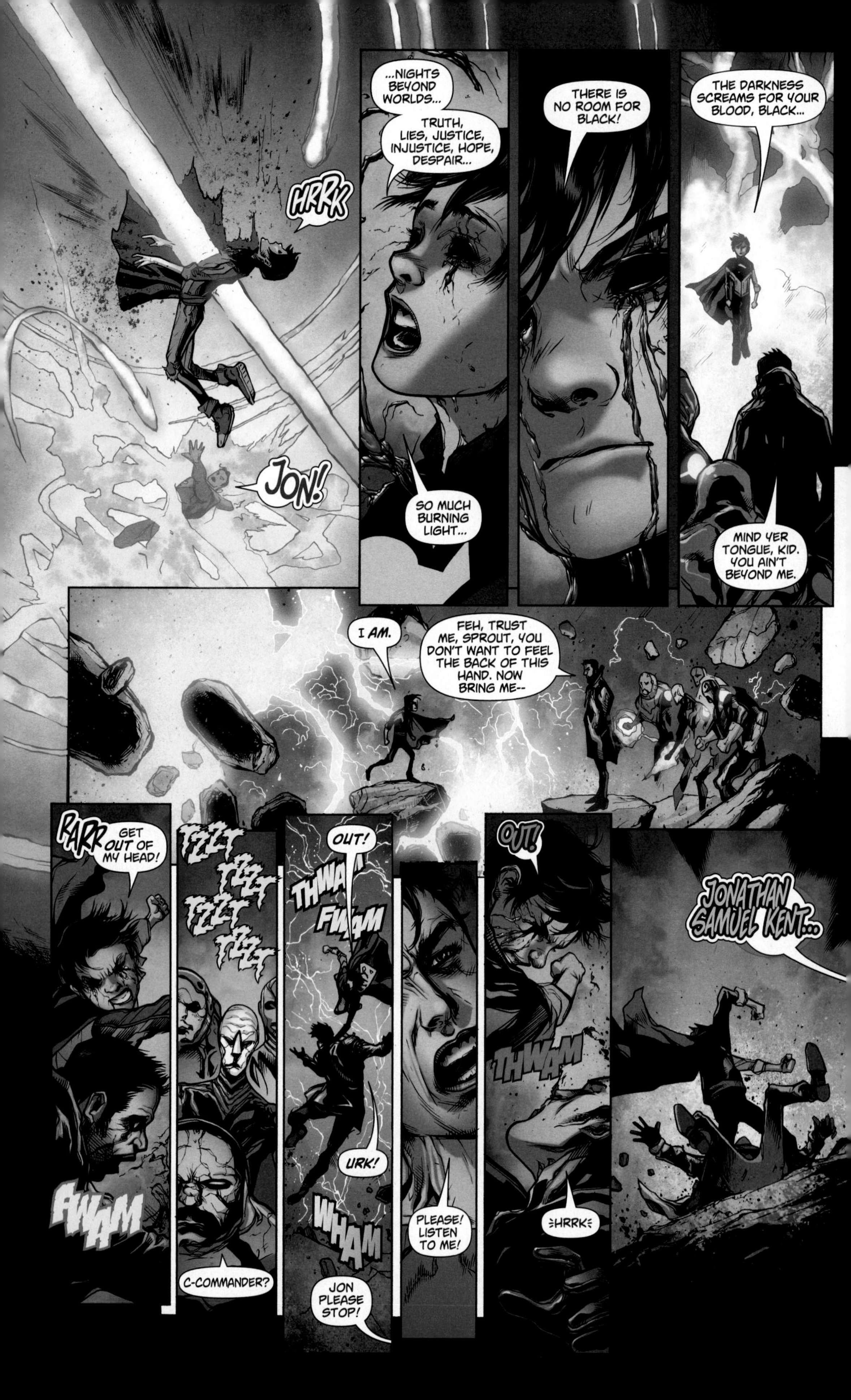

HRRK
JON!
...NIGHTS BEYOND WORLDS...
TRUTH, LIES, JUSTICE, INJUSTICE, HOPE, DESPAIR...
SO MUCH BURNING LIGHT...
THERE IS NO ROOM FOR BLACK!
THE DARKNESS SCREAMS FOR YOUR BLOOD, BLACK...
MIND YER TONGUE, KID. YOU AIN'T BEYOND ME.
I AM.
FEH, TRUST ME, SPROUT, YOU DON'T WANT TO FEEL THE BACK OF THIS HAND. NOW BRING ME--
RARR
GET OUT OF MY HEAD!
FWAM
TZZT TZZT TZZT TZZT
C-COMMANDER?
OUT!
THWAM
FWAM
URK!
WHAM
JON PLEASE STOP!
PLEASE! LISTEN TO ME!
OUT!
THWAM
HRRK
JONATHAN SAMUEL KENT...

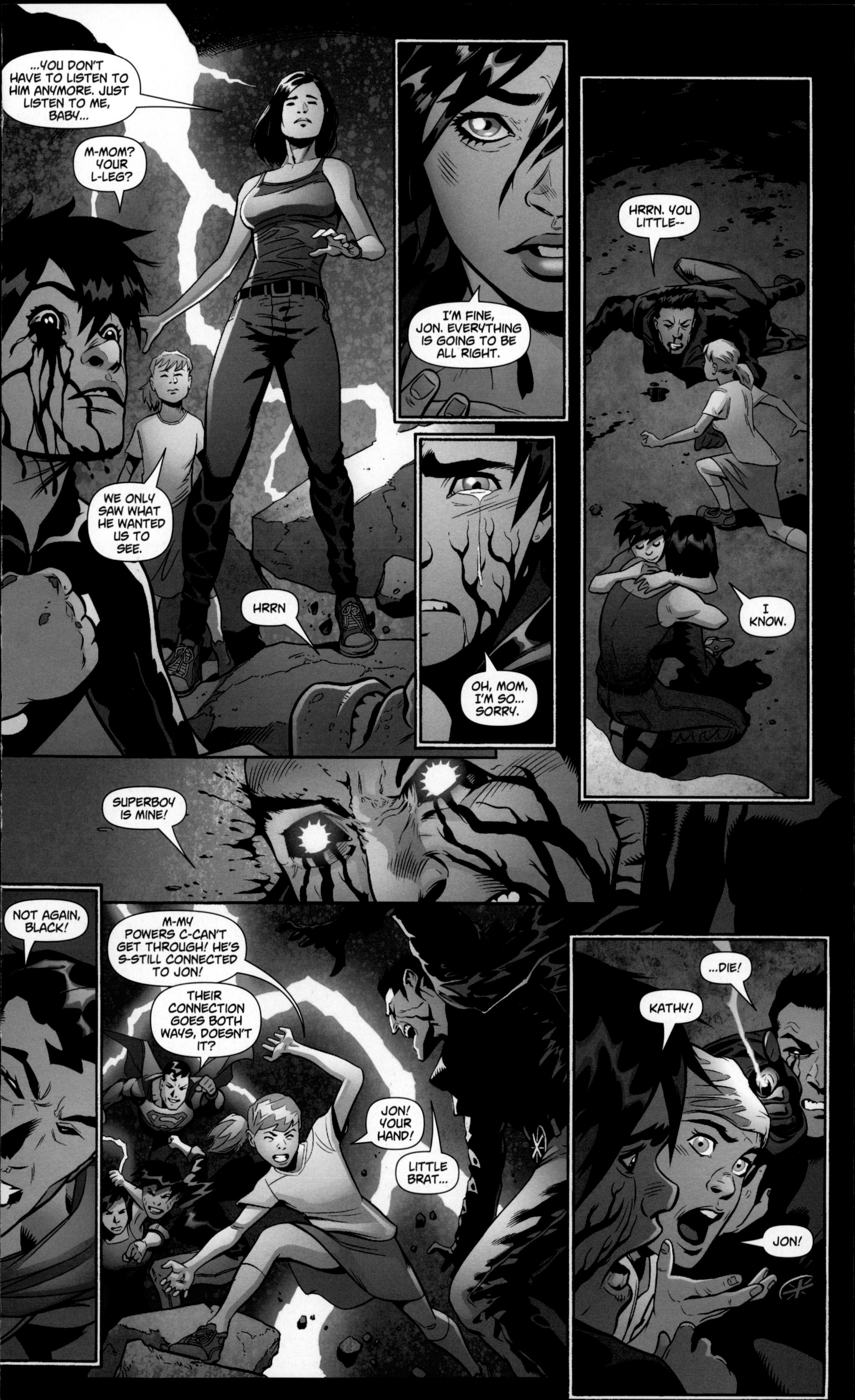
...YOU DON'T HAVE TO LISTEN TO HIM ANYMORE. JUST LISTEN TO ME, BABY...
M-MOM? YOUR L-LEG?
WE ONLY SAW WHAT HE WANTED US TO SEE.
HRRN
I'M FINE, JON. EVERYTHING IS GOING TO BE ALL RIGHT.
OH, MOM, I'M SO... SORRY.
HRRN. YOU LITTLE--
I KNOW.
SUPERBOY IS MINE!
NOT AGAIN, BLACK!
M-MY POWERS C-CAN'T GET THROUGH! HE'S S-STILL CONNECTED TO JON!
THEIR CONNECTION GOES BOTH WAYS, DOESN'T IT?
JON! YOUR HAND!
LITTLE BRAT...
...DIE!
KATHY!
JON!

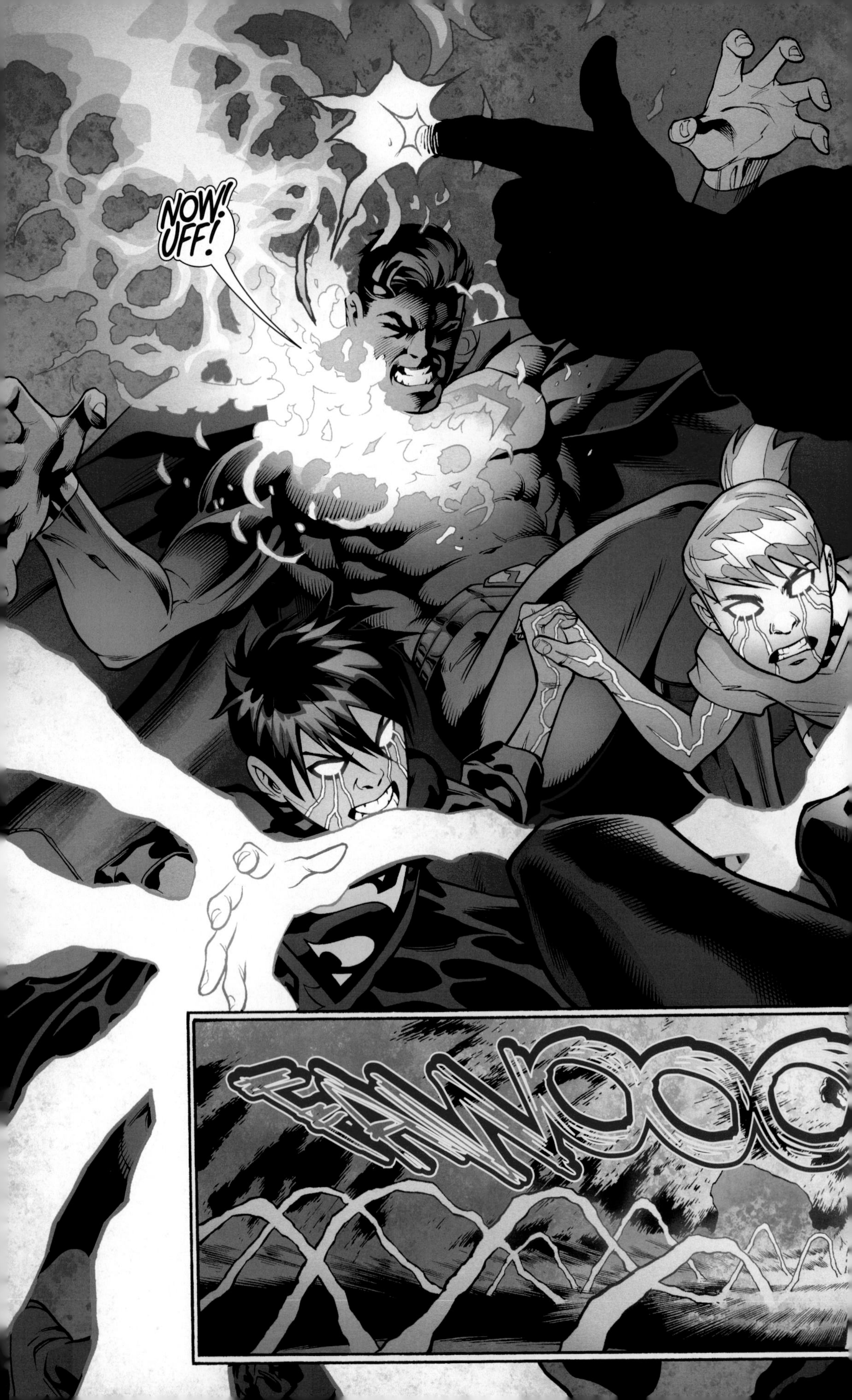
NOW! UFF!
THWOOO

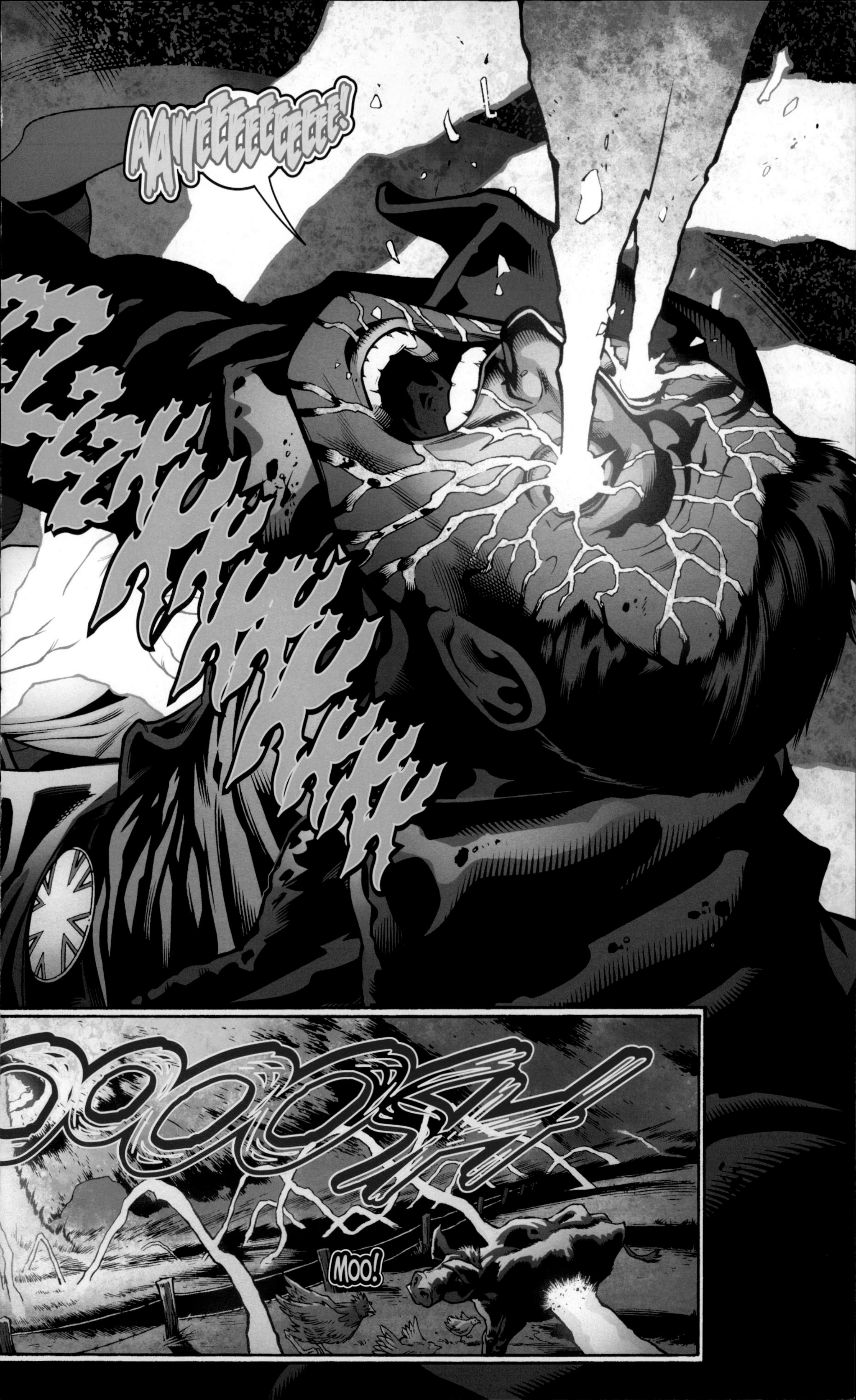
AAIIEEEEEEEEEE!
MOO!

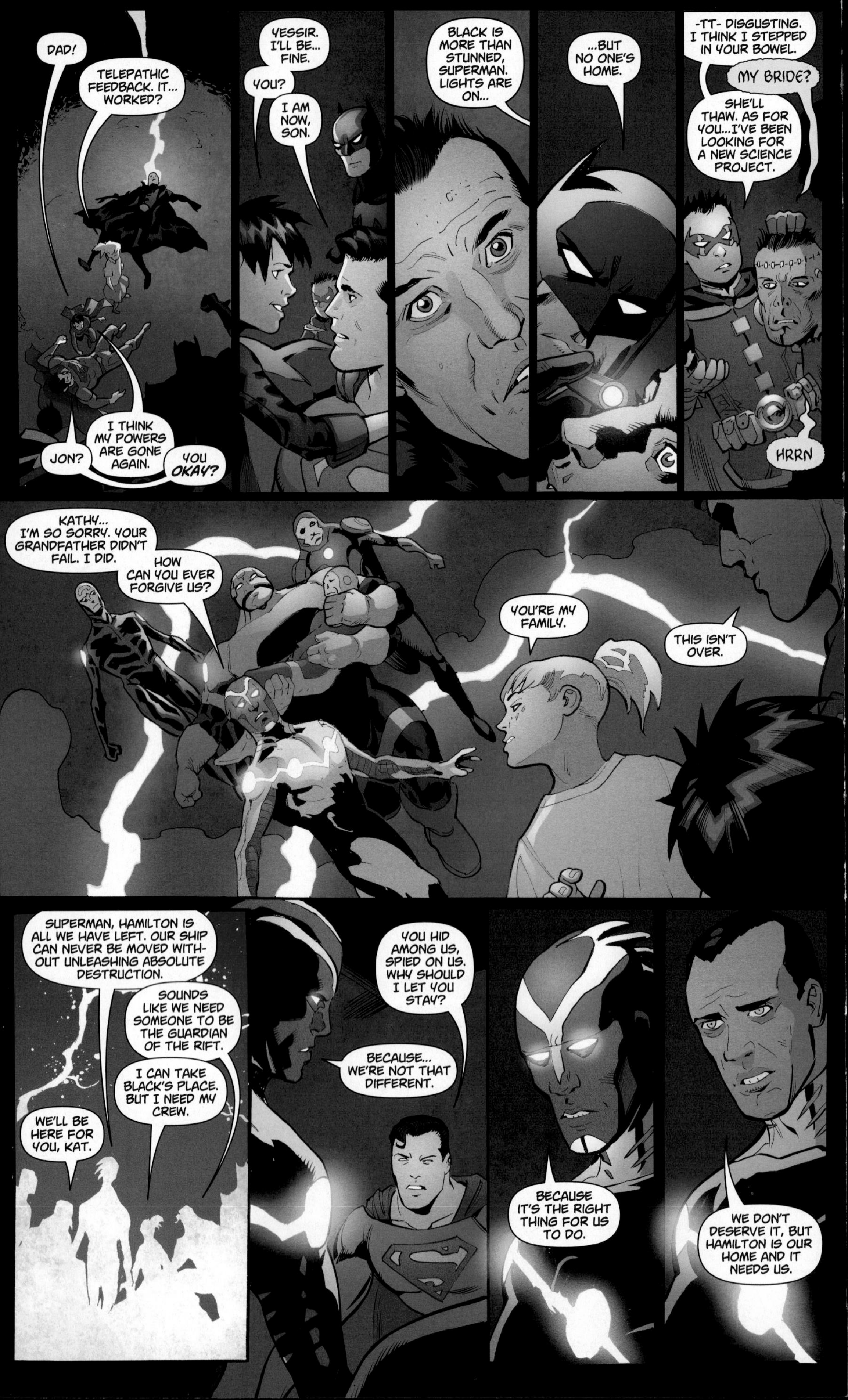
DAD!
TELEPATHIC FEEDBACK. IT... WORKED?
JON?
I THINK MY POWERS ARE GONE AGAIN.
YOU OKAY?
YESSIR. I'LL BE... FINE.
YOU?
I AM NOW, SON.
BLACK IS MORE THAN STUNNED, SUPERMAN. LIGHTS ARE ON...
...BUT NO ONE'S HOME.
-TT- DISGUSTING. I THINK I STEPPED IN YOUR BOWEL.
MY BRIDE?
SHE'LL THAW. AS FOR YOU...I'VE BEEN LOOKING FOR A NEW SCIENCE PROJECT.
HRRN
KATHY... I'M SO SORRY. YOUR GRANDFATHER DIDN'T FAIL. I DID.
HOW CAN YOU EVER FORGIVE US?
YOU'RE MY FAMILY.
THIS ISN'T OVER.
SUPERMAN, HAMILTON IS ALL WE HAVE LEFT. OUR SHIP CAN NEVER BE MOVED WITH-OUT UNLEASHING ABSOLUTE DESTRUCTION.
SOUNDS LIKE WE NEED SOMEONE TO BE THE GUARDIAN OF THE RIFT.
I CAN TAKE BLACK'S PLACE. BUT I NEED MY CREW.
WE'LL BE HERE FOR YOU, KAT.
YOU HID AMONG US, SPIED ON US. WHY SHOULD I LET YOU STAY?
BECAUSE... WE'RE NOT THAT DIFFERENT.
BECAUSE IT'S THE RIGHT THING FOR US TO DO.
WE DON'T DESERVE IT, BUT HAMILTON IS OUR HOME AND IT NEEDS US.

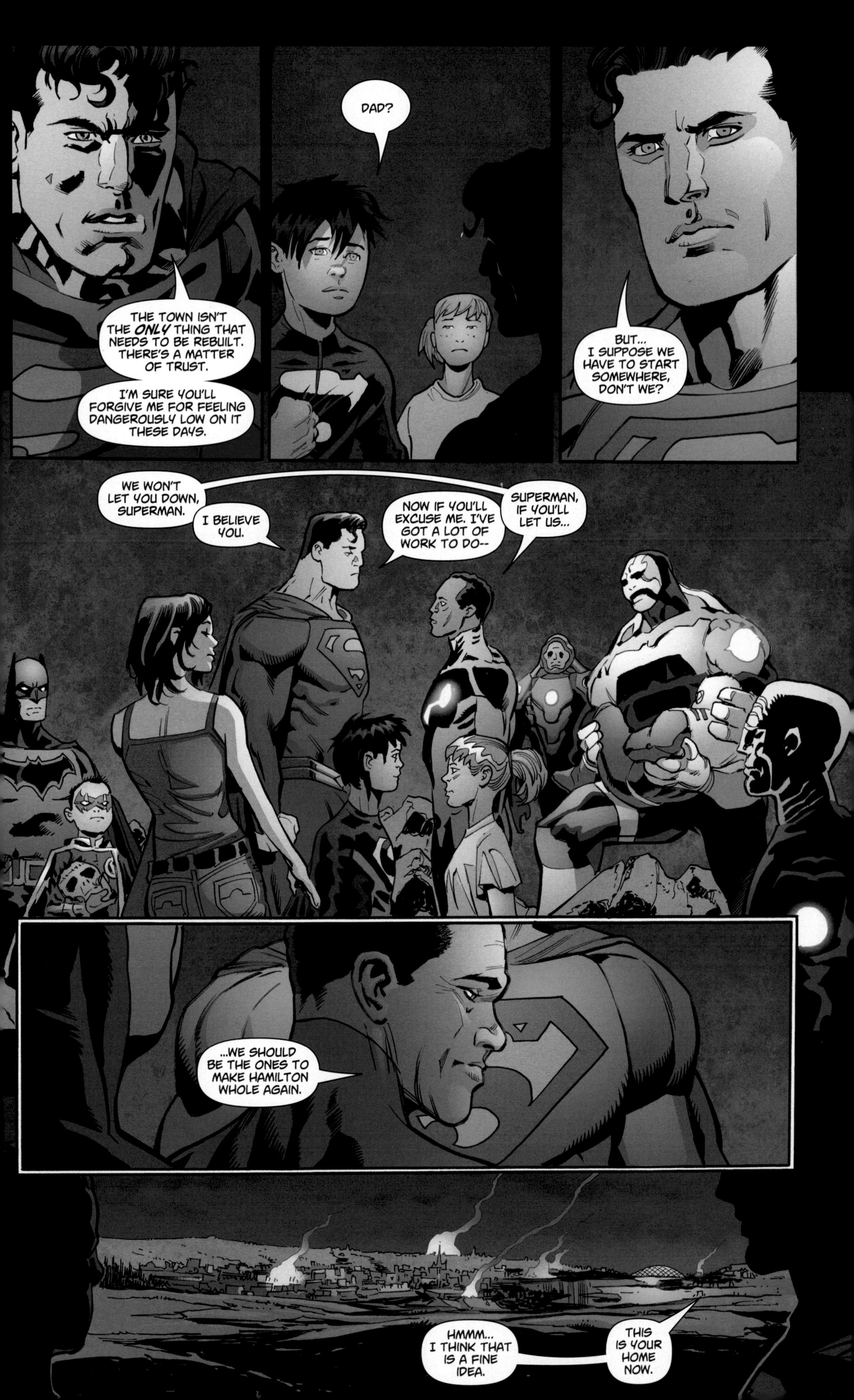
THE TOWN ISN'T THE ONLY THING THAT NEEDS TO BE REBUILT. THERE'S A MATTER OF TRUST.
I'M SURE YOU'LL FORGIVE ME FOR FEELING DANGEROUSLY LOW ON IT THESE DAYS.
DAD?
BUT... I SUPPOSE WE HAVE TO START SOMEWHERE, DON'T WE?
WE WON'T LET YOU DOWN, SUPERMAN.
I BELIEVE YOU.
NOW IF YOU'LL EXCUSE ME. I'VE GOT A LOT OF WORK TO DO--
SUPERMAN, IF YOU'LL LET US...
...WE SHOULD BE THE ONES TO MAKE HAMILTON WHOLE AGAIN.
HMMM... I THINK THAT IS A FINE IDEA.
THIS IS YOUR HOME NOW.

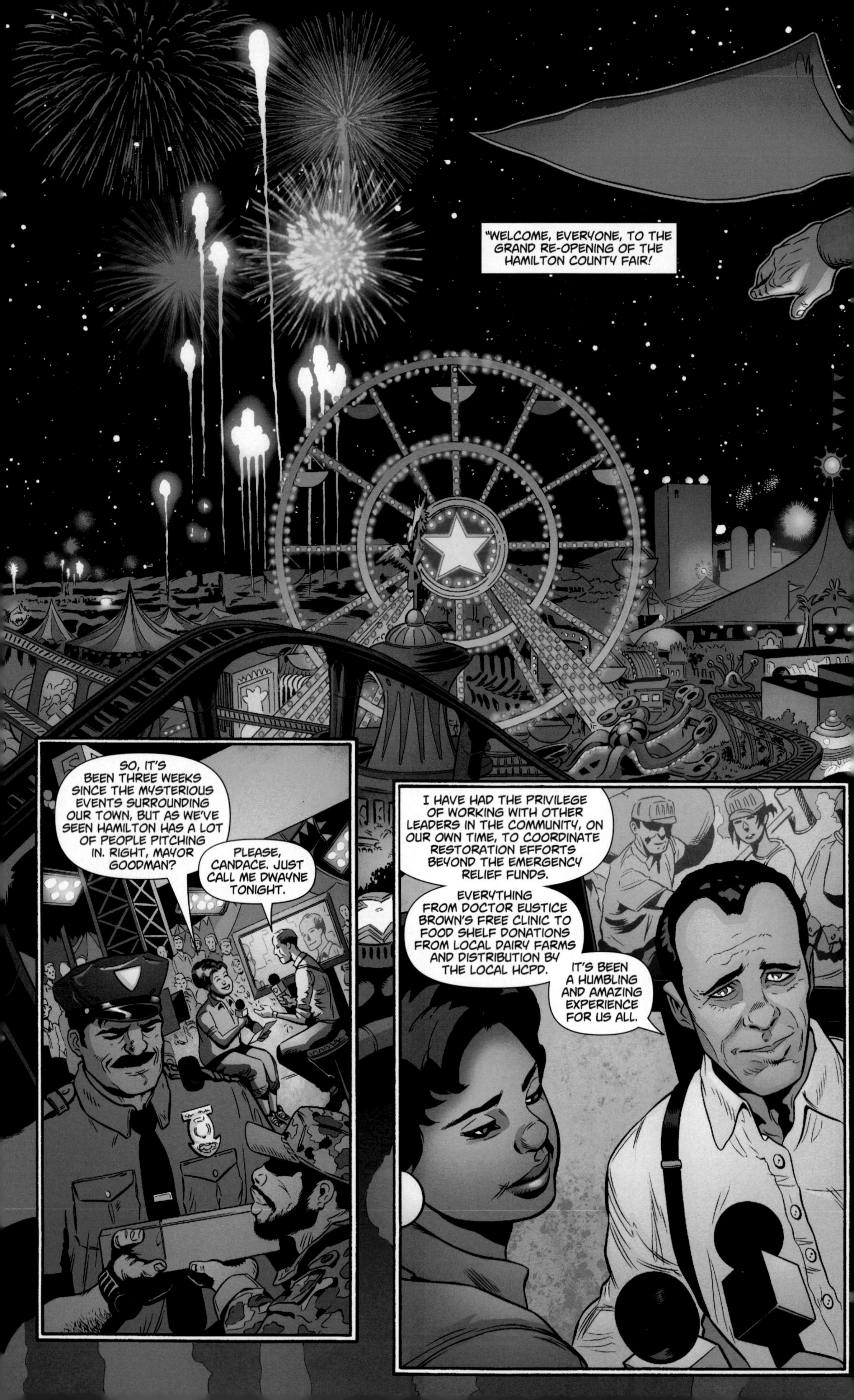
"WELCOME, EVERYONE, TO THE GRAND RE-OPENING OF THE HAMILTON COUNTY FAIR!
SO, IT'S BEEN THREE WEEKS SINCE THE MYSTERIOUS EVENTS SURROUNDING OUR TOWN, BUT AS WE'VE SEEN HAMILTON HAS A LOT OF PEOPLE PITCHING IN. RIGHT, MAYOR GOODMAN?
PLEASE, CANDACE. JUST CALL ME DWAYNE TONIGHT.
I HAVE HAD THE PRIVILEGE OF WORKING WITH OTHER LEADERS IN THE COMMUNITY, ON OUR OWN TIME, TO COORDINATE RESTORATION EFFORTS BEYOND THE EMERGENCY RELIEF FUNDS.
EVERYTHING FROM DOCTOR EUSTICE BROWN'S FREE CLINIC TO FOOD SHELF DONATIONS FROM LOCAL DAIRY FARMS AND DISTRIBUTION BY THE LOCAL HCPD.
IT'S BEEN A HUMBLING AND AMAZING EXPERIENCE FOR US ALL.

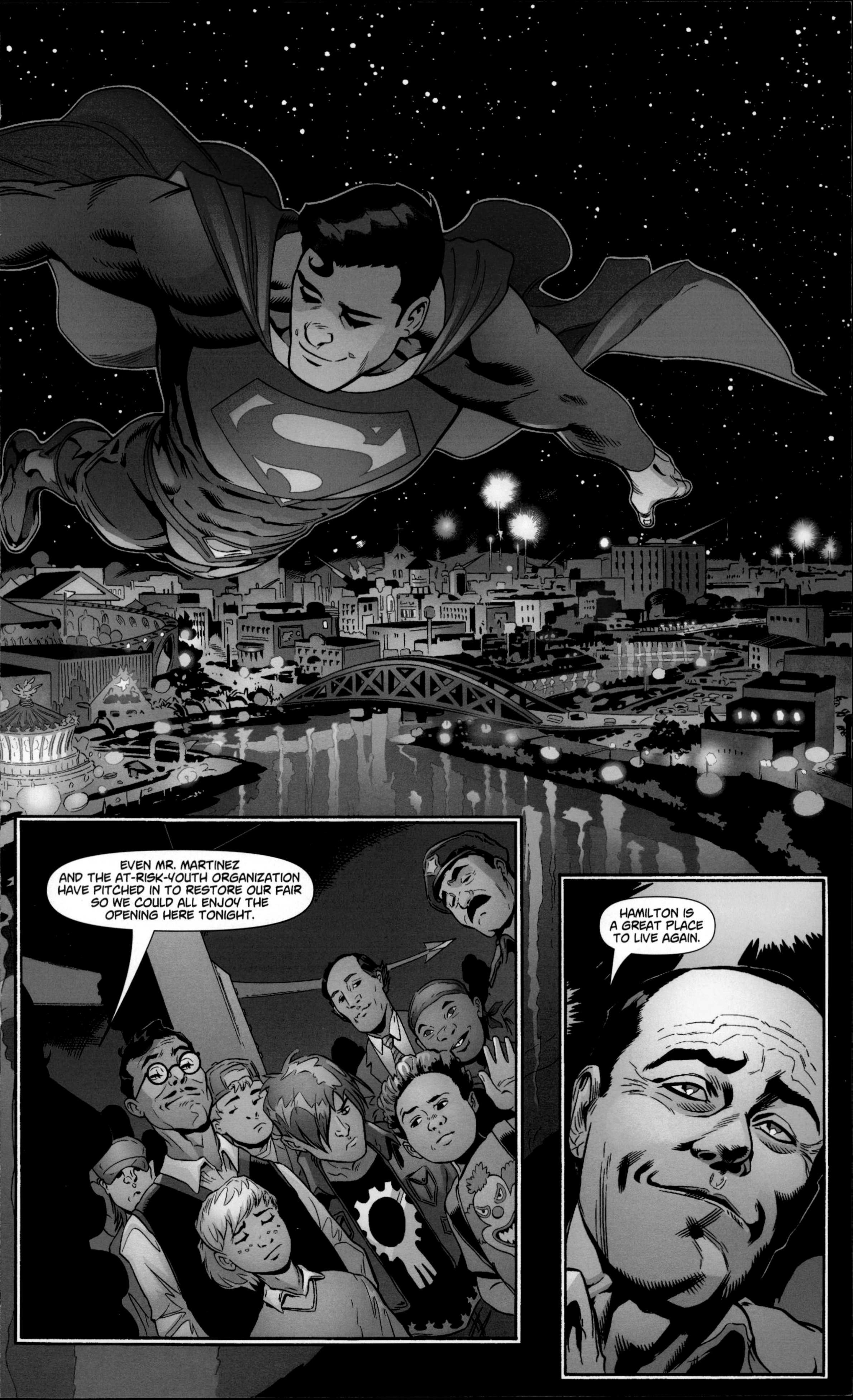
EVEN MR. MARTINEZ AND THE AT-RISK-YOUTH ORGANIZATION HAVE PITCHED IN TO RESTORE OUR FAIR SO WE COULD ALL ENJOY THE OPENING HERE TONIGHT.
HAMILTON IS A GREAT PLACE TO LIVE AGAIN.

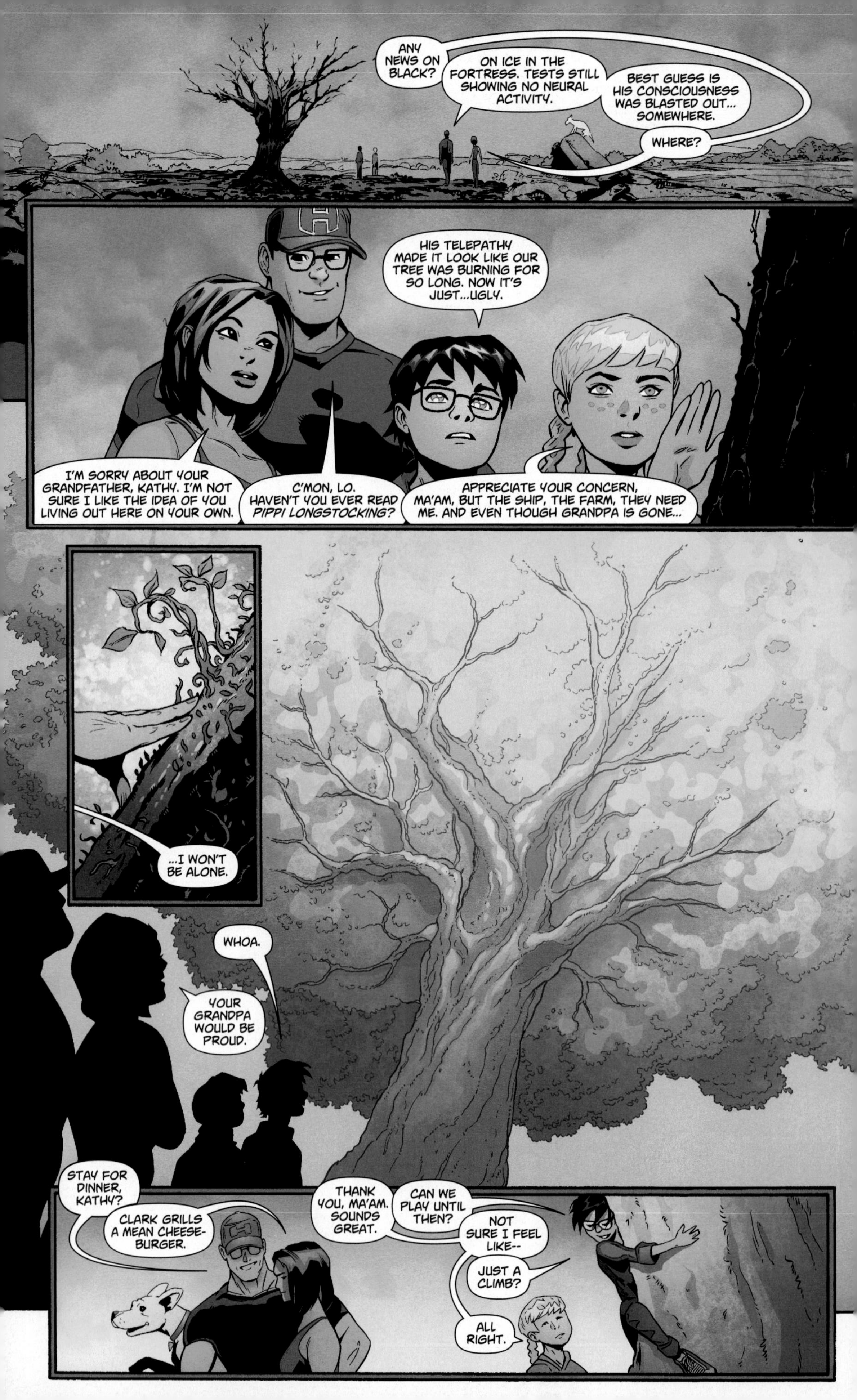
ANY NEWS ON BLACK?
ON ICE IN THE FORTRESS. TESTS STILL SHOWING NO NEURAL ACTIVITY.
BEST GUESS IS HIS CONSCIOUSNESS WAS BLASTED OUT... SOMEWHERE.
WHERE?
HIS TELEPATHY MADE IT LOOK LIKE OUR TREE WAS BURNING FOR SO LONG. NOW IT'S JUST...UGLY.
I'M SORRY ABOUT YOUR GRANDFATHER, KATHY. I'M NOT SURE I LIKE THE IDEA OF YOU LIVING OUT HERE ON YOUR OWN.
C'MON, LO. HAVEN'T YOU EVER READ *PIPPI LONGSTOCKING*?
APPRECIATE YOUR CONCERN, MA'AM, BUT THE SHIP, THE FARM, THEY NEED ME. AND EVEN THOUGH GRANDPA IS GONE...
...I WON'T BE ALONE.
WHOA.
YOUR GRANDPA WOULD BE PROUD.
STAY FOR DINNER, KATHY?
CLARK GRILLS A MEAN CHEESE-BURGER.
THANK YOU, MA'AM. SOUNDS GREAT.
CAN WE PLAY UNTIL THEN?
NOT SURE I FEEL LIKE--
JUST A CLIMB?
ALL RIGHT.

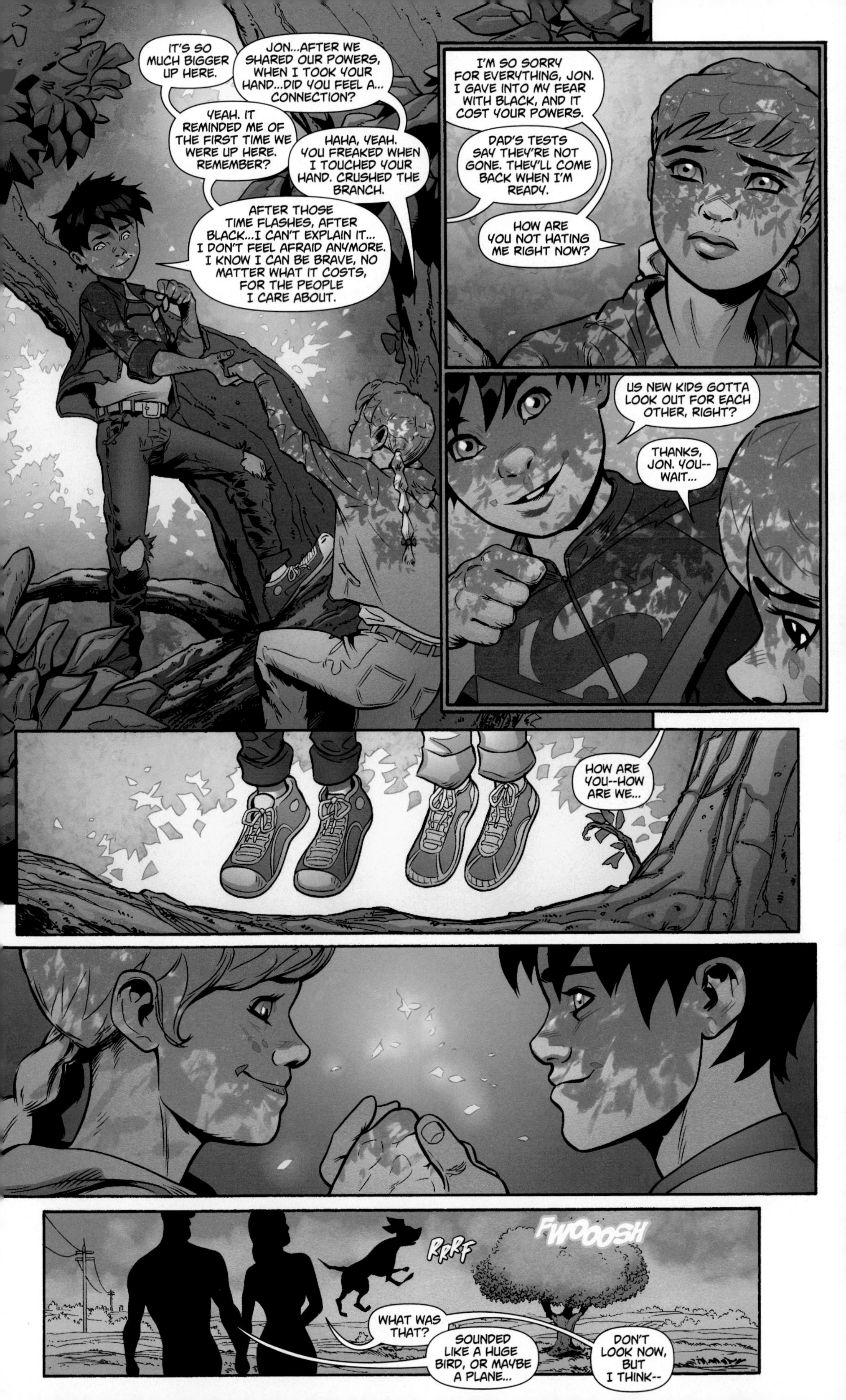
IT'S SO MUCH BIGGER UP HERE.
JON...AFTER WE SHARED OUR POWERS, WHEN I TOOK YOUR HAND...DID YOU FEEL A... CONNECTION?
YEAH. IT REMINDED ME OF THE FIRST TIME WE WERE UP HERE. REMEMBER?
HAHA, YEAH. YOU FREAKED WHEN I TOUCHED YOUR HAND. CRUSHED THE BRANCH.
AFTER THOSE TIME FLASHES, AFTER BLACK...I CAN'T EXPLAIN IT... I DON'T FEEL AFRAID ANYMORE. I KNOW I CAN BE BRAVE, NO MATTER WHAT IT COSTS, FOR THE PEOPLE I CARE ABOUT.
I'M SO SORRY FOR EVERYTHING, JON. I GAVE INTO MY FEAR WITH BLACK, AND IT COST YOUR POWERS.
DAD'S TESTS SAY THEY'RE NOT GONE. THEY'LL COME BACK WHEN I'M READY.
HOW ARE YOU NOT HATING ME RIGHT NOW?
US NEW KIDS GOTTA LOOK OUT FOR EACH OTHER, RIGHT?
THANKS, JON. YOU-- WAIT...
HOW ARE YOU--HOW ARE WE...
RRRF
FWOOOSH
WHAT WAS THAT?
SOUNDED LIKE A HUGE BIRD, OR MAYBE A PLANE...
DON'T LOOK NOW, BUT I THINK--

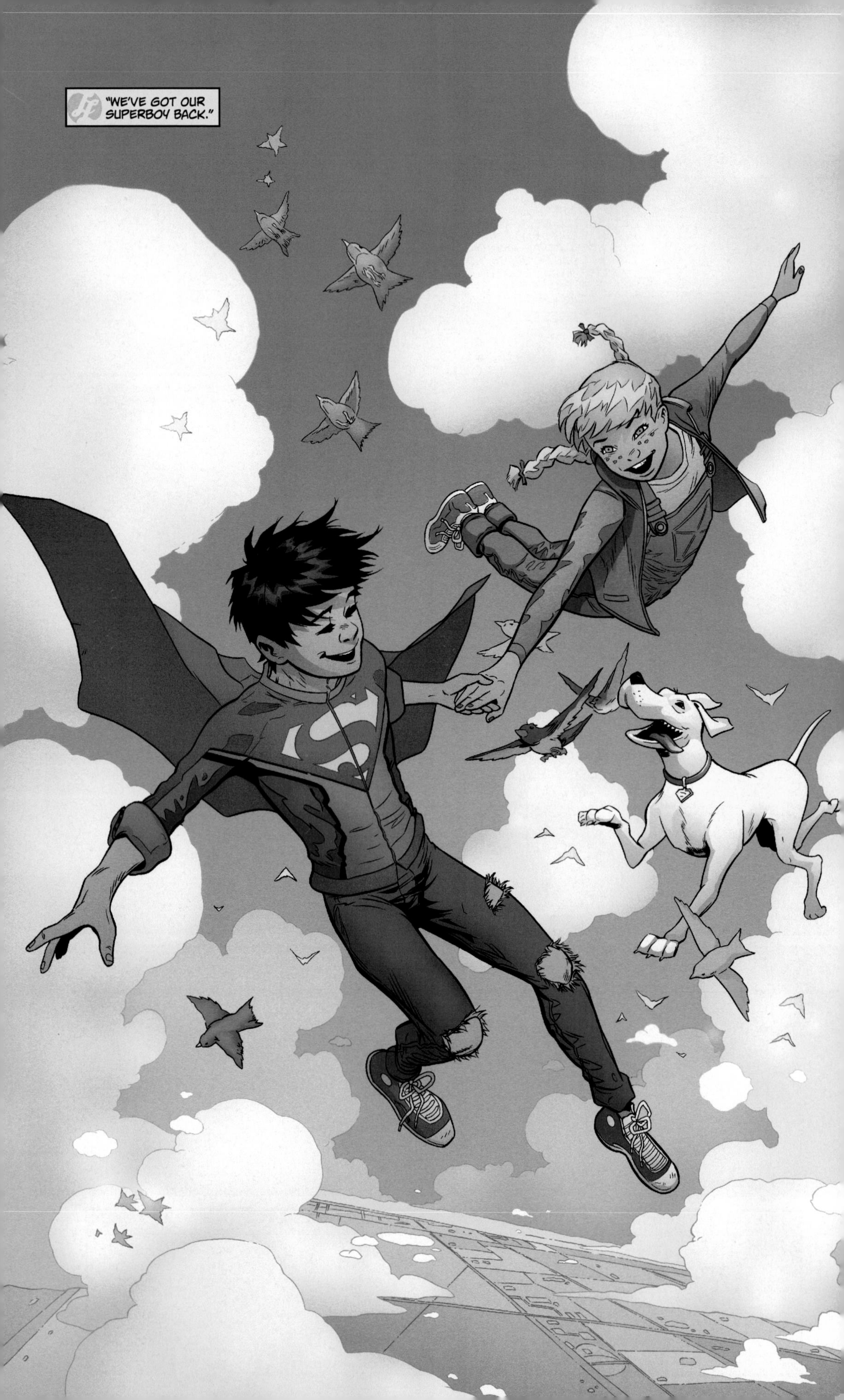
"WE'VE GOT OUR SUPERBOY BACK."

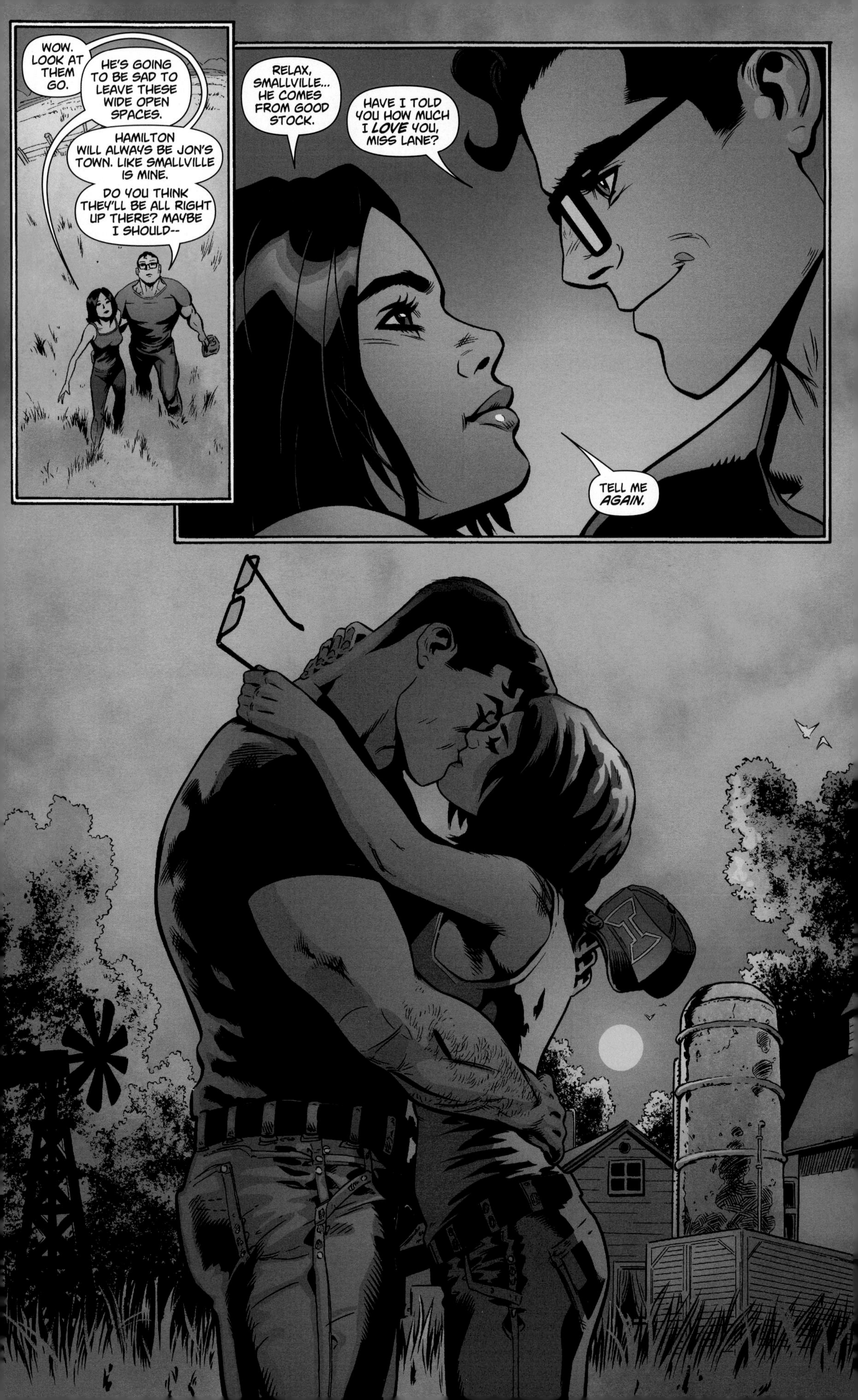

WOW. LOOK AT THEM GO.
HE'S GOING TO BE SAD TO LEAVE THESE WIDE OPEN SPACES.
HAMILTON WILL ALWAYS BE JON'S TOWN. LIKE SMALLVILLE IS MINE.
DO YOU THINK THEY'LL BE ALL RIGHT UP THERE? MAYBE I SHOULD--
RELAX, SMALLVILLE... HE COMES FROM GOOD STOCK.
HAVE I TOLD YOU HOW MUCH I LOVE YOU, MISS LANE?
TELL ME AGAIN.

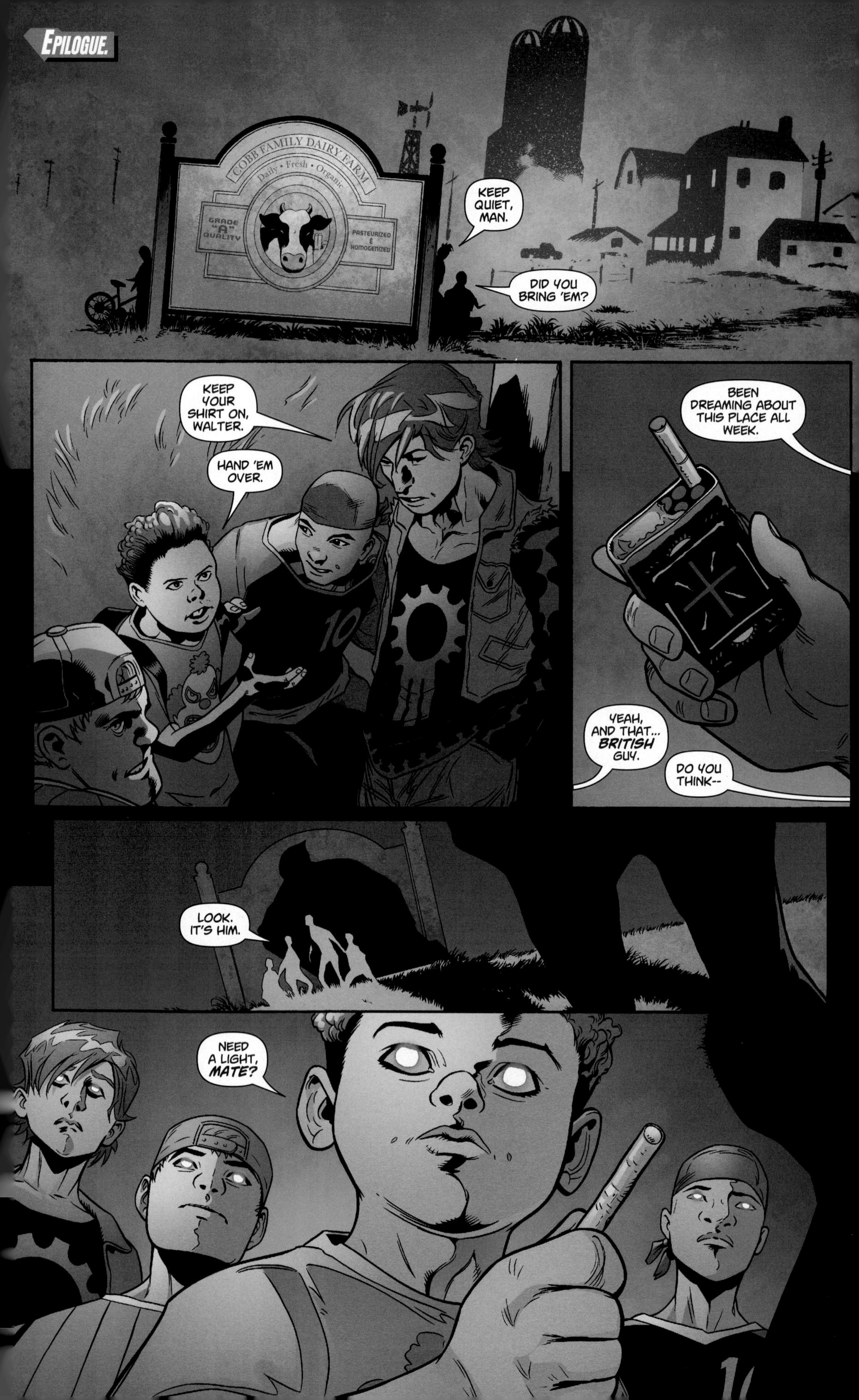
EPILOGUE.
COBB FAMILY DAIRY FARM
Daily • Fresh • Organic
GRADE "A" QUALITY
PASTEURIZED & HOMOGENIZED
KEEP QUIET, MAN.
DID YOU BRING 'EM?
KEEP YOUR SHIRT ON, WALTER.
HAND 'EM OVER.
BEEN DREAMING ABOUT THIS PLACE ALL WEEK.
YEAH, AND THAT... BRITISH GUY.
DO YOU THINK--
LOOK. IT'S HIM.
NEED A LIGHT, MATE?

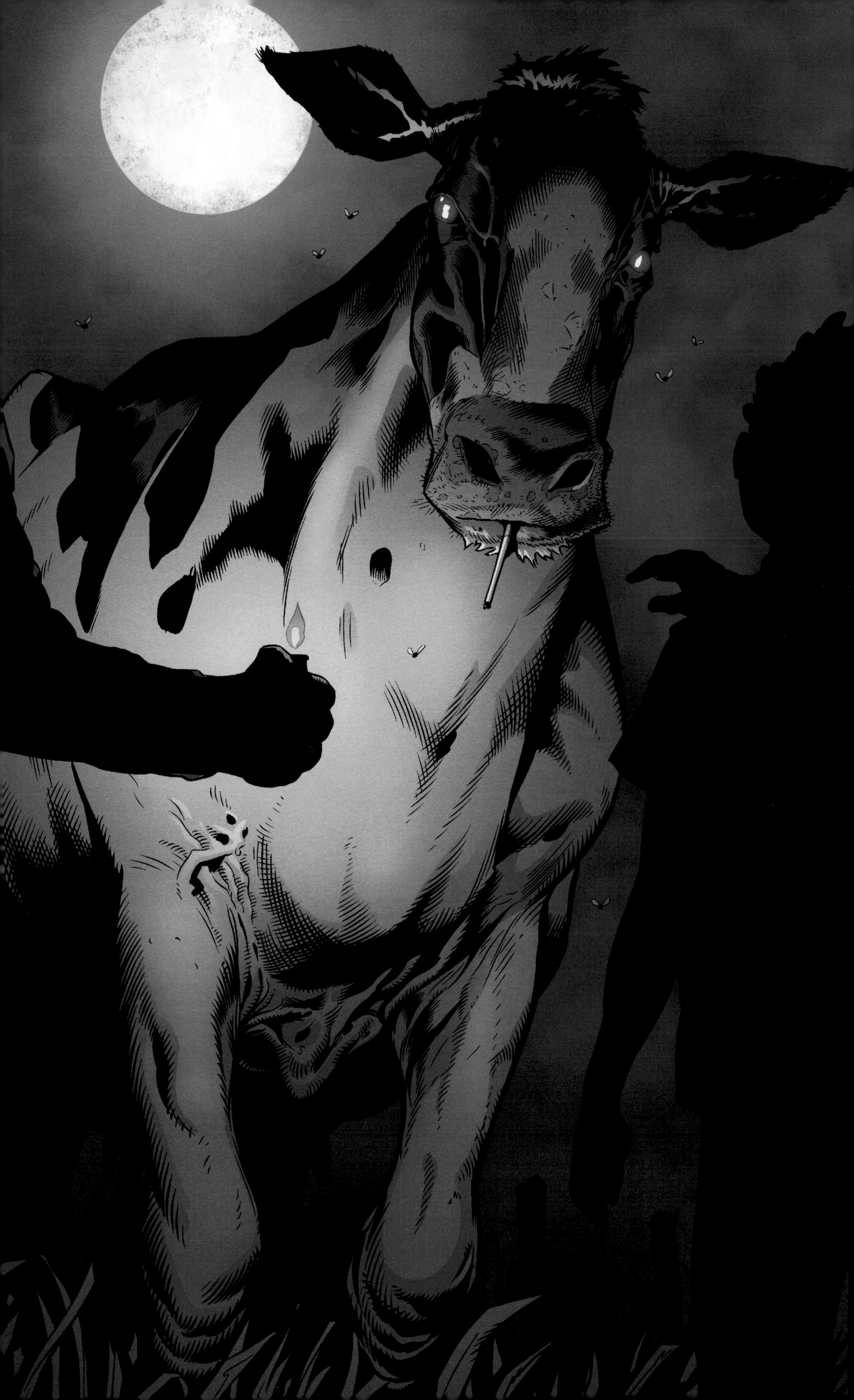

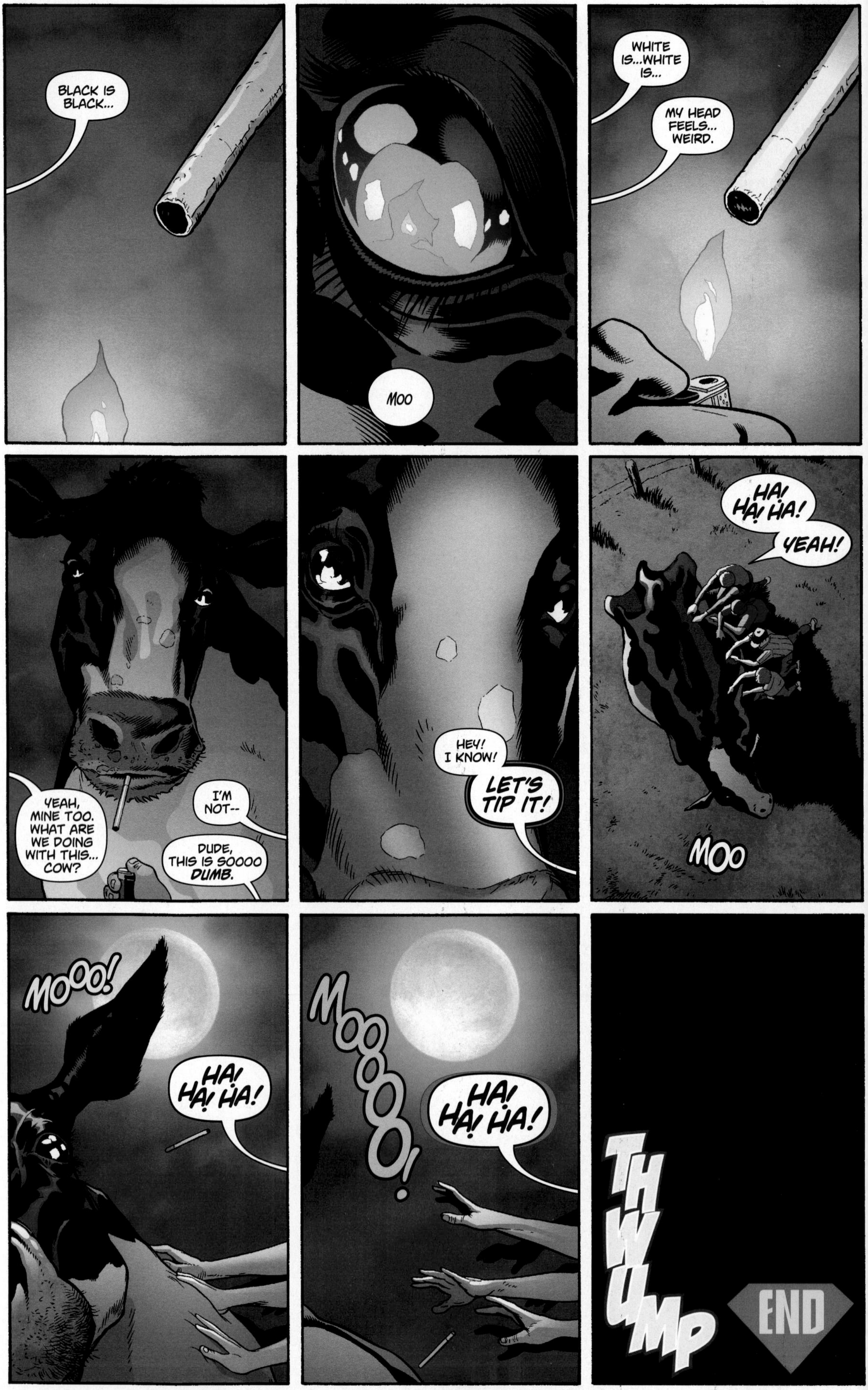
BLACK IS BLACK...
MOO
WHITE IS...WHITE IS...
MY HEAD FEELS... WEIRD.
YEAH, MINE TOO. WHAT ARE WE DOING WITH THIS... COW?
I'M NOT--
DUDE, THIS IS SOOOO DUMB.
HEY! I KNOW! LET'S TIP IT!
HA! HA! HA!
YEAH!
MOO
MOOO!
HA! HA! HA!
MOOOOO!
HA! HA! HA!
THWUMP
END

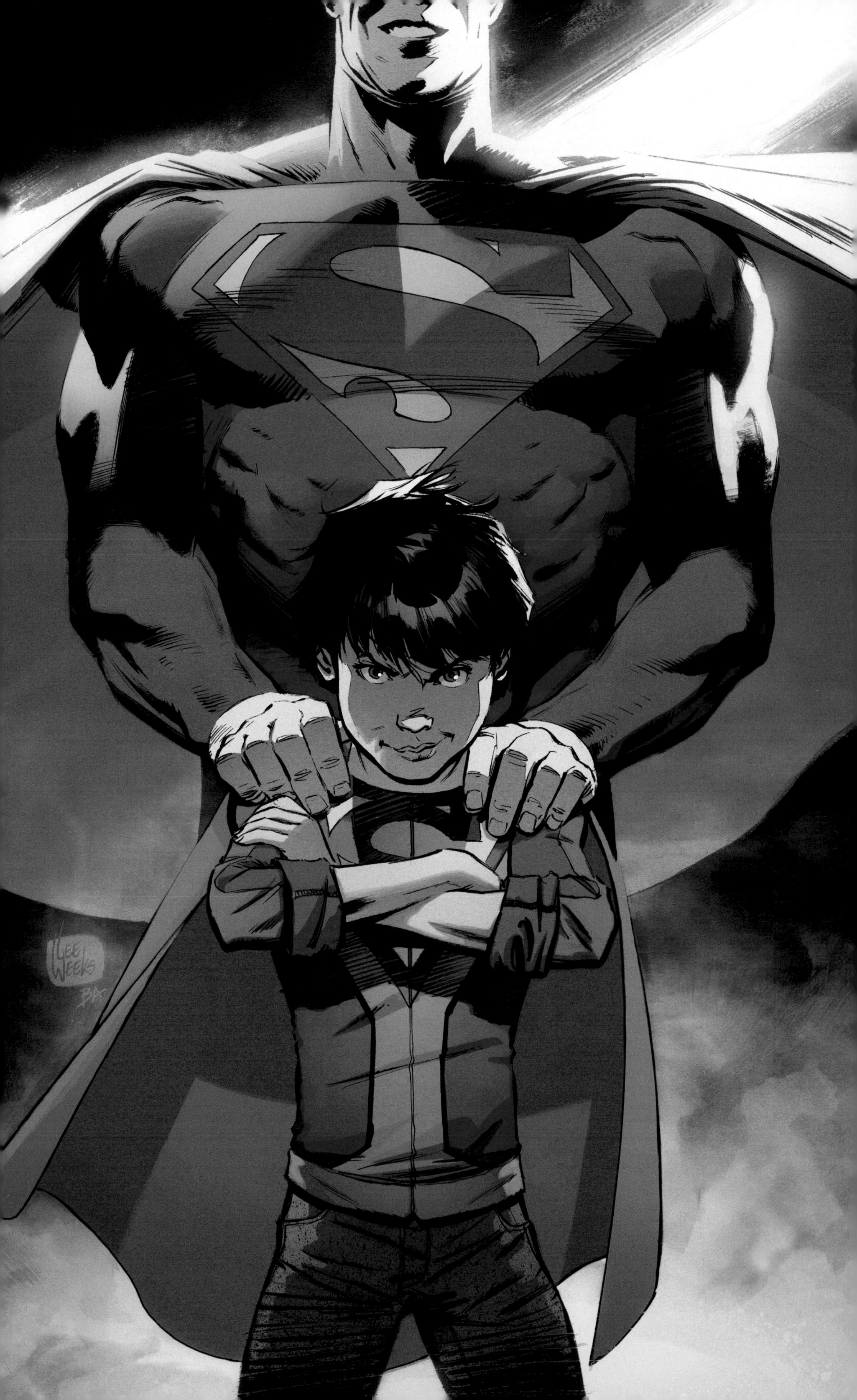
LEE WEEKS
BA

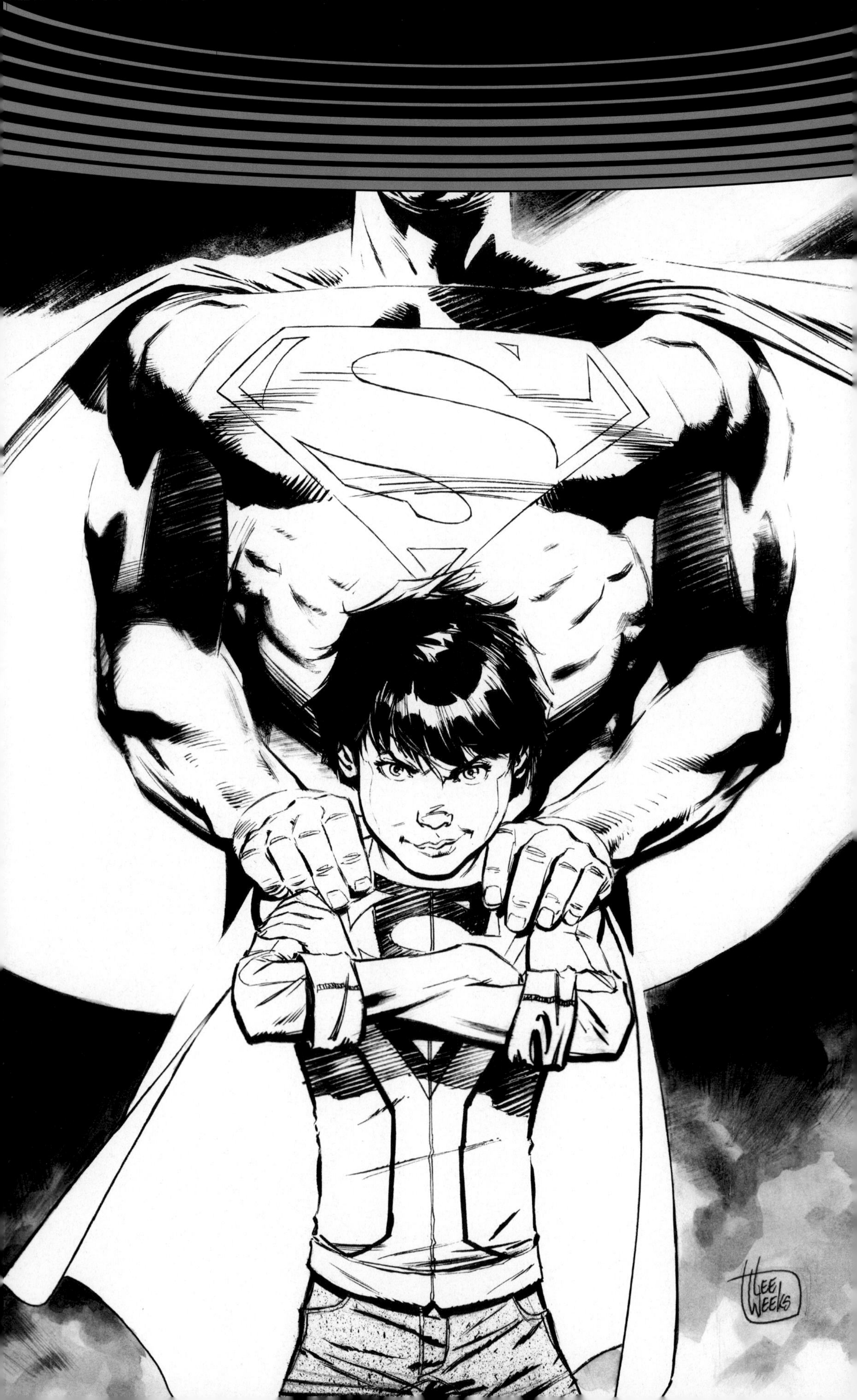
LEE WEEKS

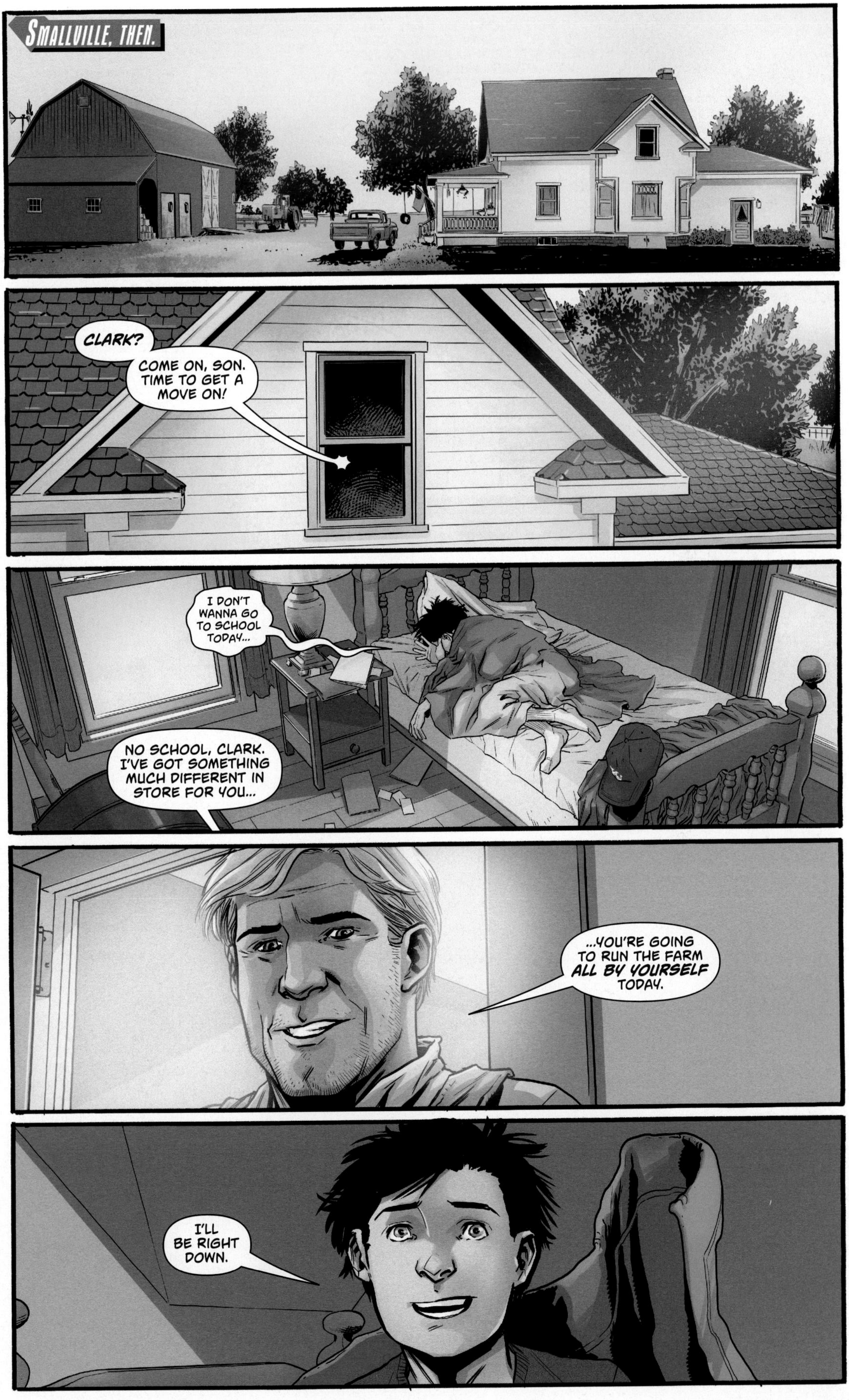
SMALLVILLE, THEN.
CLARK?
COME ON, SON. TIME TO GET A MOVE ON!
I DON'T WANNA GO TO SCHOOL TODAY...
NO SCHOOL, CLARK. I'VE GOT SOMETHING MUCH DIFFERENT IN STORE FOR YOU...
...YOU'RE GOING TO RUN THE FARM ALL BY YOURSELF TODAY.
I'LL BE RIGHT DOWN.

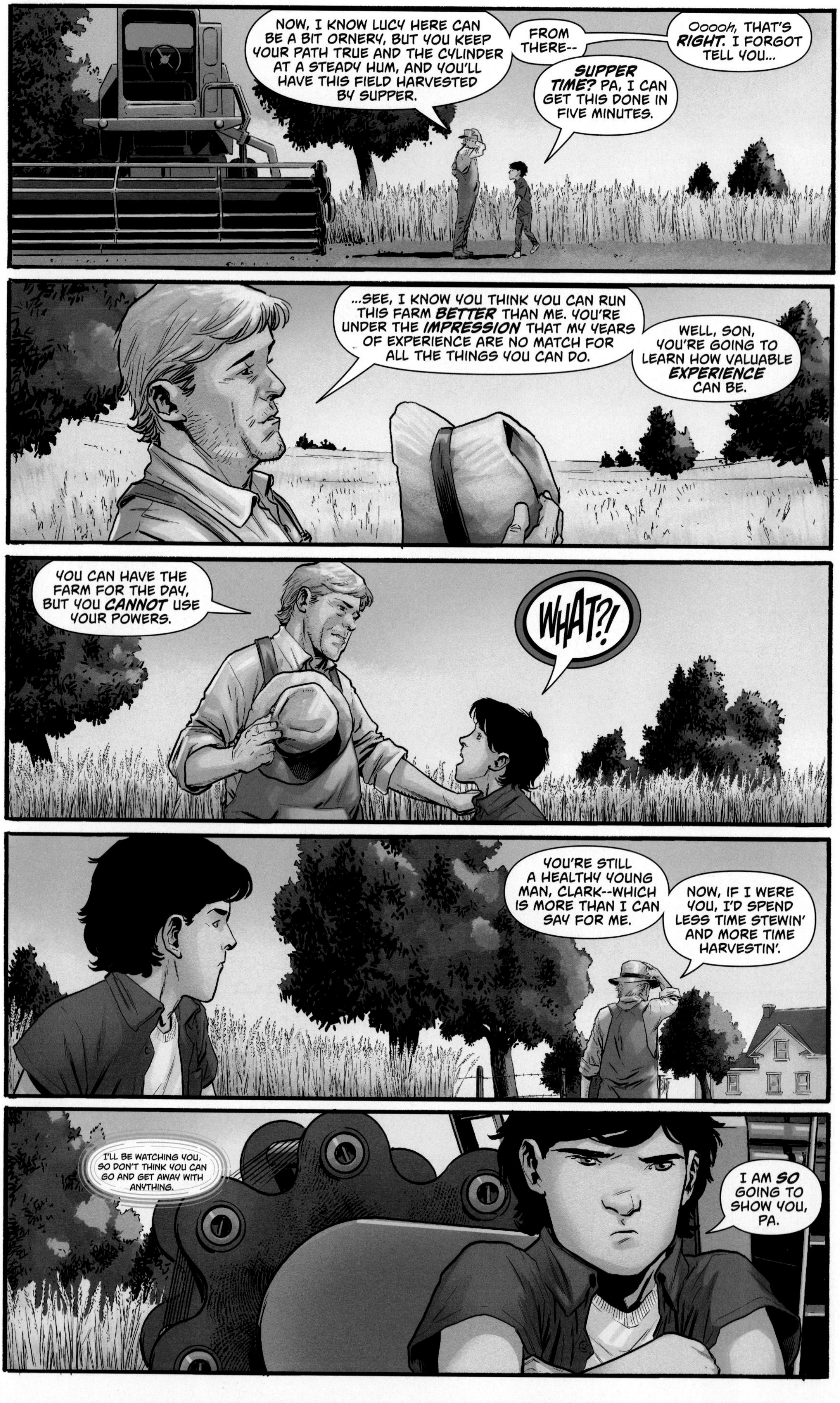
NOW, I KNOW LUCY HERE CAN BE A BIT ORNERY, BUT YOU KEEP YOUR PATH TRUE AND THE CYLINDER AT A STEADY HUM, AND YOU'LL HAVE THIS FIELD HARVESTED BY SUPPER.
SUPPER TIME? PA, I CAN GET THIS DONE IN FIVE MINUTES.
FROM THERE--
Ooooh, THAT'S RIGHT. I FORGOT TELL YOU...
...SEE, I KNOW YOU THINK YOU CAN RUN THIS FARM BETTER THAN ME. YOU'RE UNDER THE IMPRESSION THAT MY YEARS OF EXPERIENCE ARE NO MATCH FOR ALL THE THINGS YOU CAN DO.
WELL, SON, YOU'RE GOING TO LEARN HOW VALUABLE EXPERIENCE CAN BE.
YOU CAN HAVE THE FARM FOR THE DAY, BUT YOU CANNOT USE YOUR POWERS.
WHAT?!
YOU'RE STILL A HEALTHY YOUNG MAN, CLARK--WHICH IS MORE THAN I CAN SAY FOR ME.
NOW, IF I WERE YOU, I'D SPEND LESS TIME STEWIN' AND MORE TIME HARVESTIN'.
I'LL BE WATCHING YOU, SO DON'T THINK YOU CAN GO AND GET AWAY WITH ANYTHING.
I AM SO GOING TO SHOW YOU, PA.

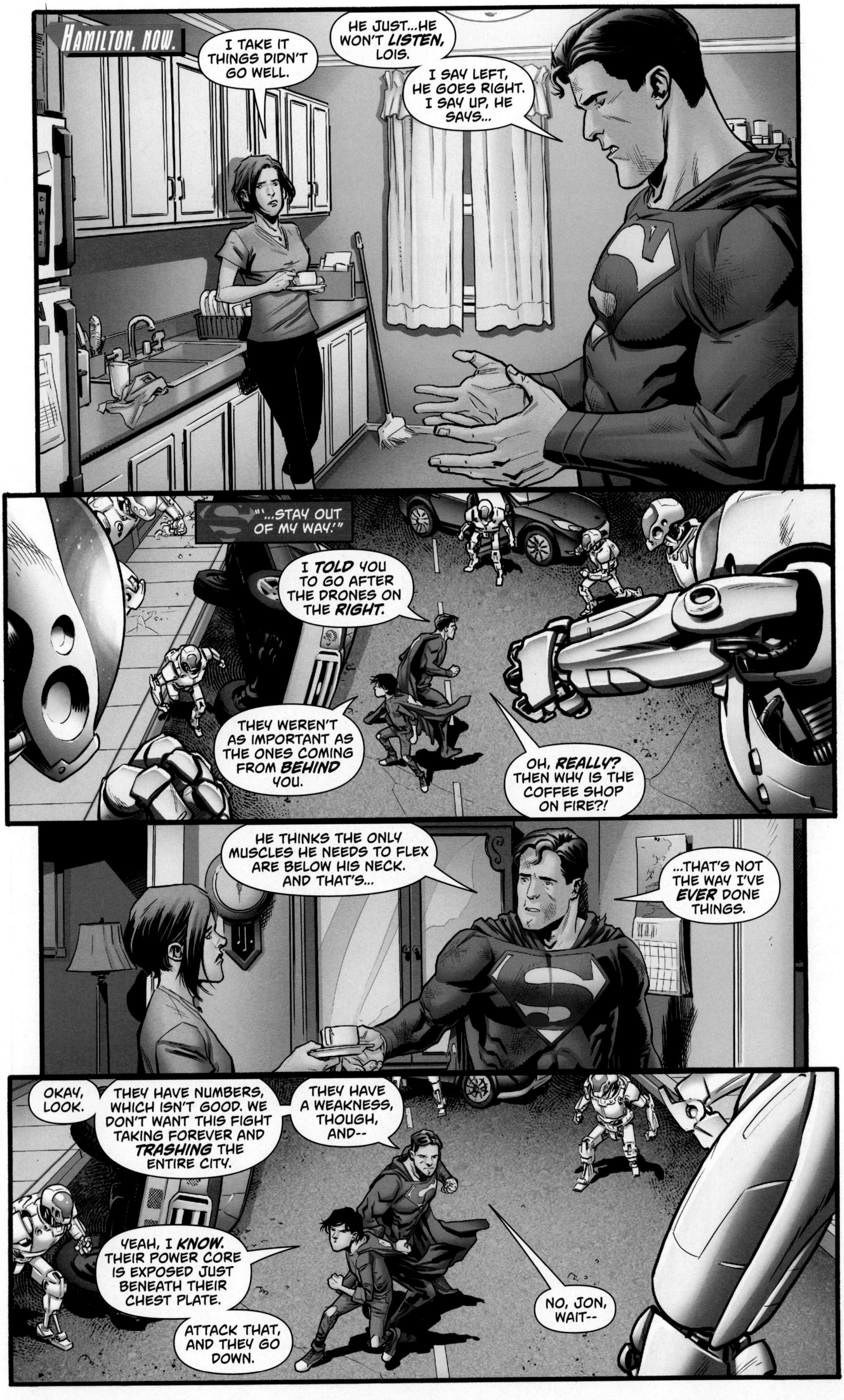
HAMILTON, NOW.
I TAKE IT THINGS DIDN'T GO WELL.
HE JUST...HE WON'T LISTEN, LOIS.
I SAY LEFT, HE GOES RIGHT. I SAY UP, HE SAYS...
"...STAY OUT OF MY WAY."
I TOLD YOU TO GO AFTER THE DRONES ON THE RIGHT.
THEY WEREN'T AS IMPORTANT AS THE ONES COMING FROM BEHIND YOU.
OH, REALLY? THEN WHY IS THE COFFEE SHOP ON FIRE?!
HE THINKS THE ONLY MUSCLES HE NEEDS TO FLEX ARE BELOW HIS NECK. AND THAT'S...
...THAT'S NOT THE WAY I'VE EVER DONE THINGS.
OKAY, LOOK.
THEY HAVE NUMBERS, WHICH ISN'T GOOD. WE DON'T WANT THIS FIGHT TAKING FOREVER AND TRASHING THE ENTIRE CITY.
THEY HAVE A WEAKNESS, THOUGH, AND--
YEAH, I KNOW. THEIR POWER CORE IS EXPOSED JUST BENEATH THEIR CHEST PLATE.
ATTACK THAT, AND THEY GO DOWN.
NO, JON, WAIT--

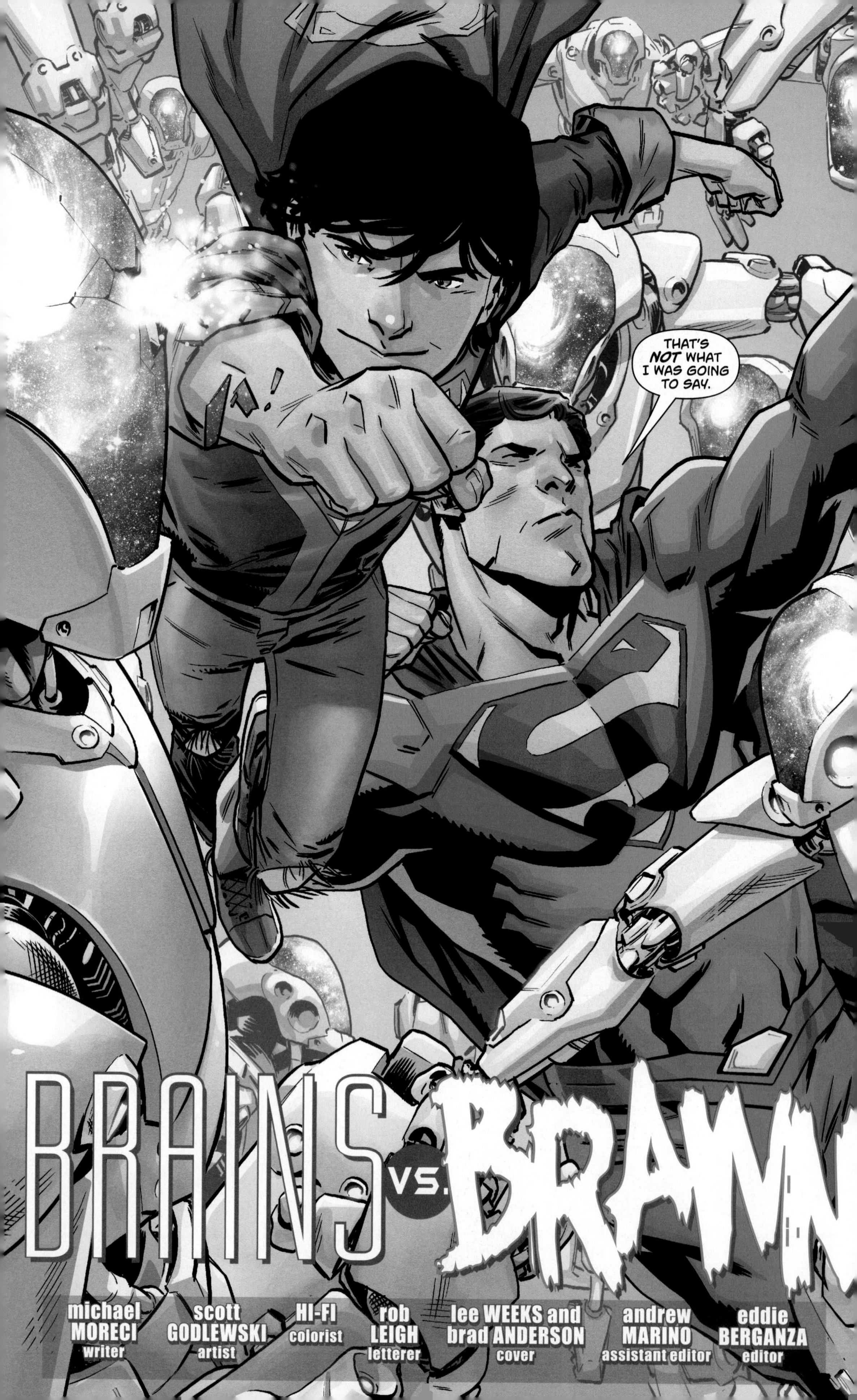
THAT'S *NOT* WHAT I WAS GOING TO SAY.
BRAINS VS.
michael MORECI writer
scott GODLEWSKI artist
HI-FI colorist
rob LEIGH letterer
lee WEEKS and brad ANDERSON cover
andrew MARINO assistant editor
eddie BERGANZA editor

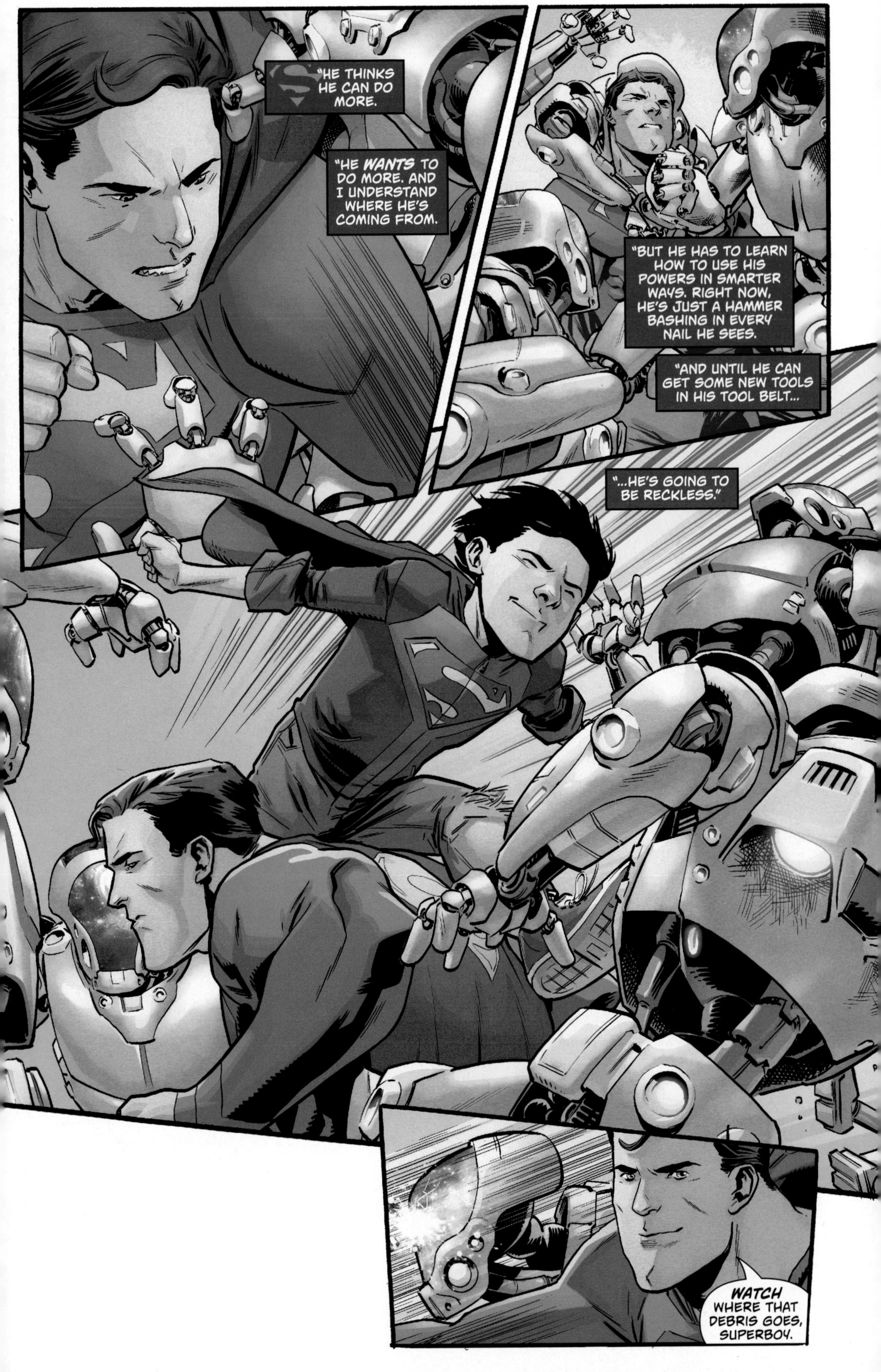
"HE THINKS HE CAN DO MORE.
"HE WANTS TO DO MORE. AND I UNDERSTAND WHERE HE'S COMING FROM.
"BUT HE HAS TO LEARN HOW TO USE HIS POWERS IN SMARTER WAYS. RIGHT NOW, HE'S JUST A HAMMER BASHING IN EVERY NAIL HE SEES.
"AND UNTIL HE CAN GET SOME NEW TOOLS IN HIS TOOL BELT...
"...HE'S GOING TO BE RECKLESS."
WATCH WHERE THAT DEBRIS GOES, SUPERBOY.

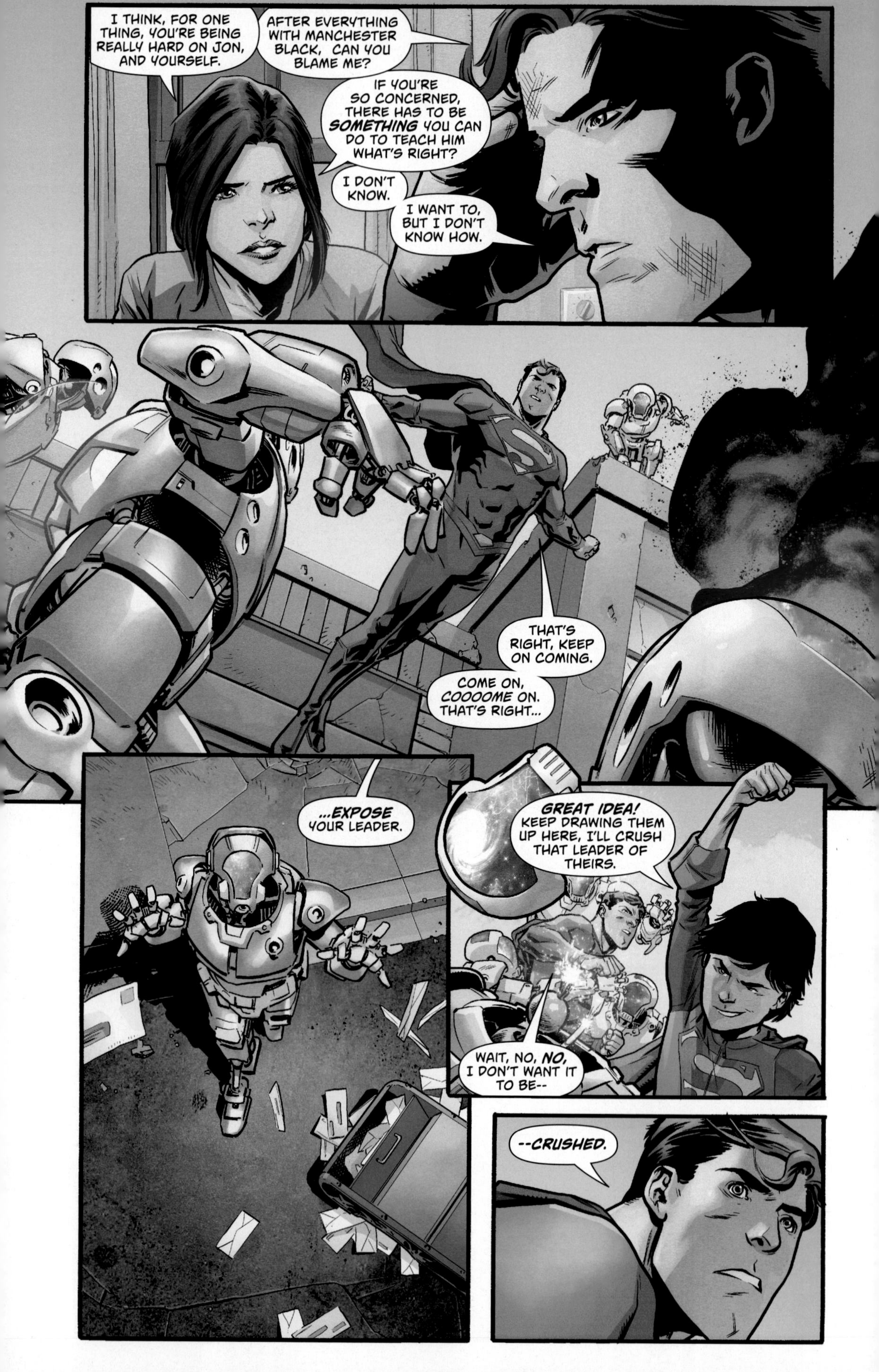

I THINK, FOR ONE THING, YOU'RE BEING REALLY HARD ON JON, AND YOURSELF.
AFTER EVERYTHING WITH MANCHESTER BLACK, CAN YOU BLAME ME?
IF YOU'RE SO CONCERNED, THERE HAS TO BE SOMETHING YOU CAN DO TO TEACH HIM WHAT'S RIGHT?
I DON'T KNOW.
I WANT TO, BUT I DON'T KNOW HOW.
THAT'S RIGHT, KEEP ON COMING.
COME ON, COOOOME ON. THAT'S RIGHT...
...EXPOSE YOUR LEADER.
GREAT IDEA! KEEP DRAWING THEM UP HERE, I'LL CRUSH THAT LEADER OF THEIRS.
WAIT, NO, NO, I DON'T WANT IT TO BE--
--CRUSHED.

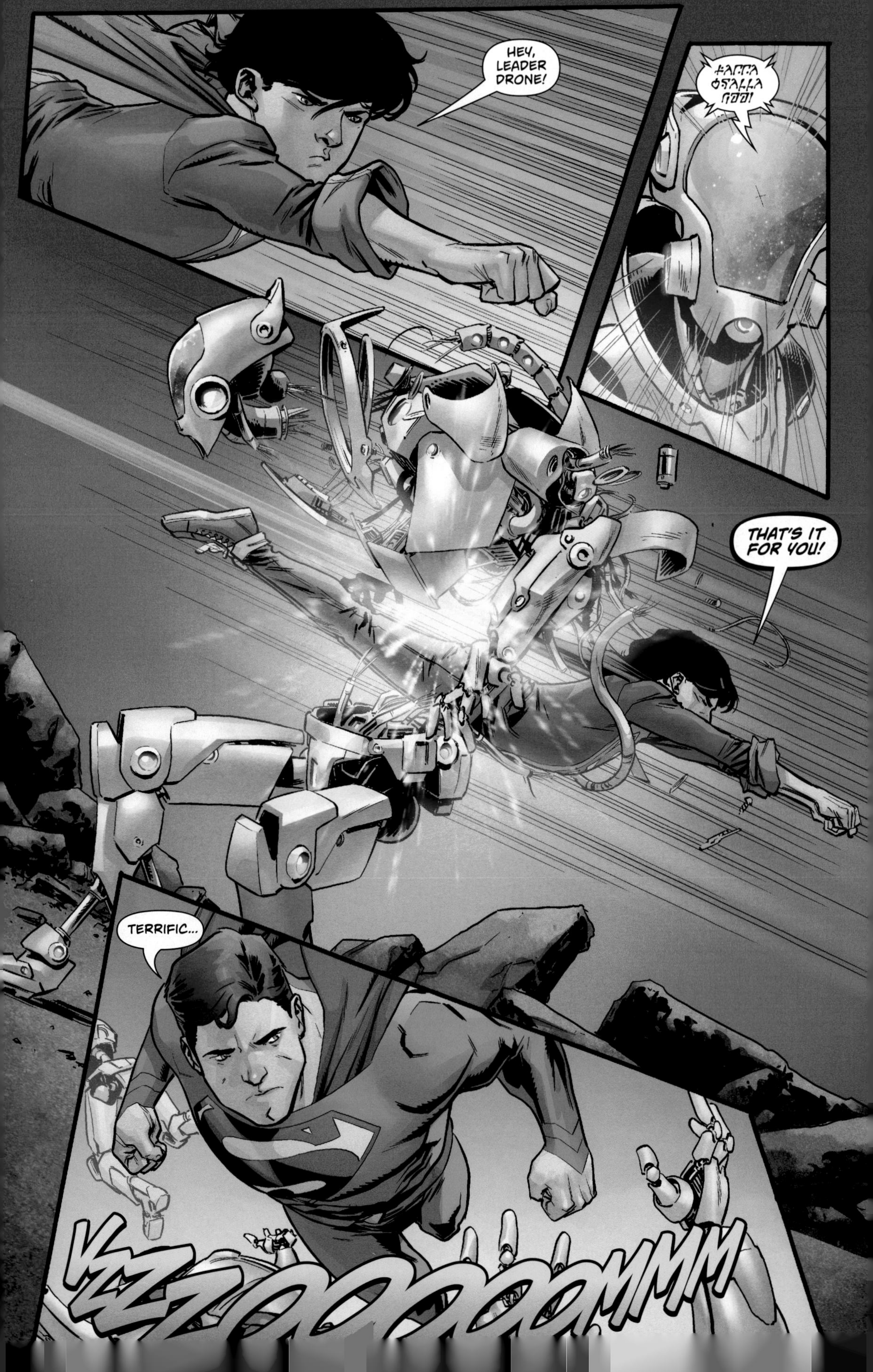
HEY, LEADER DRONE!
THAT'S IT FOR YOU!
TERRIFIC...
VZZOOOOOOMMM

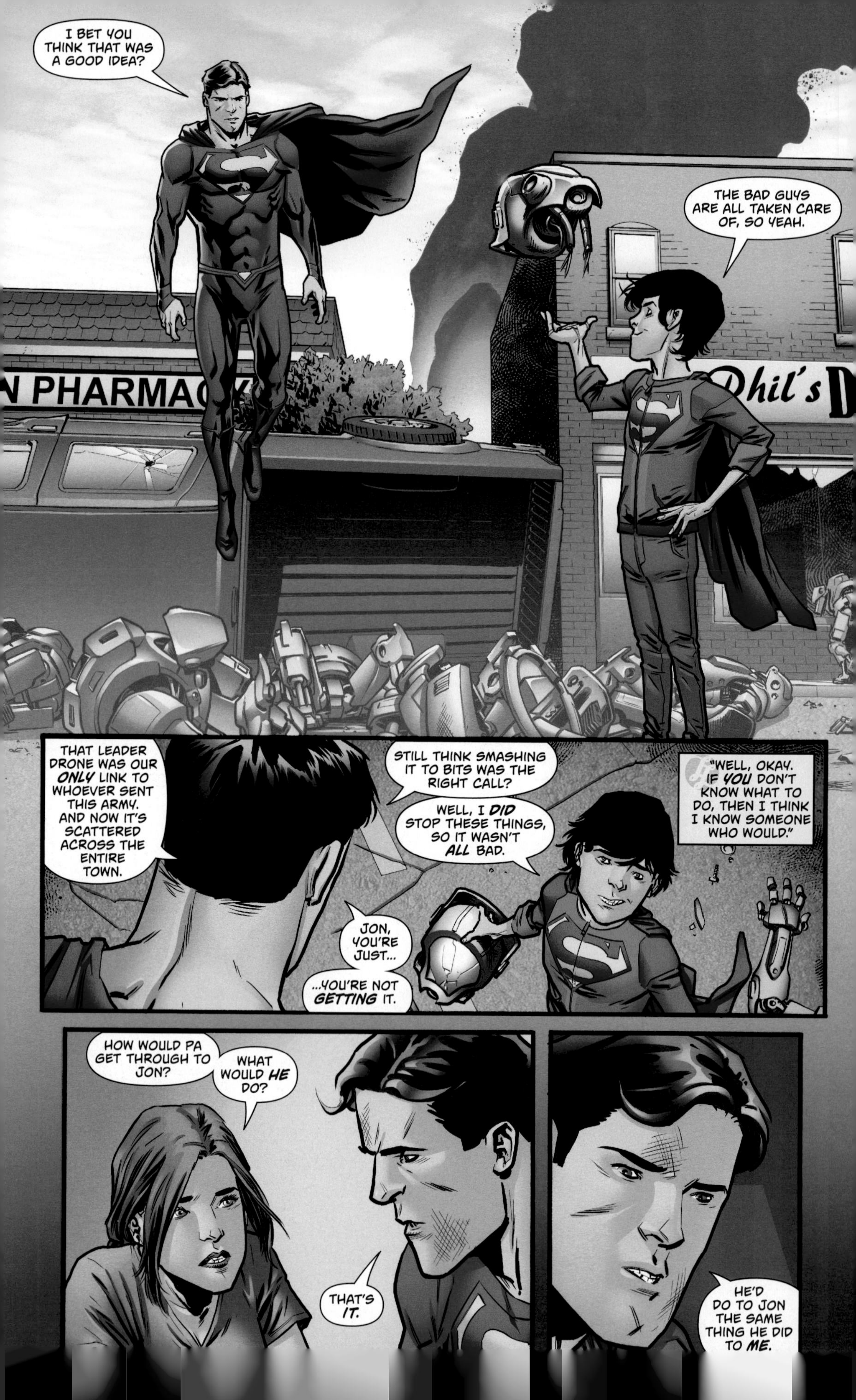
I BET YOU THINK THAT WAS A GOOD IDEA?
THE BAD GUYS ARE ALL TAKEN CARE OF, SO YEAH.
N PHARMACY
Phil's D
THAT LEADER DRONE WAS OUR ONLY LINK TO WHOEVER SENT THIS ARMY. AND NOW IT'S SCATTERED ACROSS THE ENTIRE TOWN.
STILL THINK SMASHING IT TO BITS WAS THE RIGHT CALL?
WELL, I DID STOP THESE THINGS, SO IT WASN'T ALL BAD.
"WELL, OKAY. IF YOU DON'T KNOW WHAT TO DO, THEN I THINK I KNOW SOMEONE WHO WOULD."
JON, YOU'RE JUST...
...YOU'RE NOT GETTING IT.
HOW WOULD PA GET THROUGH TO JON?
WHAT WOULD HE DO?
THAT'S IT.
HE'D DO TO JON THE SAME THING HE DID TO ME.

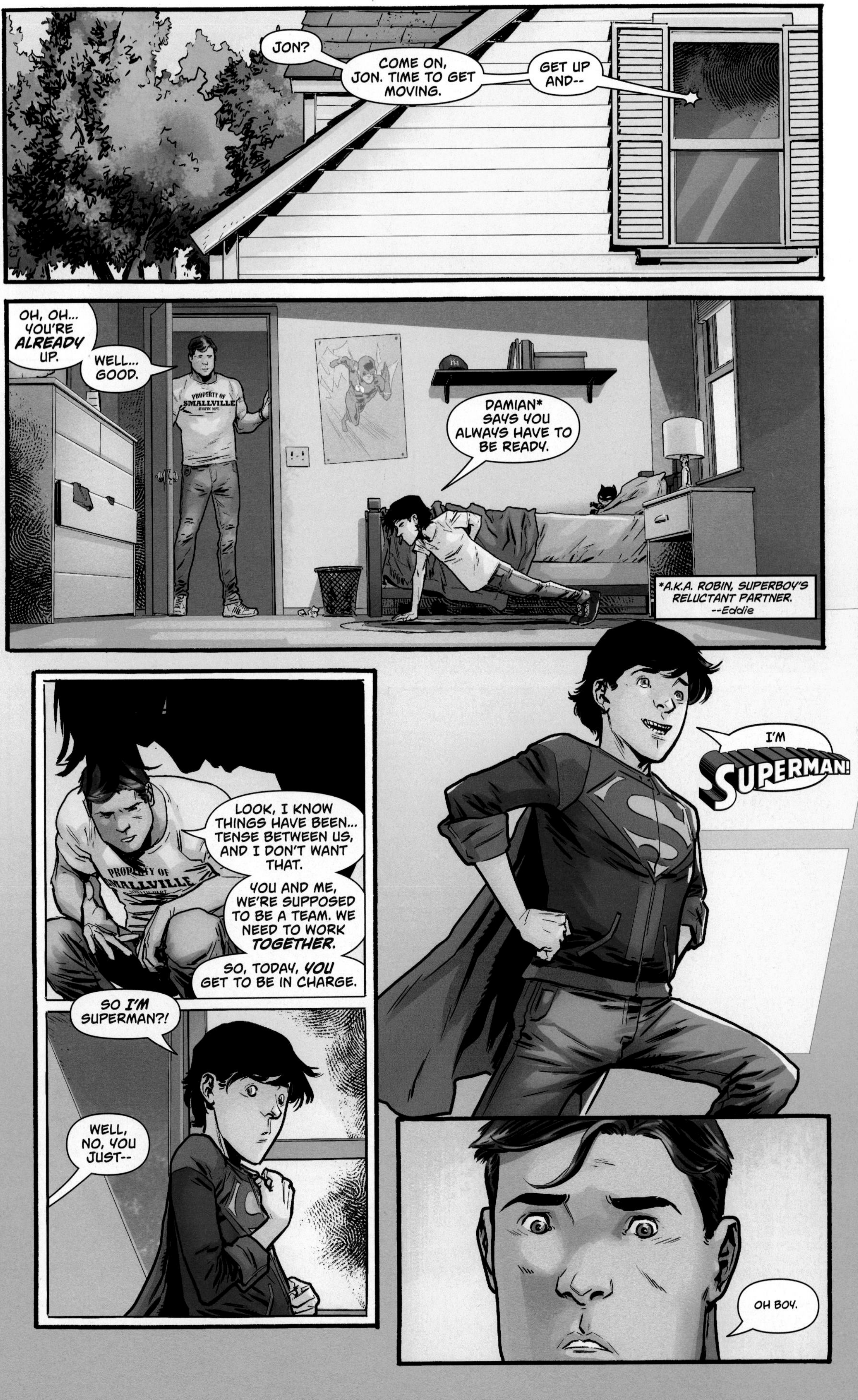
JON?
COME ON, JON. TIME TO GET MOVING.
GET UP AND--
OH, OH... YOU'RE ALREADY UP.
WELL... GOOD.
PROPERTY OF SMALLVILLE
DAMIAN* SAYS YOU ALWAYS HAVE TO BE READY.
*A.K.A. ROBIN, SUPERBOY'S RELUCTANT PARTNER. --Eddie
LOOK, I KNOW THINGS HAVE BEEN... TENSE BETWEEN US, AND I DON'T WANT THAT.
YOU AND ME, WE'RE SUPPOSED TO BE A TEAM. WE NEED TO WORK TOGETHER.
SO, TODAY, YOU GET TO BE IN CHARGE.
SO I'M SUPERMAN?!
WELL, NO, YOU JUST--
I'M SUPERMAN!
OH BOY.

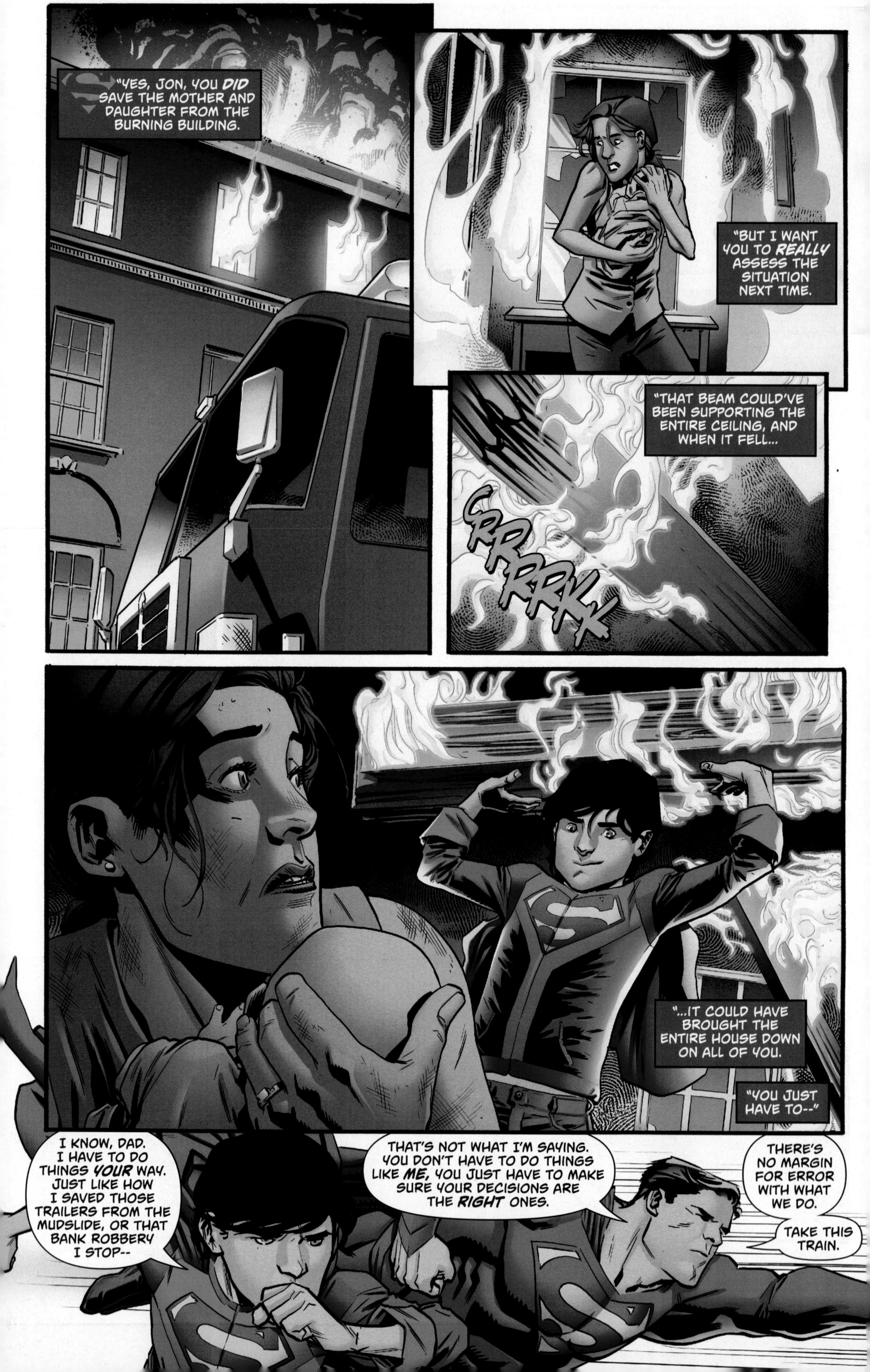
"YES, JON, YOU DID SAVE THE MOTHER AND DAUGHTER FROM THE BURNING BUILDING.
"BUT I WANT YOU TO REALLY ASSESS THE SITUATION NEXT TIME.
"THAT BEAM COULD'VE BEEN SUPPORTING THE ENTIRE CEILING, AND WHEN IT FELL...
CRRRRKK
"...IT COULD HAVE BROUGHT THE ENTIRE HOUSE DOWN ON ALL OF YOU.
"YOU JUST HAVE TO--"
I KNOW, DAD. I HAVE TO DO THINGS YOUR WAY. JUST LIKE HOW I SAVED THOSE TRAILERS FROM THE MUDSLIDE, OR THAT BANK ROBBERY I STOP--
THAT'S NOT WHAT I'M SAYING. YOU DON'T HAVE TO DO THINGS LIKE ME, YOU JUST HAVE TO MAKE SURE YOUR DECISIONS ARE THE RIGHT ONES.
THERE'S NO MARGIN FOR ERROR WITH WHAT WE DO.
TAKE THIS TRAIN.

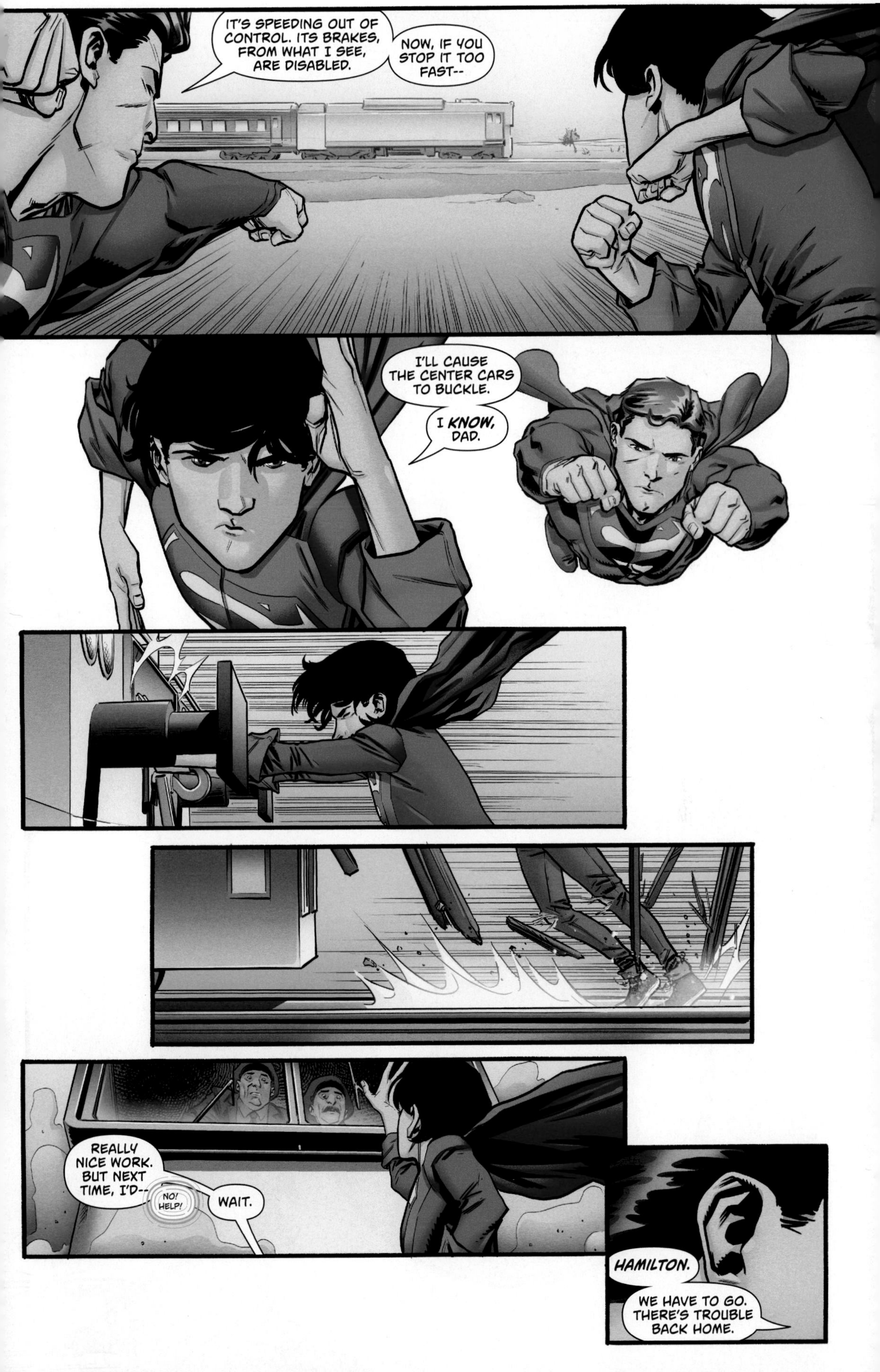
IT'S SPEEDING OUT OF CONTROL. ITS BRAKES, FROM WHAT I SEE, ARE DISABLED.
NOW, IF YOU STOP IT TOO FAST--
I'LL CAUSE THE CENTER CARS TO BUCKLE.
I KNOW, DAD.
REALLY NICE WORK. BUT NEXT TIME, I'D--
NO! HELP!
WAIT.
HAMILTON.
WE HAVE TO GO. THERE'S TROUBLE BACK HOME.

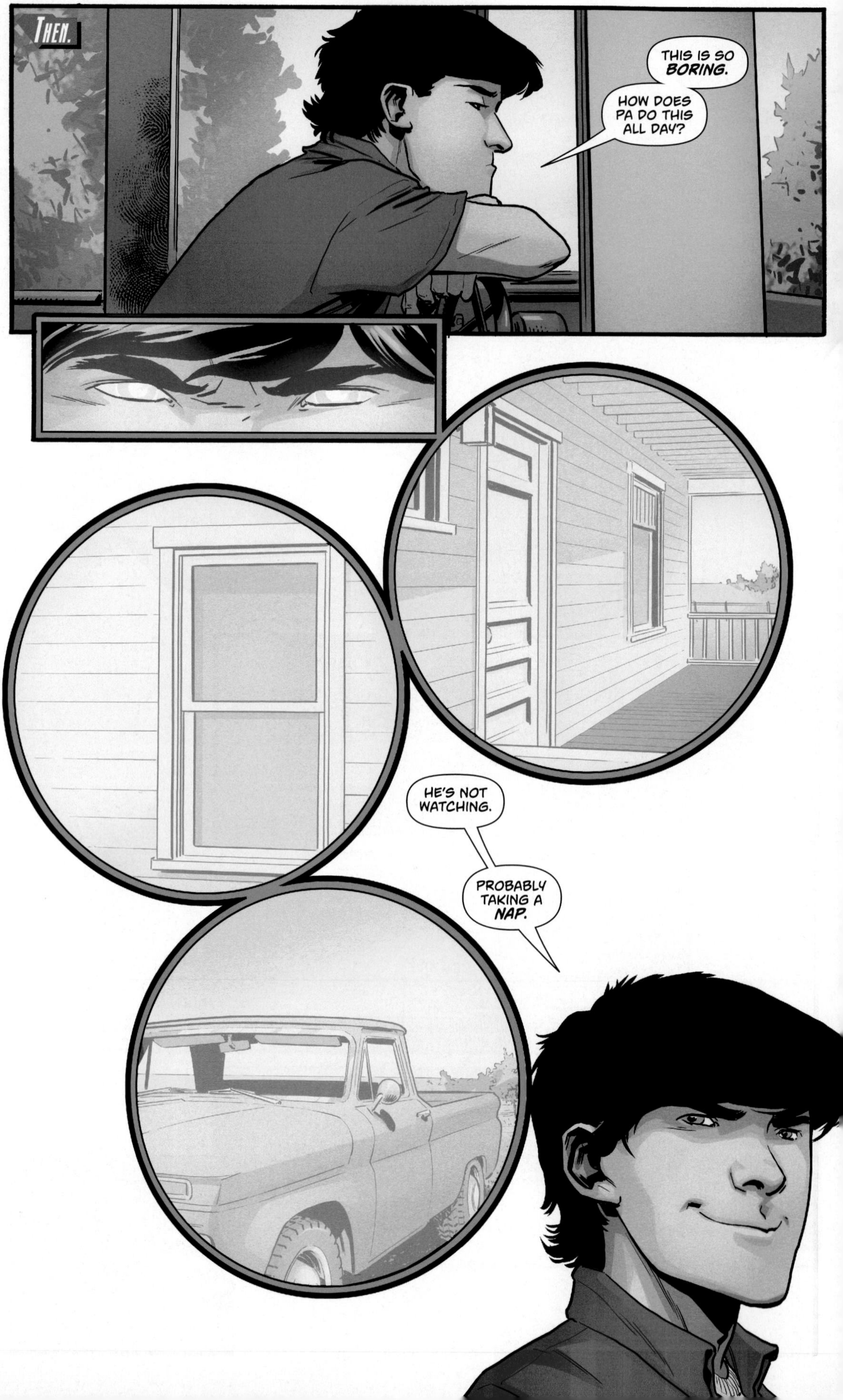
THEN.
THIS IS SO BORING.
HOW DOES PA DO THIS ALL DAY?
HE'S NOT WATCHING.
PROBABLY TAKING A NAP.

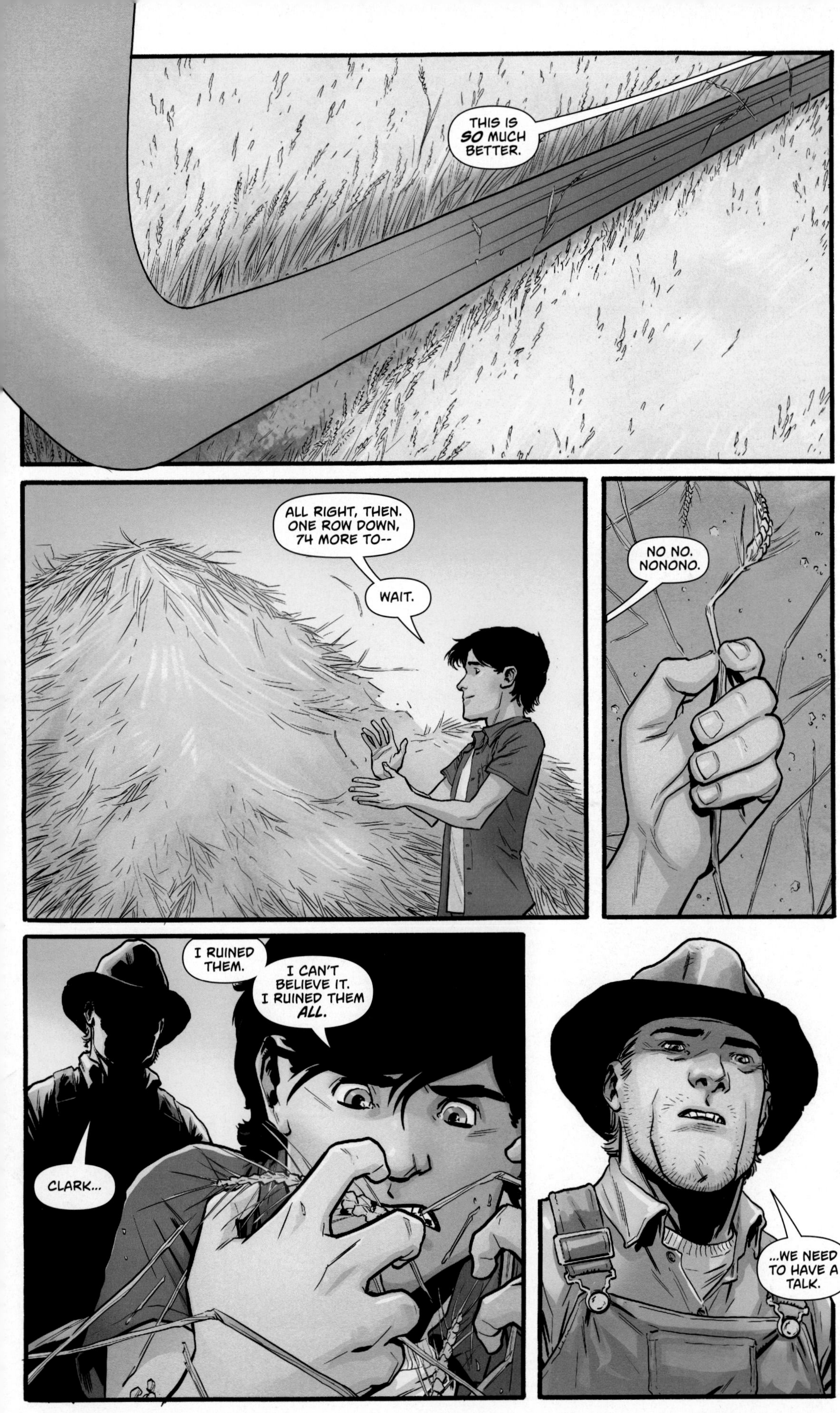
THIS IS SO MUCH BETTER.
ALL RIGHT, THEN. ONE ROW DOWN, 74 MORE TO--
WAIT.
NO NO. NONONO.
I RUINED THEM.
I CAN'T BELIEVE IT. I RUINED THEM ALL.
CLARK...
...WE NEED TO HAVE A TALK.

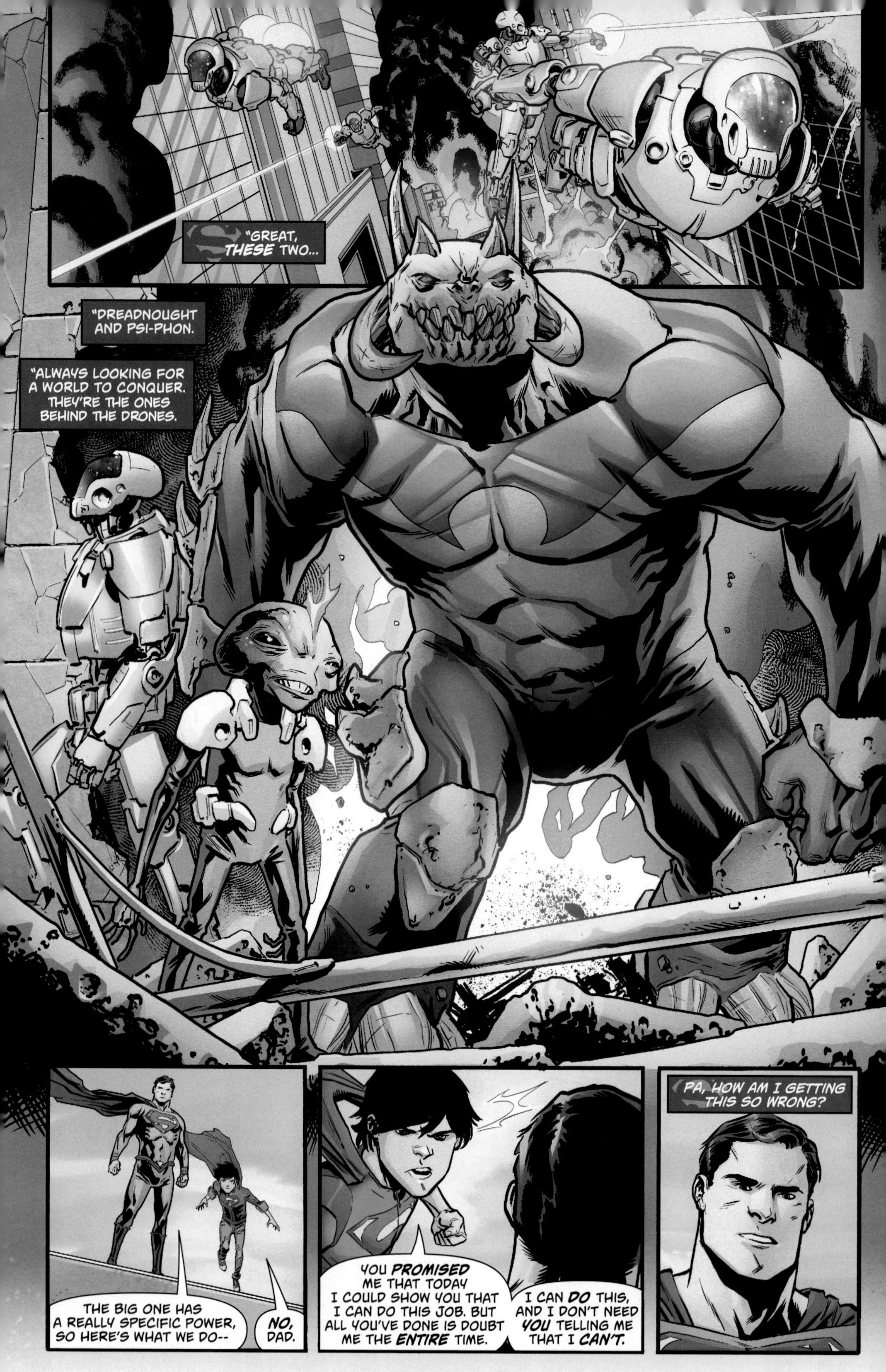
"GREAT, THESE TWO...
"DREADNOUGHT AND PSI-PHON.
"ALWAYS LOOKING FOR A WORLD TO CONQUER. THEY'RE THE ONES BEHIND THE DRONES.
THE BIG ONE HAS A REALLY SPECIFIC POWER, SO HERE'S WHAT WE DO--
NO, DAD.
YOU PROMISED ME THAT TODAY I COULD SHOW YOU THAT I CAN DO THIS JOB. BUT ALL YOU'VE DONE IS DOUBT ME THE ENTIRE TIME.
I CAN DO THIS, AND I DON'T NEED YOU TELLING ME THAT I CAN'T.
PA, HOW AM I GETTING THIS SO WRONG?

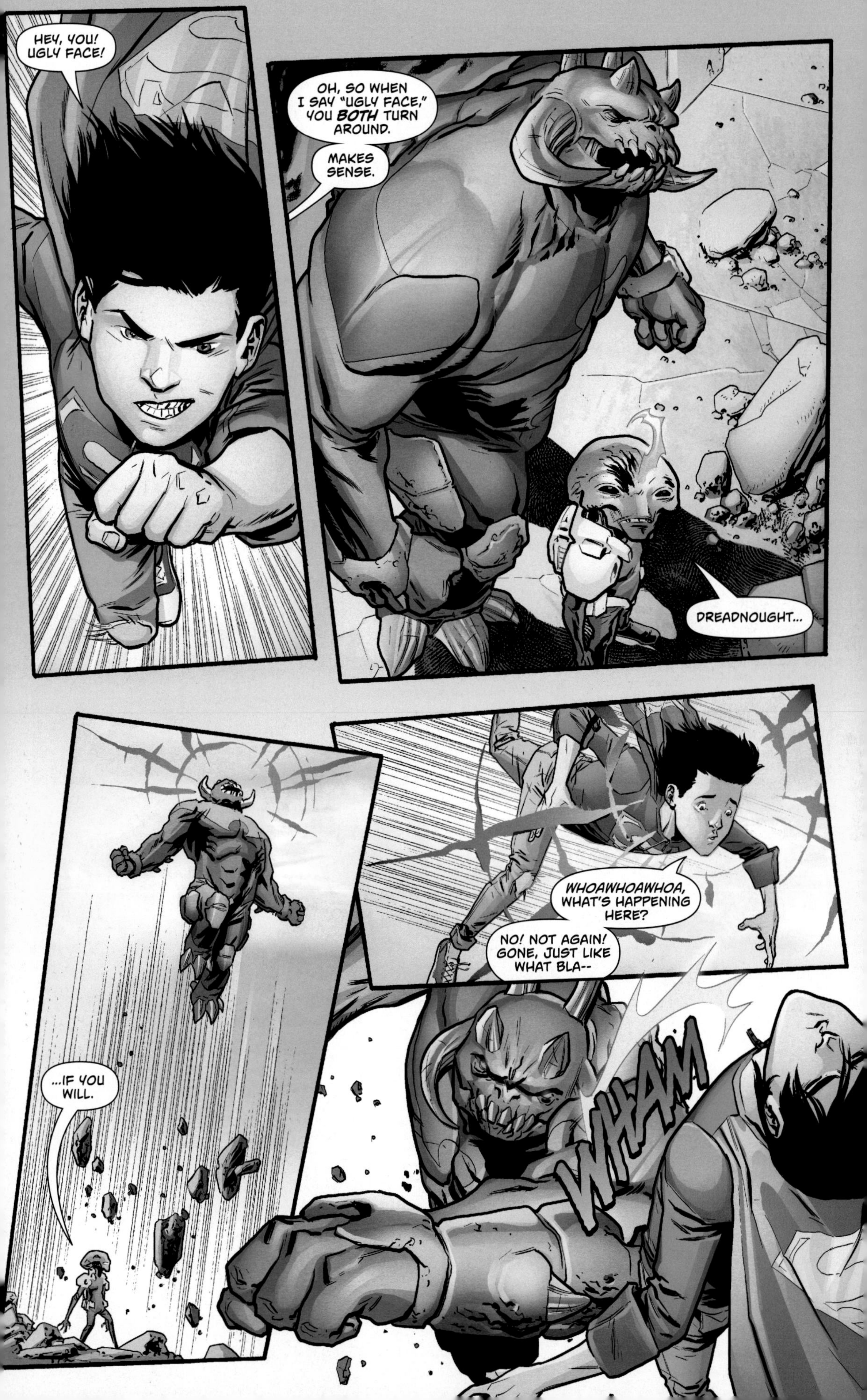
HEY, YOU! UGLY FACE!
OH, SO WHEN I SAY "UGLY FACE," YOU **BOTH** TURN AROUND.
MAKES SENSE.
DREADNOUGHT...
...IF YOU WILL.
WHOAWHOAWHOA, WHAT'S HAPPENING HERE?
NO! NOT AGAIN! GONE, JUST LIKE WHAT BLA--
WHAM

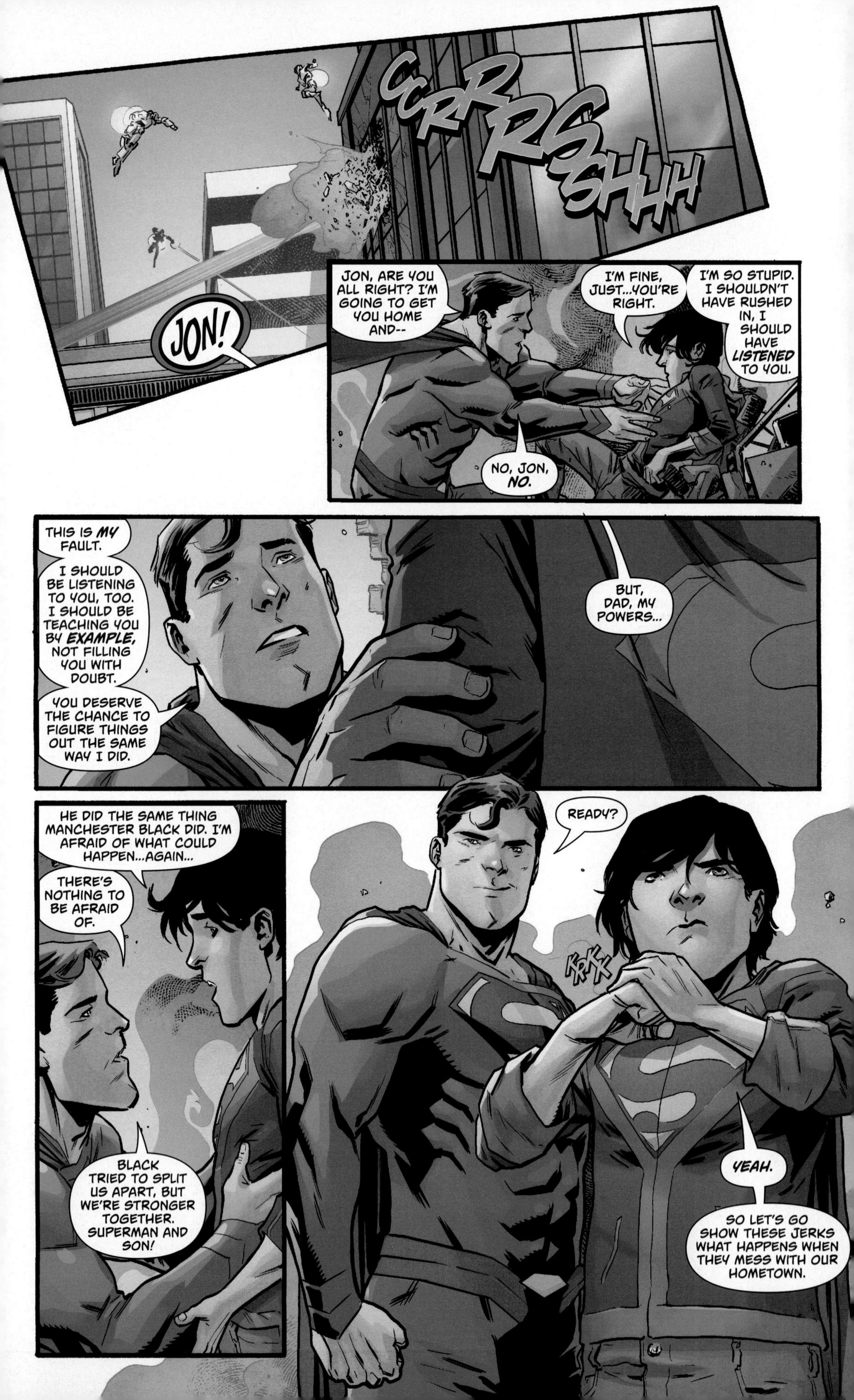
CCRRRSSHHH
JON!
JON, ARE YOU ALL RIGHT? I'M GOING TO GET YOU HOME AND--
I'M FINE, JUST...YOU'RE RIGHT.
I'M SO STUPID. I SHOULDN'T HAVE RUSHED IN, I SHOULD HAVE LISTENED TO YOU.
NO, JON, NO.
THIS IS MY FAULT.
I SHOULD BE LISTENING TO YOU, TOO. I SHOULD BE TEACHING YOU BY EXAMPLE, NOT FILLING YOU WITH DOUBT.
YOU DESERVE THE CHANCE TO FIGURE THINGS OUT THE SAME WAY I DID.
BUT, DAD, MY POWERS...
HE DID THE SAME THING MANCHESTER BLACK DID. I'M AFRAID OF WHAT COULD HAPPEN...AGAIN...
THERE'S NOTHING TO BE AFRAID OF.
BLACK TRIED TO SPLIT US APART, BUT WE'RE STRONGER TOGETHER. SUPERMAN AND SON!
READY?
KRKK
YEAH.
SO LET'S GO SHOW THESE JERKS WHAT HAPPENS WHEN THEY MESS WITH OUR HOMETOWN.

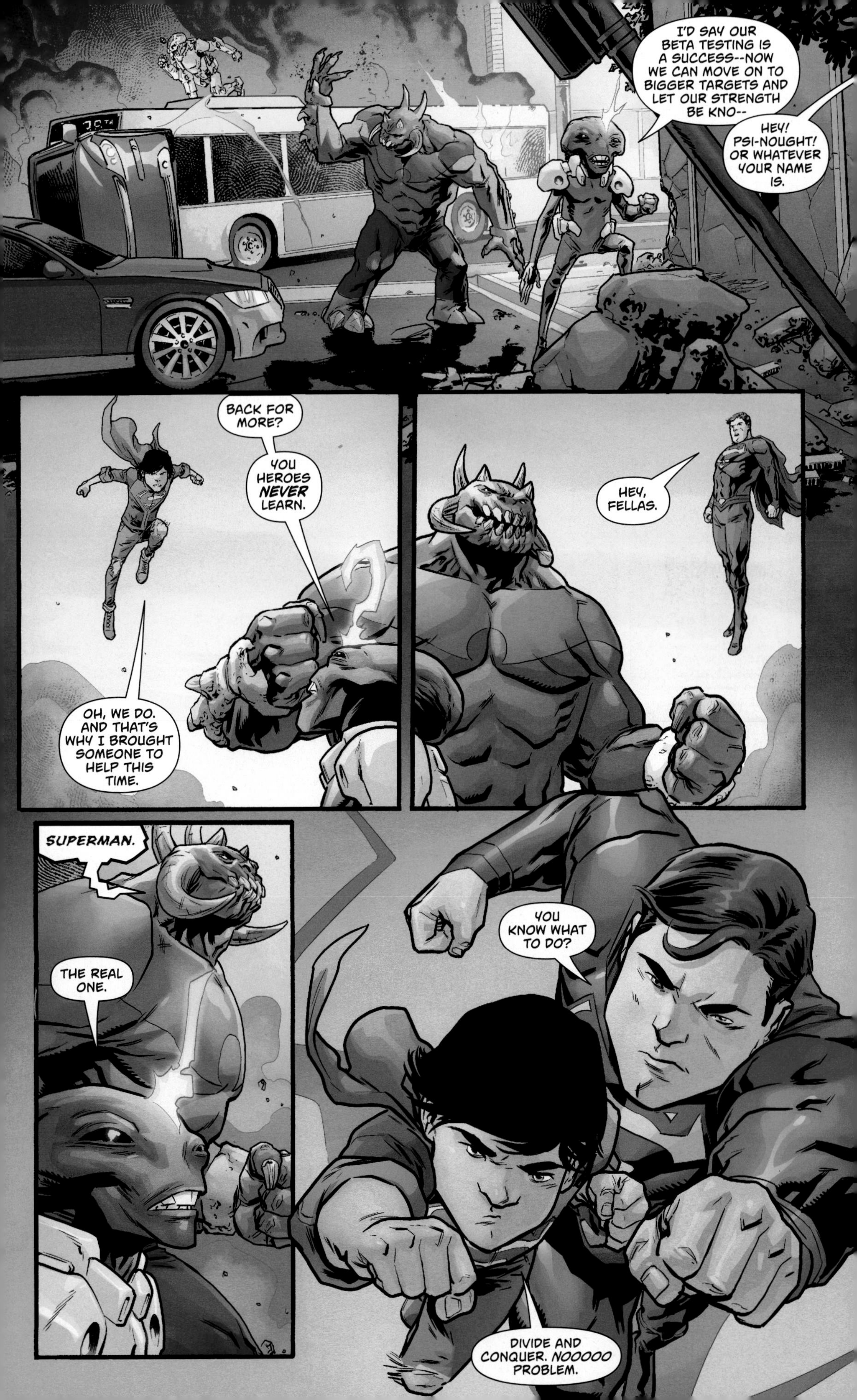
I'D SAY OUR BETA TESTING IS A SUCCESS--NOW WE CAN MOVE ON TO BIGGER TARGETS AND LET OUR STRENGTH BE KNO--
HEY! PSI-NOUGHT! OR WHATEVER YOUR NAME IS.
BACK FOR MORE?
YOU HEROES NEVER LEARN.
OH, WE DO. AND THAT'S WHY I BROUGHT SOMEONE TO HELP THIS TIME.
HEY, FELLAS.
SUPERMAN.
THE REAL ONE.
YOU KNOW WHAT TO DO?
DIVIDE AND CONQUER. NOOOOO PROBLEM.

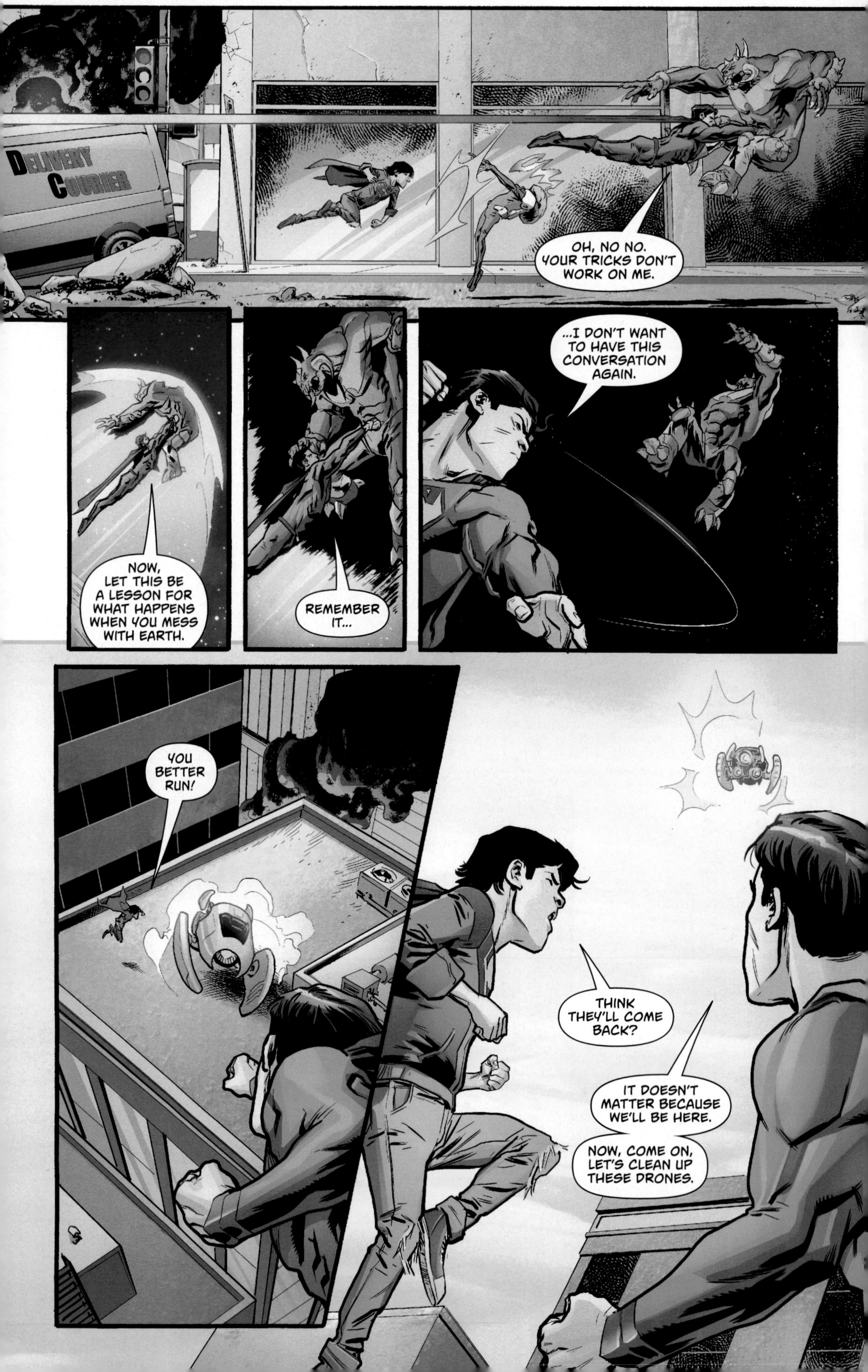
DELIVERY COURIER
OH, NO NO. YOUR TRICKS DON'T WORK ON ME.
NOW, LET THIS BE A LESSON FOR WHAT HAPPENS WHEN YOU MESS WITH EARTH.
REMEMBER IT...
...I DON'T WANT TO HAVE THIS CONVERSATION AGAIN.
YOU BETTER RUN!
THINK THEY'LL COME BACK?
IT DOESN'T MATTER BECAUSE WE'LL BE HERE.
NOW, COME ON, LET'S CLEAN UP THESE DRONES.

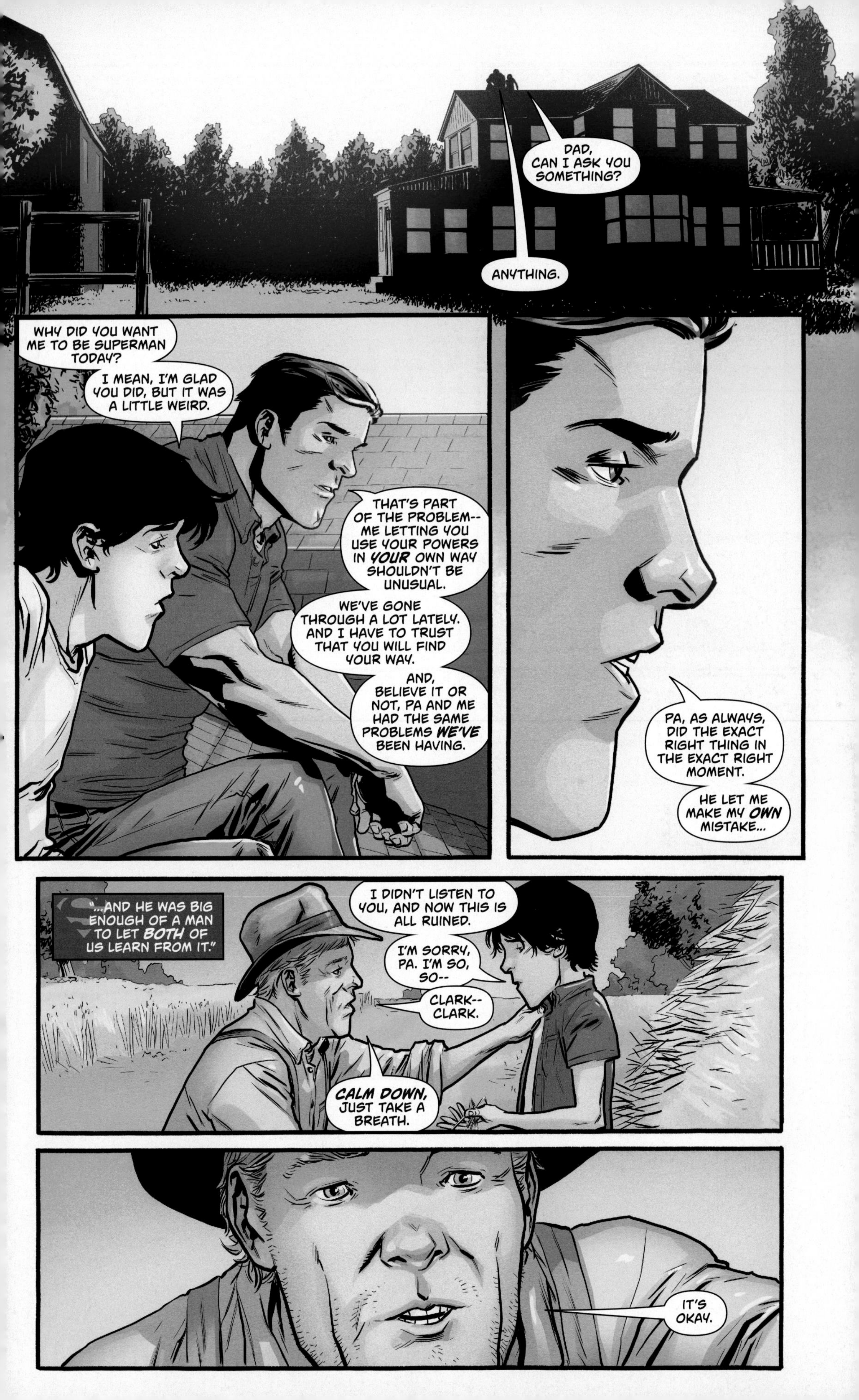
DAD, CAN I ASK YOU SOMETHING?
ANYTHING.
WHY DID YOU WANT ME TO BE SUPERMAN TODAY?
I MEAN, I'M GLAD YOU DID, BUT IT WAS A LITTLE WEIRD.
THAT'S PART OF THE PROBLEM-- ME LETTING YOU USE YOUR POWERS IN *YOUR* OWN WAY SHOULDN'T BE UNUSUAL.
WE'VE GONE THROUGH A LOT LATELY. AND I HAVE TO TRUST THAT YOU WILL FIND YOUR WAY.
AND, BELIEVE IT OR NOT, PA AND ME HAD THE SAME PROBLEMS *WE'VE* BEEN HAVING.
PA, AS ALWAYS, DID THE EXACT RIGHT THING IN THE EXACT RIGHT MOMENT.
HE LET ME MAKE MY *OWN* MISTAKE...
"...AND HE WAS BIG ENOUGH OF A MAN TO LET *BOTH* OF US LEARN FROM IT."
I DIDN'T LISTEN TO YOU, AND NOW THIS IS ALL RUINED.
I'M SORRY, PA. I'M SO, SO--
CLARK-- CLARK.
CALM DOWN, JUST TAKE A BREATH.
IT'S OKAY.

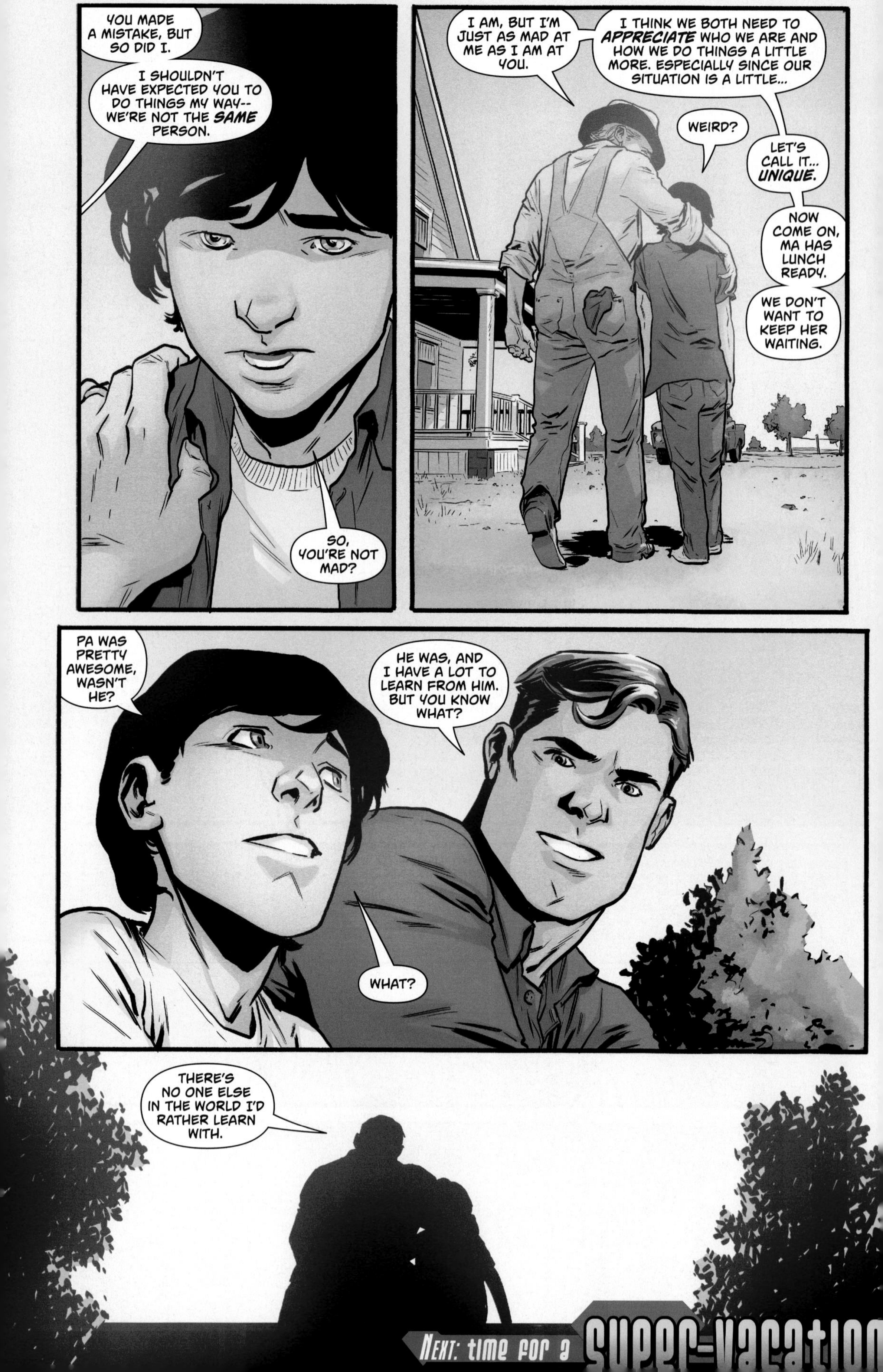
YOU MADE A MISTAKE, BUT SO DID I.
I SHOULDN'T HAVE EXPECTED YOU TO DO THINGS MY WAY-- WE'RE NOT THE SAME PERSON.
SO, YOU'RE NOT MAD?
I AM, BUT I'M JUST AS MAD AT ME AS I AM AT YOU.
I THINK WE BOTH NEED TO APPRECIATE WHO WE ARE AND HOW WE DO THINGS A LITTLE MORE. ESPECIALLY SINCE OUR SITUATION IS A LITTLE...
WEIRD?
LET'S CALL IT... UNIQUE.
NOW COME ON, MA HAS LUNCH READY.
WE DON'T WANT TO KEEP HER WAITING.
PA WAS PRETTY AWESOME, WASN'T HE?
HE WAS, AND I HAVE A LOT TO LEARN FROM HIM. BUT YOU KNOW WHAT?
WHAT?
THERE'S NO ONE ELSE IN THE WORLD I'D RATHER LEARN WITH.
NEXT: time for a SUPER-VACATION

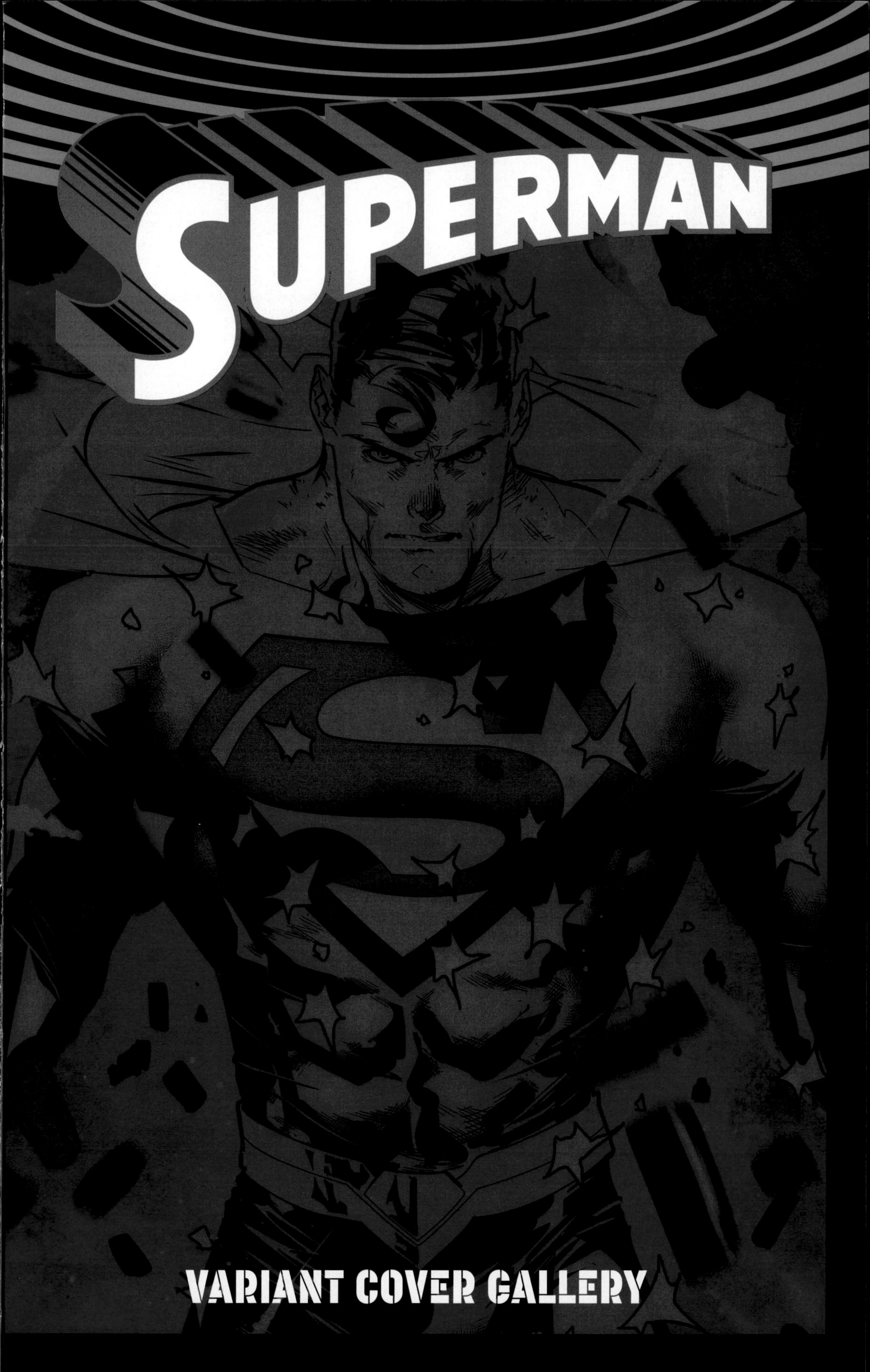
SUPERMAN
VARIANT COVER GALLERY

Variant cover art for SUPERMAN #20 by JORGE JIMENEZ and ALEJANDRO SANCHEZ

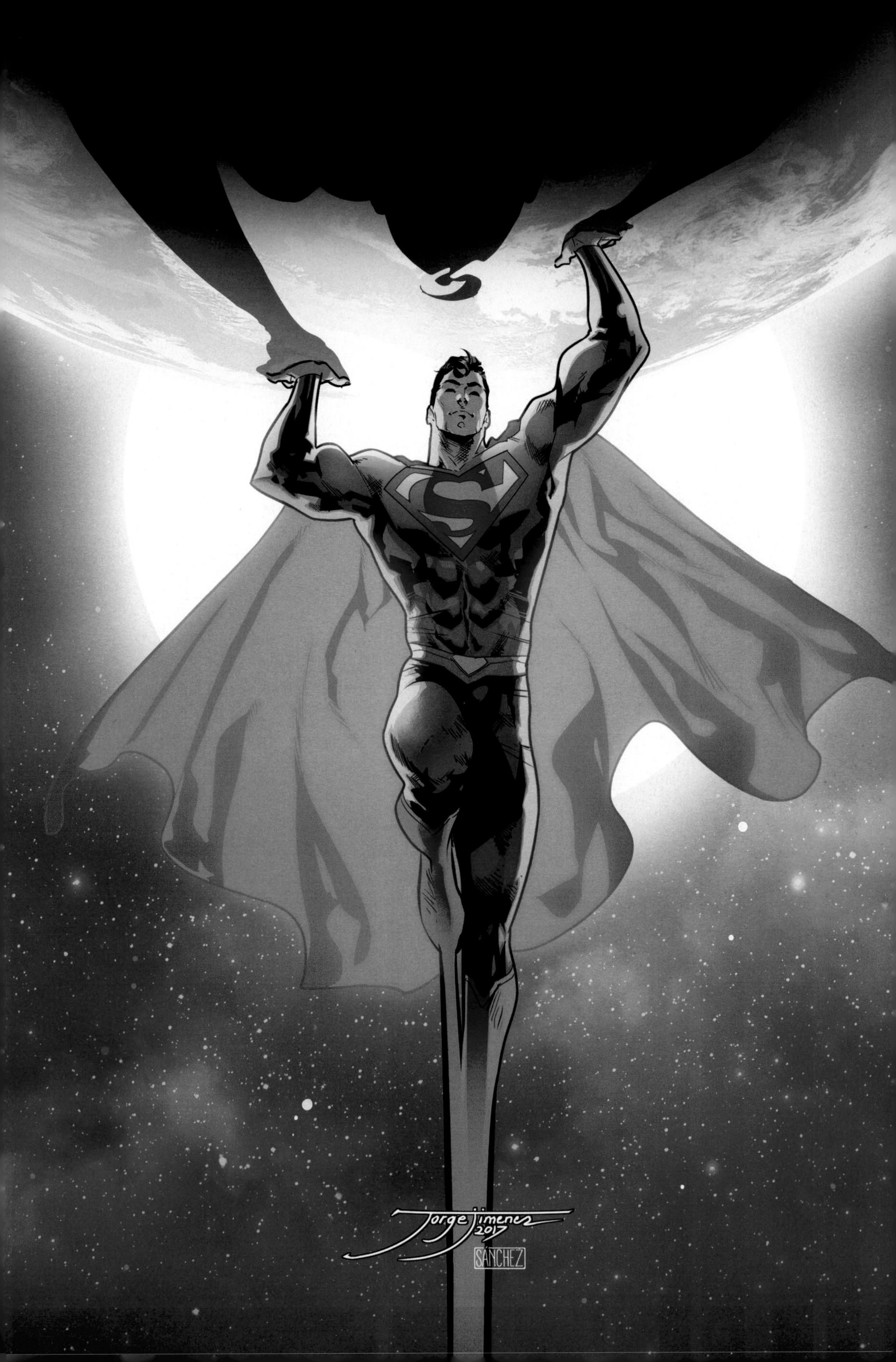

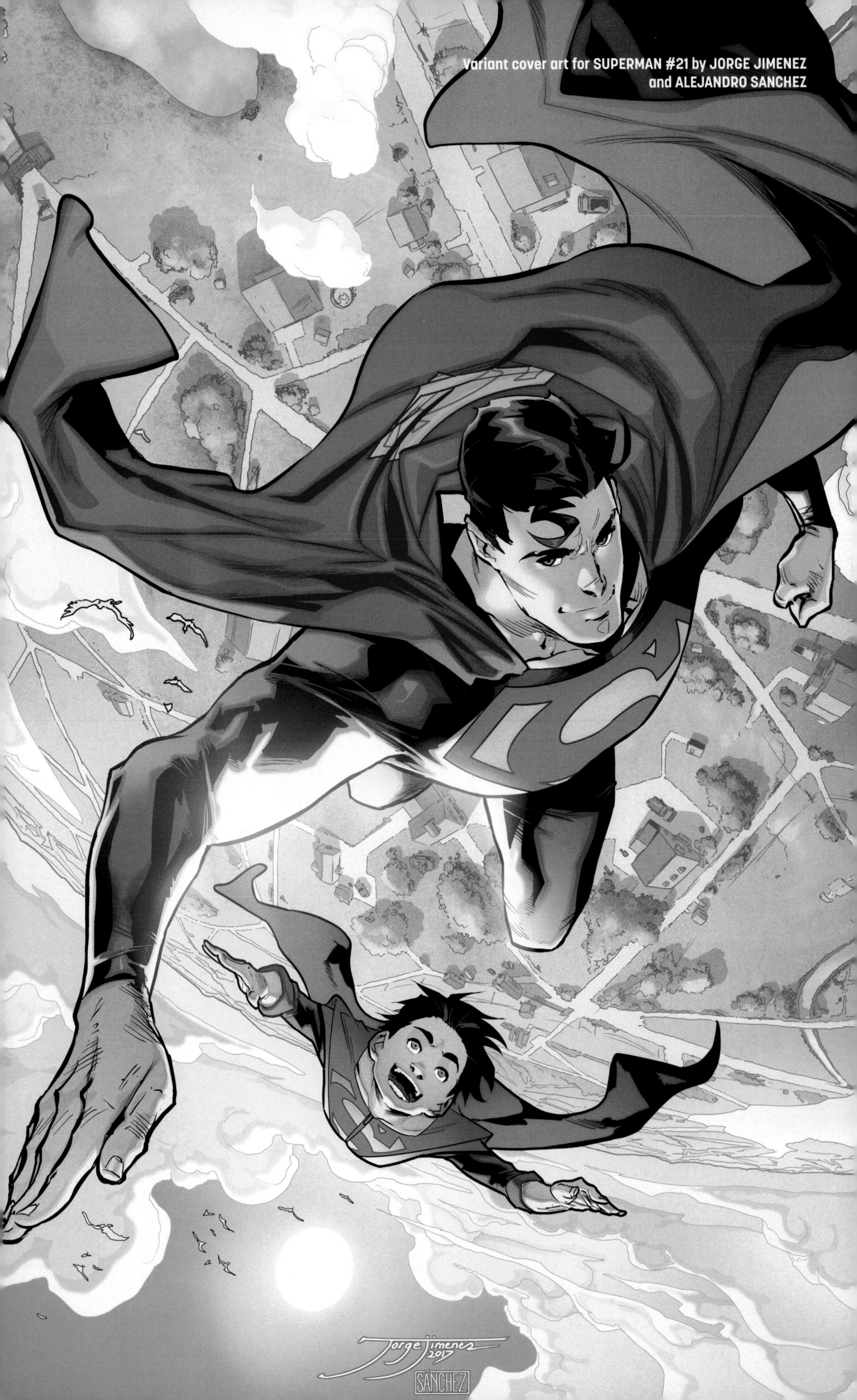
Jorge Jimenez 2017
SÁNCHEZ

Variant cover art for SUPERMAN #21 by JORGE JIMENEZ and ALEJANDRO SANCHEZ

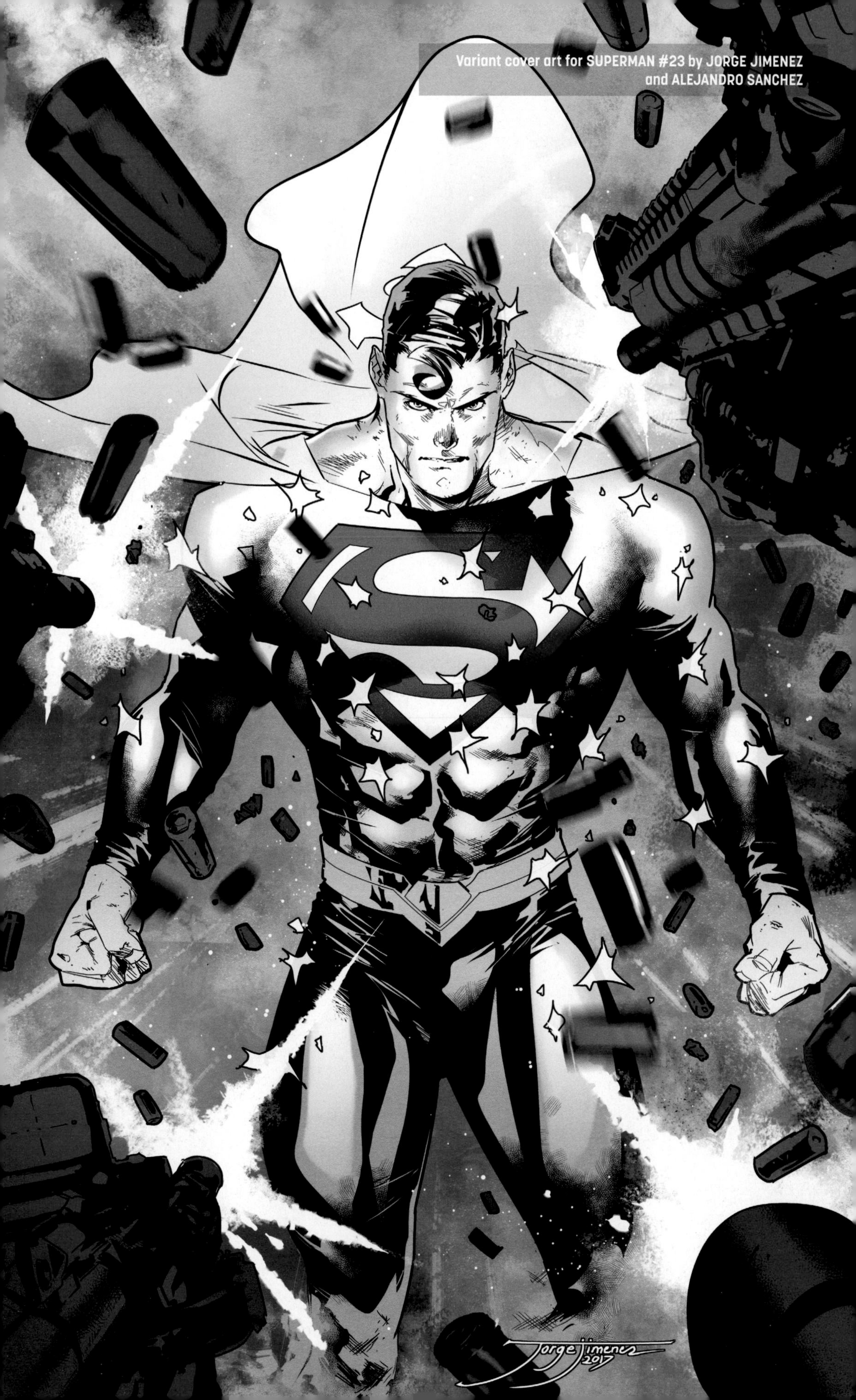
Jorge Jimenez 2017

Variant cover art for SUPERMAN #23 by JORGE JIMENEZ and ALEJANDRO SANCHEZ

Variant cover art for SUPERMAN #24 by JORGE JIMENEZ
and ALEJANDRO SANCHEZ

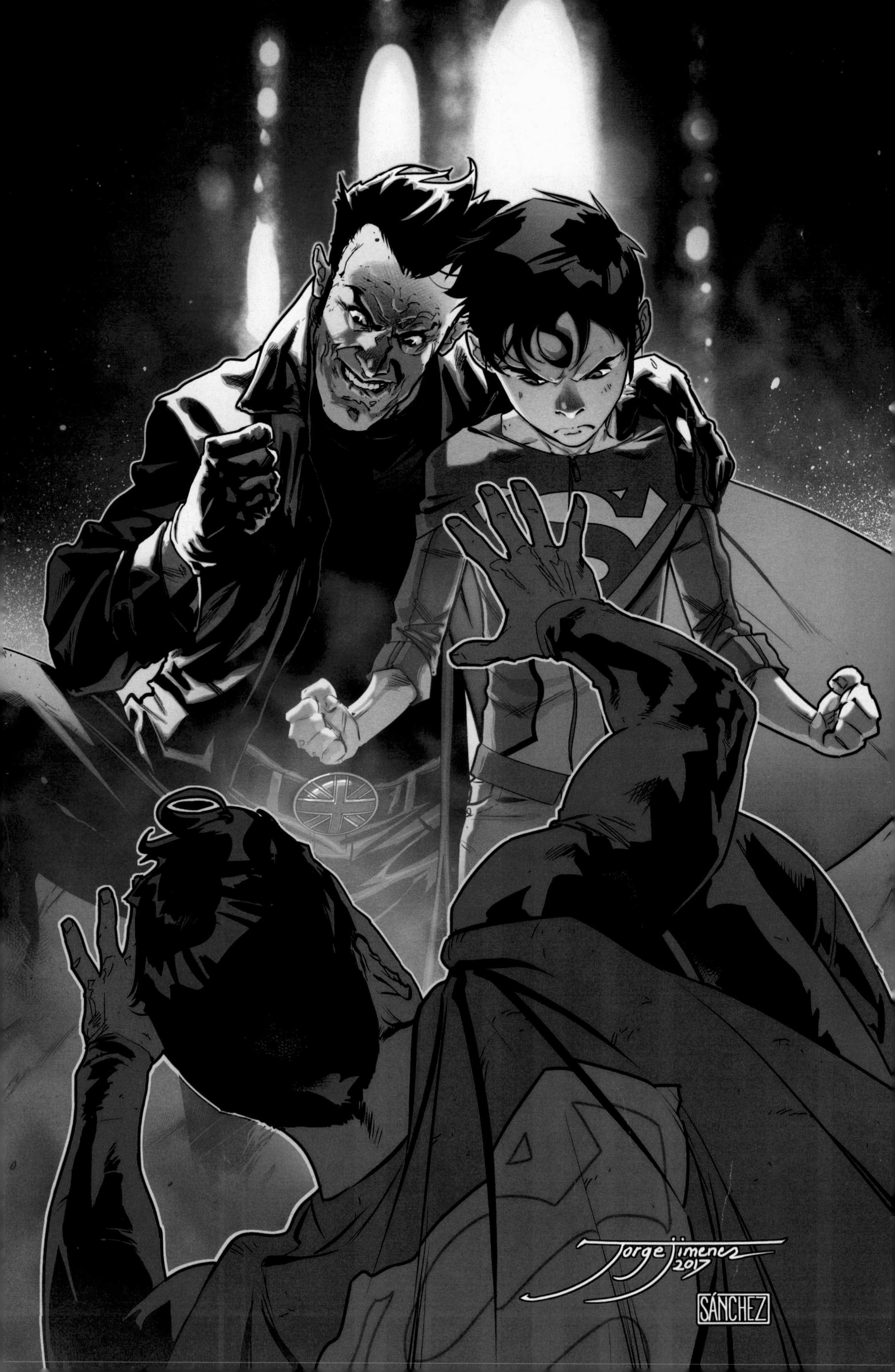
Jorge Jimenez
2017
SÁNCHEZ

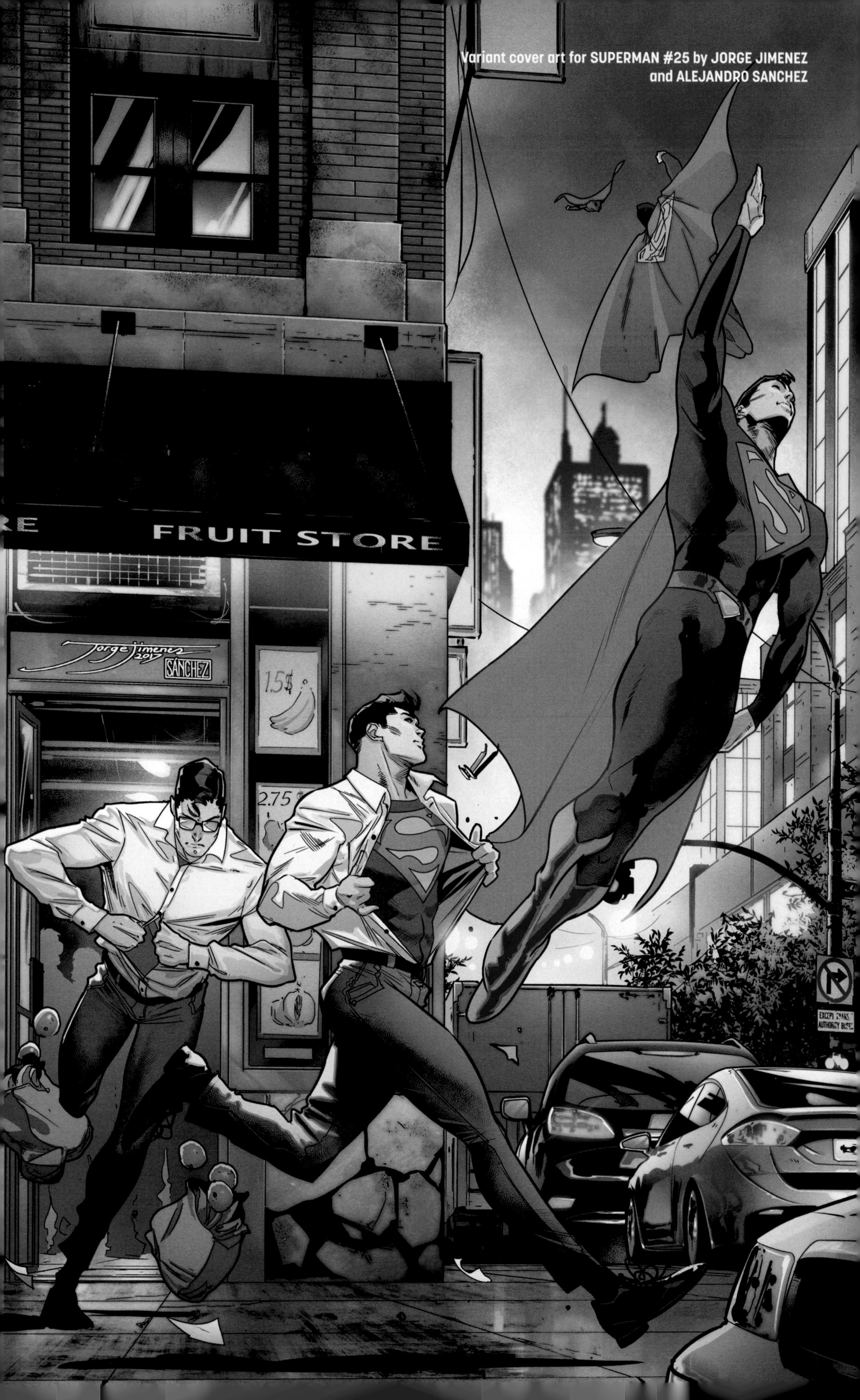
FRUIT STORE
SÁNCHEZ
1.5$
2.75

Variant cover art for SUPERMAN #25 by JORGE JIMENEZ
and ALEJANDRO SANCHEZ

Variant cover art for SUPERMAN #26 by JORGE JIMENEZ and ALEJANDRO SANCHEZ

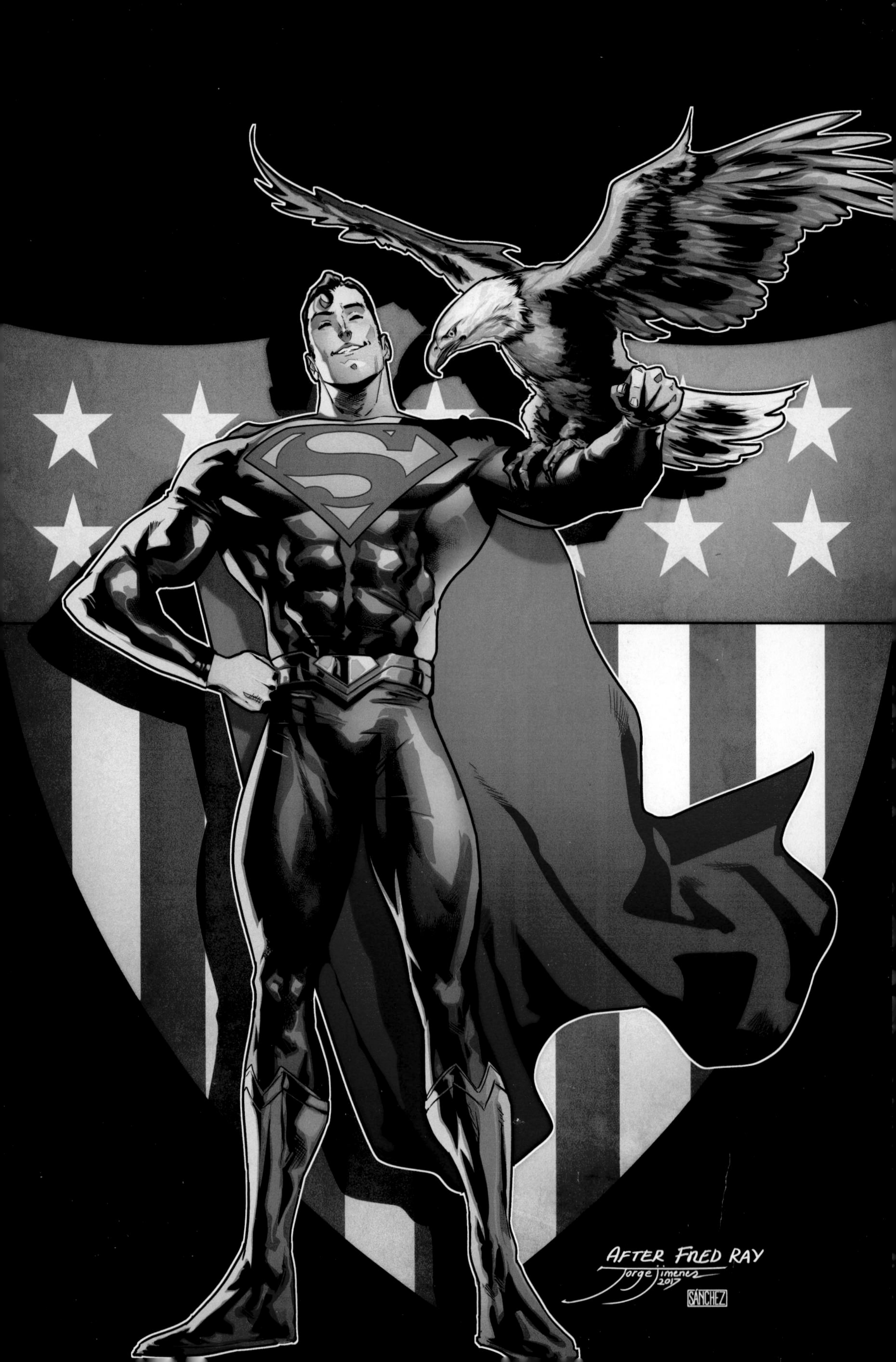

AFTER FRED RAY
Jorge Jimenez 2017
SÁNCHEZ